THE INTERNATIONAL MONETARY SYSTEM UNDER FLEXIBLE EXCHANGE RATES

THE INTERNATIONAL MONETARY SYSTEM UNDER FLEXIBLE EXCHANGE RATES

Global, Regional, and National

ESSAYS IN HONOR OF ROBERT TRIFFIN

Edited by

RICHARD N. COOPER

PETER B. KENEN

JORGE BRAGA DE MACEDO

JACQUES VAN YPERSELE

BALLINGER PUBLISHING COMPANY
Cambridge, Massachusetts
A Subsidiary of Harper & Row, Publishers, Inc.

International Standard Book Number: 0-88410-853-8

Library of Congress Catalog Card Number: 81-12861

Printed in the United States of America

Library of Congress Cataloging in Publication Data

Main entry under title:

The International monetary system under flexible
  exchange rates.

  Includes bibliographical references and index.
  1. International finance — Addresses, essays, lectures. 2. Foreign
exchange problem — Addresses, essays, lectures.
I. Triffin, Robert. II. Cooper, Richard N.
HG3881.I57673   332.4'5   81-12861
ISBN 0-88410-853-8   AACR2

CONTENTS

v

LIST OF CONTRIBUTORS

Robert Z. Aliber	Professor of International Economics and Finance, Graduate School of Business, University of Chicago
Guido Carli	Former Governor, Bank of Italy
Richard N. Cooper	Boas Professor of International Economics, Harvard University
W.M. Corden	Professor of Economics, Australian National University
Carlos F. Diaz Alejandro	Professor of Economics, Yale University
William Fellner	Resident Scholar, American Enterprise Institute; Sterling Professor of Economics Emeritus, Yale University
Hans Genberg	Professor of Economics, The Graduate Institute of International Studies, Geneva
Herbert G. Grubel	Professor of Economics, Simon Fraser University
Peter B. Kenen	Walker Professor of Economics and International Finance, Princeton University
Charles P. Kindleberger	Ford International Professor of Economics Emeritus, Massachusetts Institute of Technology
Jorge Braga de Macedo	Assistant Professor of Economics and International Affairs, Princeton University
Fritz Machlup	Walker Professor of Economics and International Finance Emeritus, Princeton University; Professor of Economics, New York University
Guillermo Ortiz	Economist, Research Department, Banco de México
Jeffrey R. Shafer	Assistant Vice-President, Federal Reserve Bank of New York
Leopoldo Solís	Vice-Governor, Banco de México
Luigi Spaventa	Professor of Economics, University of Rome
Alexander K. Swoboda	Professor of Economics, The Graduate Institute of International Studies, Geneva
James Tobin	Sterling Professor of Economics, Yale University
Edwin M. Truman	Director, Division of International Finance, Board of Governors of the Federal Reserve System
John Williamson	Senior Fellow, Institute for International Economics
Jacques van Ypersele	Chef de Cabinet of the Belgian Minister of Finance; Former Chairman of the EEC Monetary Committee

LIST OF FIGURES

LIST OF TABLES

FOREWORD

This book is composed of eighteen essays, sophisticated in analysis but practical in approach and remedy. They cover a wide range of problems associated with the now destabilized and destabilizing international monetary scene. I deliberately choose the word "scene" rather than the "system" of the title, because I do not think that the intercontinental disorganization of the decade following the collapse of Bretton Woods—with the vast masses of off-shore capital roaming the world like the legions of a huge army having lost all touch with its central command—deserves such a schematic description. That is my only quarrel with the presentation. For the rest it is admirable and makes a wholly appropriate tribute to the first seventy notable years of the life of Robert Triffin.

Professor Triffin is one of the most quietly remarkable men that I have ever known. In at least two ways he spans two worlds. He has spent most of his life in the United States, a major figure in the life and teaching of Yale, a consultant to the Council of Economic Advisers, and much involved in Latin American monetary problems. But he was born, and remains, a Belgian. In a fashion typical of the best traditions of that land which is more a meeting point than a country, Triffin feels a special responsibility for trying to make sense out of the clashing nationalisms of Europe. Equally he has been a theoretician who has always been happiest when he was trying to advance practical solutions to pressing problems.

He was the principal architect of the European Payments Union in the late 1940s. He then made an unique contribution to freeing Western Europe from the shackles of a hobbling bilateralism. Thirty years later his knowledge and experience, together with his patient optimism, were essential ingredients in the setting up of the European Monetary System (EMS). As President of the Commission of the European Communities, I tried to relaunch the idea of economic and monetary union in 1977. To begin with it fell on arid ground. But Robert Triffin was there with a watering can of intellectual refreshment. Within six months Chancellor Schmidt and President Giscard d'Estaing began to see the need for at least a limited advance. A year later the EMS was in operation. And it has worked remarkably well (although, alas, without Britain) for 2½ years. Three adjustments have been necessary, but they have been carried through quietly and efficiently. And in a turbulent monetary sea, the Europe of the Community has been an island of relative exchange rate stability. Robert Triffin has helped to get us so far and is constantly probing the possibility of necessary further advance.

The fertility of his ideas and the calm persuasiveness of his advocacy make it reasonable to compare him with Jean Monnet. But there is a difference. Monnet, with all his great gifts, saw things in black and white, with stark simplicity. Triffin comprehends all the complexity but still sees the way forward.

Roy Jenkins

London
25 October 1981

FLEXIBLE EXCHANGE RATES IN THEORY AND PRACTICE

1 FLEXIBLE EXCHANGE RATES, 1973-1980
How Bad Have They Really Been?

Richard N. Cooper

Grand claims were once made for a system of flexible exchange rates. The classic statement was by Milton Friedman (1953), and the most complete development was Egon Sohmen's *Flexible Exchange Rates: Theory and Controversy* (1961).

Robert Triffin, while never discussing flexible exchange rates in analytical detail, has over the years entertained some skepticism about their merits. His grounds for doing so revolved around the loss of discipline on fiscal and monetary authorities that flexible exchange rates permit with respect to anti-inflation policies. Triffin has also been concerned with the possibility that flexible exchange rates might lead to such turbulence in cost-price relationships that they would engender protectionist actions. He has feared the disintegrative impact that flexible exchange rates might have upon economic and, hence, upon political relations between nations, an impact that would run strongly counter to his lifelong objective of promoting economic integration among nations, and especially among European nations.[1]

By March 1981 we had eight years' experience with major currencies floating against one another in exchange markets. What can we say about this experience—and particularly against the grand claims that have been made for flexible exchange rates and Triffin's concerns about them?[2]

First, it is necessary to admit that on any comparative measure, the world's macroeconomic performance during the late 1970s, when generalized floating

1. See Triffin (1978:12, 14). In the late 1940s, however, Triffin advocated a foreign exchange auction system for nonessential transactions as a technique for eliminating the exchange controls then so prevalent (see Triffin 1966:166-68).

2. A useful review of the recent literature on flexible exchange rates can be found in Goldstein (1980).

prevailed, was worse than its performance during the final years of the adjustable peg system. For example, real economic growth was only 60 percent as rapid during 1973-1979 as it was in the preceding seven-year period; unemployment rates in industrialized countries were 50 percent higher, and inflation rates were more than double.

These lamentable developments, however, cannot be attributed to the introduction of flexible exchange rates. Post hoc does not imply propter hoc. To appreciate this, we need only recall two other factors that greatly affected economic performance during this period—the quadrupling of world oil prices in 1973-1974 and the further doubling of those prices in 1979; and the tremendous expansion of international liquidity in the period 1970-1973, the last years of the fixed exchange rate system. These factors together forced national economic policymakers to deal simultaneously with high unemployment and high inflation, a task to which our standard tools of economic management are not well suited.

If we make allowance for the severe disturbances to which the world economy was subjected during this period, I conclude that the experience under floating exchange rates has been a reasonably good one. It is worth keeping in mind that the smoothness of a ride depends on the size of the bumps on the road as well as on the quality of the shock absorbers. If we abstract from sharp day-to-day movements, floating exchange rates performed about as well as one would have expected, given the disturbances. Protectionist actions were largely avoided (indeed, major trade liberalization was agreed), and world trade continued to grow.

In what follows, I first want to make some analytical distinctions that pertain to movements in exchange rates. Then I will discuss the actual movements in exchange rates during 1973 to 1980. Following that, I consider the possibility that flexible exchange rates may have been a substantial cause of some of the disturbances experienced by the world economy during this period. I conclude with some observations about where we go from here.

REAL VERSUS NOMINAL MOVEMENTS
IN EXCHANGE RATES

One attribute of flexible exchange rates is that they can correct for differential national rates of inflation at the border, leaving all real variables unchanged. Fixed exchange rates, in contrast, lead to an alteration of relative prices among countries—or between tradable goods and nontradable goods within countries—when there are divergences in relevant national rates of inflation.

Divergences in national rates of inflation, however, are not the only source of possible disturbance to international transactions. Real disturbances—changes in the underlying demand for or supply of particular goods and services—call for correction through the price mechanism. Flexible exchange rates in some circumstances can help to bring about this adjustment. Indeed, when factor prices in nominal terms resist decline, and where some "money illusion"[3] exists, movements in exchange rates may be the most efficient way to bring about the required decline in real factor prices.

This distinction between correction for divergence in inflation rates and adjustment to changes in real variables is crucial, for it indicates that changes in nominal exchange rates under a flexible rate system can plausibly lead to a wide range of changes in "real" exchange rates (changes in exchange rates corrected for inflation differentials), from none at all to a change fully equivalent to the change in nominal rates. In contrast to the impression sometimes conveyed in a literature preoccupied with purchasing power parity, we should not be surprised, either in theory or in reality, to find a variety of changes in real rates corresponding to any given change in nominal rates. The outcome will depend inter alia on the initiating combination of disturbances.

An exchange rate is the rate at which one money exchanges for another. It therefore reflects the whole range of factors that influence the demand for money, not merely the demand for foreign goods and services. Domestic demand for foreign securities and foreign demand for domestic securities are also important factors in the foreign exchange market. Indeed, the current fashion is to treat the exchange rate as that "price" that clears the market with respect to the holding of foreign assets in national portfolios. It is admitted that over time exchange rates can have an important effect on investment at home and abroad, hence on net foreign investment, hence on foreign trade. But since the time it takes for investment flows to respond to differences in relative yield is very much longer than the time it takes for market prices to adjust to changes in asset preferences, portfolio balance considerations are thought to exercise the dominant short-run influence on exchange rates. It is only over time that changes in the current account balance, which is equal to net foreign investment, can correct portfolio imbalances with respect to the holding of foreign assets.[4]

As will become clear below, I believe it is an oversimplification to concede even dominant short-run influence of portfolio considerations on exchange rates, except tautologically. Imbalances in current payments may so influence expectations about future exchange rates (hence today's desire to hold securities) that a major role in exchange rate determination must be given to imbalances in goods and services that are perceived to be nonsustainable. These perceptions, it is true, are reflected in portfolio decisions. Thus seemingly alternative explanations for exchange rate determination, properly considered, are not alternatives at all, but different aspects of the same underlying process

---

3. "Money illusion" may in fact not involve an illusion at all. Wage earners may be willing to suffer a decline in real wages brought about through a rise in the local currency prices of imported goods even when they are not willing to accept a decline in nominal wages. For a discussion of the phenomenon, see Cooper (1977:160ff.).

4. See Branson (1980) for a formal exposition of this adjustment mechanism.

whereby perceptions are translated into expectations and expectations in turn are translated into market prices.[5]

EXCHANGE RATE DEVELOPMENTS, 1973-1980

Let us turn from these analytical considerations to the events of 1973-1980. If we abstract from week-to-week movements, exchange rate movements are not that difficult to explain. Newspapers quote bilateral exchange rates, such as that between the German mark and the U.S. dollar. What is important for a country's economy, however, is not one single exchange rate, but some average of all relevant exchange rates. This average can be called the "effective" exchange rate. It is usually a weighted average of bilateral exchange rates, where the weights correspond to the trading pattern of the country in which we are interested, or sometimes to the trade of a group of countries. (This kind of weighting obviously focuses on trade. A different set of weights would be appropriate if we were to focus exclusively or predominantly on financial transactions.) Second, as already noted, differences in national inflation rates may alter exchange rates simply to avoid affecting relative prices between or within countries. A change in an exchange rate corrected for differential inflation rates is called the change in the "real" exchange rate.

With these distinctions in mind, consider the exchange rate of the U.S. dollar during the period of floating rates. Contemporary newspaper accounts conveyed the impression that the dollar took quite a beating in exchange markets during this period. It therefore will come as a great surprise to many that the effective exchange rate of the dollar relative to currencies of other industrialized countries showed no change in December 1980 from its position in March 1973, when generalized floating began following the February 1973 devaluation of the dollar. Inclusion of the currencies of developing countries in the "effective" rate would show an appreciation of the dollar over this period.

There were some ups and downs in the value of the dollar during this period, but they were not large and they followed almost a textbook pattern in their movements. The effective rate appreciated modestly in 1973 and again in 1975-1976; it depreciated in 1977-1978 and appreciated slightly in 1979-1980 (see Table 1-1). The real effective exchange rate of the dollar (wholesale prices of manufactured goods are used to measure the relevant inflation rates) followed a similar pattern, except for an initial depreciation of the dollar in 1973, when inflation rates in other industrial countries sharply exceeded those in the United States.

The principal observation to make on these movements is that contrary to widespread impression, movements in the exchange rate of the dollar did not correct for differential rates of inflation—indeed, the United States had a better

5. These interrelations have begun to be recognized. See for example, Dornbusch (1980) and Branson's (1980) comments on it.

Table 1-1. United States, Exchange Rate, 1973-1980
(*March 1973 = 100*).

	Effective Exchange Rate[a]	*Real Effective*[b] *Exchange Rate*	*Current Account*[c] *Balance ($ billion)*
	December		
1973	101.6	95.1	7.1
1974	101.0	97.7	4.1[d]
1975	105.0	102.5	18.3
1976	106.4	101.1	4.5
1977	102.9	98.2	-14.1
1978	97.5	94.9	-14.3
1979	98.7	96.5	-0.6
1980	99.9	99.7	+0.1

a. Index of fifteen currencies of industrialized countries, weighted by the U.S. 1976 trade in manufactures with those countries.

b. Effective rate corrected for differentials in wholesale prices of nonfood manufactured goods.

c. Including government transfers.

d. Excludes a $2 billion write-off of Indian rupee holdings.

Sources: Morgan Guaranty Trust Co.; IMF, International Financial Statistics.

than average record in this regard—but rather were real, alternately improving, worsening, improving, and then again worsening the competitiveness of U.S. goods and services in international trade. Moreover, the real effective exchange rate followed a classic pattern: It declined in response to a deterioration in the current account position of the United States, and it appreciated in response to an improvement in the current account. Whatever the exact channel of causation, the relationship was a close one.

(A similar pattern can be observed for the Japanese yen. Movements in the real effective exchange rate of the yen correlate well with Japan's position on current account, with the yen generally depreciating in response to a worsening of the current account and appreciating in response to an improvement (see Table 1-2; the Japanese current account improved greatly during 1980 and was in surplus by the end of the year).

Similar effects can be discerned in movements of the German mark, although the more striking pattern there is the relative stability of the real exchange rate (except for the depreciation in 1975 and again in 1980). The mark appreciated substantially over this period, which served to offset inflation that was higher for Germany's trading partners than for Germany. Thus, in this case, in contrast to the U.S. dollar and to an extent considerably greater than for the yen, the movements in real exchange rates were far smaller than the movements in nominal exchange rates (see Table 1-3).

Establishing a visible correlation between two variables, of course, does not define the causal connection between them. By affecting the demand for foreign

Table 1-2. Japan, Exchange Rate, 1973-1980
(*March 1973 = 100*).

	$/Yen	Effective Exchange Rate[a]	Real Effective[b] Exchange Rate	Current Account[c] Balance ($ billion)
		December		
1973	96.5	93.1	106.6	-0.1
1974	89.8	85.7	90.2	-4.7
1975	88.3	86.4	84.8	-0.7
1976	88.3	91.0	88.4	3.7
1977	97.6	109.1	99.0	10.9
1978	124.4	129.6	108.0	17.6
1979	119.5	103.5	86.9	-8.7
1980	124.8	122.0	100.8	-10.8

a. Index of fifteen currencies of industrialized countries, weighted by Japan's 1976 trade in manufactures with those countries.

b. Effective rate corrected for differentials in wholesale prices of nonfood manufactured goods.

c. Including government transfers.

Sources: Morgan Guaranty Trust Co.; IMF, International Financial Statistics.

Table 1-3. West Germany, Exchange Rate, 1973-1980
(*March 1973 = 100*).

	$/DM	Effective Exchange Rate[a]	Real Effective[b] Exchange Rate	Current Account[c] Balance ($ billion)
		December		
1973	105.2	107.2	105.6	4.6
1974	109.3	111.4	104.7	10.1
1975	114.9	108.2	97.4	3.9
1976	112.2	122.4	103.8	3.6
1977	121.8	130.1	104.8	4.0
1978	140.6	135.0	105.2	8.7
1979	154.3	140.2	105.9	-6.3
1980	143.4	133.9	98.7	-15.0

a. Index of fifteen currencies of industrialized countries, weighted by Germany's 1976 trade in manufactures with those countries.

b. Effective rate corrected for differentials in wholesale prices of nonfood manufactured goods.

c. Including government transfers.

Sources: Morgan Guaranty Trust Co.; IMF, International Financial Statistics.

currency, current account imbalances could influence exchange rates directly, or as noted above, they could affect expectations about future exchange rates and hence, through attempted adjustments in portfolios, could affect today's exchange rates. Or there could be some common factor that influences both the exchange rate and the current balance. Moreover, the causation acts in both directions, with exchange rates influencing the current balance as well as the other way around. It is widely accepted, however, that a considerable period of time – perhaps as long as two years – is required before a change in the real exchange rate will have a substantial effect on the volume of trade, especially trade in manufactured goods. In the short run, a depreciation of the currency, by raising domestic currency prices of imports, will worsen the balance on goods and services (measured in domestic currency). If this condition were dominant and were to persist, the exchange market would be unstable. But if it is temporary, we have the so-called J-curve effect, whereby a movement in an exchange rate first moves the current account balance in one direction, before the volumes of imports and exports have had an opportunity to adjust fully, but over time moves the current balance in the opposite direction, after traders have had a chance to adjust to the new prices. This J-curve effect seems to have played an important role in the sharp growth of Japan's surplus during 1977 and 1978. Appreciation of the yen, induced by the growing surplus, also aggravated the surplus by raising the dollar value of exports. Moreover, an anticipated change in a currency's value may induce traders to accelerate or defer their purchases of foreign goods, so that in addition to the J-curve effect, there is actually some disequilibrating movement of goods in a period of expected exchange rate change. Again, during late 1977 and early 1978, Japanese exports may have been stimulated for a time rather than retarded by the great appreciation of the yen.[6]

The experience during these years of floating exchange rates illustrates that both real and monetary elements influenced exchange rates. Indeed, it is possible to classify countries according to the dominance of monetary or real factors. In the case of Italy, the substantial depreciation of the lira was due almost wholly to higher rates of inflation in Italy than in its major trading partners. By mid-1980 the lira had depreciated almost 50 percent since March 1973, but the real effective exchange rate was not quite 5 percent below that of the earlier period. Most of the appreciation of the German mark (DM) was also to offset differential inflation rates, although some movement in the real DM rate also occurred. At the other end of the spectrum, movements in the effective exchange rate of the dollar and the French franc (except for the very late 1970s) were largely real, with only a small part representing corrections for divergence in national inflation rates.

Japan and Switzerland fall between these extremes: A substantial part of the movement of effective exchange rates is explained by better than average per-

6. This possibility has been emphasized by Wilson and Takacs (1980).

formance of those two countries with respect to inflation, but substantial real movements in their exchange rates also took place. For example, between March 1973 and September 1978 (the peak), the effective exchange rate of Switzerland appreciated 84 percent. During the same period, the real exchange rate of the Swiss franc appreciated 34 percent, declining sharply thereafter. This large real appreciation occurred during a period in which the Swiss current account surplus was an extraordinary 5 to 6 percent of Switzerland's GNP.

The only really aberrant case among major countries—aberrant in the sense of not falling within the patterns just described—was the United Kingdom. The British pound depreciated heavily during the first several years after floating, stabilized, and then appreciated strongly, despite rates of inflation substantially in excess of those of most of its major trading partners. Indeed, in real terms the British pound appreciated 50 percent between late 1976 (a low point) and mid-1980. This appreciation was accompanied by modest but steady improvements in the current account balance. Much more important, however, was the increased production of North Sea oil, combined with a sharp rise in oil prices and Mrs. Thatcher's policy of economic retrenchment in late 1979 and 1980. This case represents a dramatic illustration of the influence of real (as opposed to monetary) economic developments on a country's exchange rate.

FLEXIBLE EXCHANGE RATES AS INSULATORS

An alleged advantage of flexible exchange rates is that they insulate national economies from disturbances coming from abroad. By the same token, they "bottle up" domestic disturbances in the originating country. On this argument, a country could neither import world inflation nor export its home-grown domestic inflation under a regime of flexible exchange rates, for movements in the exchange rates would compensate at the border for disturbances originating on the other side.

This traditional view of flexible exchange rates is a considerable oversimplification. Their powers of insulation depend very much on the nature of the disturbance, and in some instances flexible exchange rates may actually transmit disturbances across national boundaries more strongly than a system of fixed exchange rates. Flexible exchange rates are likely to be most successful at neutralizing disturbances when the disturbance is a general rise in the price level. For a small country under fixed exchange rates, a rise in the world price level would stimulate demand for national products and would lead to a rise in the domestic price level. An appreciation of the currency to offset the rise in world prices would compensate at the border, preventing either relative price or wealth effects inside the country.

A world increase in demand for the country's particular export products, in contrast, will raise incomes and stimulate domestic demand. With flexible exchange rates, its currency would appreciate and partially damp the sale of exports, as well as discouraging imports—on both counts relieving pressure on the domestic economy. But relative prices will have changed, total wealth will have been increased, and resources will have been reallocated, so the insulation provided by flexible rates is incomplete.

An increase in foreign demand for a country's securities will also lead to appreciation of its currency. That, in turn, will both diminish aggregate demand and lead to a reallocation of resources away from tradable to nontradable goods, possibly with transitional unemployment. In this instance, therefore, far from insulating the domestic economy from foreign disturbances, a flexible rate will have transmitted the disturbance more forcefully than would have been the case under a fixed exchange rate. Under a fixed rate, an increase in demand for the country's securities will be offset by the monetary authorities, who in preventing an appreciation of the currency will add to its foreign exchange reserves—that is, will export capital—in a manner that partially or even fully limits the impact of the shift in portfolio demand on the markets for goods and services and labor at home.

During the 1970s, flexible exchange rates undoubtedly insulated West Germany from imported inflation, a point much emphasized by German authorities in support of flexible rates. But changes in real economic variables are real, not monetary, and their impact can only be mitigated, not offset, by changes in exchange rates. For example, the sharp rise in the Swiss franc weakened but did not altogether stop the influence on its trading partners of Switzerland's deflationary policy during this period, a policy that was motivated by the desire to reduce the large number of foreign workers in Switzerland at the beginning of the period. By the same token, depreciation of the dollar in 1977-1978 reduced but did not eliminate the expansionary impact on the rest of the world of expansionary U.S. domestic policies.

To sum up, exchange rates during this period of floating have not been "unstable" over time, and indeed, the movements have been fully explicable in terms of correction for inflation differentials combined with a corrective response to current account imbalances.

It remains to be seen how powerful changes in real exchange rates are as an adjustment mechanism leading to the correction of imbalances. Preliminary indications are favorable. Goods and services do seem to follow a J-curve: First the imbalance worsens in response to a currency depreciation, but thereafter, with a lag, both the volume of exports and the volume of imports respond in a corrective fashion. In this respect, the experience under floating exchange rates must be considered a qualified success. Floating exchange rates do not, however, fully insulate national economies from external disturbances, nor do they fully bottle up domestic disturbances.

FLEXIBLE EXCHANGE RATES AS SOURCES OF DISTURBANCE

An assessment of flexible exchange rates would not be complete without addressing the question of whether the presence of flexible rates actually created the disturbances that plagued the world economy during this period. This is a subject for endless debate, but I believe the answer is negative. There are occasions, as noted in the previous section, when flexible exchange rates can aggravate the transmission of disturbances, especially when there are sharp portfolio shifts between foreign and domestic securities. There were episodes during the period 1973–1980 in which portfolio movements undoubtedly did disturb national economies. But it would be an error to attribute the general turmoil of the period to flexible exchange rates.

The most notable feature of the 1970s, as compared with the 1950s and 1960s, is the sharp increase in rates of inflation. But this sharp increase antedated the switch to flexible exchange rates, as did the large growth in world liquidity that supported the inflation. As Triffin has pointed out on numerous occasions, international liquidity grew enormously — doubling on most measures — between 1969 and 1972.[7] But that growth took place in a period of fixed, not flexible, exchange rates. Indeed, the introduction of flexible rates — which was resisted for years by monetary officials — was an unavoidable response to the difficulties already being experienced.

Then there was the sharp increase in oil prices in 1973–1974, following the introduction of floating exchange rates. But the price increase cannot plausibly be attributed to floating. Some observers argue that it was an autonomous action, representing a coalescence of OPEC market power in the wake of the huge increase in demand for OPEC oil during the preceding five years and the Saudi Arabian embargo associated with the Yom Kippur War. Other observers contend that the oil price increase was an endogenous response to world inflation, a reaction to the alleged decline in the real oil price in the early 1970s.[8] Whatever one's views on the hypotheses, and they are not mutually exclusive, flexible exchange rates played no role in either of them. In principle, currency instability could have been a precipitating event. But in fact the U.S. dollar (the currency in which oil prices are denominated) was relatively stable between March 1973 — after the February devaluation, a feature of the earlier adjustable peg exchange rate system — and December 1973. Its value in SDR (Special Drawing Rights) was unchanged, and it experienced only minor movements up or down against other leading currencies.

7. International monetary reserves grew from $79 billion to $159 billion during this period, and foreign liabilities of commercial banks grew from $121 billion to $217 billion (Triffin 1978: 4).

8. In fact, the real price of Saudi marker crude rose about 30 percent between 1970 and mid–1973, on the basis of the U.S. GNP deflator.

National divergences in inflation rates existed before the oil shock of 1973-1974, but that shock aggravated them. Different economies responded to that price increase in different ways. Price and wage inflation accelerated in all countries, but to differing degrees. At one extreme was the United States, where price increases accelerated more than wages; real wages actually fell in the United States, alone among industrial countries. Some countries—most notably Japan—experienced a wage explosion in the immediate aftermath of the OPEC price increase but brought wage settlements down to pre-1973 norms within two years. Still other countries—notably Britain and Italy, among others—experienced an enduring wage and price inflation. But since all of these countries had floating currencies, that fact can hardly account for the divergence in national experience. Because of the divergence in national experience, floating currencies served as a necessary shock absorber for the world economy. Without them, payments imbalances would have been far worse, and protectionist reactions—which in fact were largely avoided—would have been irresistible. Thus, flexible exchange rates can surely be credited with preserving an open world economy during this period.

It is possible that flexible exchange rates made it more difficult to control inflation in countries such as Britain and Italy, although avoidance of tariff protection or new exchange controls is no small contribution toward that end. But by the same token, flexible exchange rates contributed to the success of anti-inflation policies in other countries. This is simply a manifestation of the "bottling up" effect whereby, under flexible exchange rates, each country has to live with more of the consequences of its own behavior and actions; it cannot so easily export the consequences of its policies as it can under fixed rates.

Another source of divergence among countries was their response to the 1974-1975 world recession. The recession was led by the major countries—the United States, Japan, Germany, and Britain. Many developing countries and some smaller industrial countries cushioned the impact of the recession on their own economies (and thereby the depth of the recession itself) by continuing their policies of growth and by borrowing heavily abroad to finance it. Still other countries pursued an economic policy between these extremes.

The United States recovered from the recession with some vigor. Recovery in Japan, Germany, and Britain was more sluggish. The recovery faltered everywhere in 1976. German industrial production, for example, did not return to its 1973 peak until 1977, and in Britain and Japan 1973 levels were not restored until 1978. The United States pressed ahead with new expansionary policies in 1977 and tried, at first unsuccessfully, to persuade other major countries to do the same. This involved the much touted locomotive theory, under which the largest and financially strongest national economies—the United States, Japan, and Germany—would lead the rest of the world out of the recession and by so doing would relieve the severe financial pressures that by late 1976 were besetting many countries. A resumption of the growth of these major economies was necessary to avoid politically dangerous economic stagnation elsewhere, a revival of protectionism, and the prospect of large-scale default on outstanding debts that would have had major repercussions on the international banking system.

U.S. expansion in 1977 relieved the condition of many other countries. But failure to persuade Germany and Japan to join it in expansionist policies led to further divergence among national economic developments, which in turn was largely responsible for the large payments imbalances of 1977–1978. The United States developed exceptionally large current account deficits, while Germany and especially Japan developed large surpluses. These developments in turn played a major role in the exchange rate movements in that period. A closer coordination of economic policies would have avoided some of the exchange market turbulence in 1977–1978. Such coordination was finally achieved at the Bonn Summit meeting of July 1978, and that agreement contributed importantly to the corrective adjustment in subsequent years.[9]

There were occasions in 1977–1978 when exchange rates moved sharply and by substantial amounts in short periods of time. Exchange markets were extremely nervous, and both news and rumors moved exchange rates around erratically. Expectations were fragile rather than solidly based on economic fundamentals. In addition, there was much talk about virtuous and vicious circles, carrying the suggestion not that flexible rates had some partial feedbacks onto domestic prices, which had long been known, but that they were unstable, with depreciation leading to inflation leading to depreciation, in an endless, nonconverging spiral.

We have known for a long time that foreign trade takes one to two years to respond in volume to relative price changes. Are we collectively too impatient to wait for such adjustment processes to work? Do we need instant results? If so, there may be strong psychological, not economic, reasons for eschewing movements in exchange rates. But what are the practical alternatives?

There is no feasible alternative so long as the world economy is subject to major turbulence. The European Monetary System (EMS) is a regional arrangement designed to provide a "zone of stability" in a world that by implication is full of instability. However, even the EMS sensibly contains much more flexibility than earlier proposals for European monetary integration, especially the proposals put forward in 1969–1970 and given a strong political endorsement then by leaders in the European Community. Despite this greater flexibility, Britain declined to join the EMS, and Italy received a special dispensation under the EMS, with a much wider exchange rate band than that of other members.

Exchange rate flexibility must be managed to help stabilize expectations and to break psychological bandwagon movements. A target zone for exchange rates, such as the EMS has adopted, could help to stabilize expectations if it is credible. But it cannot be credible over a period of time so long as the relevant inflation rates diverge. Thus, we are perforce left with a somewhat ad hoc, judg-

---

9. These issues are discussed more extensively in Cooper (forthcoming).

mental system of managed floating. The monetary authorities should strive to limit radical and unjustified movements in exchange rates, which means that they will sometimes have to take large, open positions in foreign currencies. Their interventions can and should be reversed later, so as to allow exchange rates to move over time in response to market pressures. On the whole, this has been the strategy that the leading monetary authorities have followed, in collaboration with one another, and on the whole, it has worked reasonably well.

REFERENCES

Branson, William H. 1980. *Asset Markets and Relative Prices in Exchange Rate Determination.* Princeton Reprints in International Finance No. 20, Princeton, New Jersey: International Finance Section, Princeton University.

Cooper, Richard N. 1977. "Monetary Theory and Policy in an Open Economy." In A. Lindbeck and J. Myhrman, eds., *Flexible Exchange Rates and Stabilization Policy.* London: Macmillan.

_____. 1980. "Global Economic Policy in a World of Energy Shortage." In essays in honor of Walter Heller.

Dornbusch, Rudiger. 1980. "Exchange Rate Economics: Where Do We Stand?" *Brookings Papers on Economic Activity* 1.

Friedman, Milton. 1953. "The Case for Flexible Exchange Rates." In *Essays in Positive Economics.* Chicago: University of Chicago Press.

Goldstein, Morris. 1980. *Have Flexible Exchange Rates Handicapped Macroeconomic Policy?* Special Papers in International Economics No. 14, Princeton, New Jersey: International Finance Section, Princeton University.

Sohmen, Egon. 1961. *Flexible Exchange Rates: Theory and Controversy.* Chicago: University of Chicago Press.

Triffin, Robert. 1966. *The World Money Maze.* New Haven: Yale University Press.

_____. 1978. *Gold and the Dollar Crisis: Yesterday and Tomorrow.* Essays in International Finance No. 132, Princeton, New Jersey: International Finance Section, Princeton University.

Wilson, John, and Wendy Takacs. 1980. "Expectations and the Adjustment of Trade Flows Under Floating Exchange Rates: Leads, Lags and the *J*-Curve." Federal Reserve, International Finance Discussion Paper #160, April.

2 EXCHANGE RATE PROTECTION

W.M. Corden

This chapter develops the concept of exchange rate protection. The concept is familiar from popular discussion and casual references in the literature of international monetary economics, but it has not been brought explicitly into theoretical work. The chapter has been inspired by the discussion of two recent issues – namely, the Japanese current account surpluses of 1977 and 1978 and the implications of North Sea oil revenues for British industrial structure and the balance of payments.

THE SIMPLE CONCEPT AND TWO EXAMPLES

There is exchange rate protection when a country protects its tradable goods sector (export and import-competing industries) relative to its nontradable sector by devaluing its exchange rate, allowing the exchange rate to depreciate more than it would otherwise, or preventing an appreciation that would otherwise take place. This is a simple definition. It implies that a devaluation can indeed bring about the required domestic relative price change. A nominal devaluation leads to a real devaluation. It also leaves open the definition of the "otherwise" exchange rate. We shall come to both points later.

The basic idea can be represented geometrically. Figure 2-1 represents the familiar Salter (1959) diagram. We make the small country assumption, so that exportables and importables can be amalgamated into the composite good "trad-

An earlier version of this chapter was presented to a seminar of the International Economics Study Group, London, April 1978. I am greatly indebted to comments from John Black, Herbert Grubel, Anne Krueger, Peter Lloyd, Peter McCawley, John Martin, Richard Snape, and John Williamson.

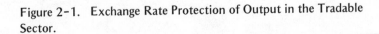

Figure 2-1.   Exchange Rate Protection of Output in the Tradable Sector.

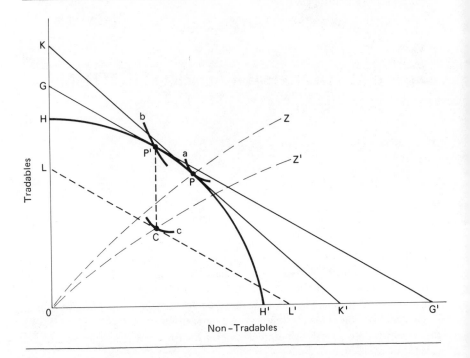

ables," shown on the vertical axis. The transformation curve between tradables and nontradables is HH', and if the current account is initially in balance, the initial point of equilibrium is P, with a domestic relative price ratio represented by the slope of KK'. This is the "otherwise" position. The assumption of initial current account balance is made for simplicity, but is not crucial to the argument.

It is desired to protect the tradable goods industry so as to bring output to P'. We now make the simple assumption (reviewed later) that the nominal price of nontradables is given. This could be the result of an exogenously determined money wage combined with a constant percentage profit margin in the non-tradable sector. We also assume, for simplicity, that foreign prices are constant. This assumption is not critical for the analysis. The desired relative price change can then be brought about by an appropriate nominal devaluation that raises the domestic price of tradables and hence alters the relative price ratio to that represented by the slope of GG'. This brings output to P', but it will also shift the pattern of absorption away from tradables, moving it from the expenditure curve OZ to OZ'. At a constant price of nontradables there will now be excess demand for nontradables, which is not a sustainable position, given that the nominal price of nontradables is to stay constant. To avoid this, aggregate demand (absorption) must be reduced appropriately – namely to OL' (in terms of nontradables) – so that we end up with absorption at C and a current account surplus of P'C.

If there is to be a continuing current account surplus and there are no offsetting private capital outflows (as we are assuming), the monetary inflows have to be sterilized. In terms of Figure 2-1, the level of absorption has to be kept down to OL'. In the absence of sterilization, the money supply and hence the absorption level would steadily increase until the surplus disappeared. The difficulties of sterilization in the absence of a fiscal surplus are well known. In the presence of capital mobility, sterilization would lead to offsetting capital inflows as the domestic interest rate steadily rose, and in any case, a continuous surplus and continuous sterilization would not be compatible with stock equilibrium of the private sector. Thus, it has to be assumed that the current account surplus is matched by a budget surplus, this continuing budget surplus being the way in which the lower level of absorption is maintained. The government steadily redeems its debt, and when there is no more left to redeem, it builds up liquid balances with the central bank. This is, of course, not a situation of public stock equilibrium. Furthermore, at some time in the future there must be budget and current account deficits – which antiprotect the tradables sector – as the foreign exchange reserves accumulated during the period of exchange rate protection are used up. But we are concerned here only with the first period. Thus, this chapter is strictly limited to a short-term analysis.[1]

The objective of exchange rate protection is often to maintain employment in the tradables sector in response to some exogenous shock that would otherwise have caused employment in that sector to fall. The motive may be short term, the object being to maintain employment temporarily. Such a case is represented in Figure 2-2. Initially the transformation curve is JJ', and equilibrium is at R. A productivity improvement in the tradables sector causes the curve to rise vertically to HJ'. If there were to be no net resource shift between the two sectors, output would have to move to P', vertically above R. In the movement from R to P' there is no change in output of nontradables. Now the question is where output would settle if the exchange rate (or the money price of nontradables) were flexible and full employment were maintained. Suppose this "otherwise" position were at P. Exchange rate protection would ensure that output moves to P' so as to prevent a decrease in employment in tradables.[2] To explore the position of P relative to P' further, let us consider two special cases.

1. A two-period analysis broadly in the same framework as the present chapter (i.e., using the Salter model as a starting point) can be found in Razin (1980).

2. This sentence assumes that constancy of output of nontradables also means constancy of employment in that sector, and hence also constancy of employment in tradables.

Figure 2-2. Protection of Employment After a Productivity
Improvement.

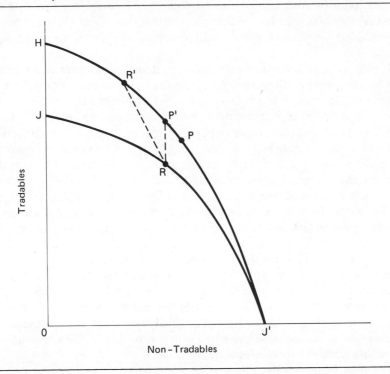

Non - Tradables

1. There is a windfall oil discovery requiring no significant extra resource use.
   The output of tradables rises by a uniform amount independent of the
   resources in the tradable industries.[3] The slope at P' will be equal to the
   slope at R, and with the nominal price of nontradables given, the exchange
   rate will be the same at P' as at R. The "otherwise" position P will be to the
   right of P' (as in Figure 2-2), provided the marginal propensity to absorb

---

It assumes that output and employment always move in the same direction (apart from the
effects of the productivity improvement itself).

   This would be so either (a) in a two-mobile-factors model where the productivity improvement is Hicks neutral or (b) in a model where labor is the only mobile factor. In the
more general two-factor case, with the productivity improvement factor biased, constancy
of output of nontradables can be associated with one factor moving into that sector and the
other out. This is described tautologically here as zero net resource shift. Thus the complica-
tion to note is that in the general case, constant employment in tradables could mean a position to the left or right of P'.

   3. The curve JH' would be vertically displaced above JJ' by a uniform amount and
would have a kink vertically above J'.

nontradables is positive. Exchange rate protection—which is designed to move the production point from P to P'—keeps the exchange rate constant when it would otherwise have appreciated. It will ensure that the absorption point remains at R and that the whole of the oil windfall finances a payments surplus.

2. There is a factor-neutral and scale-neutral proportional productivity increase in the tradables industry. This is the case represented in Figure 2-2. The slope at P' will be steeper than that at R, and if the nominal price of nontradables is given, the exchange rate at P' will be appreciated relative to that at R. Hence some appreciation is required if employment in tradables is to remain constant. A constant exchange rate would actually mean an increase in employment in tradables.[4]

This time the "otherwise" point P could be to the right or to the left of P'. Two opposing factors are at work in determining its position relative to P'. A positive marginal propensity to absorb nontradables would tend to draw resources out of tradables (and so push P to the right of P'); on the other hand, the fact that resources in tradables are now more productive is likely to draw resources into them (and so push P to the left of P'). If the first effect is stronger, P will be to the right of P', and a need for exchange rate protection in favor of tradables will arise. The earlier "oil" case was an extreme case where resources in tradables were no more productive than before at the margin because the whole of the output gain was a windfall.

THREE-GOOD MODEL: BOOMING SECTOR
AND LAGGING SECTOR

The tradable-nontradable model used so far does not fully capture the most common reason for exchange rate protection—to protect one part of the tradables sector when there is a productivity improvement or windfall gain in another part. Hence, there is need for a model with three sectors.

We divide the tradables sector into two parts—a booming sector and a lagging sector. The booming sector is where there is a large productivity improvement or a minerals windfall. The productivity improvement may be in value terms and not in physical terms, the world price of the booming sector's output having risen even though physical productivity is constant (the oil price case). In Japan the booming sector is the progressive, dynamic part of export-oriented manufacturing. In Britain, Norway, and all the OPEC countries it is the oil sector. In the case of the Netherlands it is the natural gas sector, and in Australia it is the minerals sector. The lagging sector in these countries consists of all other export industries as well as import-competing industries. The objective of actual or pro-

---

4. It would bring output to R' on the Rybczynski line RR', the slope of JH' at R' being the same as the slope of JJ' at R'.

posed exchange rate protection is to protect the lagging sector. There has been discussion of this issue in all these countries (see McKinnon 1976; Gregory 1976; Snape 1977; Forsyth and Kay 1980; Corden 1981).

This model can also be adapted for the Swiss case, where a real appreciation has been generated by exogenous (or speculative) private capital inflows rather than by a boom in some export industries. Exchange rate protection would avoid the appreciation and keep the current account balance unchanged, the exogenous private capital inflow being matched by an increase in official reserves or by private capital outflow induced by monetary policy (fall in the interest rate). In this case, the private sector exporting money or short-term bonds is the booming sector.

Let us now consider how a productivity improvement in the booming sector affects the lagging sector adversely (in the absence of exchange rate protection). As before, the nominal price of nontradables is held constant. The conclusions below follow from a formal model where there is a specific factor in each industry and one mobile factor used in all three industries (see Snape 1977; Corden and Neary 1980). An adverse effect for the lagging sector means that its output and, with it, the real rent of its specific factor fall.

Spending Effect

The extra income from the productivity increase will be spent partly on nontradables, so that at constant relative prices, excess demand for nontradables and a balance of payments surplus (domestic excess supply of tradables) would result. In the absence of intervention, the exchange rate would then appreciate to restore equilibrium, and this appreciation will lower the output of the lagging sector, employment in that sector, and the income of the specific factor there.

It should be noted that the extra income resulting from the productivity improvement will be spent in part directly by the factors of production in the booming sector and in part indirectly through extra tax revenues from the booming sector allowing increased government expenditures or reductions in other taxes. The indirect spending effect dominates in the case of British North Sea oil. When tax remissions and the benefits of extra government services are taken into account, there may finally be a net gain to the specific factor in the lagging sector even though its pretax income from employment will fall.

Direct Resource Movement Effect

Insofar as the productivity improvement raises the marginal product of the mobile factor in the booming sector, it will lead to resource movements of this factor out of the lagging sector, and lower the rent received by the specific factor in that sector. It should be noted that this effect does not operate through the exchange rate.

Indirect Resource Movement Effect

If the marginal product of the mobile factor in the booming sector is raised, there will also be a movement of the mobile factor out of the nontradables sector, which will create excess demand for nontradables, hence reinforcing the spending effect by giving rise to further appreciation that has an adverse effect on the specific factor in the lagging sector.

These results can be summarized as follows. The rent of the specific factor in the lagging sector must fall as a result of the productivity improvement in the booming sector unless (1) all the extra income from the productivity improvement is spent on tradables and (2) the marginal product of the mobile factor in the booming sector is not raised by the productivity improvement. If either some of the extra income is spent on nontradables or the marginal product of a given quantity of the mobile factor is raised by the improvement (or if both conditions apply), the real rent of the specific factor in the lagging sector will fall. Note that the real income of the mobile factor may rise or fall. These results can be generalized in a more imprecise form to a model with more than three factors—for example, where there are several mobile factors employed in different proportions to each other (different factor intensities) in the three industries.

Exchange rate protection in its extreme form would completely prevent the appreciation that would otherwise take place. It would be associated with a reduction in absorption that completely offset the spending effect and, in addition, offset the indirect resource movement effect on the demand for nontradables. The resultant balance of payments surplus would be equal to the reduction in absorption. Some adverse effect on specific factors in the lagging sector through the direct resource movement effect would remain. Exchange rate protection might, of course, not be complete and may be only a short-term policy.

It can be clearly established that exchange rate protection is not first best. Assume to begin with that it is desired to protect the whole tradables sector relative to nontradables, and take this as given. Thus, the basic protection motive is not queried at this stage. The first-best policy is then to subsidize the purchase of tradables, financing this by a tax on the purchase of nontradables, or alternatively, to subsidize the production of tradables, financing this by a tax on the production of nontradables. In Figure 2-1, this would bring the economy to P'. The inevitable cost of protection in this case is represented by the movement from indifference curve a to curve b. Note that with a given nominal price of nontradables, a purchase subsidy cum tax would have to be associated with a depreciation of the exchange rate to induce production to shift appropriately and maintain equilibrium in the market for nontradables, while a production subsidy cum tax would require an appreciation for the same reason.

The use of the exchange rate as the method of protection brings the economy to the current absorption point C and to a welfare level below that of curve b

but above that of curve c. The additional cost resulting from the balance of payments surplus can be termed the absorption contraction cost. There is such an additional cost because we are assuming that the level of official reserves (and of private holdings of foreign bonds and equities) was initially optimal; in other words, if there were no exchange rate protection motive, it would be optimal for the current account to be in balance. The welfare level will thus be below b, but it will be down to curve c only if (improbably) an increase in official reserves or in private holdings of foreign bonds or equities yielded no benefits at all (in the case of the reserves, yielding no interest receipts and no increased sense of security, and being eventually confiscated by the reserve currency country or completely devalued by inflation).

Let us next turn to the more relevant three-sector model and assume that the given objective is to protect not all tradables but only the lagging sector. The first-best policy is then to subsidize directly production of lagging industries. While this will yield an inevitable cost of protection, the use of the alternative device of exchange rate protection would impose two additional costs or by-product distortions. First, by protecting all tradable industries, whether booming or lagging, it would unduly increase the size of the booming sector (above the increase that would take place in any case). Second, by generating a surplus, it would impose the absorption contraction cost.

With regard to the direct subsidy for lagging industries, one might visualize it being financed primarily out of the revenue raised from the booming industries (a case of British industrial policy being financed by North Sea oil). But it must be stressed that the availability of extra revenue does not alter the fact that a cost of protection in the Pareto-efficiency sense is likely to be imposed when industries are subsidized for income maintenance or similar reasons.

THE IDENTIFICATION PROBLEM AND BRITAIN'S NORTH SEA OIL

Can one determine empirically when there is exchange rate protection? Let us first consider this question in the absence of interest-rate-responsive private capital movements, so that exchange rate protection will manifest itself in official exchange rate intervention policies.

The identification problem arises because one is concerned with assessing the motivation of such intervention policies. If there were no reason for a country ever to accumulate official reserves other than to depreciate the exchange rate for the sake of protecting part or all of the tradables sector, the fact of reserves accumulation would be the indicator of protection. We would at least have a quantitative indicator, which might provide a basis for estimates of the extent of depreciation brought about by this protection. But the accumulation of official reserves may have other purposes. In any particular case, one needs to estimate how much of the reserves accumulation reflects an official view that the absolute size of the reserves stock is too low in relation to the level of trade or of the GNP and in relation to other assets (or other criteria affecting judgments of reserves adequacy) and how much is the by-product only of maintaining or attaining a desired exchange rate. The "otherwise" situation referred to earlier would be the result of pursuing a reserves accumulation policy motivated by the first set of considerations – that is, one that is concerned with the optimal accumulation of reserves irrespective of the exchange rate result.[5]

It has to be noted that a clear distinction between exchange rate protection and the optimal accumulation of reserves cannot always be made. Reserves may be accumulated optimally at a given time not only to achieve a long-term stock target but also to smooth out fluctuations in absorption and generally to avoid instability. This relates to the discussion in the next section. Awkwardly, this motive cannot be entirely distinguished from exchange rate protection because, as mentioned later, exchange rate protection may be designed to avoid a temporary fall in prices facing lagging industries, a fall that would generate misleading resource allocation signals.

The identification of motive is even more difficult once we allow for private capital movements. A government that wishes to extend exchange rate protection to its industries need not intervene in the foreign exchange market at all. It can run a fiscal surplus and redeem some of its debt. While the resulting reduced expenditure will tend to appreciate the exchange rate, the actual or incipient rise in the interest rate will have the opposite effect, tending to depreciate the rate. If the capital flow effect outweighs the goods market effect (as is assumed in most simple models with capital mobility), the fiscal surplus will have brought about exchange rate protection without intervention in the foreign exchange market. One must then assess the motive for the fiscal surplus.

The identification problem arises in a case such as Britain's where the North Sea oil windfall is expected to be fairly short term. An optimal savings policy may call for most of the gains to be saved. If the savings are invested in domestic real assets, there will still be the spending effect and the associated appreciation (in the absence of exchange rate protection). But if it is thought optimal to invest in liquid assets, the reserves will be built up even without any exchange rate protection motivation. If the whole of the windfall were invested in liquid assets (and hence yielded a current account surplus to that extent), the spending effect would be zero and the exchange rate would appreciate only if there were any indirect resource movement effect. The lagging sector would lose because of this and any direct resource movement effect. In Britain's case, these two effects are likely to be small.

---

5. The vast literature on the demand for official reserves is relevant here. See the surveys by Grubel (1971), Williamson (1973), and de Beaufort Wijnholds (1977). The present chapter is not concerned with the many issues raised there but only with one additional reason that is not dealt with in this literature – why reserves may be accumulated (or reduced) by a country.

One might conclude that in Britain's case the much-discussed issue of exchange rate policy in response to North Sea oil divides up into three issues: (1) How much of the windfall is to be saved and how much consumed, supposing that there is no particular concern with adverse effects on lagging industries? (2) How much of the savings is to be invested in real assets domestically and how much in liquid assets, again disregarding effects on lagging industries? (3) What concern is there for possible adverse effects on lagging industries (the exchange rate protection issue)?

In considering issues 1 and 2, a possible ratchet effect must be allowed for. First, suppose that the windfall is consumed, in the form of either public or private consumption—in the latter case, perhaps, because of tax remissions that raise after tax real personal incomes. Later consumption may have to fall back again. If there is a downward rigidity of public consumption and of after tax real wages (a ratchet effect), a problem will be stored up for later. It may lead later to an inevitable balance of payments deficit and to unemployment. It may be wiser not to allow consumption to rise so far that it will later have to be reversed. This is an argument for investing, rather than consuming, the windfall. It is not necessarily an argument for investing the windfall in liquid assets, as distinct from domestic real assets, and so avoiding an appreciation.

Next, suppose it is decided to increase spending domestically, for either consumption or real investment. The exchange rate will appreciate, which will raise real incomes of factors specific to or intensive in nontradable industries, notably labor. If the real wage is flexible upwards but rigid downwards, again, trouble will be stored up for the future, when the exchange rate moves back again. This consideration may be an argument for avoiding or moderating an appreciation and investing instead in liquid assets. It must be distinguished from the exchange rate protection motive. It is concerned with avoiding a temporarily favorable effect for nontradables, as distinct from avoiding an unfavorable effect for lagging industries.

EXCHANGE RATE PROTECTION AND
THE THEORY OF PROTECTION

How does exchange rate protection fit into the existing theory of protection? Exchange rate protection uniformly raises the domestic prices of all tradables relative to the prices of all nontradables. This relative price change has effects not only on the output pattern and on income distribution, but also (when combined with the appropriate change in absorption) on the balance of payments.

By contrast, much of standard protection theory does not include nontradables at all. It is concerned with shifts in the pattern of output within the tradable goods sector, usually between importables and exportables. More recently, nontradables have been introduced into the theory of protection. But it is always assumed that the balance of payments is kept unchanged as a result of protection (Corden 1971: chs. 4, 5). This is normally thought of as happening through exchange rate adjustment. The assumption is part of the familiar dichotomy between the real theory of international trade and the monetary or balance of payments theory, with variations in the balance of payments being permitted only in the latter. Thus, in the existing theory of protection, the instrument of protection policy is the tariff or some similar device, while the exchange rate adjusts to attain a constant balance of payments. By contrast, with exchange rate protection, the exchange rate is the instrument of protection policy, and the balance of payments effect becomes a residual.

It has been shown in the theory of protection that in a model with an importable, an exportable, and a nontradable, a tariff will protect the importable not only relative to the exportable, but also relative to the nontradable. One can calculate a net protective rate that represents the rate of protection of the importable relative to the nontradable (Corden 1971: ch. 5). But this does not represent general protection of tradables relative to the nontradable, since, when the exchange rate adjustment takes place, the exportable is antiprotected relative to the nontradable by the tariff. Hence, in spite of the concept of the net protective rate, exchange rate protection is not part of the existing theory of protection.

Let us now turn to reasons for exchange rate protection. These are similar to those for "ordinary" protection and need to be analyzed in the same way. The fact that there are reasons does not mean that they are good reasons.

Probably the most common explanation for exchange rate protection is sectional real income maintenance, the sections concerned being factors specific to or intensive in the lagging industries. This motive is usually short term, a response to sudden shocks that, in the absence of protection, would reduce real incomes of particular sections of the community markedly. This might be described as the expression of a "conservative social welfare function" by policymakers.[6] Alternatively, one might see such income maintenance policies not as the fruits of a coherent "social welfare function" that is concerned to shelter losers in an economy but as a response to sectional pressures intensified by the prospect of, or actual, real income losses.

Real wages in the lagging industries may be rigid downwards, and labor may be immobile. An argument for protection designed to maintain total employment can then be made. It would also apply if labor were mobile and the lagging industries were labor intensive.[7]

---

6. The argument that a principal motive for protectionist policies is the pursuit of a "conservative social welfare function" is set out in Corden (1974: 88–90, 107–109).

7. It was argued above that if the windfall were temporary, it might be undesirable to allow an appreciation because it would raise real incomes in nontradables, which would lead to unemployment in that sector later, when the exchange rate movement has to be reversed. This should be combined with the present argument. If there is downward real wage rigidity (and other things are equal), an appreciation will cause unemployment now in the lagging industries and unemployment later in nontradable industries. This is the familiar argument for preventing price fluctuations because of ratchet effects.

The windfall in the booming industries may be known to be temporary by the government and by "informed" observers, so that there ought not to be any long-term resource shifts out of the temporarily lagging industries. It has been argued (for example, in Britain) that an appreciation would set up signals that would induce such undesirable resource shifts. Exchange rate protection is needed to produce the right signals. This argument implies that private decision-makers are influenced by current rather than expected profitability or that their expectations are based on inferior information.

All of these arguments apply to the protection of lagging industries within the tradables sector, rather than to the protection of tradables as a whole. It is more difficult to think of arguments for protecting all tradables relative to nontradables. A neophysiocratic tendency in Britain to glorify manufacturing relative to services on account of supposed differential growth effects has at times been transformed into an argument for protecting tradables relative to nontradables.

Possibly an infant industry argument for protection of manufacturing might be used. It may apply particularly to exports of manufactures in the form of a "long-term market development argument." Sometimes the German surplus has been justified, from Germany's point of view, in these terms. When the infant industry argument refers to the protection of manufacturing relative to services it is subject to the same sorts of qualifications that apply when, as is more usual, it refers to manufacturing relative to agriculture (see Corden 1974:ch. 9).

Incidentally, one can also envisage a situation of reverse exchange rate protection: The nontradables sector is protected at the expense of the tradables sector through the avoidance of a devaluation and thus the prolongation of a balance of payments deficit. The motive might be to maintain incomes of persons employed in nontradables (e.g., in the public sector). If labor is mobile between the sectors and nontradables are relatively labor intensive, protection of nontradables will raise real wages above the level they would otherwise be. In that case, devaluation may be avoided because it would either lower real wages or, with real wage rigidity, create unemployment.

To return to the protection of the lagging tradables sector, given that such protection is desired, how does exchange rate protection compare with tariffs and export subsidies for these industries? First, tariffs and export subsidies for the lagging industries ("ordinary" protection) shift the pattern of consumption away from lagging toward booming industries when it is only desired to affect prices facing producers. They thus impose a consumption distortion cost within the tradables sector as a whole that exchange rate protection avoids. Second, exchange rate protection creates two by-product distortions that ordinary protection avoids: (1) The booming sector is protected relative to nontradables when protection of the booming sector is certainly not desired, and (2) there is the absorption contraction cost because of the balance of payments surplus. Thus, at the a priori level, one cannot choose between the two devices, though one might wish to give a heavy weight to the absorption contraction cost, in which case exchange rate protection would be inferior.

Other considerations are also relevant in choosing between these policies. Protection may be intended to be temporary. The chances of exchange rate protection being temporary may be greater than the chances of tariffs and export subsidies being removed in due course. Administratively, exchange rate manipulation and tariffs are both easier than various kinds of subsidies. Furthermore, there are strong international rules against export subsidies. In comparing tariffs with exchange rate adjustment, three considerations may possibly favor use of the latter from the point of view of the government, at least in the short term. First, tariffs need generally to be legislated, while the exchange rate can be freely manipulated by the monetary authorities. Second, international commitments may prevent increases in tariffs. Third, tariff increases and the imposition of import quotas are more obviously protective than exchange rate depreciation and hence are more likely to provoke international retaliation.

UPWARD FLEXIBILITY OF NOMINAL WAGES: THE STORY RETOLD

Instead of assuming the nominal price of nontradables constant one could have assumed a constant nominal wage. The general argument would still stand: a devaluation would raise the relative price of tradables.[8]

Alternatively, one might prefer to assume that the nominal wage is rigid downwards but flexible upwards. If one starts in an equilibrium situation and then aims to protect tradables, it would still be necessary to devalue if one desired to maintain the level of employment. A reduction of absorption on its own would create unemployment without bringing down the price of nontradables. But the matter is quite different for the case on which we have been focusing, where a productivity improvement in the booming sector would, in the absence of exchange rate protection, lead to an appreciation. Let us retell this story with the assumption of a firmly fixed exchange rate and with upward flexibility of nominal wages and prices.

Again, we start with a productivity improvement in the booming sector and initially assume no policy designed to shelter the lagging sector. The extra demand for nontradables generated by the spending effect and the indirect resource movement effect will raise nominal wages and prices of nontradables. The higher wages will raise the costs of the lagging sector and hence affect profits in that sector adversely. In our earlier story, this adverse result was brought about by appreciation combined with constant wages. A policy designed to avoid this adverse cost effect (a policy equivalent to exchange rate protection) would consist of an offsetting policy of reducing absorption that ensured that demand for nontradables and labor did not rise in the first instance. There would

---

8. This would be so if labor and capital were mobile between the sectors and nontradables were relatively labor intensive or if only labor were mobile while capital is specific to each sector. It would not be so in the improbable case where nontradables are relatively capital intensive (see Jones and Corden 1976).

then be no rise in nominal wages. If the initial source of the extra demand in the absence of such a policy had been wholly the spending effect, the aim would be to keep absorption constant, with extra private spending by the booming industry possibly being offset by reduced public spending. Alternatively, the higher income of the booming sector may be largely siphoned off by taxes (as in the case of Britain's North Sea oil), while government expenditure is held constant.

It is certainly a significant point that the basic analysis of this chapter applies even when the nominal exchange rate is fixed, provided nominal wages are flexible upwards. Exchange rate protection consists in this case not of preventing appreciation but of preventing a rise in nominal wages. The crucial variable is the real exchange rate and not the nominal exchange rate.

One might also consider the case where the nominal exchange rate is an instrument of policy but where nominal wages and prices of nontradables are flexible upwards. As explained above, with a fixed exchange rate, the extra spending resulting from the booming sector's boom would have led to an inflationary rise in wages. The question is whether this would have been allowed or whether it would have been deliberately avoided by appreciation. In our earlier account, with rigid nominal wages or prices of nontradables, the appreciation was needed to avoid excess demand for nontradables. Now it is needed to avoid an inflationary adjustment. In both cases the spending effect of the boom leads to appreciation and to an adverse effect on the lagging sector, and exchange rate protection is the policy of avoiding this.

LARGE COUNTRY MODEL: HOW EXCHANGE RATE TARGETS CAN BECOME COMPATIBLE

The analysis needs to be extended to the large country case. The small country assumption has allowed the analysis to focus on the protectionist country itself, with the rest of the world being a sponge that absorbs any surplus or deficit that this country wishes to generate. Since exchange rate protection appears to have been practiced to some extent by the capitalist world's largest economies — notably, Germany and Japan — this is clearly not an adequate approach, though it is a beginning. The following discussion is particularly relevant to the issues that were debated in relation to the large Japanese current account surpluses of 1977 and 1978.

A two-country model, where neither country is small, brings out the essential issues. The two countries could be thought of as Japan and the United States. In such a model it would not be possible for each country to fix independently a target real exchange rate for itself. Given its own real exchange rate, a particular balance of payments surplus or deficit will be generated. But one country's deficit must be the other's surplus. The implicit idea that countries have real exchange rate or current account targets gives rise to the popular view that the international monetary system requires policy coordination.

The noncoordinated system can be rescued by departing from the fixed target approach. It can be shown that it is possible to have a two-country equilibrium without policy coordination. Instead of having a fixed real exchange rate or current account target for each country, each country can be assumed to take the interest rate into account when it formulates its exchange rate or balance of payments policy. Thus, the size of the current account target becomes a positive function of the interest rate. A country will seek to accumulate less foreign exchange reserves the lower the interest rate it expects to obtain on these reserves. Similarly, a country planning a deficit will bear in mind that the lower the foreign interest rate, the less the cost of this deficit—that is, the less the gain foregone in running down foreign exchange reserves or the greater the cost of foreign borrowing. If a country's current account target is achieved not by intervention in the foreign exchange market but by fiscal policy (an increased fiscal surplus generating a higher current account surplus and an increased fiscal deficit similarly increasing a current account deficit), the idea is that fiscal policy would take into account the interest rate.

Applying this interest rate consideration to the exchange rate protection concept, it can be said that exchange rate protection has a cost to a country and that this cost varies with the interest rate. The cost of this form of protection is the cost of excess lending abroad for the sake of protecting the tradables sector. The lower the interest rate obtainable, the greater the cost of exchange rate protection for the surplus country and thus the less exchange rate protection it will seek. Similarly, as pointed out above, the lower the interest rate, the more the deficit country will wish to borrow.

A world equilibrium model can then be built where the interest rate becomes endogenous—as it must be in a two-country model. Suppose that at the existing interest rate, Japan's target current account surplus is greater than the U.S. target current account deficit. In other words, at the existing interest rate, Japan wishes to buy more financial assets than the United States wishes to sell. Each target, and especially that of Japan, may be influenced by the exchange rate protection consideration. In this particular case there will be an excess demand for financial assets, and hence the interest rate—a single world interest rate—will fall. This will raise Japan's cost of exchange rate protection and hence reduce her target current account surplus. Similarly, the U.S. target deficit will increase since borrowing will be cheaper. In this way, the decline of the interest rate will bring the two current account targets together and hence make their exchange rate policies compatible.

SUMMARY

The purpose of this chapter has been to discuss various aspects of exchange rate protection—defined as a policy designed to protect tradables relative to nontradables. It has been stressed that the concern is with the real exchange rate, that exchange rate protection requires an appropriate reduction in absorption, and that it will yield a balance of payments surplus (or lesser deficit than otherwise). A common reason for exchange rate protection is to maintain employment, output, or profitability in "lagging" tradables industries when there is a boom in one part of the tradables sector. This is the case of British North Sea oil, and effects of a sectional boom on the lagging industries are detailed in the section on the three-good model.

It has been noted that the first-best way of protecting a lagging sector is by direct subsidies. The use of exchange rate protection imposes the absorption contraction cost (excessive lending abroad) and also unduly increases the size of the booming sector.

There is some difficulty in identifying exchange rate protection in practice. It is a matter of uncovering the motives for intervention in the foreign exchange market or of a fiscal surplus that lowers the domestic interest rate and depreciates the exchange rate: Is it to build up foreign exchange reserves to an optimal level, or is it to protect producers of tradables? This matter is discussed with respect to Britain's North Sea oil. There may be some argument in favor of the accumulation by Britain of foreign financial assets—and hence not allowing as much real appreciation as otherwise—because of the temporariness of the oil income. If British absorption is raised now, it may be difficult to get it down again later. Furthermore, optimal savings policy may justify some extra accumulation of assets.

The relation between exchange rate protection and the concept of "ordinary" protection has also been spelled out. The main point is that ordinary protection is concerned with resource (and income distribution) shifts within the tradables sector, while exchange rate protection is concerned with protection of the whole tradables sector relative to nontradables. The reasons for protection are similar in both cases, and particular weight has been given in this chapter to the "conservative social welfare function" motive. A comparison has also been made between the method of ordinary protection (tariffs or export subsidies) and exchange rate protection to achieve given protection of a lagging tradables sector. Each method imposes particular distortion costs, and in general it cannot be said that one method must be preferable, though the likely importance of the absorption contraction cost suggests that exchange rate protection may, in total, have a greater cost.

It has been noted that exchange rate protection can apply even in a fixed exchange rate system, bearing in mind that the concern is with the real exchange rate. This is so when a rise in nominal wages and prices of nontradables that would otherwise have taken place in response to a sectional export boom is avoided by a policy of preventing an increase in absorption. The object is to prevent a rise in costs and hence a fall in profits and employment in lagging tradables industries. Finally, a two-country model, where both countries have exchange rate protection or current account targets and the problem of incompatibility of targets arises, is briefly discussed. The main point is that an international equilibrium (in which the targets become compatible) would be achieved if the world interest rate—which is endogenous in the model—affects the target levels.

REFERENCES

Corden, W.M. 1971. *The Theory of Protection.* Oxford, England: Oxford University Press.

_____. 1974. *Trade Policy and Economic Welfare.* Oxford, England: Oxford University Press.

_____. 1981. "The Exchange Rate, Monetary Policy and North Sea Oil: The Economic Theory of the Squeeze on Tradables." *Oxford Economic Papers* 33 (July): 23–46.

Corden, W.M., and J.P. Neary. 1980. "Booming Sector and De-Industrialisation in a Small Open Economy." Unpublished.

de Beaufort Wijnholds, J.A.H. 1977. *The Need for International Reserves and Credit Facilities.* Leiden, The Netherlands: Martinus Nijhoff.

Forsyth, Peter J., and J.A. Kay. 1980. "The Economic Implications of North Sea Oil Revenues." *Fiscal Studies* 1 (July): 1–28.

Gregory, Robert G. 1976. "Some Implications of the Growth of the Mineral Sector." *Australian Journal of Agricultural Economics* 20 (August): 71–91.

Grubel, Herbert G. 1971. "The Demand for International Reserves: A Critical Review of the Literature." *Journal of Economic Literature* 9 (December): 1148–66.

Jones, Ronald W., and W.M. Corden. 1976. "Devaluation, Non-flexible Prices, and the Trade Balance for a Small Country." *Canadian Journal of Economics* 9 (February): 150–61.

McKinnon, Ronald I. 1976. "International Transfers and Non-traded Commodities: The Adjustment Problem." In D.M. Leipziger, ed., *The International Monetary System and the Developing Nations.* Washington, D.C.: Agency for International Development.

Razin, Assaf. 1980. "Capital Movements, Intersectoral Resource Shifts, and the Trade Balance." *Seminar Paper* No. 159. Stockholm: Institute for International Economic Studies, University of Stockholm, October.

Salter, W.E.G. 1959. "Internal and External Balance: The Role of Price and Expenditure Effects." *Economic Record* 35 (August): 226–38.

Snape, Richard H. 1977. "Effects of Mineral Development on the Economy." *Australian Journal of Agricultural Economics* 21 (December): 147–56.

Williamson, John. 1973. "Surveys in Applied Economics: International Liquidity." *Economic Journal* 83 (September): 685–746.

3 THE VALID CORE OF RATIONAL EXPECTATIONS THEORY AND THE PROBLEM OF EXCHANGE RATE RELATIONS

William Fellner

INTRODUCTION AND SUMMARY

I had the good fortune to serve on the Yale faculty for the two decades during which Robert Triffin developed much of his original, perceptive, and influential thinking about international economic problems. He did so without ever giving up his interest in what is usually described as general economic theory. Happy recollections of the close contacts we had during those years make me appreciative of this opportunity to express a few thoughts on problems about which we would, I am sure, have had many personal discussions had these problems developed in their present form at that time.

This chapter suggests the existence of a link between two areas of economic analysis by recognizing that the valid core of rational expectations theory – the core that in other writings I described as the credibility hypothesis[1] – has a bearing on the problem of desirable exchange rate relations among countries. This link exists because exchange rate movements within a group of countries depend on the relation of their domestic policies to each other. Hence, consistency in living up to exchange rate commitments, the results of which are promptly observable, is apt to influence expectations concerning the complex relation of general domestic policies within a group. Yet this is a matter of relativities within any group, rather than of the standards observed by any member of a

1. Of my more recent writings on this, I refer to Fellner (1976, 1979, 1980). The volume of which Fellner (1980) is a part includes several papers by contributors to the development of rational expectations theory and several papers by critics. The papers had been written for a conference held at the American Enterprise Institute in February 1980.

group. Thus, using this method for increasing the credibility of the relation of domestic policies to each other is desirable only to the extent that it involves anchoring this intragroup relation to the policies of at least one major participant whose domestic policy behavior is considered desirable and firmly credible.

The conclusion will be that once the determination of at least one major country – preferably of a subgroup of countries – to a return to noninflationary demand policies has acquired firm credibility, a system usually described as limited exchange rate flexibility has a good chance of adding credibility to the declared intention of other countries also to return to the same policies. Such an exchange rate system has often been nicknamed "band and crawl." As compared to "fixed rate" systems of the past, such a system involves widened margins between intervention points and gradual and limited adjustability of the range bordered by intervention points.

However, in the absence of a consistently kept and credible commitment of any major participant to return to a policy of price level stability, establishing the exchange rate relations so described runs a substantial risk of becoming an engine of coordinated inflationary policies. In the environment existing at the time of this writing, that risk is in fact substantial. While this is an environment that is hopefully not here to stay, the need to anchor any such exchange rate relations in at least one major currency the management of which is credibly noninflationary even aside from exchange rate relations remains an essential condition.

This condition poses a problem that would not have to be faced in circumstances in which the conditions of a reasonably satisfactory functioning of the gold standard would be satisfied because, when that is the case, exchange rate stability and a good approximation to price level stability can be achieved at one stroke. However, for reasons on which I will not elaborate in this chapter, and that are connected with trends in supply and demand in the gold market, I feel convinced that coupling a return to noninflationary demand management with the restoration of any variety of the gold standard does not at present describe a feasible program. What the more distant future might bring in this regard I consider an open question that should not be closed by calling everyone attempting to explore it a "gold bug." Yet at present a world of "fiat money" needs to be taken for granted, and in the given circumstances, I regard as crucial the problem of "anchoring" any desirable regularization of exchange rate relations to a dependably well-behaved currency (or to several such currencies). As long as that is not possible, institutionally regularized exchange rate relations would create significant difficulties that are avoided by floating rates. Whether in such circumstances "management" of the float is justified is a question the answer to which also depends on whether the "management" is undertaken in such a way as to help the market participants to form rational expectations.

THE VALID CORE OF "RATIONAL EXPECTATIONS"

Distinguishing the Valid Core from Other Claims

There is no room here for surveying systematically the major contributions or the points of disagreement that have received attention in recent writings on rational expectations. I will instead summarize some of the conclusions to which an appraisal of these writings has led me, focusing on aspects of these debates that bear on the subject of the present essay.

The valid and essential core of the rationality hypothesis in the theory of expectations is not of recent origin. What has recently come to be regarded as the "rational expectations school" has thrown additional light on this valid core, but it has also added at least two claims that do not belong to what I regard as the valid core of the basic rationality hypothesis.[2] I will first describe briefly what I consider the valid core and then comment on the additional claims that I consider unconvincing. Subsequently I will relate the conclusions derived from this analysis to the main topic of the present essay.

The "valid core" can be expressed in general terms as maintaining that a detectable structure of relations among economic variables will be figured out by the market participants. Thus, if all structural relations were clearly detectable and credible—if they all were unequivocally recognizable by intelligent and well-informed people whose services are presumably available for a fee to the less intelligent or less well informed—then all deviations from the equilibrium path of the economy would result merely from the fact that the structural relations include error terms of a stochastic nature. To me it seems important to recognize that the stochastic terms that, as is generally admitted, would cause deviations from the economy's equilibrium path do so not only at the time when they produce "residuals" (as compared to probabilistically expected values) but more or less at all times. This is because the existence of stochastic terms would in any event be known to the public, and most market participants are not risk neutral. The equilibrium path implied in these propositions is determined by the

2. The concept of the "rational expectations school" is not well-defined. I list a number of contributions, some of which do make claims that I exclude from the "valid core"; others either qualify these claims to some extent or at least admit the possibility that qualifications may be needed; still others (particularly those by Phelps, Taylor, and Fischer) stress some specific qualifications effectively and elaborate on these. Nevertheless, the distinctive views at present commonly associated with the "rational expectations school" do include these claims—essentially the claim to have demonstrated (1) the neutrality of a generally identifiable systematic component of demand policy and (2) the inability of demand policy to influence the real variables of the economy.

A selective list of articles bearing out the content of the preceding paragraph includes Haberler (1980); Lucas (1972, 1973, 1975); Barro and Fischer (1976); Barro (1978); Sargent and Wallace (1976); Phelps and Taylor (1977); Fischer (1977); Taylor (1979); and McCallum (1979).

intended real supply prices of the available inputs and by the value placed on the output obtainable from these inputs. Deviations from the equilibrium path of the economy are deviations from a path so defined. These are the deviations that would be caused exclusively by the stochastic terms in the usual sense if all structural relations were clearly detectable by intelligent individuals—that is, if the relevant "models" were truly credible.

In my appraisal the rationality hypothesis, when reduced to its valid core, needs to stress, however, that there often exist legitimate differences between the market participants' appraisals of the basic structural relations connecting the variables. To the extent that these relations are not unequivocally recognizable by all intelligent people, risk allowances will be greater than they would otherwise be and the deviations from the economy's equilibrium path will also be greater. There is obviously a difference between the role of error terms in the decision process relating to an experiment with coins whose properties all intelligent people assess identically—say, with guaranteed fair coins or their equivalents in some properly devised experiment—and the role of error terms in an experiment with coins about whose properties there exist substantial "legitimate" differences of views prior to the tossing. If fair coins are tossed a limited number of times, the knowledge that the ratio of heads to tails is unlikely to be precisely unitary will influence decisionmakers even in an experiment so described, but that influence will be much smaller than the influence of imperfections of foresight (uncertainty) if the properties of the coins are a matter of guesswork.

Moving from the general level of structural relations among economic variables to the policy variables with which we shall be mainly concerned in this chapter, the valid core of the rationality hypothesis in expectations theory suggests that a clearly detectable system adopted by the authorities for setting the level of policy variables will be figured out and understood by the markets. Thus, given such a detectable system underlying the conduct of policy, only the effect of stochastic elements will be unpredictable. To express the same proposition in other words: Were it not for the stochastic terms, the authorities managing a clearly recognizable demand policy would not affect the path of the real variables, but would merely influence the price level. The stochastic terms would in any event have an effect on the real variables, particularly because the public is not risk neutral, but that is all.

If, on the other hand, demand policy has no clearly detectable design—if the public can make only vague guesses about any "system" that it will be possible to read into the policy behavior of the authorities in retrospect—then demand policy will have a major "real" effect, reflecting itself in large deviations from the equilibrium path. As concerns the subject matter of the present chapter, this is the main proposition following from what I regard as the valid core of rationality hypothesis.

What I have described as the valid core does not include two of the claims made by the rational expectations school as this is nowadays usually interpreted.

One of the claims that in my appraisal does not belong in the valid core is that it is generally useful to divide the movement of the demand policy variables into a systematic component that has no effect on the real variables because it is figured out by the public and a stochastic component that alone does have a "real" effect. It is unconvincing to attribute such "real neutrality" to an alleged systematic component of the movements of policy variables in circumstances in which a systematic component can be figured out only in the spurious sense that market participants are kept guessing about what the policymakers are about to do, with the result that significantly differing guesses will be made by market participants, all of whom will attach large risk allowances to their guesses. "Real neutrality" of a systematic component of the movement of demand policy variables is a valid proposition—it is that at least in an acceptable approximation to reality—only to the extent that the component can be clearly detected and that all intelligent market participants will thus figure it out in very nearly the same fashion. The claim that demand policies generally have a neutral systematic component is in my appraisal unrealistic.

Another claim of the rational expectations school, as that description is nowadays usually interpreted, is that as a result of the "real neutrality" of the systematic component of demand policy and as a result of the fact that the admittedly nonneutral stochastic component is uncontrollable, the authorities in charge of demand policy are generally incapable of influencing the real variables of the economy. This claim I also exclude from the valid core, because the claim would not be generally acceptable even on the assumptions on which the systematic component would be clearly and unequivocally detectable and hence would possess "real neutrality." Even in that event, the stochastic terms would presumably be serially correlated, and in a stochastic world in which market participants are not risk neutral, some of the cost and price decisions would be made in the markets well ahead of time. Thus, if demand policy can be made to take effect promptly enough, it could make use of the knowledge that is conveyed only shortly before each period by the serial correlation of error terms. Demand policy could make use of this knowledge to offset disturbances that tend to develop because of cost and price commitments made at an earlier time without the benefit of the knowledge conveyed by the serial correlation of the stochastic term.

Hence, as concerns the propositions usually associated with the "rational expectations school," I do not attribute validity to any generalized version of the proposition asserting the real neutrality of a distinguishable component ("systematic" component) of demand policy, and I do not attribute validity to the proposition asserting that demand policy is generally incapable of exerting a desired influence on the course of the economy's real variables. At the same time I feel convinced that in the postwar period, the most influential theoretical constructs—constructs that have mostly developed along neo-Keynesian lines—have paid far too little attention to the valid core of the rationality hypothesis in expectations theory. These constructs have paid far too little attention to the fact that the public does indeed see through clearly detectable characteristics of the relations among economic variables. From this a number of nontrivial conclusions follow. I will start with two "negative" conclusions before turning to the positive content of this chapter.

Two Negative Propositions Following From the Valid Core

While policy efforts to reduce measured unemployment rates by inflationary methods—policy efforts oriented to the Phillips trade-off—do have some clearly detectable characteristics, they cannot have a detectable design in the sense required for keeping an economy close to its equilibrium path. Under such a policy the public does, of course, detect easily enough that an inflationary price trend is developing. The inflationary stimulus therefore requires the accommodation of a rate of inflation that tends to steepen, yet preventing this tendency from getting out of hand at an early stage calls for interrupting full accommodation occasionally. This inevitably is done at unpredictable stages of the process and to an unpredictable extent, with the result that whereas the public becomes aware of the steepening tendency of the inflation, it remains in great uncertainty about all details of the course of events that are essential to intelligent decision-making. The efficiency of the system is thereby significantly reduced.

Restoring reasonable predictability and credibility after such inflationary interludes requires reestablishing a practically noninflationary price trend, because the usual promise of policymakers to stabilize an already existing appreciable inflation rate is a clearly noncredible promise. This promise amounts to asserting that while the authorities are at present shying away from the discomfort of reducing the now observable inflation rate, they will on the next occasion accept the even greater discomfort of reducing any higher inflation rate—a promise that will rightly be disbelieved, with the result that cost trends will continue to show a steepening tendency. It is not possible to return to the neighborhood of an equilibrium path without accepting the difficulties of an adjustment period during which inflation is reduced to insignificance.

The second negative proposition to be derived from the valid core is that the usual neo-Keynesian models—often referred to as standard models—stipulate an unconvincing relationship between past wage and price increases on the one hand and current and future wage and price increases on the other. For any given degree of "slack" of resources, these models imply that price expectations, and therefore current wage increases, are determined by past price increases, with unchanging positive coefficients linking the past to the present increases. It is not astonishing that these models have proved seriously misleading.

If demand policy has a generally detectable design, this neo-Keynesian specification is unconvincing because any design or system underlying such policy practices is practically certain to have characteristics different from those that would carry the past over into the present and into the future in this particular fashion. To take an illustration, a policy that has been figured out by the markets as aiming for a practically horizontal price trend clearly does not establish this kind of mechanical link between the past and the future when deviations occur from the trend. If, on the other hand, the policy has no clearly detectable design—if, for example, demand policy is oriented to short-term Phillips trade-offs—then, for the reasons discussed above, it will create an environment of high uncertainty in which the public may conceivably have no better way of guessing about the future than to project the recent past into the next periods, but in such an environment the coefficients linking the past to the future will prove highly unstable.

A Positive Conclusion for Anti-inflationary Policy

The positive conclusion is that a consistent and credible demand policy aiming for price stability will, after an adjustment period, succeed in conditioning price expectations and cost trends to a behavior consistent with the desired price stability. Adverse effects on output—stagflationary tendencies—will be limited to an adjustment period the duration of which depends on how long it takes to establish the credibility of the policy and on how long the carryover effects of past cost commitments continue to cause difficulties to the sellers of goods. On the other hand, if a demand policy aiming for general price stability does not succeed in establishing credibility, then cost trends will not adjust, and the main result of the policy will be reflected in adverse effects on output and employment rather than in favorable effects on the price trends.

I now turn to the bearing of this analysis on international monetary relations. The relevance of these conclusions for the problem of exchange rate systems develops from the fact that successful anti-inflationary domestic policy in a group of countries implies very moderate exchange rate movements as compared to those observed in the recent past in the Western world. This is known to the markets, and the market participants take it into account in developing their expectations. The problem of promptly observable exchange rate movements thus has a bearing on the credibility of domestic policy programs within a group of countries.

EXCHANGE RATES AND THE OBJECTIVE OF RETURNING TO PRICE LEVEL STABILITY

The Environment Requiring Floating Rates

"Debasing the currency" for the sake of achieving various financial objectives of governments has a long history, but only in the post–World War II era has it become routine practice in a good many important developed economies to adopt inflationary policies for the specific purpose of raising the level of output and employment. In the United States this practice dates back no further than the mid-1960s. For reasons discussed above, such policies can succeed only for a short period. They soon lead to high inflation and high unemployment in an environment of substantial uncertainty and of unfavorable productivity trends— results that have by now become observable in many countries. Nevertheless, exchange rates could be kept reasonably stable among countries engaging in policies of this kind if these countries decided to coordinate their inflationary policies to the extent needed for achieving exchange rate stability. The fact of the matter, however, is that some countries have so far been capable of resisting these domestic policy pressures to a much greater extent than others. The emergence of such a "spectrum" violates the conditions of exchange rate stability and favors floating.

In an environment in which acceptance of the difficulties of an adjustment period is postponed further and further and in which some countries are more resistant than others to domestic inflationary policy pressures, it is, of course, in principle possible to make the inevitable exchange rate adjustments administratively and to do so by changing from time to time the officially set levels at which the exchange rates are held by the support operations of the central banks. I am very skeptical about this procedure because there is no general presumption that the authorities would mostly be able to avoid situations in which the markets get ahead of them and there is no presumption that, when an attempt is made to correct disequilibrium, the administratively adjusted rates would in fact be equilibrium rates.

Floating rates thus describe the currency relations best suited to the requirements of an international community the members of which are striving in different degrees for the short-term payoff of inflationary policies. Floating has made it possible to avoid the currency crises, including the temporary suspensions of market activities, that occur when, under fixed but administratively adjustable rates, excess demand emerges as a result of insufficient flexibility of these administered rates. At the same time, floating has enabled countries whose political processes are less biased toward inflationary methods than those of others to remain less inflationary in fact.

When is the Management of Floating Rates Justified?

From what has been said, it does not follow as a general proposition that the authorities should abstain from "managing" the float by occasional official interventions in the currency markets. But the conclusion does indeed suggest that such ad hoc support operations will be useful only if followed by policy measures that would subsequently have the desired effect even aside from the support operations. Authorities that acquire the reputation of engaging in interventions if, and only if, at the same time they are adopting such domestic measures as well are apt to add to the credibility of their determination to adopt these domestic measures and to follow through on them; and in that event, the effects of these domestic measures are apt to be anticipated by the markets under the influence of the interventions at an earlier stage than would otherwise be the case.

This is one of the policy problems that needs to be appraised in view of the importance of credibility effects. The appropriate domestic policies would in due time bring the exchange rates to a level consistent with those policies even in the absence of currency interventions, yet currency movements inconsistent with those policies reflect lack of conviction in the markets that the domestic policies in question will in fact be carried out, and it is more difficult (more "costly") to carry out these domestic policies in an environment of distrust in which trends in wage rates, interest rates, and raw material prices adjust slowly. This is why credibility can be increased by currency market interventions whose effects are promptly noticeable and are rightly believed to be appropriate and to bring the authorities gains if the announced domestic policy plans are carried out (and to be inappropriate and to cause the authorities losses in the contrary case).

Differently expressed, whereas in general there is no reason to assume that the authorities know better than the markets, they do in many cases know better or sooner what they themselves are about to do, and interventions credibly expressing a commitment to adopt a course of action may help to make that course become effective more promptly. On the other hand, interventions based on the conception that the mere sale and purchase of currencies by the authorities have a lasting effect on exchange rates are certain to miscarry. Hence a case exists for the management of floating rates when the currency interventions are consistently followed up by the appropriate domestic policies.

What to me seems no more than a "favorite game" of the critics of floating as the regime suitable to the general policy environment of the past decade is the identification of episodes during which the market produced sharp fluctuations of specific exchange rates, with reversals following soon after a steep rise or decline. The existence of such episodes proves nothing about the merits and limitations of floating. The policies of the decade have kept the markets in substantial uncertainty concerning the presumptive path of a great many important variables in all Western economies. The generally harmful consequences of this have been made particularly weighty by the fact that the U.S. inflation rate has been one of the ill-behaved variables and that while this rate has clearly been rising in the Western international inflation spectrum, it has remained unpredictable within uncomfortably large ranges. This has created an incentive in many countries to reduce the dollar component of the portfolios held. It was to be expected that in such circumstances exchange rate variations should reflect the uncertainties of the environment and that many of these variations should appear to be unjustified in retrospect. There is no presumption that official agencies or their professional forecasters would have had better foresight than the markets concerning those fluctuations that central bank interventions have not in fact smoothed out.

Institutionalized Exchange Rate Systems
and the Problem of Credibility

It might be tempting to conclude from these considerations that the float would describe the most desirable exchange rate regime even if in the conduct of their domestic affairs major countries succeeded in putting an end to the era of inflationary efforts for the sake of short-run benefits. It might be argued that in an essentially noninflationary world, even freely floating exchange rates would show a good deal of stability or at least would move very gradually. While this argument cannot be brushed aside, it has the weakness of disregarding an adjusted version of what I described above as the case for the management of floating rates when the currency interventions are followed up by domestic policies. I will argue that an adjusted version of this principle suggests giving consideration to a specific type of exchange rate relation for a future noninflationary group of countries, along the lines of proposals for widened margins and crawling support point ranges (band and crawl schemes), extensively discussed at an earlier stage of the debate, mostly prior to the collapse of the Bretton Woods system.

The view I am expressing implies that in the "foreseeable future," as this is to be interpreted for the present purpose, it will be impossible to resurrect any version of the gold standard as the basis of currency relations. During the era of its dominance, the gold standard established very nearly fixed exchange rates (rather than wide band and crawling parity arrangements) among the participating countries. The gold standard subordinated to exchange rate fixity any price level objectives the countries may have had, although it must have been clear at that time too that major instability of the price level is very damaging. The absence of a direct concern for price level objectives under the gold standard seemed regrettable to some of the most significant economists of that era, including among others Irving Fisher and "the Keynes of the twenties," and including before them also Marshall.[3] Yet this problem of priorities was of much smaller importance at that time because movements of the general price level

---

3. Even with the references here limited to these three authors of that era, comparing the suggestions made for giving price stability more prominence would have to be the subject matter of a separate article. For Fisher's ideas about the "compensated dollar," see primarily Fisher (1920: ch. IV), though in that book he refers also to pre–World War I publications that express essentially the same ideas in less-developed form. For Keynes' ideas, see Keynes (1924: 154ff.; 1930: II, 388 ff.).

As for Marshall, he repeatedly expressed himself on the conflict between the gold standard and general price stability and stressed the importance of the latter. He considered his practical suggestion to establish a system of symmetalism (which in his earlier writings he called true bimetalism) merely a minor step toward stabilizing the purchasing power of money in the sense of stabilizing the quantity that a money unit buys of some composite of goods (in that case, of a fixed composite of a quantity of gold and of a quantity of silver)

compatible with the system were quite minor as compared to highly damaging price level movements – particularly of the inflationary kind – that could develop quite easily in countries that would agree to keep their exchange rates fixed while maintaining inconvertible currencies (fiat money). Keeping exchange rates fixed with the currencies consisting of inconvertible paper money does not in itself guarantee even a crude approximation to a stable price level. The world of the gold standard was different in that regard. When in exceptional phases of that era major price level movements did occur (as they did in times of war), the incompatibility of those movements with the system became promptly apparent, and the aftermath included painful readjustments.[4]

Given the conditions that will prevail in any foreseeable future, the priority of price level stability over exchange rate stability would have to be clearly recognized, and the specific content of any exchange rate commitment would therefore have to be made dependent on what exchange rate movements are at all likely to be compatible with a reasonable approximation to general price stability in the participating countries. Authorities committing themselves to an exchange rate system that permitted merely these "compatible" movements of the rates could thereby add to the credibility of their basic commitment to price level goals. As was argued above, it is unconvincing to object to this proposition on the grounds that if "incompatible" exchange rate movements develop and the authorities fail to intervene in the currency markets, then a consistent price-level-oriented policy will in due time teach the markets a lesson in any event. It is unconvincing because the "incompatible" exchange rate movements are symptoms of the lack of credibility of basic price level commitments, and to enforce the basic commitment in an environment of lack of credibility has unfavorable output effects that are avoided if the price level commitment does possess credi-

---

rather than of gold alone. The principle he favored was that of stabilizing the general purchasing power of money, though at that time he probably did not consider it practical to adjust the monetary system in such a way as to achieve this objective. See, for example, Marshall (1887; 1923: 49).

4. Lumping together all phases of the period from 1879 to the collapse of Bretton Woods (the first of these dates being that at which the United States returned to gold after the Civil War), the gold and the gold exchange standard did include some periods in which the U.S. price level rose at a rate higher than what may reasonably be called moderate, but these periods clearly demonstrate that sustained substantial inflation was at that time incompatible with systems belonging in the gold standard category. In the United States, the inflation of World War I was followed by almost fifteen years of partially offsetting deflation and in 1934 by a significant upward revaluation of gold. The inflation of World War II and the brief inflationary phase of the Korean War were followed neither by offsetting deflation in the United States nor by a revaluation of gold in terms of the dollar but by a renewed flare-up of inflation after 1965 and soon thereafter by a collapse of the system. For the entire period 1879–1965, the average yearly compound rate of increase of the consumer price level was 1.4 percent. (For the period preceding that for which the present official Bureau of Labor Statistics estimates are regularly published, I used series E135 of the *Historical Statistics of the United States* I: 210–11.)

bility and the cost trends therefore do adjust to it. The behavior of exchange rates is promptly observable, while the policy adjustments required for achieving more fundamental objectives are subject to lags.

The Exchange Rate Implications of Noninflationary Policies in a Group of Countries

This raises the question of what exchange rate behavior is likely to prove a corollary of price level stability in a group of countries aiming for that objective. This question cannot be answered with a generality that includes taking account of situations in the nature of "emergencies." In a political crisis by which some countries are much less affected than the others, price stability is in principle compatible with very substantial swings of exchange rates, though this qualification loses part of its significance if we recognize that in such circumstances price stability is also very difficult to maintain in the countries under consideration. More generally, the possibility always exists of major sudden changes in international portfolio preferences that would bring about large swings in exchange rates, regardless of whether the price levels in the various countries do or do not change significantly. No exchange rate system can be devised that would withstand all storms that may hit the international community. This is to be taken for granted in all speculations such as the present.

But something can be said about the "normal" relationship among the currencies of countries following noninflationary policies. In particular something can be said about the main "normal" reasons why stability of the general price level in all participating countries is incompatible with strictly fixed exchange rates and yet is very unlikely to have as its corollary more than a very gradual change in currency rates extending possibly over long periods.

What I have in mind here can be illustrated by sustained differences between national productivity trends, assuming that the steeper trends are largely concentrated in the traded goods sectors. Alternatively, I could have illustrated my proposition with a sustained trend in the composition of international demand toward the products of a specific country, but while such shifts need not be associated with steeper productivity trends (including product improvement) in the favored country, that association does in fact often exist. Assuming productivity trends that in the traded goods sector remain steeper over an extended period in one country than in the others, either the currency rate of that country would have to rise in order to keep its price level constant or expansionary demand policy would have to be used in the steep productivity country to raise its general price level relative to that of the other countries, which we assume to be noninflationary. If neither of these two things happen, the steep productivity country would become a surplus country. Moreover, the surplus itself would have a rising trend: The difference between the productivity levels of the countries would be rising from period to period because trend differentials cumulate.

This needs to be offset. It can be offset by a rising trend in the steep productivity country's currency rate or in the domestic prices of that country, because both of these also cumulate in terms of levels (currency rate levels or price levels).

With constant exchange rates, the price trends would remain the same in the traded goods sector of the steep productivity country as in that of the other countries. This implies that as a result of a productivity trend differential that is concentrated in the traded goods sector, this sector of the economy becomes more profitable than the country's nontraded goods sector. Other things equal, the result will be a transfer of resources from the country's nontraded to its traded goods sector and the emergence of a surplus in the country's current account unless demand is managed in the country in such a way that prices in its nontraded goods sector rise and its profitability is thereby maintained. The nontraded goods prices of the steep productivity country are the only ones free to rise in the circumstances here described, and their rise will raise the steep productivity country's general price level on any reasonable definition of the "general" price level. If this is to be avoided, the exchange rate of the country's currency needs to rise in order to prevent a progressive transfer of resources from the nontraded to the traded goods sector and to prevent correspondingly raising disequilibrium in the international accounts.

The size of the yearly productivity trend differentials we have in mind here may in some cases amount to several percentage points over extended periods. The exchange rate adjustments required for preventing the emergence of price trend differentials is quite likely to be adequately taken care of by some version of the schemes involving widened margins between intervention points and limited adjustments ("crawls") of the range between these points. Such a scheme would also take care of most other inconsistencies between price level and exchange rate stability if at least one major participant's commitment to price level stability is assured and credible. Some participants could, of course, misuse such a scheme for generating an inflation rate compatible with "crawling downward" in relation to a noninflationary country at the permissible rate. But if the permissible yearly rate was, say, 2 or 3 percent, not even a country so misusing the provisions could develop an inflationary record comparable to those we nowadays observe over most of the international inflation spectrum. Countries that consistently followed up intervention with the domestic policies required to limit their exchange rate movements in relation to any noninflationary country would increase their own noninflationary credibility by such interventions.

It is not possible to turn this proposition around by requiring strict exchange rate stability, in the more rigorous sense in which it existed in the heyday of the gold standard, and permitting that degree of general price increase relative to a credibly noninflationary country that is consistent with strict exchange rate stability. This would not describe an internally consistent construct, because the "credibly noninflationary country" may turn out to be the steep productivity trend country, the currency of which would be crawling upward under limited exchange rate stability. In the event of strict exchange rate stability, this country would have to become inflationary—an inconsistent set of assumptions.

The requirement that there should be at least one credibly noninflationary major country to which the exchange rate arrangements and the policy coordination here discussed are anchored is crucial for arriving at the conclusions of this chapter. This must be a country—preferably a nucleus of a larger group of countries—not suspect of being pulled up in the inflation spectrum by its partners in an exchange rate system. At present this requirement is not satisfied. Hopefully one may look toward a future in which it will be, but this involves more than coping with problems of relativity or coordination within the international community.

The unrealistic view is occasionally expressed that something can be gained by merely aiming for an average of recently observed national inflation rates through coordinating the policies of countries located high with countries located lower in the inflation spectrum. This view disregards the fact that, for reasons explained in section one, appreciable inflation rates cannot be stabilized.

REFERENCES

Barro, Robert J. 1978. "Unanticipated Money, Output and the Price Level." *Journal of Political Economy* (August).

Barro, Robert, and Stanley Fischer. 1976. "Recent Developments in Monetary Theory." *Journal of Monetary Economics* 2 (April): 133–67.

Fellner, William. 1976. *Towards a Reconstruction of Macroeconomics: Problems of Theory and Policy.* Washington, D.C.: American Enterprise Institute.

_____. 1979. "The Credibility Effect and Rational Expectations: Implications of the Gramlich Study." *Brookings Papers on Economic Activity* 1.

_____. 1980. "The Valid Core of Rationality Hypotheses in the Theory of Expectations." *Journal of Money, Credit, and Banking* (November): supplement.

Fischer, Stanley. 1977. "Long-Term Contracts, Rational Expectations and the Optional Money Supply Rule." *Journal of Political Economy* 85 (February): 191–205.

Fisher, Irving. 1920. *Stabilizing the Dollar.* New York: Macmillan.

Haberler, Gottfried. 1980. "Rational and Irrational Expectations." In *Wandlungen in Wirtschaft und Gesellschaft: Die Wirschafts- und die Sozialwissenschaften vor neuen Aufgaben: Festschrift in Honor of Walter Adolf Jöhr.*

Keynes, John Maynard. 1924. *A Tract on Monetary Reform.* London: Macmillan.

_____. 1930. *A Treatise on Money.* London: Macmillan.

Lucas, Robert E., Jr. 1972. "Expectations and the Neutrality of Money." *Journal of Economic Theory* 4 (April): 103–24.

_____. 1973. "Some International Evidence on Output–Inflation Tradeoffs." *American Economic Review* 63 (June): 326–34.

_____. 1975. "An Equilibrium Model of the Business Cycle." *Journal of Political Economy* 83 (December): 1113–44.

Marshall, Alfred. 1887. "Preliminary Memorandum [to the] Commission on the Value of Gold and Silver." Reprinted in *Official Papers.* p. 31. 1926. London: Macmillan.

_____. 1923. *Money, Credit and Commerce.* London: Macmillan.

McCallum, Bennett T. 1979. "The Current State of the Policy Ineffectiveness Debate." *American Economic Review* 69 (May): 240–45.

Phelps, Edmund S., and John B. Taylor. 1977. "Stabilizing Powers of Monetary Policy under Rational Expectations." *Journal of Political Economy* 85 (February): 163–90.

Sargent, Thomas J., and Neil Wallace. 1976. "Rational Expectations and the Theory of Economic Policy." *Journal of Monetary Economics* 2 (April): 169–83.

Taylor, John B. 1979. "Staggered Wage Setting in a Macro Model." *American Economic Review* 69 (May): 108–13.

4 EFFECTS OF INTERVENTION AND STERILIZATION IN THE SHORT RUN AND THE LONG RUN

Peter B. Kenen

INTRODUCTION

Academic views about flexible exchange rates are even more volatile than the rates themselves. At the start of the current float, in 1973, there was much criticism of official intervention. What we want, said the critics, is a "clean" float rather than a "dirty" float. Five years later, in 1978, there was much criticism of the United States because of its reluctance to intervene in the support of the dollar.

The recent move toward more management and, therefore, more intervention should not surprise or disappoint Robert Triffin. "On balance," he wrote, "stabilizing interventions by the Central Bank itself, with their implicit bias toward internal monetary adjustments, would often present advantages over private stabilizing interventions with their implicit bias toward neutralization" (Triffin 1960:85). This brief passage is especially interesting today, because it anticipates the debate that has begun concerning the effects of sterilized and nonsterilized intervention.

In a thoughtful paper on official intervention under floating exchange rates, Mussa (1980) weighs the several arguments for intervention and finds some of them persuasive. But he comes down strongly on the side of nonsterilized intervention. Intervention will not have long-lasting influence, he says, if central banks sterilize its money supply effects.

This chapter was written while I was Ford Visiting Research Professor at the University of California, Berkeley. I am grateful to Polly Allen, Jeffrey Frankel, Jorge de Macedo, and Jerry Stein for comments on an earlier version.

Intervention can affect exchange rates temporarily by changing expectations about economic policies:

> The argument that official intervention is required to correct for the defects of private speculation, specifically excessive variation caused by "bandwagon effects," is not especially convincing, particularly in view of the possibility that official intervention may itself be responsible for the purported defects of private speculation. There is, however, a valid case for official intervention on the grounds that the authorities may have better knowledge of their own future policy intentions than private market participants. Official intervention may be called for in circumstances where the credibility of the authorities is in question and it is necessary to "buy credibility" by committing the assets of the central bank to the support of its intended future policy. (Mussa 1980: 4)

But intervention can affect exchange rates permanently only by changing the quantity of money:

> [It] is clear from the general principles of the "asset market view" of exchange rates why [nonsterilized] intervention should be of first order importance for the behavior of exchange rates. It is much less clear, from general analytical principles, that [sterilized] intervention, which has no effect on the domestic money supply, should have a significant effect on the behavior of exchange rates, particularly in the long run. In fact, an analysis of the principal channels through which [sterilized] intervention may be presumed to operate suggests that while such intervention may be able to affect the behavior of exchange rates in the short run, it has at best very modest capacity to affect their behavior in the long run. (Ibid.: 25)

Mussa does not provide a formal model containing the channels to which he refers. His model, however, is implicit in his presentation.

Setting aside the effects of intervention on expectations, Mussa goes on to treat spot intervention as a form of monetary policy. A spot purchase of foreign currency by the central bank resembles an ordinary open market purchase of domestic securities in that it increases the money supply and therefore reduces the long-run equilibrium price of the domestic currency. By implication, a spot purchase that is offset (sterilized) by an open market sale of domestic securities cannot affect the long-run equilibrium price of the domestic currency, because it does not affect the money supply.

Mussa's treatment of official intervention is thus based on a simple monetarist model of exchange rate determination in which supplies of assets other than money are unimportant. Transactions in foreign currency are equivalent to transactions in domestic securities, because changes in supplies of domestic securities do not affect the exchange rate. Mussa's conclusions do not reflect the "general principles" of the asset market approach to exchange rate theory but derive from a special case.

I shall examine the effects of official intervention in a more general asset market model of exchange rate determination. It is a streamlined version of the portfolio balance model developed by Allen and Kenen (1980).[1] Our model is useful for the purpose because it contains several channels through which exchange rates influence behavior in goods and asset markets and because the conduct of monetary policy is carefully specified. Furthermore, it can be solved for short-run effects (those taking place before flows of assets have had time to alter the corresponding stocks) and separately for long-run effects (those pertaining to comparisons of stationary states where all flows of assets cease and stocks come to be constant). In consequence, it allows us to pursue the two-way distinction drawn by Mussa between sterilized and nonsterilized intervention on the one hand and between short-run and long-run effects on the other. Finally, the model includes Mussa's monetarist model as a limiting case. When domestic and foreign bonds are perfect substitutes, changes in supplies of domestic bonds do not influence exchange rates.

The model can be used to study shifts in expectations, but I shall not go that far. Instead, I shall assume that expectations are stationary, so as to exclude all expectational effects from my conclusions about intervention and set aside the issues raised in the first quotation from Mussa's paper. I want to concentrate on those raised in the second.

I present the model in the following section and solve it for short-run and long-run effects in section three. I interpret the solutions in section four, with particular reference to Mussa's distinction between sterilized and nonsterilized intervention, and return to his special case in the final section, where I show what happens with perfect substitutability. These are my main conclusions:

• When foreign and domestic bonds are not perfect substitutes, intervention can have permanent effects on the exchange rate even when it is sterilized completely. There is indeed one instance, examined below, in which sterilized intervention is equally effective in the short run and the long run, whereas nonsterilized intervention is effective in the short run but much less effective in the long run.

• When foreign and domestic bonds are perfect substitutes, sterilized intervention is ineffective in the long run. But it is also ineffective in the short run, apart from any influence it may exert on expectations. Official intervention can affect exchange rates only when it is allowed to alter the money supply — when the central bank employs the foreign exchange market to carry out its monetary policy.

---

1. I use the simplified version of the model presented in Chapter 7 of Allen and Kenen (1980), where there are no nontraded goods, but go further by simplifying the notation and eliminating fiscal policies and goods market disturbances that do not affect asset markets in the short run (because the demand for money is made to depend on wealth but not on income).

THE MODEL

Consider an economy whose households hold three assets—domestic money, domestic (government) bonds, and foreign bonds denominated in foreign currency. Denote their holdings by L^h, B^h, and F^h, and make them depend on interest rates and wealth:

$$L^h = L(r_0, r_1, W^h), \quad L_0 < 0, L_1 < 0, 0 < L_W < 1 \qquad (4.1)$$

$$B^h = B(r_0, r_1, W^h), \quad B_0 < 0, B_1 > 0, 0 < B_W < 1 \qquad (4.2)$$

$$\pi F^h = F(r_0, r_1, W^h), \quad F_0 > 0, F_1 < 0, 0 < F_W < 1 \qquad (4.3)$$

where r_0 is the interest rate on the foreign bond, r_1 is the interest rate on the domestic bond, W^h is household wealth in home currency, and π is the home currency price of the foreign currency (the spot exchange rate), and where

$$W^h = L^h + B^h + \pi F^h \qquad (4.4)$$

By implication, $L_0 + B_0 + F_0 = 0$, $L_1 + B_1 + F_1 = 0$, and $L_W + B_W + F_W = 1$.

Household wealth can be described by the history of saving, S, and the history of capital gains and losses on bond holdings. As bonds are bills in this model, however, there can be no capital gains or losses on account of fluctuations in bond prices (interest rates). Therefore,

$$W^h = \int_0^t S\,dt + \int_0^t V\left(\frac{\dot{\pi}}{\pi}\right) dt \qquad (4.5)$$

where $V = \pi F^h$.[2] Saving is made to rise with interest rates and income and, following Metzler (1951), to fall with wealth[3]:

$$S = S(r_0, r_1, Y^d, W^h), \quad S_0 > 0, S_1 > 0, 0 < S_Y < 1, S_W < 0 \qquad (4.6)$$

where Y^d is disposable income and is defined by

$$Y^d = Y + r_1 B^h + r_0 \pi F^h - T^h \qquad (4.7)$$

Here, Y is gross domestic product, and T^h is the lump sum tax collected by the government.

---

2. Note that $V > 0$ (because $F > 0$). This economy is a foreign currency creditor. On the importance of this point for the behavior of the model, see Allen and Kenen (1980: 204–205).

3. The wealth effect plays a role in this model analogous to the role of the real balance effect in a monetary model; an increase of wealth raises consumption (absorption) by reducing saving. A negative wealth effect can be justified, of course, only for a stationary economy in which households take a life cycle view of their need to save and there are no legacies.

The supply of money is given by the balance sheet of the central bank:

$$L = B^c + \pi R - W^c \tag{4.8}$$

where L is the stock of money, B^c is the stock of domestic bonds held by the central bank, R is the stock of foreign exchange reserves measured in foreign currency, and W^c is the history of capital gains and losses on the bank's foreign exchange reserves:

$$W^c = \int_0^t \pi R \left(\frac{\dot{\pi}}{\pi} \right) dt \tag{4.9}$$

Changes in B^c represent open market operations in the domestic bond. Changes in R represent interventions in the foreign exchange market. When interventions are not sterilized, R changes by itself, changing the money supply by the same amount. When interventions are completely sterilized, R and B^c change by opposite amounts, leaving the money supply unaffected. (Hereafter, B^c and R are written as $\bar{B}^c$ and $\bar{R}$ because they are policy determined.) The market-clearing equation for domestic money is

$$L^h - L = 0 \tag{4.10}$$

The supply of the domestic (government) bond is given by the history of budget deficits and surpluses. In this chapter, however, the budget is always balanced, so that B is fixed at $\bar{B}$. Furthermore, foreigners do not hold the domestic bond, so that the market-clearing equation is

$$B^h + B^c - \bar{B} = 0 \tag{4.11}$$

The supply of the foreign bond is infinitely elastic at the interest rate r_0 (which is written hereafter as $\bar{r}_0$).

The economy produces a single good, Q, priced at p_1 in domestic currency. Its output is

$$Q = f(p_1) \tag{4.12}$$

In the simplest of classical economies, $f'(p_1) = 0$; in the simplest of Keynesian economies, $f'(p_1) > 0$.[4] Gross domestic product is defined by

$$Y = p_1 Q \tag{4.13}$$

There are three sources of demand for the domestic good—households, foreigners, and the government. Household demand is given by

$$c^h = c^h(p_1, \pi p_0, C), \ c_1^h < 0, \ c_0^h > 0, \ c_C^h > 0 \tag{4.14}$$

---

4. In the simple classical economy, the money wage rate is flexible, and the supply of labor is fixed. In the simple Keynesian economy, the money wage rate is fixed, and the supply of labor is perfectly elastic at that money wage. Combining these assumptions with profit maximization by domestic producers, we obtain the conditions in the text. For details, see Allen and Kenen (1980: ch. 2 and App. A).

where p_0 is the foreign currency price of the foreign good and C is domestic consumption in domestic currency:

$$C = Y^d - S \qquad (4.15)$$

Assume that $c^h (\dots)$ is homogeneous of zero degree in prices and consumption and that the consumption elasticity is unity. Foreign demand is given by

$$c^f = c^f \left(\frac{p_1}{\pi}, p_0, C^f \right), \ c_1^f < 0, \ c_0^f > 0, \ c_C^f > 0 \qquad (4.16)$$

where C^f is foreign consumption in foreign currency and is fixed at $\overline{C}^f$. Let $c^f (\dots)$ have properties identical to those of $c^h (\dots)$. Government demand is fixed at $\overline{G}$ in nominal terms. Therefore, the market-clearing equation for the domestic goods is

$$c^h + c^f + (\overline{G}/p_1) - Q = 0 \qquad (4.17)$$

The economy is not small in the market for its export good. It is small in the market for its import good. The supply of that good is infinitely elastic at its fixed foreign currency price (written hereafter as $\overline{p}_0$).

To close the model, we need the government budget. Outlays are $\overline{G}$ on domestic output, $r_1 B$ on interest, and T^f on transfers to foreigners. Receipts are tax revenues, T^h, and the interest income of the central bank, $r_1 B^c$. As the budget is balanced at all times,

$$\overline{G}_1 + r_1 B^h + T^f - T^h = 0 \qquad (4.18)$$

The lump sum tax, T^h, is manipulated to balance the budget (i.e., to offset variations in $\overline{G}, r_1 B^h$, and T^f). Transfers to foreigners are manipulated to offset interest income earned on the foreign bond [5]:

$$T^f = r_0 \pi F^h \qquad (4.19)$$

These assumptions allow us to rewrite disposable income as

$$Y^d = p_1 f (p_1) - \overline{G} \qquad (4.20)$$

and to show that saving must be equal to the current account balance, which is equal in turn to the trade balance.

The model outlined above can be written compactly, beginning with the three market-clearing equations:

$$L (\overline{r}_0, r_1, W^h) - (\overline{B}^c + \pi \overline{R} - W^c) = 0 \qquad (4.21)$$

---

5. This assumption is, of course, quite arbitrary, but serves to simplify the model substantially. It can be relaxed without impairing the chief conclusions of this paper (see Allen and Kenen 1980:279–85).

$$B(\bar{r}_0, r_1, W^h) + \bar{B}^c - \bar{B} = 0 \tag{4.22}$$

$$c^h(p_1, \pi p_0, Y^d - S) + c^f\left(\frac{p_1}{\pi}, p_0, \bar{C}^f\right) + (\bar{G}/p_1) - f(p_1) = 0 \tag{4.23}$$

But equation (4.20) defines Y^d as a function of p_1 and $\bar{G}$ when the government budget is balanced; equation (4.5) defines W^h as a function of the histories of S and π; equation (4.9) defines W^c as a function of the history of π; and equation (4.6) defines S as a function of $\bar{r}_0, r_1, Y^d$, and W^h. Accordingly, the three market-clearing equations can be solved for changes in π, r_1, and p_1 (or nominal income, Y) resulting from changes in $\bar{B}^c, \bar{R}, \bar{r}_0, \bar{G}, \bar{p}_0, \bar{C}^f$, and other exogenous disturbances.

THE SOLUTIONS

As income does not directly affect the demands for bonds and money, equations (4.21) and (4.22) can be solved separately from equation (4.23) to give the impact (short-run) of various disturbances. Differentiating them (but holding $\bar{r}_0$ and $\bar{B}$ constant),[6]

$$\begin{bmatrix} B_1 & B_W \\ L_1 & L_W \end{bmatrix} \begin{bmatrix} \delta r_1 \\ V\left(\frac{\delta \pi}{\pi}\right) \end{bmatrix} = \begin{bmatrix} -1 & 0 \\ 1 & 1 \end{bmatrix} \begin{bmatrix} \delta \bar{B}^c \\ \pi \delta \bar{R} \end{bmatrix} - \begin{bmatrix} \delta B^a \\ \delta L^a \end{bmatrix} \tag{4.24}$$

where δB^a is an autonomous shift of household demand from the foreign bond to the domestic bond and δL^a is an autonomous shift of demand from the foreign bond to domestic money.

The solutions for the changes in the interest rate are

$$\delta r_1 = -(1/H)[(B_W + L_W)\delta\bar{B}^c + (B_W)\pi\delta\bar{R}^n$$

$$- (L_W)\pi\delta\bar{R}^s + (L_W)\delta B^a - (B_W)\delta L^a] \tag{4.25}$$

where $\pi\delta\bar{R}^n$ denotes a nonsterilized purchase of foreign exchange, $\pi\delta\bar{R}^s$ denotes a sterilized purchase, and $H = B_1 L_W - L_1 B_W > 0$. (The solution for $\pi\delta\bar{R}^n$ is the solution for $\pi\delta\bar{R}$ by itself. The solution for $\pi\delta\bar{R}^s$ is the solution for $\pi\delta\bar{R}$ combined with the solution for $\delta\bar{B}^c = -\pi\delta\bar{R}$, an open market sale of the domestic bond to offset the money supply effect of the foreign exchange purchase.) The signs of these effects are listed in Table 4-1. They are interpreted in the next section.

6. Here and hereafter, the operator δ is used to denote impact (short-run) effects, while d is used to denote steady-state (long-run) effects.

Table 4-1.   Short-run Effects of Disturbances and Policies.

Effect on	$\delta \bar{B}^c$	$\pi \delta \bar{R}^n$	$\pi \delta \bar{R}^s$	δB^a	δL^a
r_1	$-$	$-$	$+$	$-$	$+$
π	$+$	$+$	$+$	$-$	$-$
p_1	$+$	$+$	$+^*$	$-^*$	$-$

*Assuming that $S_W L_1 > S_1 L_W$.

The solution for the changes in the exchange rate are

$$\left(\frac{\delta \pi}{\pi}\right) = (1/HV)\left[(-F_1)\,\delta \bar{B}^c + (B_1)\,\pi \delta \bar{R}^n - (L_1)\,\pi \delta \bar{R}^s \right.$$
$$\left. + (L_1)\,\delta B^a - (B_1)\,\delta L^a \right] \tag{4.26}$$

The signs of these effects are also listed in Table 4-1. Notice that nonsterilized intervention causes a larger depreciation than an equal amount of sterilized intervention. Defining the effect of nonsterilized intervention as $(\delta \pi/\pi)^n$ and the effect of sterilized intervention as $(\delta \pi/\pi)^s$ and setting $\pi \delta \bar{R}^n = \pi \delta \bar{R}^s$, we have

$$\left(\frac{\delta \pi}{\pi}\right)^n - \left(\frac{\delta \pi}{\pi}\right)^s = (1/HV)(B_1 + L_1)\,\pi \delta \bar{R}^n$$

and $B_1 + L_1 = -F_1 > 0$. The difference is, of course, the same as the effect of an open market purchase shown in equation (4.26).

Differentiating equation (4.23) but holding $\bar{G}$, $\bar{p}_0$, and $\bar{C}^f$ constant, we obtain this expression for the change in the price of the domestic good:

$$\left(\frac{\delta p_1}{p_1}\right) = (1/N)\left[(u_\pi - m_1 S_W V)\left(\frac{\delta \pi}{\pi}\right) - (m_1 S_1)\,\delta r_1\right] \tag{4.27}$$

where $N = (u_t + \sigma N_Y)$; and $N_Y = S_Y + m_0(1 - S_Y)$, where m_0 and m_1 are the marginal propensities to spend on imported and domestic goods, respectively, and where u_π, u_t, and σ are (positive) combinations of goods market parameters.[7] Substituting the arguments of equations (4.25) and (4.26) for the changes in r_1 and π,

7. To be precise, $m_1 = p_1 c_C^h$, and $m_0 = 1 - m_1$, while $u_t = p_1 c^h e_0^h - p_1 c^f e_0^f$, where e_0^h and e_0^f are the (positive) cross-price elasticities of domestic and foreign demands for the domestic good, and $u_\pi = u_t + p_1 c^f$. Finally, $\sigma = Y[1 + f'(p_1)(p_1/Q)]$, which measures the effect of a change in p_1 on nominal gross domestic product. Note that N_Y is the simple Keynesian multiplier (the sum of the marginal propensities to save and import defined with respect to disposable income). It can be shown, moreover, that $u_\pi > 0$ (because $u_t > 0$), which satisfies the Marshall–Lerner–Robinson condition (see Allen and Kenen 1980:54). The exchange rate term, $u_\pi - m_1 S_W V$, in equation (4.27) contains an expenditure-switching (elasticities) effect, u_π, and an expenditure-changing (absorption) effect, $-m_1 S_W V$. The latter has three parts: (a) A depreciation of the domestic currency raises

$$\left(\frac{\delta p_1}{p_1}\right) = (1/NHV)\left\{m_1 V\left[S_1(B_W + L_W) + S_W F_1\right] - F_1 u_\pi\right\}\delta\bar{B}^c \quad (4.28)$$

$$+ (1/NHV)\left[m_1 V(S_1 B_W - S_W B_1) + B_1 u_\pi\right](\pi\delta\bar{R}^n - \delta L^a)$$

$$+ (1/NHV)\left[m_1 V(S_W L_1 - S_1 L_W) - L_1 u_\pi\right](\pi\delta\bar{R}^s - \delta B^a)$$

The effects of an open market purchase and of nonsterilized intervention are unambiguous. The effect of sterilized intervention is not, because $S_W L_1 \gtrless S_1 L_W$. Here and hereafter, however, I shall assume that $S_W L_1 > S_1 L_W$, which is to say that desired saving (absorption) is relatively sensitive to changes in wealth, and the demand for money relatively sensitive to the interest rate. Using language made familiar by recent work on fiscal policy in a closed economy, I assume that "crowding out" does not dominate.[8] The signs listed in Table 4-1 reflect this assumption.

It is not hard to prove that this model is stable—that saving falls monotonically to zero in the course of the response to an exogenous disturbance, causing stocks of wealth and assets to converge to constant levels. Accordingly, the steady-state solutions are meaningful, and they are obtained as follows: The changes in the interest rate and nominal wealth are obtained from equations (4.21) and (4.22). The change in disposable income is obtained from the changes in the interest rate and wealth, using equation (4.6) and the steady-state condition that $S = 0$. The change in p_1 is obtained from the change in disposable income, using equation (4.20). Finally, the change in the exchange rate is obtained from the price and income changes, using equation (4.23). Impact effects on the exchange rate are decided by behavior in the bond and money markets. Long-run effects come from the goods market, given the price and income changes produced by disturbances and domestic policies. This proposition is the analogue of the assertion that "purchasing power parity" obtains only in the long run.

Proceeding in this fashion, one can show that the long-run changes in r_1 are the same as those supplied by equation (4.25). The interest rate is unaffected by the dynamic adaptation that follows a disturbance. The long-run change in nominal wealth is given by

$$dW^h = (1/H)\left[(-F_1)d\bar{B}^c + (B_1)\pi d\bar{R}^n - (L_1)\pi d\bar{R}^s\right. \quad (4.29)$$

$$+ (L_1)dB^a - (B_1)dL^a]$$

---

wealth by $V(\delta\pi/\pi)$, the capital gain on foreign bonds held by domestic households; (b) the increase in wealth reduces desired saving by $S_W V(\delta\pi/\pi)$, raising consumption by the same amount; and (c) the increase of consumption raises the demand for the domestic good by the fraction m_1.

8. See, for example, Blinder and Solow (1973). In Allen and Kenen (1980: esp. ch.5), we show that a number of familiar propositions in international monetary theory, including those pertaining to the influence of capital mobility on the effectiveness of monetary and fiscal policies, depend crucially on this same assumption.

Table 4-2. Long-run Effects of Disturbances and Policies.

Effect on	$d\bar{B}^c$	$\pi d\bar{R}^n$	$\pi d\bar{R}^s$	dB^a	dL^a
r_1	−	−	+	−	+
W^h	+	+	+	−	−
p_1	+	+	+*	−*	−
π	+	+	+*	−*	−

*Assuming that $S_W L_1 > S_1 L_W$.

Moving directly to the change in p_1 obtained from the change in disposable income,

$$\left(\frac{dp_1}{p_1}\right) = -(1/\sigma S_Y)[(S_1) dr_1 + (S_W) dW^h] \tag{4.30}$$

Substituting the arguments of equations (4.25) and (4.29) for the changes in the interest rate and wealth,

$$\left(\frac{dp_1}{p_1}\right) = (1/H\sigma S_Y)[S_1(B_W + L_W) + S_W F_1] d\bar{B}^c \tag{4.31}$$

$$+ (1/H\sigma S_Y)(S_1 B_W - S_W B_1)(\pi d\bar{R}^n - dL^a)$$

$$+ (1/H\sigma S_Y)(S_W L_1 - S_1 L_W)(\pi d\bar{R}^s - dB^a)$$

Finally, the change in the exchange rate is given by

$$\left(\frac{d\pi}{\pi}\right) = [(u_t + m_0 \sigma)/u_\pi]\left(\frac{dp_1}{p_1}\right) \tag{4.32}$$

so that the sign of the change in π is the same as the sign of the change in p_1.[9]
The signs of the changes in r_1, W^h, p_1, and π are listed in Table 4-2 and are interpreted in the next section.

EFFECTS OF NONSTERILIZED AND STERILIZED INTERVENTIONS

The comparative static results obtained in the previous section are most readily explained with the aid of a simple asset market diagram. In Figure 4-1, the curve WW traces the sets of combinations of r_1 and W^h that clear the bond mar-

9. In the classical variant of the model, $\sigma = Y$. In the absence of government spending, moreover, $Y = Y^d$, while $Y^d = C$ in the steady state, because there is no saving. Thus, $m_0 \sigma = m_0 C$, which measures the value of imports. But trade is balanced in the steady state, so that $m_0 C = p_1 c^f$, and this means in turn that $u_t + m_0 \sigma = u_\pi$. By implication, $(d\pi/\pi) = (dp_1/p_1)$ in the classical variant; "purchasing power parity" holds in the long run when there are no goods market disturbances. For a more general proof, comprising the case in

Figure 4-1.   Effects of Nonsterilized Intervention.

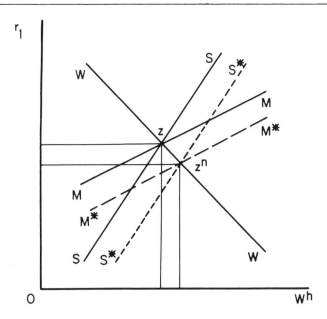

ket; it is downward sloping because an increase in wealth raises the demand for bonds ($B_W > 0$) and must therefore be offset by a reduction in the interest rate ($B_1 > 0$). The curve MM traces the sets of combinations that clear the money market; it is upward sloping because an increase in wealth raises the demand for money ($L_W > 0$) and must therefore be offset by an increase in the interest rate ($L_1 < 0$). Finally, the curve SS traces the sets of combinations at which saving is zero, given the steady-state level of disposable income; it is upward sloping because an increase in wealth reduces saving ($S_W < 0$) and must therefore be offset by an increase in the interest rate ($S_1 > 0$). When "crowding out" does not dominate, SS is steeper than MM.[10]

---

which government spending is not zero but is fixed in real terms rather than nominal terms, see Allen and Kenen (1980: App. C).

10. These are the equations for the three asset market curves:

• Bond market equilibrium (WW):

$$dr_1 = - (B_W/B_1) dW^h - (1/B_1)(d\overline{B}^c + dB^a)$$

• Money market equilibrium (MM):

$$dr_1 = - (L_W/L_1) dW^h + (1/L_1) [(\pi d\overline{R} + dB^c) - dL^a]$$

• Zero saving (SS):

$$dr_1 = - (S_W/S_1) dW^h - (S_Y/S_1) dY^d$$

When SS is steeper than MM, $(S_W/S_1) < (L_W/L_1)$, so that $S_W L_1 > S_1 L_W$.

As asset markets clear instantaneously in this model, short-run equilibria in the bond and money markets are defined by intersections of WW and MM. As saving is zero in the steady state, long-run equilibria are defined by intersections of WW, MM, and SS. When short-run equilibrium is displaced from some such point as z in Figure 4-1, where the three curves intersect, to a point above the SS curve, households will start to save at the initial level of disposable income, and absorption (consumption) will fall; when it is displaced to a point below the SS curve, households will start to dissave, and absorption will rise.

Income and the exchange rate do not appear explicitly in Figure 4-1, but it tells us much about the way that they behave.

What does it say about the behavior of income? As income rises with absorption, a disturbance that displaces asset market equilibrium to a point below the original SS curve raises nominal income above its initial level. Furthermore, a new SS curve must pass through the new equilibrium point, and this tells us what must happen to income in the long run. When the new SS curve lies below the old, the steady-state level of disposable income must be higher than it was before. The interest rate is lower at each point on the new SS curve, and disposable income is thus higher, because saving must be zero on any SS curve. But nominal income rises with disposable income when, as here, there are no changes in taxes other than those needed to keep the budget balanced. Summing up, the location of the new asset market equilibrium point, above or below the original SS curve, tells us how income responds in the short run and where it must wind up in the long run if asset market curves do not shift again.

What does it say about the behavior of the exchange rate? In the short run, before flows can influence stocks, there is only one way to alter nominal wealth—by changing the home currency value of the foreign bonds held in household portfolios. This is, in fact, the short-run function of an exchange rate change, which means that the sign of the short-run change in wealth gives us the sign of the short-run change in the exchange rate. The stock of wealth cannot rise instantaneously unless there is a depreciation of the domestic currency (an increase in π, the price of the foreign currency). With the passage of time, of course, wealth will respond to saving as well as the exchange rate. But the sign of the permanent change in the exchange rate can be inferred from the shift in the SS curve, because the long-run equilibrium level of the exchange rate depends on the long-run level of p_1 and, therefore, the long-run level of nominal income. When the new SS curve lies below the old, for example, so that there must be a permanent increase in nominal income and, therefore, a permanent increase in p_1, there must be a permanent depreciation of the domestic currency.[11]

---

11. This inference, like the one above concerning the long-run change in income, depends on the assumption that $\bar{G}$ is constant. A change in $\bar{G}$ would alter the relationship between Y^d and Y, changing the relationship between Y^d and p_1. The relationship between p_1 and π, moreover, would be altered by a goods market disturbance.

Starting at point z in Figure 4-1, where the three curves intersect, let us examine the effects of nonsterilized intervention. A purchase of foreign currency ($\pi d\overline{R} > 0$) adds to the assets of the central bank and raises the money supply. The MM curve shifts downward to M*M*, raising wealth and reducing the interest rate. The increase in wealth testifies, of course, to a depreciation of the domestic currency—which is what one would expect in the foreign exchange market, where the central bank has bought foreign currency and thus sold domestic currency. The decrease in the interest rate is what one would expect in the domestic bond market; the increase in wealth resulting from the depreciation of the domestic currency raises the demand for the domestic bond, and there has been no change in the supply, so that the interest rate must fall to clear the market.

As the new short-run equilibrium point, z^n, lies below the original SS curve, households start to dissave, raising absorption and nominal income, the result recorded in Table 4-1. With the passage of time, of course, wealth must be affected by dissaving, but asset market equilibrium remains at z^n, because WW and M*M* stay in place. The stock of wealth and the interest rate do not change. The SS curve, however, is displaced to S*S*, which says that there must be a permanent increase in disposable income, a permanent increase in p_1, and a permanent depreciation of the domestic currency. The permanent depreciation, moreover, must be larger than the initial depreciation; the price of foreign currency must rise through time to raise the home currency value of foreign bonds held in households' portfolios and thus to stabilize the stock of wealth in the face of the dissaving that takes place on the way to the new steady state (for more on these dynamics, see Allen and Kenen 1980: ch. 6).

To sum up, a nonsterilized purchase of foreign exchange has short-run and long-run effects on the economy. The interest rate falls, nominal income rises, and the domestic currency depreciates, immediately and permanently.

What happens with sterilized intervention? The answer is given by Figure 4-2. There is no change in the position of the MM curve, because there is no change in the money supply. But the WW curve shifts upward to W*W*, because the central bank must make an open market sale of domestic bonds if it is to make room for its purchase of foreign currency without affecting the money supply. Asset market equilibrium is displaced to z^s. There is an instantaneous increase in wealth, just as there was in Figure 4-1, which says that the domestic currency depreciates. But the interest rate rises instead of falling, because of the increase in the supply of the domestic bond. When SS is steeper than MM, as in Figure 4-2, the point z^s lies below the old SS curve, and households begin to dissave, raising absorption and nominal income. Furthermore, the SS curve gives way to S*S*, which means that disposable income must be higher in the new steady state, that p_1 must be higher too, and that there will be a permanent depreciation of the domestic currency. When "crowding out" does not dominate, then, sterilized intervention raises the interest rate rather than reducing it, but it raises

Figure 4-2.   Effects of Sterilized Intervention.

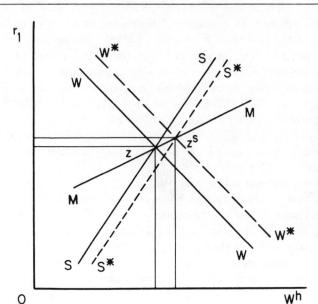

nominal income nonetheless and causes the domestic currency to depreciate, on impact and permanently.[12] There is no clear-cut qualitative distinction of the type that Mussa (1980) draws between the short-run effects of sterilized intervention and its long-run effects.

Consider, next, the consequences of official intervention designed to stabilize the exchange rate in the face of a shift of household demand from the foreign bond to the domestic bond. Setting $(\delta\pi/\pi) = 0$, I solve equation (4.26) for the requisite amounts of intervention: $\pi\delta\bar{R}^n = -(L_1/B_1)\delta B^a$, and $\pi\delta\bar{R}^s = \delta B^a$. In both instances, the central bank must buy foreign currency to keep the domestic currency from appreciating. If it engages in sterilization, the requisite purchase will be larger,[13] and the side effects will be quite different. With nonsterilized intervention, equations (4.25) and (4.27) give

---

12. As in the case of nonsterilized intervention, the permanent depreciation will be larger than the initial depreciation, because wealth must be kept constant in the face of dissaving. When SS is flatter than MM, by contrast, the point z^s will lie above the SS curve, so that households will begin to save. Furthermore, the SS curve will shift upward, which says that disposable income must fall, reducing p_1 and causing the domestic currency to appreciate. The long-run change in the exchange rate will be opposite in sign to the short-run change.

13. This is because $-(L_1/B_1) = [L_1/(L_1 + F_1)] < 1$.

$$\delta r_1 = -(1/B_1)\delta B^a < 0$$

and

$$\left(\frac{\delta p_1}{p_1}\right) = -(m_1 S_1/N)\delta r_1 > 0$$

The interest rate falls, raising nominal income and the price of the domestic good. With sterilized intervention, $\delta r_1 = (\delta p_1/p_1) = 0$. There are no side effects. Furthermore, the long-run effects are different, including the effects on the exchange rate itself. With nonsterilized intervention, equations (4.25) and (4.29) give $dr_1 = \delta r_1 < 0$ (the long-run and short-run effects are the same), and $dW^h = 0$. In consequence, equations (4.30) and (4.32) give

$$\left(\frac{dp_1}{p_1}\right) = -(S_1/\sigma S_Y)dr_1 > 0$$

and

$$\left(\frac{d\pi}{\pi}\right) = [(u_t + m_0\sigma)/u_\pi]\left(\frac{dp_1}{p_1}\right) > 0$$

An act of intervention that prevents appreciation in the short run leads to depreciation in the long run! With sterilized intervention, by contrast, $dr_1 = dW^h = 0$, so that $(dp_1/p_1) = (d\pi/\pi) = 0$. An act of intervention that prevents appreciation in the short run stabilizes the exchange rate in the long run too.

The differences between the two types of intervention are shown in Figure 4-3. The shift of demand between bonds is represented by the movement of the bond market curve from WW to $W^a W^a$. In the absence of any intervention, asset market equilibrium would be displaced from z to z^a. The domestic currency would appreciate. The effects of nonsterilized interventions are described by the movement of the money market curve from MM to $M^n M^n$, a movement large enough to keep wealth constant in the fact of the shift in demand and thus to keep the exchange rate constant in the short run. At the new equilibrium point, z^n, the interest rate is lower, and z^n lies below the SS curve, so that absorption rises in the short run, raising nominal income. The SS curve must shift downward, which means that disposable income must be higher in the new steady state, along with nominal income, and that the domestic currency must depreciate eventually.

The effects of sterilized intervention are even easier to show. As it does not affect the money market curve but acts instead on the bond market curve, intervention to stabilize the exchange rate serves merely to shift the bond market curve back from $W^a W^a$ to WW. Asset market equilibrium returns to point z, and there are no side effects at all, in the short run or the long run.

Consider, finally, the effects of intervention designed to stabilize the exchange rate in the face of a shift of household demand from the foreign bond

Figure 4-3. Effects of a Shift of Demand Between Bonds with Nonsterilized and Sterilized Intervention.

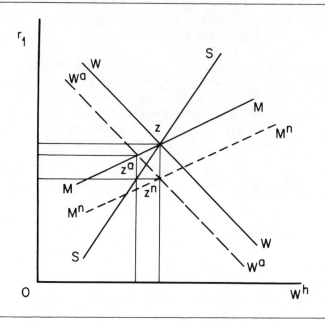

to domestic money. Here, equation (4.26) gives $\pi\delta\bar{R}^n = \delta L^a$, and $\pi\delta\bar{R}^s = -(B_1/L_1)\delta L^a$. Once again, the central bank must buy foreign currency to keep the domestic currency from appreciating, and when it engages in sterilization, the amount of intervention must be larger. In this instance, however, involving an increase in the demand for money, nonsterilized intervention is preferable, because it raises the supply of money. With nonsterilized intervention, there are no effects on the interest rate or nominal income in the short run or the long run and no change in the long-run level of the exchange rate. With sterilized intervention, by contrast, the interest rate rises in the short run and the long run, depressing nominal income and the price of the domestic good, so that the domestic currency must appreciate eventually.

These examples lead to a general conclusion. Nonsterilized intervention is the optimal response to a disturbance that impinges directly on the domestic money market. It can stabilize the exchange rate in the short run and the long run without affecting wealth or income. Sterilized intervention is the optimal response to a disturbance that impinges directly on other asset markets but not on the money market.[14]

14. A shift of household demand from the domestic bond to domestic money ($\delta L^a = -\delta B^a$) would cause the domestic currency to appreciate. From equation (4.26), $(\delta\pi/\pi) = -[(L_1 + B_1)/HV]\delta L^a = (F_1/HV)\delta L^a < 0$ (because $F_1 < 0$). But exchange market inter-

SUBSTITUTABILITY AND STERILIZATION

Is there any case in which Mussa would be right about the effects of sterilized intervention? There is one in which he is half right but has therefore to be half wrong. When domestic and foreign bonds are perfect substitutes in households' portfolios, sterilized intervention cannot have any permanent effect on the exchange rate, which is why Mussa is half right. But it cannot have any impact effect either, which is why Mussa is half wrong.

When domestic and foreign bonds are perfect substitutes, $-F_1 \to \infty$, so that $B_1 \to \infty$ (I assume that L_1 is unaffected). Therefore, $H \to \infty$ in equation (4.25), so that $\delta r_1 \to 0$. The domestic interest rate cannot change unless there is a change in the foreign interest rate. Furthermore, equation (4.26) becomes

$$\left(\frac{\delta \pi}{\pi}\right) = (1/L_W V)(\delta \bar{B}^c + \pi \delta \bar{R}^n - \delta L^a) \qquad (4.33)$$

Sterilized intervention has no effect on the exchange rate, even in the short run. (Note that δB^a has also vanished from the exchange rate equation, because it has no economic meaning in this special case. When the two bonds in the model are perfect substitutes, there can be no shift of demand between them.) Turning to the short-run change in p_1, equation (4.28) becomes

$$\left(\frac{\delta p_1}{p_1}\right) = [(u_\pi - m_1 S_W V)/NL_W V] (\delta \bar{B}^c + \pi \delta \bar{R}^n - \delta L^a) \qquad (4.34)$$

When sterilized intervention has no effect on any asset market variable, it can have no effect on saving (absorption), the price of the domestic good, or nominal income. And when it does not influence saving or income, it cannot affect the path of the economy. The steady-state values are unchanged.

Look more closely at equations (4.33) and (4.34). Nonsterilized intervention and an open market operation have the same effects on the exchange rate, the price of the domestic good, and thus the level of nominal income. This is because they operate in the same fashion—by altering the money supply. Open market operations in the domestic bond do not affect the interest rate on that bond. In other words, perfect substitutability between the two bonds converts our asset market model from a portfolio balance model into a simple monetarist model of the type implicit in Mussa's analysis.

---

vention is not the optimal response, because this disturbance does not impinge directly on the foreign exchange market. The optimal response is an open market purchase of domestic securities, as it would raise the supply of money to meet the increase in demand, reduce the supply of bonds to meet the decrease in demand, and stabilize the exchange rate in the process. Conclusions similar to those drawn in the text are found in Kouri (1980).

REFERENCES

Allen, Polly R., and Peter B. Kenen. 1980. *Asset Markets, Exchange Rates, and Economic Integration.* London and New York: Cambridge University Press.

Blinder, Alan S., and Robert M. Solow. 1973. "Does Fiscal Policy Matter?" *Journal of Public Economics* 2: 319–37.

Kouri, Pentti J.K. 1980. "Monetary Policy, the Balance of Payments, and the Exchange Rate." In David Bigman and Teizo Taya, eds., *The Functioning of Floating Exchange Rates.* Cambridge, Massachusetts: Ballinger Publishing Company.

Metzler, Lloyd A. 1951. "Wealth, Saving and the Rate of Interest." *Journal of Political Economy* 59 (April): 930–46.

Mussa, Michael. 1980. "The Role of Official Intervention." Paper prepared for the Group of Thirty, New York.

Triffin, Robert. 1960. *Gold and the Dollar Crisis.* New Haven: Yale University Press.

5 PORTFOLIO DIVERSIFICATION ACROSS CURRENCIES

Jorge Braga de Macedo

Over twenty years after Robert Triffin, the Cassandra of the dollar standard,[1] proposed a reserve system based on an international reserve asset, there is still no agreement in sight about implementing a "world money" standard. Nevertheless, it turns out that the cosmopolitan spirit underlying Triffin's proposal is enlightening in the investigation of portfolio diversification across assets denominated in different currencies.

In fact, more and more economic agents, from multinational firms and banks to monetary authorities, consume – or are affected by the consumption of – bundles of goods and services produced in different countries and hold portfolios of assets denominated in different currencies. This internationalization of portfolios has spread in an environment where real returns on financial assets denominated in the major currencies have been highly volatile. The variability of observed real returns can be attributed to the divergent rates of inflation across countries and to the changes in relative prices that have occurred in the floating rate period. In such an environment, an index of value appropriate for consumers and investors with an international horizon can be defined as the purchasing power of a currency over goods and services produced in different countries. In section one, this index, introduced in earlier work with Pentti Kouri, is set forth and used to interpret recent trends in the relative attractiveness of major currencies.

Earlier versions of this chapter were presented in seminars at the IMF in August 1978 and more recently at Warwick (England); INSEAD (France); and the GSB/NYU. Comments from the participants, the members of my Ph.D. committee, my co-editors, and David Meerschwam – as well as financial support from the Ford Foundation – are gratefully acknowledged. Errors are my own.

1. See Leonard Silk, *The New York Times*, October 6, 1971, who, recalling the 1959 Elsinore meeting where the prediction was first stated, likened Triffin to Hamlet's father.

Armed with an index of value to find the relevant real return for the international investor, we proceed in section two to derive an optimal portfolio rule. A crucial assumption underlying the optimal portfolio rule is that world financial markets are perfectly integrated with continuous and costless trading, so that real returns on short bonds denominated in different currencies can be assumed to be generated by continuous stochastic processes. In order to be able to present an intuitive and computationally convenient derivation of the portfolio rule, it is also assumed that the stochastic processes are serially independent (no matter how short the time interval) with constant instantaneous means and variances and that the consumption preferences of the international investor can be described by a separable utility function with a constant relative degree of risk aversion.[2] Under these restrictive assumptions, as is well known, the portfolio rule is independent of the consumption rule, and the optimal portfolio is the sum of a minimum variance portfolio and of a zero net worth speculative portfolio dependent on real returns and scaled by risk aversion.[3] A two-country, two-asset model is used to express the minimum variance portfolio as the difference between the vector of constant expenditure shares and a zero net worth hedging portfolio depending on the covariance between exchange rate changes and inflation rates as well as on consumption preferences. It is also shown that the degree of relative risk aversion determines whether an increased demand for goods produced in one country will increase the demand for the currency of that country, as is required for the stability of both the textbook flow model of the foreign exchange market and the portfolio approach to exchange rate determination emphasizing the "wealth transfer" effect.

Optimal portfolios for eight major currencies are computed in the third section, using actual quarterly changes in their purchasing powers. The time-invariant parameters that transform real return differentials into portfolio proportions are reported for alternative weighting schemes and degrees of relative risk aversion. The findings are relevant for the problem of optimal reserve diversification by central banks, insofar as those institutions can be assumed to pursue a risk averse strategy of maximizing real returns with consumption preferences given by expenditure patterns.[4] For example, recent estimates of the share of dollars in world official reserves, being somewhere between 60 and 70 percent, depending on coverage,[5] are not much higher than the optimal dollar share would be

2. The consumption and portfolio rules for the general N country non–Brownian motion case are derived in Macedo (1981).

3. This was first shown by Kouri (1975) in a center periphery monetary world that was a stylized representation of the Bretton Woods system.

4. For an application of this framework to the central bank of a less-developed country, when real returns are equalized, see Healy (1980b), who estimates the optimal reserve portfolios of four LDCs and contrasts them with popular alternatives like pure dollar holdings, expenditure shares, and SDR weights.

5. Heller and Knight (1978) report an 80 percent dollar share in 1976; Branson (1980b) quotes a dollar share of the same magnitude in 1978.

if the world's expenditure share on U.S. goods were about 40 percent and an investor had a degree of relative risk aversion close to unity. Other implications, as well as suggestions for future research, are taken up in the conclusion of the chapter.

INDEXES OF PURCHASING POWER DESCRIBED

We begin by deriving an optimal price index for the international consumer in terms of the standard maximization problem of the household. The utility function is assumed to be homothetic and loglinear so that relative risk aversion is unity. While the assumption of constant expenditure shares is an important drawback for the application of such indexes over long periods of time,[6] it is nevertheless convenient for the purpose of handling the optimizing foundations of international currency diversification in a well-known framework.[7]

Consider the static consumption problem in an environment where goods produced in different countries are not perfect substitutes for each other, so that each good j is also indexed by its country of origin i, where country i produces M_i goods and there are N countries. If the utility function of the "representative" international consumer ℓ is as assumed, then an indirect utility function, V^ℓ, separable between expenditure, E_k, and prices can be derived such that the purchasing power of currency k for that consumer, denoted by Q_k, is the measure of the utility of an extra unit of currency k, or

$$Q_k = \frac{\partial V^\ell}{\partial E^k} = \prod_{i=1}^{N} \prod_{j=1}^{M_i} (P_{ij} S_{ki})^{-\alpha_i \beta_j^i}$$

where P_{ij} is the price of good j, $j = 1, \ldots, M_i$, in the currency of country i, $i = 1, \ldots, N$;

S_{ki} is the price of the currency of country i in terms of the currency of country k;

β_j^i is the share of good j in the expenditure on the M_i goods produced in country i;

α_i is the share of goods produced in country i in total expenditure of consumer ℓ;

$$\sum_{j=1}^{M_i} \beta_j^i = 1, \text{ and } \sum_{i=1}^{N} \alpha_i = 1 \ .$$

6. McKinnon (1979:130–31) uses such indexes computed by Kawai for the period 1953–1977.

7. Other specifications of the utility function could provide exact or at least "superlative" indexes (see Diewert 1976; and further discussion in Macedo 1979).

The purchasing power of currency k is the inverse of the geometric average of prices expressed in currency k using the expenditure shares as weights. The purchasing power of money, applied to any particular good, is of course the inverse of the price of that good.

Since all goods produced in country i are priced in domestic currency (and thus exchange rates are not indexed over j), the purchasing power of currency k can be decomposed into an index of the purchasing power of "world money" and a multilateral effective exchange rate for currency k. The effective exchange rate, S_k^e, is defined as the expenditure-weighted average price of currency k in terms of all the other currencies, whereas S_{ki} was defined above as the price of currency i in terms of currency k. An increase in S_k^e therefore represents an effective appreciation of currency k. Using currency N as the numeraire, we can express S_k^e as:

$$S_k^e = \prod_{i=1}^{N} (S_k/S_i)^{-\alpha_i} = S_k^{-(1-\alpha_k)} \prod_{i \neq k}^{N} S_i^{\alpha_i}$$

where $S_i = S_{iN} = S_i/S_N$ $i = 1, \ldots, N-1$ and $S_N = 1$.

Thus S_k^e can be seen as the ratio between the average price of foreign currencies, $\prod_{i \neq k}^{N} S_i^{\alpha_i}$, and the price of currency k in terms of currency N, raised to the power of $\sum_{i \neq k} \alpha_i = 1 - \alpha_k$. Note that if the expenditure share of goods from country k it is negligible for the international consumer or if it is used as the standard of reference, we obtain the usual effective exchange rate index where bilateral exchange rate indexes are weighted by their importance in the foreign trade of the home country.[8]

We now define the world price level as a weighted average of domestic currency prices

$$P = \prod_{i=1}^{N} \prod_{j=1}^{M_i} P_{ij}^{\alpha_i \beta_j^i}$$

What we called the purchasing power of "world money" is the inverse of P, which will be denoted by Q.[9] The reason why Q can be seen as the purchasing power of a basket of currencies is that since there are only $N-1$ exchange rates, the N effective rates S_k^e multiply to 1 if the same country weights α_i are used.

8. Rhomberg (1976) has a thorough discussion of the indexes of effective exchange rates in use at the time. See also *World Financial Markets* (August 1976: 14, technical note) and below in the text.

9. Since July 1974 the Special Drawing Rights of the IMF satisfy this notion of "world money." See below in the text.

In other words, in the same way that the numeraire has a bilateral rate of 1, world money has an effective rate of 1.

Therefore the purchasing power of currency k is obtained by multiplying the purchasing power of world money by the effective exchange rate for currency k, or

$$Q_k = Q S_k^e .$$

This index of the purchasing power of currency k can be used to compute the purchasing power of any asset i, the domestic currency price of which is A_k^i, in terms of a particular international consumption basket, which would simply be

$$Q_k^{Ai} = A_k^i Q_k .$$

The purchasing power of bonds, of equities, of gold, or of raw materials would be defined in this way. An international "real wage" could similarly be defined as the purchasing power of labor in country k in terms of a given international consumption basket.

The notion of the purchasing power of a currency can be usefully applied without an explicit knowledge of the (constant) expenditure shares of a given consumer-investor, depending on the purpose at hand. For example, a multinational firm producing one particular good might be interested in the purchasing power of different currencies over that good, say j, produced in N different countries or over these N different products; this would be obtained by setting $\beta_j^i = 1$ for all i.[10]

Alternatively, the domestic expenditure shares β can be given implicitly by an available price index, so that the only explicit choice of weights will refer to the expenditure shares across national outputs, given by α. In that case, a decision has to be made about the relevant price index. This has been a long-standing subject of controversy in connection with the purchasing power parity hypothesis.[11] Keynes and Triffin, among others, favored broadly based indexes, such as the consumer price index or the value-added deflator, in the definition of an "equilibrium" exchange rate. The basic reason was that indexes of relative prices with too large a share of traded goods—such as wholesale price indexes—would move too closely with the exchange rate. As a consequence, they claimed that such a "real" exchange rate would understate the departure from presumed base period purchasing power parity.[12] Recent evidence on the substantial movements

10. The demand structure underlying the IMF Multilateral Exchange Rate Model is roughly one where there are M products produced in N countries so that $M_i = M$ for all i (see Armington 1969; and below in the text).

11. Officer (1976) and Katseli (1979) have useful surveys of the PPP literature.

12. See Keynes (1923) and Triffin (1937). Triffin (1957:71, n. 1) states that wholesale prices are "totally irrelevant and misleading" for competitiveness calculations.

in relative costs and prices for manufactures has revived the interest in comparisons based on traded goods prices as well as unit labor costs and made real exchange rates quite popular both in policy discussions[13] and in attempts at quantifying long-run trends in international competitiveness.[14] Nevertheless, it should be pointed out that the comparison underlying the construction of "real" exchange rates cannot be grounded on optimizing behavior, because the preferences of the national and international consumer–investor may be presumed to be different. This is clear from the framework above, where a "real" effective exchange rate of currency k is nothing but the ratio of the purchasing power of currency k from the perspective of an international investor, and the purchasing of currency k from the perspective of a national investor, defined as consuming a national basket, or $\alpha_k = 1$. This ratio can be written as

$$\tilde{S}_k^e = Q_k / Q_k^d$$

where Q_k^d is the purchasing power of currency k when the consumer is such that $\alpha_k = 1$.

Using the definition of S_k^e, we see that the "real" effective exchange rate of currency k is just the relative price of domestic and world output in the same units, and as before, when it increases there is real effective appreciation of the domestic currency. We can express $\tilde{S}_k^e$ as

$$\tilde{S}_k^e = \prod_{i=1}^{N} (P_i S_k / P_k S_i)^{-\alpha_i}$$

where

$$P_i = \prod_{i=1}^{M_i} P_{ij} \beta_j^i \quad i = 1, \ldots, N$$

In this context, an intermediate case may be mentioned. Consider a "foreign" consumer–investor, defined as being located in country k but consuming only goods of country i, so that $\alpha_i = 1$. The purchasing power of currency k for such an agent, denoted by Q_k^i, is simply the purchasing power of currency k for the domestic consumer–investor of country i, $1/P_i$, times the bilateral exchange rate, or

$$Q_k^i = (S_i / S_k) P_i^{-1}$$

---

13. They have been reported monthly in *World Financial Markets* since November 1978 and in *International Financial Statistics* since January 1979. An early example of the use of such indexes for policy purposes (reported in *Business Week*, April 3, 1978) is Dornbusch (1978). A more recent analysis is given by Cooper in Chapter 1 of this volume.

14. Historical perspectives on various countries are taken by Diaz (in Chapter 11 of this volume), Macedo (1980), and Branson (1980a).

The real bilateral exchange rate between currency i and currency m can therefore be expressed as a ratio of the purchasing powers of the same currency for investors located in the two different countries, including the case where one of them is the domestic country. For example,

$$\tilde{S}_{im} = \frac{Q_k^m}{Q_k^i} = \frac{P_i S_m}{P_m S_i} \quad \text{for all } k$$

Finally, because the ratio of two nominal effective exchange rates is always the bilateral rate, the ratio of the purchasing powers of two currencies is also the bilateral rate.

In order to illustrate the application of the framework developed above, monthly indexes of the purchasing power of major currencies from April 1973 to April 1978 are plotted in Figure 5-1. The consumption horizon of the hypothetical international investor was taken to be eight industrial countries, Canada, France, Germany, Italy, Japan, Switzerland, the United Kingdom, and the United States. Keeping in the Triffin spirit, the β weights were assumed to be the ones used in constructing the consumer price indexes of the eight countries. Several alternative schemes for the α weights will be discussed below, but in Figure 5-1, weights given by the shares of the countries' incomes in 1975 world dollar income were used in the computation of the monthly indexes of the purchasing power of the eight currencies and world money (with base 100 in April 1973). End of month exchange rates, rather than monthly averages, were used in order to come closer to prices at which actual transactions take place.

As already mentioned, the choice of the α weights depends "on the particular policy objective" (Rhomberg 1976:87; see also *World Financial Markets* May 1978 and May 1979). Since the concept of an international investor requires that a rigorous comparison between the purchasing powers of different currencies be possible, however, we do not consider weights obtained from the perspective of a particular country. Table 5-1 presents three alternative weighting

Table 5-1. Alternative Weighting Schemes (*percent*).

	XM	MERM	Y
Canada	8.0	5.8	5.0
France	12.2	17.4	9.6
Germany	19.4	15.3	13.3
Italy	8.2	7.8	5.0
Japan	13.4	8.5	15.9
Switzerland	3.2	1.9	1.7
United Kingdom	11.1	6.0	6.7
United States	24.5	37.3	42.7

Notes: *XM* = total trade.
         MERM = IMF Multilateral Exchange Rate Model.
         Y = Income.

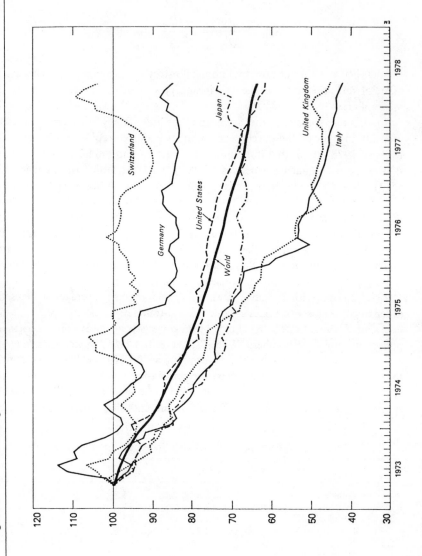

Figure 5–1. Purchasing Powers of Selected Currencies, April 1973–April 1978 (*April 1973 = 100*).

schemes. The "trade weights," labeled XM in the first column, are measures of the average openness of the economy, using exports and imports. The "MERM weights" in the second column are measures of marginal openness or "sensitivity."[15] Finally, the weights of the third column, obtained from shares in 1975 dollar incomes, are a prima facie measure of relative size.[16] Note that aside from the United States, only France shows marginal openness larger than average openness. The United States and Japan rank highest on income weights. Import weights for the United Kingdom are the highest, but the income share is higher than the MERM share. Canada, Germany, Italy, and Switzerland show a ranking typical of smaller open economies (total trade first, MERM second, and income last), even though Germany ranks a close third on the income scale.

If we attach α weights to the national consumer price indexes, we find that there is hardly any difference in the aggregate between these three weighting schemes. In fact, the values of the indexes of the purchasing power of world money computed from total trade weights, income weights, and MERM weights were 120.1, 119.0, and 118.9, respectively, in January 1970, and 62.8, 63.9, and 63.8, respectively, in April 1978, with base 100 in April 1973. The effect of the weighting scheme can also be seen in Table 5-2, where the mean annualized percentage changes of the indexes are reported for the period April 1973-April 1978 together with the standard deviations. The mean rate of change using income weights is always between the mean changes using total trade weights and MERM weights and is generally closer to the latter. Similarly, the ranking of the variances is almost the same for income and MERM weights.

Many other weighting schemes could be discussed,[17] but one is particularly relevant for the international perspective taken here. It has to do with the relative use of a particular currency in world payments. This measure is relevant only for the five major currencies—the U.S. dollar, the Deutsche mark, the pound sterling, the French franc, and the yen. Indeed, even though the SDR

15. The sensitivity-openness issue was first addressed in Cooper (1968) and has become a popular topic in international political economy. See Keohane and Nye (1977) and Macedo and Peaslee (1971), expanded in Macedo (1977), for example.

16. The XM weights refer to the sum of average exports and imports in dollars during the period 1973-1977. The income weights are derived from gross domestic product in 1975 domestic prices converted into dollars at the average yearly exchange rate and averaged from 1973 to 1977. The MERM weights are derived from the size of the effect of a 10 percent depreciation of the domestic currency in the total balance in dollars, at the scale of world trade in 1977. From the relative size of these total effects, bilateral shares are derived that, after adjustment for the initial trade imbalance is made, are used to obtain bilateral weights for the effective exchange rates reported in *International Financial Statistics*—see Artus and McGuirk (1978) and Artus and Rhomberg (1973). In Table 5-1, column 2, we take the main diagonal of the share matrix, so that the weights give a ranking of the eight countries according to one measure of "sensitivity" to external developments.

17. See Macedo (1979:11 ff.) for a discussion of four other weighting schemes—namely export and import shares, export shares in manufactures using the IMF World Trade Model, and MERM "high elasticity" weights.

Table 5-2. Mean and Standard Deviation of Quarterly Changes
in Purchasing Powers, for Alternative Weighting Schemes, April
1973-April 1978 (*in percent p.a.*).

	Mean			Standard Deviation		
	XM	MERM	Y	XM	MERM	Y
Canada	-12.20	-11.64	-11.97	13.88	12.95	11.57
France	-9.78	-9.18	-9.41	12.20	12.29	14.05
Germany	-2.77	-2.12	-2.36	15.46	16.74	17.91
Italy	-17.33	-16.76	-17.01	15.74	15.48	16.19
Japan	-6.05	-5.44	-5.76	12.84	13.45	12.67
Switzerland	1.17	1.83	1.56	16.87	17.99	18.81
United Kingdom	-15.00	-14.38	-14.67	13.60	14.55	14.62
United States	-9.98	-9.42	-9.74	11.11	9.72	8.37

Table 5-3. SDR and Income Weights (*percent*).

	Weights in SDR Basket			Income Weights (from Table 5-1)
	1974[a]	1978[a]	1980[b]	
United States	47	49	42	48
Germany	18	18	19	15
United Kingdom	13	11	13	8
Japan	11	11	13	18
France	11	11	13	11

a. Relative weights based on the shares of the five currencies in the sixteen-currency
basket; actual rates in interest rate calculation.

b. Actual weights in five-currency basket and in interest rate calculation.

basket was based for several years on sixteen currencies, the interest rate was
computed on the basis of an average of these five currencies (see Polak 1979:
643). Advocates of a greater commercial use of the SDR have long proposed the
reduction of the number of currencies in the basket from sixteen to five,[18] and
the step was taken officially by the IMF in September 1980. Table 5-3 contrasts
these weights with the implicit ones established in July 1974 and July 1978, as
well as with the implicit income weights for the five currencies using the shares
in the third column of Table 5-1.

The reversal of the ranking of Japan, a larger economy and a smaller currency
area, and of the United Kingdom, a smaller economy and a larger currency area,

18. While the possibility of a private use of SDRs was raised in the Committee of
Twenty in connection with intervention (see IMF 1974:123), the "simplified SDR" as a
means of promoting its commercial use was proposed in *World Financial Markets* (August
1975) on the basis of the implicit weights of July 1974. These weights were used in Kouri
and Macedo (1978:129) to compute optimal portfolios.

are noteworthy in the contrast of columns 1 and 4 of Table 5-3. Comparing the first three columns, the decline of the two reserve currencies of the Bretton Woods system from 60 to 55 percent and the increase in the share of the Deutsche mark are apparent, but it is the stability of these shares that appears striking in light of the volatility of the foreign exchanges since 1974.

We now turn to an interpretative account of the period, using the indexes of purchasing power presented in Figure 5-1. During the five-year period, the downward trend in the purchasing power of world money is particularly noteworthy. The variations of the purchasing powers of the various currencies follow closely those of their nominal effective exchange rates, with built-in depreciation of about 7.25 percent per annum over the eight years from 1970. Thus, the only currency for which purchasing power increased was the Swiss franc (3.7 percent). The largest decline in purchasing power was for the Italian lira (57.8 percent), closely followed by the pound sterling (54.5 percent). The Deutsche mark lost 15.1 percent of its purchasing power.[19] In Figure 5-2 we show the "real" effective exchange rates of the same currencies. The difference between national and international purchasing power is evident in the greater variability of these indexes, even though there are discernible trends in the real world price of domestic consumption baskets, particularly for the United States and Japan. In fact, the yen shows a much higher domestic inflation than the decline in its international purchasing power might have led one to predict, given that the weight of the yen in world money is the second largest (16 percent). The real appreciation of the yen (which would have been much smaller had only traded goods prices been included)[20] was largely offset after mid-1978, while the decline in the purchasing power of the yen has continued at roughly the same pace. Finally, Figure 5-3 displays another measure in the relative attractiveness of the U.S. dollar by comparing its purchasing power for the "national" investor, which is just the inverse of the U.S. consumer price index (line labeled United States); the purchasing power of the U.S. dollar for the international investor (line labeled World—the same as the line labeled United States in Figure 5-1); and the purchasing power of the U.S. dollar for "foreign" investors located in Italy, the United Kingdom, Germany, and Switzerland. These four lines are simply the increase of the dollar value of the domestic price level, so that the purchasing power of the dollar is lower in the low inflation than in the high inflation countries.

19. The remaining values were Canada (54.9), France (61.3), Japan (73.7), and the United States (61.9).

20. Thus on May 15, 1978, the real effective rate of the yen with 1976 bilateral manufactures trade shares as weights and March 1973 as base was 109.1, using wholesale prices of manufactures, and 132.7, using consumer prices. Using export unit values leads to a real depreciation of 9 percent (see *World Financial Markets* May 1978). The IMF values are 107.7 for relative wholesale prices in 1978 relative to 1973 and 123.6 for relative value-added deflators during the same interval.

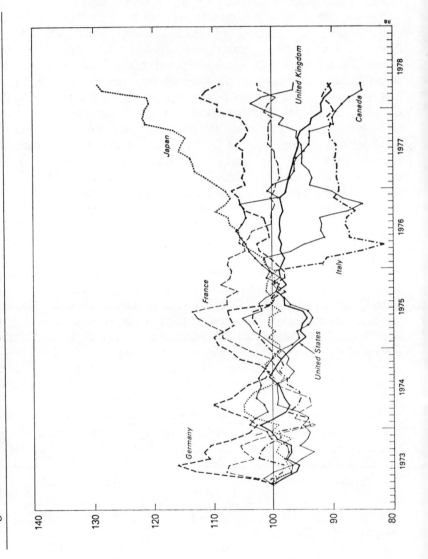

Figure 5-2. Real Effective Exchange Rates, April 1973 - April 1978 (April 1973 = 100).

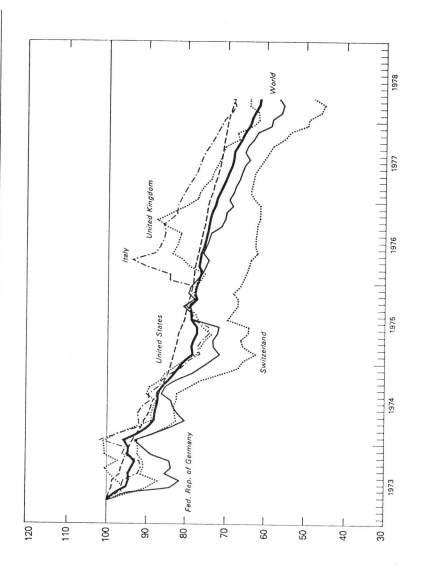

Figure 5-3.   The Purchasing Power of the U.S. Dollar, April 1973–April 1978 (*April 1973 = 100*).

TIME-INVARIANT PORTFOLIO RULES DERIVED

The indexes of purchasing power were derived in the previous section from the static optimization problem of an international consumer with an homothetic loglinear utility function (the so-called Bernoulli case), but they can also be derived in the less restrictive framework of continous time intertemporal consumption and investment optimization under uncertainty (see Merton 1975, and references therein). Thus, in this section we retain the homotheticity of the utility function, but we allow nonunitary relative risk aversion. In order to preserve the separation between the consumption and investment decisions typical of the classic mean variance framework (see Markowitz 1958; and Tobin 1965), prices and exchange rates are assumed to be stationary and lognormally distributed. While, as indicated, these assumptions are quite restrictive, they are sufficient for the computation of optimal portfolios in the next section.

Since the purpose of this section is illustrative, we restrict the investor to a two-country, two-good model and confine the N country case to the chapter appendix. Consider the problem of maximizing the expected value of a utility function U with constant relative risk aversion $1 - \gamma$, which is linear in the mean and variance of the real return on two assets:

$$U = x_1 (R_1 + dq_1) + x_2 (R_2 + dq_2)$$
$$- \frac{1}{2} (1 - \gamma) [x_1 (R_1 + dq_1) + x_2 (R_2 + dq_2)]^2$$

where x_i is the proportion of wealth invested in the asset denominated in currency i, $i = 1, 2$; R_i is the known nominal return on the asset denominated in currency i; and dq_i is the proportional change in the purchasing power of currency i.

The solution to Max $E(U)$ subject to $x_2 = 1 - x_1$ is an optimal portfolio obtained by adding a minimum variance portfolio, denoted by the column vector x^m, which is independent of risk aversion and of real returns, and a zero net worth speculative portfolio, denoted by the column vector x^s, which is scaled by risk aversion and chosen by comparing the real return on each asset to the real return on the minimum variance portfolio as a whole. Writing these portfolios in full, we obtain:

$$
\begin{bmatrix} x_1 \\ x_2 \end{bmatrix} = \begin{bmatrix} x_1^m \\ x_2^m \end{bmatrix} + \frac{1}{1 - \gamma} \frac{1}{\omega_1^2 \omega_2^2 - 2\omega_{12}^2} \begin{bmatrix} \omega_2^2 & -\omega_{12} \\ -\omega_{12} & \omega_1^2 \end{bmatrix} \begin{bmatrix} 1 - x_1^m & -x_2^m \\ -x_1^m & 1 - x_2^m \end{bmatrix} \begin{bmatrix} r_1 \\ r_2 \end{bmatrix}
$$

and

$$
\begin{bmatrix} x_1^m \\ x_2^m \end{bmatrix} = \frac{1}{\omega_1^2 \omega_2^2 - 2\omega_{12}^2} \begin{bmatrix} \omega_2^2 - \omega_{12} \\ \omega_1^2 - \omega_{12} \end{bmatrix}
$$

where ω_i^2 is the variance of changes in the purchasing power of currency i, $i = 1, 2$; ω_{12} is the covariance between purchasing power changes; and $r_i = R_i + E(dq_i)$ is the expected real return in the asset denominated in currency i. The logs of the purchasing powers of the two currencies are expressed as

$$q_1 = -\alpha_1 p_1 - \alpha_2 p_2 - (1 - \alpha_1) s$$

$$q_2 = -\alpha_1 p_1 - \alpha_2 p_2 + \alpha_1 s$$

An increase in s means that currency 1 depreciates relative to currency 2.

Now, denoting means by ν_i and π and variances by ζ_i^2 and σ^2, proportional changes in prices and exchange rates are given by the following linear functions of the stochastic processes du_i and dz:

$$dp_i = \nu_i \, dt + \zeta_i \, du_i \quad i = 1, 2$$

$$ds = \pi dt + \sigma dz$$

The processes du_i and dz are serially independent no matter how short the time interval and normally distributed with mean zero and unit variance, so that, as assumed, prices and exchange rates are stationary and lognormally distributed. Using the fundamental theorem of stochastic calculus, we can derive the proportional rate of change of the purchasing power of the two currencies and the covariance between purchasing power changes to obtain the result that the sum of the variances of purchasing power changes is equal to the variance of the change in the bilateral exchange rate, or

$$\omega_1^2 + \omega_2^2 - 2\omega_{12} = \sigma^2$$

Using this result to simplify the speculative portfolio, and denoting the vector of real returns by r, we rewrite it in terms of a matrix Σ, which depends only on the variance of the exchange rate:

$$x^s = \frac{1}{1 - \gamma} \Sigma r$$

and

$$\Sigma = \frac{1}{\sigma^2} \begin{bmatrix} 1 & -1 \\ -1 & 1 \end{bmatrix}$$

Now, using matrix notation and denoting the vector of expenditure shares by α, we rewrite the minimum variance portfolio as

$$x^m = (I - \Phi) \alpha$$

where

$$\Phi = \begin{bmatrix} \zeta_1 \rho_1 / \sigma & \zeta_2 \rho_2 / \sigma \\ -\zeta_1 \rho_1 / \sigma & -\zeta_2 \rho_2 / \sigma \end{bmatrix}$$

In this expression, the matrix Φ measures the ratio of the covariance of prices and exchange rates to the variance of exchange rates. A high correlation coefficient could thus be offset by an exchange rate variance sufficiently higher than the variance of prices. If exchange rates and prices are uncorrelated or if price changes are perfectly anticipated, Φ becomes a zero matrix. Lower variance of exchange rates relative to prices would make weights in the minimum variance portfolio differ more from expenditure shares. In fact, the condition for the share of currency 1 in the minimum variance portfolio (x_1^m) to be larger than the expenditure share for country 1 is given by

$$\alpha_1 \left(1 - \frac{\zeta_1 \, \rho_1}{\zeta_2 \, \rho_2} \right) < 1 \quad \text{as} \quad \rho_2 < 0$$

This condition will hold when $\rho_1 < 0$, so that currency 1 is a good hedge because its price level is negatively correlated with the exchange rate. Given that, as purchasing power parity would lead one to predict, $\rho_1 > 0$, the smaller the covariance term in country 1 relative to country 2, the more likely that $x_1^m > \alpha_1$, given α_1.

In the "textbook" view of the foreign exchange market, in which the demand for foreign currency per unit of time is derived from the supply and demand for exports and imports, an increase in the demand for foreign goods generates a greater demand for and supply of foreign exchange, if the "elasticities condition" holds. A similar condition holds when there is a demand for foreign currency at a given time, as implied by the portfolio approach to exchange rate determination. Here, given real returns, the condition for a marginal increase in α_1 to increase the share of currency 1 in the minimum variance portfolio is

$$\sigma > \zeta_1 \, \rho_1 - \zeta_2 \, \rho_2$$

which will generally be true even if $\rho_1 > 0$ and $\rho_2 < 0$ because the variance of exchange rate changes tends to be much larger than the variance of inflation rates.

The effect on total portfolio proportions has, however, to take into account that real return differentials depend on the variance of exchange rate changes as well as on their covariance with price changes. In fact, the difference between real and nominal differentials can be written as

$$dq_1 - dq_2 = \left\{ -\pi + \sigma^2 + [\alpha_1 (-\sigma^2 + \zeta_1 \, \rho_1 \, \sigma) + \alpha_2 \, \zeta_2 \, \rho_2 \, \sigma] \right\} dt - \sigma dz$$

Noticing that the term in square brackets is nothing but $-x_1^m \, \sigma^2$, the speculative portfolio of currency 1 becomes

$$x_1^s = \frac{1}{1 - \gamma} \left[\frac{\hat{R}}{\sigma^2} - x_1^m \right]$$

where $\hat{R} = R_1 - R_2 - \pi + \sigma^2$; and, using matrix notation introduced earlier for the minimum variance portfolio, the total portfolio proportions can be written as:

$$x = -\frac{\gamma}{1-\gamma} (I - \Phi) \, \alpha + \frac{1}{1-\gamma} \, \frac{\hat{R}}{\sigma^2} \begin{pmatrix} 1 \\ -1 \end{pmatrix}$$

The condition for a marginal increase in α, to increase the share of currency 1 in the total portfolio given that it increases the share of currency 1 in the minimum variance portfolio, is therefore that the relative degree of risk aversion be greater than 1 ($\gamma < 0$).

If the investor has a Bernoulli utility function ($\gamma = 0$), the covariance term in the speculative portfolio exactly offsets the minimum variance portfolio. Then the total portfolio, independent of preferences, is given by $x_1^B = \hat{R}/\sigma^2$, where B refers to the Bernouilli investor.

If the investor is less risk averse, the weight of the speculative portfolio is correspondingly increased. Taking the case discussed in a letter of Gabriel Cramer to Daniel Bernouilli (quoted in Samuelson 1977), let $\gamma = 1/2$, giving

$$x_1^C = -x_1^m + 2\hat{R}/\sigma^2$$

where C refers to the Cramer investor.

In that case, the result that $\partial x_1^C / \partial \alpha_1 > 0$ would require that the effect of an increase in the demand for goods of country 1 be associated with a lower share of currency 1 in the minimum variance portfolio. In terms of the above condition, we would have

$$\sigma < \zeta_1 \rho_1 - \zeta_2 \rho_2$$

There is, however, some agreement that relative risk aversion is probably higher than the Bernouilli watershed, perhaps as large as 2. In that case ($\gamma = -1$), and we have

$$x_1^P = \frac{1}{2} (x_1^m + \hat{R}/\sigma^2)$$

where P refers to the "Samuelson presumption."[21] It is clear that the condition for the effect on the minimum variance portfolio to be positive applies to the effect on the total portfolio as well.

21. See Samuelson (1977: 39, n. 7). Krugman (1981) argues that this condition is restrictive. It is, however, usual in the finance literature and also underlies some of the results in Weiss (1980).

OPTIMAL PORTFOLIOS FOR EIGHT
INDUSTRIAL COUNTRIES

We now compute the optimal portfolio proportions that would have obtained if in April 1978 an international investor with given expenditure shares and constant relative risk aversion had applied the time-invariant portfolio rule derived in the previous section to observed returns and ex post covariances of prices and exchange rates in the eight country world of section one.

The assumption that the covariance structure of exchange rate changes and inflation is stationary is a strong one. Rather than assuming that the investor expects the change in purchasing power next period to be the same as the change in purchasing power this period, as implied by the stochastic processes used in section two, forecasting rules could be postulated that would make the filtered covariance structure stationary.[22]

Impressionistic evidence on whether the covariance structure was stationary from October 1973 to April 1978 is at best mixed. For example, the variance of exchange rate changes seems to have declined in the cases of the French franc, the Deutsche mark, and the yen. The lira and the Swiss franc show jumps rather than a downward trend. The Canadian dollar is quite stable, but with an upward jump in late 1976, and sterling shows a great deal of variation, with a slight upward trend. Covariances between prices and exchange rates are typically dominated by the exchange rate variance. Filtering techniques are, however, an equally ad hoc alternative, particularly if different auto regressive or moving average processes are used for each series. While evidence for the experience to the end of 1980 yields similar portfolios and thus suggests that covariances might tend to stabilize, the assumption that they did has to be made mostly on grounds of convenience (see further discussion in Branson 1980b:192).

From the previous section, we know that the "capital position" of the international investor is given by the portfolio proportions that minimize the variance of the return. This portfolio is the equivalent of the "risk-free" asset in domestic finance. We also know that the optimal portfolio rule involves computing a minimum variance portfolio, x^m, dependent on mean real returns.

The quarterly change in the purchasing power of each currency in terms of consumer prices is used to deflate the nominal return on money market instruments denominated in the eight different currencies. Using call money rates when readily available, the mean and standard deviation of nominal returns in percent per annum are reported in the first two columns of Table 5-4. Mean real returns, for the three different weighting schemes, obtained by adding the changes in purchasing powers from Table 5-2, are also reported in Table 5-4.

---

22. This was one of the procedures used in the simulations of Healy (1980a:209-20), who fits different integrated moving average processes to the exchange rate series and prefers the results to the ones obtained from sample averages.

Table 5-4.   Rates of Return, April 1973-April 1978.

	Nominal		Mean Real Return for Three Weighting Schemes		
	mean	s. d.	XM	MERM	Y
Canada	7.55	1.12	-4.09	-4.65	-4.42
France	9.56	2.10	.39	-.21	-.21
Germany	6.10	3.22	3.99	3.33	3.74
Italy[a]	11.14	2.80	-5.61	-6.18	-5.87
Japan	8.51	2.91	3.07	2.46	2.75
Switzerland[a]	5.52	1.24	7.34	6.69	7.08
United Kingdom	9.78	2.28	-4.60	-5.22	-4.89
United States	7.13	2.36	-2.28	-2.84	-2.61

a. Government bond yield. Others are call money rates.

It is apparent that the differences across weighting schemes are slight. Indeed the ranking of relative returns (indicated in Table 5-8 below) is the same, independent of the weighting scheme. Therefore, in spite of the fact that, as shown in the previous section, real return differentials depend on the minimum variance portfolio, mean real returns are not too sensitive empirically to differences in preferences.[23]

The minimum variance portfolio is given by the deviation between the expenditure shares α and a zero net worth weighted average of these shares, where the weights for the N-1 currencies are given by the covariance between changes in exchange rates and in prices in the N-1 countries. The share of the Nth currency in this zero net worth component of the minimum variance portfolio is simply minus a weighted sum of the covariance between the N-1 exchange rate changes and domestic inflation rates relative to the variance-covariance matrix of exchange rate changes. Using the notation of the previous section, we obtain the Φ matrix by multiplying the seven-by-eight covariance matrix between dollar exchange rate changes and inflation rates (both in number per quarter) in the eight countries by the inverse of the variance-covariance matrix of dollar exchange rate changes (in number per quarter) and by using the fact that total minimum variance portfolio proportions sum to 1. As indicated, the Φ matrix measures departures from anticipated inflation. Because $\Phi\alpha$ measures the difference between the expenditure shares and the minimum variance portfolio proportions, in the case of anticipated inflation we would have that $x^m = \alpha$. For the special case of an investor consuming only goods produced in country i ($\alpha_i = 1$), anticipated inflation in country i means that the investor will only hold currency i ($x_i^m = 1$), because the ith column of the Φ matrix will be 0. The Φ matrix is reported in Table 5-5 in percentage terms, so that the numbers are comparable to the weights in Table 5-1.

23. The reason why the variance and covariance enter has to do with Jensen's inequality. On the empirical magnitude of the effect, see McCulloch (1975) and references therein.

Table 5-5. The Φ Matrix (percent).

	Canada	France	Germany	Italy	Japan	Switzerland	United Kingdom	United States
Canada	-1.0	-7.7	-11.1	21.3	-40.8	-7.0	-7.9	-11.1
France	-2.7	-0.1	-7.1	-0.4	3.8	-4.9	-24.0	-1.6
Germany	3.0	-1.9	1.3	-8.4	-8.1	4.6	2.6	2.3
Italy	-3.8	-1.2	5.5	15.0	2.4	-1.0	2.5	-5.6
Japan	4.5	8.2	3.2	14.5	20.8	20.3	4.5	4.8
Switzerland	-1.2	-0.6	2.7	-6.9	4.9	0.8	13.1	1.1
United Kingdom	0.2	0.1	-4.1	-1.6	-8.1	-6.6	5.0	-1.6
United States	1.0	3.3	9.6	-33.6	25.0	-6.3	4.2	11.8

Note: Columns may not add to 0 because of rounding.

Take the example of an investor consuming only Japanese goods (α_{JA} = 100). Then the percentage of each currency in the minimum variance portfolio is given by subtracting the fifth column of Table 5-5 from the vector of expenditure shares, to obtain a portfolio where 79 percent is held in yen, 41 percent in Canadian dollars, 8 percent in Deutsche marks and in pounds sterling–the total of 136 percent being obtained by borrowing 25 percent in U.S. dollars, 8 percent in Swiss francs, 4 percent in French francs, and 2 percent in lira. Relative to the expenditure share, therefore, this Japanese national investor basically exchanges yen and U.S. dollars for Canadian dollars, Deutsche marks and pounds sterling.

The diagonal element gives a measure of how the "domestic" currency performs as a hedge against inflation. If the diagonal element is positive, as in the case of Japan, the national investor will borrow domestic currency to increase the foreign component of the minimum variance portfolio. If the diagonal element is negative, as in the case of Canada (first column of Table 5-5), the domestic currency is a superior hedge against inflation, and an investor consuming only Canadian goods would borrow in yen, Deutsche marks, and U.S. dollars to increase the domestic currency share to 101 percent and hold lira, French francs, and Swiss francs. Another way of looking at the diagonal elements of the Φ matrix is as a measure of the "own" effect–that is, of the effect of an increase in the share of expenditure on the goods of a particular country on the share of the respective currency in the minimum variance portfolio. For example, the increase in the share of yen is 0.79 (1 - 0.208) times the increase in the share of expenditure on Japanese goods.[24] The own effect being greater than or (as in the case of France) equal to 1 is an indication that the hypothesis of a "preferred monetary habitat" need not rely on transactions costs, even when broadly defined to include regulations requiring payments in domestic currency. The departure from the "preferred habitat" in the case of Japan, Italy, the United States, the United Kingdom, and less so, Germany and Switzerland is also based purely on portfolio considerations.[25] Similarly, the effect of an increase in the share of Japanese goods would increase the share of Canadian dollar in the minimum variance portfolio by a factor of 0.41 and the share of Deutsche marks and pounds sterling by a factor of 0.08, while it would decrease the share of U.S. dollars by a factor of 0.25. These effects are, of course, the same as the minimum variance portfolio proportions for a "Japanese" investor. Other significant cross-effects are $\partial x_{US}^m / \partial \alpha_{IT}$ = 0.34, $\partial x_{FR}^m / \partial \alpha_{UK}$ = 0.24, and $\partial x_{JA}^m / \partial \alpha_{SZ}$ = -0.20. Increases in the share of Italian goods increase the share of dollars, and

24. Including the effect from the speculative portfolios as well, we obtain $-0.79(\gamma/1-\gamma)$, or about 0.4 if $\gamma = -1$.

25. In Kouri and Macedo (1978), in a world of five countries using wholesale prices from April 1973 to August 1977, the quarterly own effect for France and Japan was substantially below 1, and the own effect for Germany, the United Kingdom, and the United States substantially higher. Traded goods price changes were mostly unanticipated.

increases in the share of British goods increase the share of French francs, whereas increases in the share of Swiss goods decrease the share of yen.

While all columns of the $I - \Phi$ matrix give the minimum variance portfolio of the respective national investor, the eighth column is particularly interesting because it also gives the minimum variance portfolio for every investor if purchasing power parity obtains.[26] In this special case, the minimum variance portfolio would include long positions of 88 percent in U.S. dollars and 11 percent in Canadian dollars and short positions in all the "strong" currencies whose exchange rates show a positive correlation with U.S. inflation. This is in sharp contrast with the minimum variance portfolios actually obtained with the three weighting schemes reported in Table 5-6: The combined North American portfolio ranges from 37 (XM) to 46.5 percent (MERM) rather than the 99 percent implied by the acceptance of the purchasing power parity hypothesis.

Another way of interpreting the Φ matrix is in terms of elasticities of the shares in minimum variance portfolio with respect to the shares in expenditure. By multiplying each element of the $I - \Phi$ matrix by the ratio of the expenditure share from Table 5-1 and the minimum variance portfolio share from Table 5-6, we obtain a matrix of elasticities. The higher the elasticity, the greater the effect of a proportional increase in the expenditure share on the portfolio share. For example, an increase of 10 percent in the share of Japanese goods consumed (to 17.5 percent) would imply an increase of 16 percent in the share of yen in the minimum variance portfolio (to 9.1 percent). Similarly, the own elasticity for Canada is 0.28, the cross-elasticity of the French franc with respect to expenditure on British goods is 0.13, the U.S. dollar-Italy elasticity is 0.05, and the yen-Swiss franc elasticity is -0.04.

Turning to the speculative portfolio, the augmented inverse of the variance-covariance matrix of exchange rate changes, denoted in the previous section as the Σ matrix, is reported in Table 5-7 in percent per annum. The diagonal ele-

Table 5-6. Minimum Variance Portfolios for Alternative Weighting Schemes (*percent*).

	XM	MERM	Y
Canada	18.6	15.4	18.1
France	16.5	20.5	12.5
Germany	19.9	15.5	13.7
Italy	7.2	8.0	5.7
Japan	5.1	1.0	7.8
Switzerland	1.0	0.6	-0.4
United Kingdom	13.2	7.9	9.1
United States	18.4	31.1	33.5

Note: Columns may not add to 100 because of rounding.

26. If, on top of this, inflation is known in the Nth country, the minimum variance portfolio disappears as analyzed in Kouri (1977).

Table 5-7. The Σ Matrix.

	Canada	France	Germany	Italy	Japan	Switzerland	United Kingdom	United States
Canada	9.76							
France	1.65	2.98						
Germany	-1.10	-1.38	3.23					
Italy	1.08	-0.60	-0.11	1.48				
Japan	1.00	0.25	-0.84	-0.08	2.60			
Switzerland	-0.98	-0.36	-1.64	0.12	-0.20	2.61		
United Kingdom	0.06	-0.26	0.06	-0.31	-0.40	-0.42	1.66	
United States	-11.46	-2.28	1.78	-1.58	-2.34	0.88	-0.40	15.39

Note: Columns and rows may not add to 0 because of rounding.

ments of the Σ matrix measure the own effect of changes in real rates of return, and the off-diagonal elements indicate the degree of substitutability or complementarity between currencies. The large own effect of the U.S. dollar, and to a lesser degree of the Canadian dollar, is apparent. As shown in the last column of Table 5-8, the Canadian dollar rate exhibits a much smaller variance than any of the other seven dollar rates and has therefore a larger own effect. The large value for the U.S. dollar comes from the sum of the cross-effects of the dollar and the remaining currencies—namely, the Canadian dollar. In fact, the two North American currencies are strong substitutes for each other. An increase in the real return differential of one leads to a decline in the share of the other in the speculative portfolio of 11.5 percent/1 - γ. The degree of substitutability between the Deutsche mark and the Swiss franc is smaller (1.6 percent), smaller in fact in absolute value than the degree of complementarity between the U.S. dollar and the Deutsche mark.[27]

Note also that the magnitude of own and cross-effects as given by the Σ matrix in Table 5-7 is larger than the difference in real rates of return in Table 5-4. As a consequence, when the vectors of real return (in percent per annum) are premultiplied by Σ, we obtain the same speculative portfolio for the three weighting schemes at two decimal points. In Table 5-8, the portfolio proportions of speculative currency holdings are reported in decreasing order, together with the variance of changes in the exchange rates against the dollar (in percent per annum.). As mentioned above, the ranking of real returns from Table 5-4 is also reported in Table 5-8.

Table 5-8. Speculative Portfolio for the Bernouilli Investor
and Variance of Dollar Exchange Rate Changes.

	Rank of Real Return (Table 5-4)	x^s (percent)[a]	σ^2 (percent per annum)
Canada	6	-28	0.2
France	4	-3	1.1
Germany	2	-2	1.5
Italy	8	-8	1.2
Japan	3	7	0.7
Switzerland	1	15	1.4
United States	5	28	–
United Kingdom	7	-9	1.0

a. Rounded to offset the effects of different weighting schemes on the decimals.

27. This complementarity, pointed out in Kouri and Macedo (1978), is also found in Healy (1980a) when the sample mean is used. When a weighted average of past exchange rate changes or ARIMA techniques are used, however, the complementarity is between the Deutsche mark and Canadian dollar. This ambiguity does not justify empirical applications of a two-country framework where assets are forced to be substitutes. Such a framework has, however, been used to discuss the "dollar overhang" in Dornbusch (1980).

The dominant share of the U.S. dollar (28 percent) in the speculative portfolio is exactly offset by a short position in Canadian dollars. The high positive covariance between the two rates implied by the strong cross-effects leads the investor to borrow substantially in the currency with a slightly lower rate of return. Given the ranking of real returns, the 15 percent long position in Swiss francs and the 7 percent long position in yen are no surprise. The short position in Deutsche marks, while a direct consequence of the complementarity with the U.S. dollar and the strong substitutability with the Swiss franc, is harder to motivate empirically and indeed disappears when more recent observations are included.

The percentages indicated in Table 5-8 are the speculative portfolio for the Bernouilli investor ($\gamma = 0$). The higher the relative degree of risk aversion, the smaller will be the contribution of this speculative portfolio to total portfolio proportions. Indeed, the minimum variance portfolio of Table 5-6 becomes the total portfolio when risk aversion becomes infinite. In practice, values of γ of about -10 are enough to make the speculative portfolio negligible. When $\gamma = -1$ (the "Samuelson presumption"), the percentages shown in Table 5-8 are cut in half, and they are doubled for the Cramer investor ($\gamma = 1/2$).

Total portfolio proportions for the three different weighting schemes and three degrees of risk aversion are reported in Table 5-9. For the Bernouilli investor, the total share of the U.S. dollar ranges from 46 to 62 percent and the share of the Deutsche mark from 12 to 18 percent. The high share of the French franc when the MERM weights are used is also noteworthy. But the startling feature of Table 5-9, particularly with respect to the United States and Canada, is the sensitivity of the proportions to assumptions about risk aversion. The share of the U.S. dollar, for example, almost doubles from the high to the low risk aversion cases using MERM and income weights and more than doubles when trade weights are used. Increasing risk aversion would ultimately bring the total portfolio proportions very close to the minimum variance portfolio and therefore to an optimum portfolio that would be entirely independent of returns. Optimum portfolio proportions would then become akin to the weighting schemes underlying the SDR standards described in Table 5-3. Indeed, using the "Samuelson presumption" and total trade weights, we find that the shares of the Deutsche mark and of the French franc are higher than in the 1980 definition (23 instead of 19 percent and 18 instead of 13 percent, respectively), while the share of the dollar is slightly lower (39 instead of 42 percent), and the shares of the pound and of the yen are still equal to each other, but also slightly lower (10 instead of 13 percent).

Figure 5-4 shows the difference between the optimal dollar share and the expenditure share as a function of risk aversion. It is not surprising that in this case the optimal portfolio should be lower than the actual. Aside from political considerations that may enter in the central banks' reserve management poli-

Table 5-9. Total Portfolios for Three Weighting Schemes and Three Degrees of Risk Aversion (percent).

	XM			MERM			Y		
	$\gamma = -1$	$\gamma = 0$	$\gamma = \frac{1}{2}$	$\gamma = -1$	$\gamma = 0$	$\gamma = \frac{1}{2}$	$\gamma = -1$	$\gamma = 0$	$\gamma = \frac{1}{2}$
Canada	4.6	-9.4	-37.4	1.4	-12.6	-40.6	4.1	-9.9	-37.9
France	15.0	13.5	10.5	19.0	17.5	14.5	11.0	9.5	6.5
Germany	18.9	17.9	15.9	14.5	13.5	11.5	12.7	11.7	9.7
Italy	3.2	-0.8	-8.8	4.0	0.0	-8.0	1.7	-2.3	-10.3
Japan	8.6	12.1	19.1	4.5	8.0	15.0	11.3	14.8	21.8
Switzerland	8.5	16.0	31.0	8.1	15.6	30.6	7.1	14.6	29.6
United Kingdom	8.7	4.2	-4.8	3.4	-1.1	-10.1	4.6	0.1	-8.9
United States	32.4	46.4	74.4	45.1	59.1	87.1	47.5	61.5	89.5

Note: Columns may not add to 100 because of rounding.

Figure 5-4. Difference Between the Dollar Share in the Optimal Portfolio and in Consumption Depending on Relative Risk Aversion.

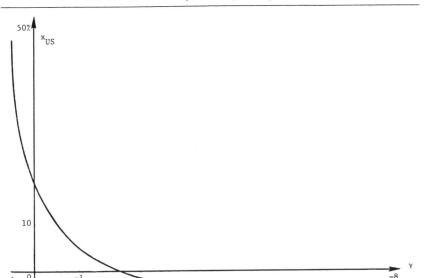

cies,[28] this framework entirely abandons the presumption that transactions costs and regulations imply a "preferred monetary habitat" for the domestic currency. It would therefore take a degree of risk aversion of about 3 (γ = -2) for substantial further diversification out of dollars to have been optimal, given the real return structure of April 1978. This result holds true when more recent observations are included.

CONCLUSION

Even though an explicit test of the framework presented above is beyond the scope of this chapter—in part because available data on actual currency proportions in central banks are highly aggregated across countries—the use of the indexes of purchasing power and of the optimal portfolio proportions can yield

28. As argued by Heller and Knight (1978), Ben-Bassat (1980), and Aliber (in Chapter 9 of this volume), particularly for central banks of developed countries. There is at least one case where reserve management is explicitly based on return–risk considerations, and that is the Monetary Authority of Singapore.

a great deal of insight on the problems and proposed reforms of the present international monetary system. Previous findings like the strong substitution between the U.S. and the Canadian dollars, the complementarity between the U.S. dollar and the Deutsche mark, and the large importance of the U.S. dollar in a world without the economies of scale of the vehicle currency were confirmed in a more general framework. Significant departures from purchasing power parity and the related presence of significant unanticipated inflation in Japan, Italy, and the United States, and the United Kingdom were other findings of interest. While all these conclusions certainly should be further examined with indexes using traded goods prices and a closer examination of the degree to which covariances are stationary, other uses could be cited for the framework developed here. These include the computation of the real forward premiums, taking into account the cross-effects given by the Σ matrix; the investigation of a weighting scheme that would make a given portfolio optimal; the analysis of the effects of nominal return differentials; and above all, the exploration of market equilibrium.

To sum up, the framework developed in this chapter shows the importance of the microeconomic foundations of a "world money" standard and provides a guide for currency diversification policy on the part of large organizations, in particular central banks—a policy that single exchange rate models have to neglect entirely. In this respect, it is a step in the direction of providing an empirically implementable theoretical framework for thinking about world monetary issues in the global terms that have been advocated by Robert Triffin. Let us hope that dollar shares computed in this chapter would not be too far from optimal in Triffin's world.

APPENDIX
THE OPTIMAL PORTFOLIO RULE IN THE N COUNTRY CASE

The maximization problem can be written as

$$\text{Max } E(U) = E(x'r) - \frac{1}{2} bV(x'r)$$

subject to $x'e = 1$, where $x = (x_1 \ldots x_N)'$ is the vector of portfolio proportions; $r = (r_1 \ldots r_N)'$ is the vector of real returns; e is a N column vector of 1s; and b is the relative degree of risk aversion.

Since nominal returns R_i are known, the variance of mean return can be written as

$$V(x'r) = E(x'rr'x) = x'\Omega x$$

where $\Omega = [\omega_{ij}] = E(dq_i dq_j)^2$ is the N-by-N variance covariance matrix of changes in purchasing powers denoted by dq_i.

Note that in the two-country case described in the text, we have, respectively

$$dq_1 = \left\{ -\alpha_1 \nu_1 - \alpha_2 \nu_2 - (1-\alpha_1)\pi + \frac{1}{2} \left[\alpha_1 (1+\alpha_1)\zeta_1^2 + \alpha_2 (1+\alpha_2)\zeta_2^2 \right. \right.$$

$$\left. + 2\alpha_1\alpha_2\zeta_1\zeta_2\rho_{12} + (1-\alpha_1)(2-\alpha_1)\sigma^2 + 2(1-\alpha_1)(\alpha_1\zeta_1\sigma\rho_1 + \alpha_2\zeta_2\sigma\rho_2)] \right\}$$

$$dt - \alpha_1\zeta_1 du_1 - \alpha_2\zeta_2 du_2 - (1-\alpha_1)\sigma dz$$

and

$$dq_2 = \left\{ -\alpha_1 \nu_1 - \alpha_2 \nu_2 + \alpha_1 \pi + \frac{1}{2} \left[\alpha_1 (1+\alpha_1)\zeta_1^2 + \alpha_2 (1+\alpha_2)\zeta_2^2 \right. \right.$$

$$\left. + 2\alpha_1\alpha_2\zeta_1\zeta_2\rho_{12} - \alpha_1 (1-\alpha_1)\sigma^2 - 2\alpha_1(\alpha_1\zeta_1\sigma\rho_1 + \alpha_2\zeta_2\sigma\rho_2)] \right\}$$

$$dt - \alpha_1\zeta_1 du_1 - \alpha_2\zeta_2 du_2 + \alpha_1\sigma dz$$

where ρ_{12} is the correlation coefficient between du_1 and du_2; ρ_i is the correlation coefficient between du_i and dz; and ν_i, ζ_i, π, and σ were defined in the text.

The mean instantaneous expected change is given by the expressions in curly brackets, and by Ito's multiplication rule, the expressions in square brackets give the instantaneous variance. The covariance is given by

$$\omega_{12} = \alpha_1^2\zeta_1^2 + \alpha_2^2\zeta_2^2 + 2\alpha_1\alpha_2\zeta_1\zeta_2\rho_{12} - \alpha_1(1-\alpha_1)\sigma^2 - 2\alpha_1^2\zeta_1\sigma\rho_1$$

$$- 2\alpha_1\alpha_2\zeta_2\sigma\rho_2 + \alpha_1\zeta_1\sigma\rho_1 + \alpha_2\zeta_2\sigma\rho_2$$

Since in this case dq_i and ω_{ij} are given, we find the optimal portfolio by differentiating the maximand with respect to the decision variables x_i, imposing the constraint, and accepting short sales, so that x_i can be negative. We form the Lagrangean

$$L = x'r - \frac{1}{2} b\, x'\Omega x + \lambda(x'e - 1)$$

Differentiating L with respect to the vector of instruments, we find the $N+1$ first-order conditions as

$$\frac{\partial L}{\partial x} = r - b\Omega x + \lambda e = 0$$

$$\frac{\partial L}{\partial x} = x'e - 1 = 0$$

The variance-covariance matrix being nonsingular, we can solve for x, and using the constraint, we obtain

$$\lambda = (b - e'\,\Omega^{-1}\,r)/e'\,\Omega^{-1}\,e$$

so that, eliminating λ from the N first-order conditions, we have:

$$r - b\Omega x + \frac{1}{e'\,\Omega^{-1}\,e}\,(b - e'\Omega^{-1}r)e = 0$$

Solving for x and factoring r, we obtain the portfolio rule

$$x = \frac{\Omega^{-1}e}{e'\,\Omega^{-1}\,e} + \frac{1}{b}\,\Omega^{-1}\left[I - e\,\frac{e'\,\Omega^{-1}}{e'\,\Omega^{-1}\,e}\right]r$$

In this derivation it is obvious that the speculative portfolio is chosen by comparing the real return on each asset to the return of the minimum variance portfolio (this is further elaborated in Macedo 1979:23). Using the notation in the text and recalling that $b = 1 - \gamma$, we see that

$$\frac{\Omega^{-1}e}{e'\,\Omega^{-1}\,e} = (I - \Phi)\alpha$$

$$\Omega^{-1}\left[I - e\,\frac{e'\,\Omega^{-1}}{e'\,\Omega^{-1}\,e}\right] = \Sigma$$

REFERENCES

Armington, Paul S. 1969. "A Theory of Demand for Products Distinguished by Place of Production." *IMF Staff Papers* 16 (March): 159–78.

Artus, Jacques R., and Anne K. McGuirk. 1978. "A Revised Version of the Multilateral Exchange Rate Model." IMF Research Department. 16 May. Draft.

Artus, Jacques R., and Rudolf R. Rhomberg. 1973. "A Multilateral Exchange Rate Model." *IMF Staff Papers* 20 (November): 591–611.

Ben–Bassat, Avraham. 1980. "The Optimal Composition of Foreign Exchange Reserves." *Journal of International Economics* 10 (May): 285–95.

Branson, William H. 1980a. "Trends in U.S. International Trade and Investment since World War II." In Martin S. Feldstein, ed., *The American Economy in Transition.* Chicago: University of Chicago Press.

_____. 1980b. "Comment" on Dornbusch (1980). *Brookings Papers on Economic Activity* 1.

Cooper, Richard N. 1968. *The Economics of Interdependence.* New York: McGraw-Hill.

Diewert, W.E. 1976. "Exact and Superlative Index Numbers." *Journal of Econometrics* 4 (May): 115–45.

Dornbusch, Rudiger. 1978. "Statement." U.S. House of Representatives, Hearings on the Conduct of Monetary Policy Committee on Banking, Finance and Urban Affairs. 7 March.

_____. 1980. "Exchange Rate Economics: Where Do We Stand?" *Brookings Papers on Economic Activity* 1.

Healy, James P. 1980a. "The Asset Market Determination of Exchange Rates in a Multi-Country Setting." Ph.D. dissertation, Princeton University.

_____. 1980b. "The Optimal Diversification of Foreign Exchange Reserves for a Less Developed Country. IMF. August. Draft.

Heller, H. Robert, and Malcolm Knight. 1978. *Reserve Currencies Preferences of Central Banks.* Essays in International Finance No. 131, Princeton, New Jersey: International Finance Section, Princeton University.

International Financial Statistics. Various issues.

International Monetary Fund. 1974. *International Monetary Reform, Documents of the Committee of Twenty.* Washington, D.C.

Katseli, Louka T. 1979. *The Reemergence of the Purchasing Power Parity Doctrine in the 1970s.* Special Papers in International Economics No. 13, Princeton, New Jersey: International Finance Section, Princeton University.

Keohane, Robert E., and Joseph S. Nye. 1977. *Power and Interdependence.* Boston: Little Brown.

Kouri, Pentti J.K. 1975. "Essays on the Theory of Flexible Exchange Rates." Ph.D. thesis, MIT.

_____. 1977. "International Investment and Interest Rate Linkages Under Flexible Exchange Rates." In R. Aliber, ed., *The Political Economy of Monetary Reform.* London: Macmillan.

Kouri, Pentti J.K., and Jorge Braga de Macedo. 1978. "Exchange Rates and the International Adjustment Process." *Brookings Papers on Economic Activity* 1: 111–50.

Krugman, Paul R. 1981. "Consumption Preferences, Asset Demands and Distribution Effects in International Financial Markets." NBER Working Paper No. 651, March.

Macedo, Jorge Braga de. 1979. "Porfolio Diversification Across Currencies." Economic Growth Center Discussion Paper No. 319. Yale University, September.

_____. 1980. "Portuguese Currency Experience: An Historical Perspective." *Estudos em Homenagem ao Prof. Doutor J.J. Teixeira Ribeiro.* Vol. IV. Coimbra: Boletim da Faculdade de Direito.

_____. 1981. "Optimal Currency Diversification for a Class of Risk Averse International Investors." Discussion Paper in Economics No. 12. Woodrow Wilson School, Princeton University, June.

Macedo, Jorge Braga de, and James Peaslee. 1974. "Monetary and Political Aspects of Optimal Economic Interdependence." Term paper for R. Triffin's Berkeley College Seminar, Yale University, Fall 1971. (Adapted in J.B. de Macedo, *Interdependencia Economica, Sistema Monetário Internacional e Integracāo Portuguesa.* Lisbon: National Development Bank, 1977.)

Markowitz, Harry. 1958. *Portfolio Selection.* New Haven: Yale University Press.

McCulloch, J. Huston. 1975. "Operational Aspects of the Siegel Paradox." *Quarterly Journal of Economics* 89 (February): 170-72.

McKinnon, Ronald I. 1979. *Money in International Exchange: The Convertible Currency System.* Oxford: Oxford University Press.

Merton, Robert C. 1975. "Theory of Finance from the Perspective of Continuous Time." *Journal of Financial and Quantitative Analysis* (December): 659-74.

Officer, Lawrence H. 1976. "The Purchasing-Power-Parity Theory of Exchange Rates: A Review Article." *IMF Staff Papers* 23 (March): 1-60.

Polak, J. Jacques. 1979. "The SDR as a Basket of Currencies." *IMF Staff Papers* 26 (December): 627-53.

Rhomberg, Rudolf R. 1976. "Indices of Effective Exchange Rates." *IMF Staff Papers* 23 (March): 88-112.

Samuelson, Paul A. 1977. "St. Petersburg Paradoxes: Defanged, Dissected and Historically Described." *Journal of Economic Literature* 15 (March): 24-55.

Solnik, Bruno H. 1974. "An Equilibrium Model of the International Market." *Journal of Economic Theory* 8 (August): 500-24.

Tobin, James. 1965. "The Theory of Portfolio Selection." In F. Hahn and J. Brechling, eds., *The Theory of Interest Rates.* New York: Macmillan.

Triffin, Robert. 1937. "La théorie de la surevaluation monétaire et la devaluation belge." *Bulletin de l'Institut de Recherches Economiques* (Louvain) (November): 19-52.

_____. 1957. *Europe and the Money Muddle.* New Haven: Yale University Press.

Weiss, Lawrence. 1980. "A Model of International Trade and Finance." *Quarterly Journal of Economics* 95 (September): 277-92.

World Financial Markets. Various issues.

6 GROWTH RATES, TRADE BALANCES, AND EXCHANGE RATES

Fritz Machlup

Few writers in the field of international monetary economics have had the deep insights and sharp foresights of Robert Triffin, the man whom I wish to honor by this modest contribution to the area of his special interest. Trade balances and exchange rates are two key words in the universe of his knowledge. The first element of the triad shown in the title of my chapter—growth rates— has not figured prominently in Triffin's work: He has not explored, as far as I know, the effects of disparate growth rates upon trade balances and equilibrium exchange rates. This will deprive me of the pleasure of pointing to his superior wisdom in avoiding many fallacies that have snared some of our respected colleagues. Triffin did not commit himself on the subject of this chapter, and this explains why references to his work will be absent from the pages that follow.

STATEMENT OF THE PROBLEM

The literature under review relates to the effects that divergent rates of economic growth are liable or likely to have on the trade balances of the countries concerned (if foreign exchange rates are kept unchanged) or on exchange rates (if these are determined by free market forces). The problem is of pragmatic significance, because it bears on national and international policies. It is also of intellectual interest to historians of economic thought. It is one of those instances where academic and official specialists find a particular answer to be cogent and "obvious" and fail to realize that some of their fellow specialists have pronounced the diametrically opposite, but equally "obvious," conclusion. Moreover, none of the partisans of the contradictory opinions seems to be aware of the fact that these pronouncements have long since been refuted and devas-

101

tated by more judicious theorists. This lack of awareness, unfortunately, seems to be endemic in the economic profession: The contents of the journals of years past are disregarded or forgotten. Fallacies refuted and "safely" buried reemerge every few years, because the refutations are buried in old journal issues no longer consulted by the newer generation.

These charges need to be substantiated. First I list the two contradictory positions and their refutation. I then point out that lack of clarity in the use of terms and of tacit assumptions may be largely responsible for the confusion.[1]

Thesis. More rapid growth strengthens the trade balances of the faster growing countries and weakens the trade balances of the others.

Antithesis. · More rapid growth weakens the trade balances of the faster growing countries and strengthens the trade balances of the others.

Synthesis. Whether more rapid growth will strengthen or weaken the trade balances of the faster growing countries depends on several conditions, of which the most decisive are the monetary policies of the countries concerned.

Obscurities. These statements all suffer from insufficient specifications of growth and monetary policies and from failure to stipulate whether foreign exchange rates are fixed, managed, or freely floating. It stands to reason, however, that all three positions tacitly assume fixed exchange rates and I would have to replace the words "trade balances" with "exchange rates" if the latter were freely determined in competitive markets for currencies supplied and demanded exclusively by exporters and importers of merchandise. As to monetary policies, I strongly suspect that the contradiction between thesis and antithesis is due chiefly to opposite but nonexplicit assumptions regarding relative expansions in the supplies of national moneys. The thesis is evidently based on the assumption that the more rapid real growth is not matched or exceeded by monetary expansion; the antithesis evidently takes it for granted that the faster real growth is associated with (induced, made possible by) even faster monetary expansion. The expression "faster" or "slower" monetary expansion suffers from an especially awkward ambiguity in that it seems to disregard induced changes in the demand for money balances. The references to growth rates suffer from several ambiguities, to be discussed later in the chapter. Some of the worst misunderstandings can be traced to tacit assumptions regarding supply-determined growth and demand-determined growth, where the opposing parties entertain opposite views regarding the possibility of controlling the rate of real growth by means of "demand management."

1. This may be the place to thank Richard Cooper and Peter Kenen, two of the editors of this volume, for their critical comments on the first draft of this chapter. Although they can be credited for many improvements in my formulations, they should not be held accountable for remaining weaknesses.

That this sketch of contradictory positions and of the underlying and disturbing obscurities is not exaggerated may be documented by quoting two highly respectable recent sources. Concerning the effects of "more rapid growth and technological advance abroad," Clarke (1980:29) states: "More rapid advance in many foreign countries than in the United States tended to weaken the country's merchandise trade balance." The antithesis, that more rapid growth abroad could strengthen, not weaken, the external position of the United States, finds strong expression in the annual reports of the International Monetary Fund (IMF) and in the periodic surveys of the Organization for Economic Cooperation and Development (OECD). The IMF report for 1978 states: "Since the divergence in rates of economic growth is one of the main causes of the present external imbalances, it is essential to achieve more coordination in this field" (p. 16); and further, "most industrial countries other than the United States— and especially the major surplus countries—should aim for growth rates . . . significantly higher than the actual rates . . ." (p. 17). Clearly, the writers of this statement attributed the weakness of the external balances of the United States to its higher rate of growth or to what they thought to be the unduly slow growth of its trading partners—especially the surplus countries, Germany and Japan.

THE THESIS AS EXPLANATION
OF DOLLAR STRENGTH

Theories holding that disparities in rates of economic growth are responsible for imbalances in trade and/or for movements in the exchange rates among the currencies of the countries concerned were heatedly debated at various periods in the past. The thesis that faster growth strengthens and slower growth weakens a country's balance of trade was strongly argued and defended in the days of dollar shortage, or dollar strength, in the late 1940s and early 1950s. Some of the protagonists thought that the causal connection was so simple—perhaps self-evident—that no detailed explanation was needed. The country with the faster growth in output and/or productivity (the difference was usually not considered) "surely" must have a stronger currency. Why? Because faster growth made it a more "powerful" economy, or because it had more goods to supply to the more slowly growing countries, which "consequently" would have trouble finding the foreign exchange to pay for their increased imports. Even these poor reasons were sometimes not spelled out. It was simply taken for granted that the country with the faster growth in output and/or productivity would have a surplus in its trade balance, and this was, of course, the logical counterpart of a trade deficit for the more slowly growing countries. If the United States had the more rapid growth, it followed that the other countries had to suffer dollar shortage.

Thomas Balogh, a major protagonist of this position, wanted to show not only the cause but also the cure of the dollar shortage. He had rather peculiar remedies to propose. Monetary restraint on the part of deficit countries was regarded as cruel as well as unhelpful, and hence, commercial policy was proposed as the most effective remedy: The poor Europeans should adopt more stringent trade restrictions of a discriminatory sort. Foreign exchange controls, discriminating against U.S. imports, were thought to be the most effective remedy (Balogh 1950). Other currency doctors were hoping that the Europeans would eventually be able to overcome the sluggishness of their growth and reduce or close the productivity gap; in the meantime, their plight could be alleviated by a generous supply of investment, loans, and grants from the rich Americans.

At that early stage of the debate, the different concepts of growth had not yet been clarified. Those who attributed the dollar shortage to the superior economic strength of the United States and its "consequent" export surpluses were not sure how to specify that superior strength. Balogh spoke of "faster technical progress," more "aggressiveness in managerial leadership," "overwhelmingly dominant power," "advantages of greater size and wealth," "rapid development" rendering "most industries in poorer and smaller countries obsolete," greater "competitive power," "monopoly positions," and favorable "terms of trade," but he probably saw the main cause for the troublesome U.S. surpluses in its faster growth of productivity (Balogh 1946, 1950). John H. Williams, another protagonist of this position, was not any clearer, but at least in one statement he pronounced that "over time, if there are divergent rates of growth of productivity, the trade will be progressively less favorable to the countries less rapidly advancing in productivity (Williams 1954:14). By "less favorable" he meant the trade balance—not the terms of trade—since it was dollar shortage he wanted to explain.

The thesis that faster growth of productivity could strengthen the trade position of the country concerned was partly rejected, partly qualified, by a highly sophisticated argument advanced by John R. Hicks. He distinguished between dollar shortages that could be avoided through appropriate monetary policies and others that had such profound structural causes that monetary policies would be of no avail. Thus, a U.S. trade surplus or a European trade deficit would not yield to treatment by compensatory monetary measures if the cause was found in an "import-biased" growth of productivity in the United States. If American productivity increased in the industries producing import substitutes, the consequent damage to European exporters could not be offset, reduced, or cured by any monetary adjustment (Hicks 1953). Hicks' diagnosis was that the American economy had been developing superior technologies in the goods previously imported from Europe and that this was responsible for European trade deficits and chronic dollar shortages.

THE THESIS REJECTED

The theories asserting that faster growth in general, or at least faster growth of productivity in particular sectors of the economy, would lead to surpluses in balances of trade of the fast-growing countries, were critically analyzed by several writers. Haberler (1948), Robertson (1954), Johnson (1954), Machlup (1954), Streeten (1955), and Komiya (1969) were among those who denied that disparities in rates of economic growth or of advances in economic productivity were strategic factors in determining the imbalances of trade of the countries involved or the relative strength of their currencies. They argued that faster growth in a country would be compatible with the emergence of a deficit, a surplus, or an even balance in its trade accounts, depending on the monetary policies of the countries concerned. It is the relative growth of money supply and aggregate spending in the various countries that is decisive in the determination of changes in their trade balances and/or exchange rates.

Not that other conditions besides monetary policies are entirely irrelevant. It may make a difference whether economic growth is the result of increases in the labor force, accumulation of capital, improvements in techniques of production and management, or intersectoral shifts of productive resources. And it may also make a difference whether technical advances occur chiefly in export industries or in import-competing industries or are well distributed over most sectors of the economy. However, all these differences are likely to impinge only on the rate of monetary expansion that would be too fast, too slow, or just right for the external balance to be unchanged at fixed exchange rates or for flexible exchange rates to remain stable. The mentioned conditions behind real growth or growth of productivity are by and large beyond the reach of governmental policy, whereas monetary expansion can be controlled, at least within limits, by the authorities. Of course, things are not easy for the authorities in as much as the rates of "adequate" monetary expansion are likely to be different in the short run, in the medium run, and in the long run.

If one accepts the proposition that the nonmonetary characteristics of real growth have a bearing on the influence that a given expansion of the money supply will have on the external balance and/or the exchange rate, one cannot consistently reject an analysis of the consequences that real growth and structural changes in the course of such growth are likely to have upon external balance with zero expansion of the money supply or with such expansion as matches the increase in the labor force or in real output or some such limiting ratio. Where the purveyors of the original thesis had gone wrong was in failing to specify what was happening on the side of money. It is impossible to say how the external position of a country or its currency will change as a result of faster growth of output or productivity unless one stipulates the relative rates of monetary expansion.

THE ANTITHESIS AS EXPLANATION
OF DOLLAR WEAKNESS

The rejection of the thesis was soon forgotten. When, in the 1970s, it became necessary to explain dollar glut, or dollar weakness, academic and official theorists resorted again to the notion that disparities in growth rates were behind the large imbalances in foreign trade and conspicuous movements of foreign exchange rates. The thesis, however, was now converted into its obverse: The reincarnation of the theory that growth rate disparities caused external imbalances had its sign inverted; unbeknown to its proponents, the thesis had given place to the antithesis.

According to this antithesis, faster growth would now lead not to a surplus but to a deficit position; countries with higher growth rates would find themselves faced with deficits in their trade balances and/or with weakened and weakening currencies. Again, some of the theorists affirming a causal connection between divergent growth rates and external imbalances consider the proposition self-evident and thus do not take the time to explain it. Countries growing more slowly must "of course" get into surplus and have their currencies strengthened.

In the absence of explicit arguments in support of the antithesis, one has to construct one's own set of definitions and assumptions that could make the asserted effects plausible. The "growth" occurring at different rates in different countries is not, as in the earlier thesis, something that happens as a result of changes in technology and managerial organization or of differences in supply of physical and human capital; instead, it is an increase in the use of (idle or underemployed) resources induced by an increase in effective demand. In other words, faster growth, in this scenario, is brought about by fiscal and monetary expansion effecting an increase in aggregate spending. This, however, explains only nominal growth; in order to explain real growth of total output, the assumption must be made that wage rates and product prices increase less than aggregate spending. Wage inertia is supposed to ensure such a lag: There was a time when "money illusion" was thought to guarantee that all additional spending would lead to additional production with hitherto underemployed resources. Later it was thought that as much as 90 percent of the increase in nominal GNP would be "real" and 10 percent would take the form of price inflation. Now a group of empirical researchers think that the division of the demand pull between real growth and price lift may be something like 67:33 in the first year, with a possible catch-up of the price inflation in the long pull, and there are those who hold that, owing to rational expectations, all of the increase in nominal GNP will be absorbed by wage and price inflation without much of a lag. Some more sophisticated economists admit that all these possibilities exist, and just which outcome is most probable depends on the starting point of the demand pull.

The connection between demand-induced growth and trade deficits and/or currency depreciation is quite simple: One merely has to add the assumption that an increase in effective demand raises the demand for imports (and may also reduce the supply of exports), so that the countries with faster expansions of monetary demand will have their trade balances worsened and/or their currencies weakened, and the countries with slower expansion will have their trade balances improved and/or their currencies strengthened.

The assumptions regarding the wage and price lag behind the spending pull can, without being "implausible," vary between infinity and zero. Thus, the assumptions regarding the effectiveness of "macroeconomic growth policies" can vary between 100 percent and zero. If this is agreed, how is it possible for so many honest and intelligent economic advisers still to speak of specified growth targets "to be aimed at" by national governments? Yet they go on doing this, and they admonish governments to set their targets higher and, for example, to aim at growth rates 2 or 3 percent above those of last year or two years ago. Some of these advisers see an important difference between recovery from a growth recession (or an employment recession) and long-term real growth. Yet they allow their fellow economists and, particularly, their clients (government, legislature, international organization) to speak of growth even when only the question of short-term recovery should be addressed. (I shall return to the difference between short-term expansion of output and employment and long-term growth of productive capacity.) Most of the growth rate boosters believe that real growth can be controlled.

A WIDE CHOICE OF GROWTH RATES

Over the years we have learned that "growth" can refer to a great many things and that, in speaking of growth rates, it is wise to be specific about just which growth is being referred to. The rates of growth of several (theoretically meaningful but not always statistically obtainable) magnitudes would be on the list of the teacher of growth economics: (1) money stocks, (2) monetary demand, (3) real demand, (4) total product at current cost or market prices, (5) total product adjusted for price changes (real product), (6) real product per head, (7) real product per worker in the labor force, (8) real product per worker employed, (9) real product per labor hour, and (10) real product per unit of productive factors (including capital and land). These ten growth rates of aggregate magnitudes would have to be supplemented by some sectoral subaggregates if the analysis had to extend beyond macroeconomics. And, in any case, the time dimensions of the expansions or increases in magnitudes ought not to be disregarded.

Several of the listed macroeconomic magnitudes are purely theoretical and have no clear operational definitions. The greatest difficulties arise with the identification of demand and supply. Since expenditures are the same as receipts and quantities purchased are the same as quantities sold, the use of statistical proxies—expenditures standing in for demand and measured product for supply—is apt to erase the essential difference between the concepts of demand and supply. This makes it difficult to obtain evidence about the roles that changes and reactions on the demand side and on the supply side play in determining the outcome. Yet, even without these serious handicaps, the large number of options in selecting magnitudes for measuring growth rates interferes with clear thinking and unambiguous talking about growth.

If, for example, the theorists in the 1950s spoke of disparities or divergences in the growth of (average) productivity, they could have meant any of five magnitudes in the list above (6, 7, 8, 9, or 10). In addition, there is the question of the statistical proxy for real product: Should it be gross national product, gross domestic product, net national or domestic product, or some other aggregate? Think of improvements in quality and substitutions of new products for old ones—changes that cannot be measured and are therefore not reflected in "measured output." They may play important roles in comparative advantages in production and trade. The most likely candidate for selection, in the context of the arguments, as the representative rate of growth of productivity seems to be item 9 on the list, real product per labor hour. Any good economist will quickly realize, however, that growth in this magnitude may be offset, in its effect on competitiveness in foreign trade, by increases in hourly wage rates. The theorists who supported the thesis that faster growth of productivity would result in trade surpluses of the fast-growing countries evidently assumed that other things, including wage rates, would remain unchanged.

The theorists of the 1970s who supported the antithesis that faster growth would be liable to give trade deficits to the countries in question were most likely thinking of magnitudes 2, 3, 4, or 5. Their reasoning evidently was that total product was determined by demand and that the expansion of demand that induced or allowed the increase in domestic production would lead also to an increase in the demand for imports. Hence they concluded that fast-growing countries would find their trade in deficit and/or their currencies depreciating.

Bearing in mind that statistical concepts may be very inadequate counterparts of theoretical constructs, we may nevertheless take a glance at statistical comparisons among several growth rates (see Table 6-1). Nominal GNP, real GNP, real GNP per capita, real GNP per member of the labor force, and real GNP per worker employed are taken here as proxies for items 4, 5, 6, 7, and 8. I select five years in which the growth rate (read: percent rate of change from the previous year) of nominal GNP was almost the same. This rate was associated, however, with very different growth rates of the other four magnitudes.

Much as one tries to resist the temptation to read theories into statistical figures, one cannot help being impressed by the increasing differences between the rates of growth of nominal and real GNP: The gap between the two rates increased conspicuously over time. Thus, the same 8.2 percent growth of nom-

Table 6-1.   Rates of Growth of Gross National Product in the United States (*percent changes from previous year*).

Year	(1)	(2)	(3)	(4)	(5)
1959	8.4	6.0	4.3	4.9	3.7
1965	8.2	5.9	4.6	4.0	3.5
1971	8.3	3.0	1.9	1.3	2.5
1974	8.2	-1.6	-2.3	-4.1	-3.6
1975	8.2	-1.0	-1.7	-2.7	0.4

(1) Nominal GNP total.
(2) Real GNP total.
(3) Real GNP per head of population.
(4) Real GNP per member of labor force.
(5) Real GNP per gainfully employed.
Source: U.S. Department of Commerce.

inal GNP that was associated with a 5.9 percent increase in real GNP in 1965 went with a 1.6 percent decrease in real GNP in 1974.

Comparisons with the various relatives (ratios to population, labor force, and employment) show little regularity. It is surely but a statistical coincidence that the rates of change of real GNP per worker in the labor force and per worker employed are virtually the same in 1965 and 1975 but with the signs reversed (+4.0, -4.1; +3.5, -3.6, respectively). The fact that the rates of growth (or change) are sometimes larger, sometimes smaller for product per head of population compared with product per member of the labor force is easily explained: The labor force increases sometimes more slowly, sometimes faster than population. Similarly, since labor force and employment may change at different rates, it is not surprising to see GNP per worker in the labor force change sometimes faster, sometimes more slowly than GNP per worker employed.

One conclusion from the few rates shown in the tabulation may be warranted: The same increase in total expenditures for goods and services measured in GNP need not be associated with similar changes in the other magnitudes and not even with the same direction of change. An increase in expenditures may be linked with negative growth of real output as a total or as a ratio to other magnitudes significant in the economics of growth.

RECOVERY VERSUS LONG-TERM GROWTH

I have promised to return to the difference between two kinds of increase in GNP: Short-term recovery from a recession and long-term sustainable growth. If an increase in real output is due only to an increase in the rate of employment of a given labor force, such increase is necessarily limited. Assume that only 92 percent of the labor force is employed and that 95 percent is regarded as the full-employment mark; the increase in GNP due to "recovery" of the employment rate cannot go on once the "gap" between actual and potential output is closed. Good economists have therefore agreed (though many seem to have forgotten) not to speak of growth as long as GNP increases only thanks to the reabsorption of the jobless into the labor force. The term "real growth," in this (more enlightened) glossary, refers only to increases in productive *capacity*.

One difficulty with this distinction is that it depends largely on judgments of what rate of unemployment should be regarded as full employment, and what part of an increase in GNP can reasonably be attributed to a growth in productive capacity (and its utilization). If measurements of capacity, or of its increase, were reliable—based on the size and quality of the labor force and on the size and efficiency of the capital stock—the concept of potential output would be empirically useful. Unfortunately it is not. Changes in the composition of the labor force with regard to skill, efficiency, perseverance, exertion of effort, etc., are not measurable and are in fact disregarded by the statisticians. (The number of years workers have spent at school is not an acceptable proxy for any of these attributes.) Changes in the stock of capital equipment and its efficiency are likewise not subject to quantification. Accumulation of capital measured by the money outlays for its construction is not a good substitute for establishing the real contribution capital can make to total output. In lieu of estimates of genuine increases in productive capacity, statisticians and econometricians have used historical data for employment and output to concoct an unacceptable proxy for "potential output," a proxy that neglects changes in the quality and composition of human resources and in the size, quality, and composition of real capital.

The general idea of separating increases in GNP resulting from demand-induced reemployment of workers made jobless in the preceding recession from increases resulting from supply-induced growth of capacity makes good economic sense in theory even if statistical data do not suffice to make the distinction in reality. Several differences may be significant:

1. In a recovery, the average productivity of labor may increase, especially because some of the employed labor had been insufficiently utilized during the recession and can now be used more nearly to capacity. The consequent reduction in labor cost per unit of output may counteract any tendencies of increased demand to pull up product prices.

Counterargument: In a later phase of the recovery, this tendency may be offset by the employment of workers of lower efficiency. The less efficient had been favored candidates for being layed off in the recession and are now being rehired; moreover, during the period of their inactivity many may have lost some of their previous skills.

2. In a recovery, starting from high rates of unemployment, increased hiring need not lead so soon to union demands for wage increases as would be the case if employers' demand for more labor increased beyond the full-employment mark.

Counterargument: This notion is associated with the belief in a trade-off between inflation and unemployment, as pictured in the popular Phillips curve. If it were true that wage boosts are rare and modest as long as unemployment is high, but frequent and sharp when "full employment" is approached, recovery and real growth would be truly different. With inflationary experiences and consequent inflationary expectations, however, the difference is apt to disappear: Wage rates are likely to be pushed up with any kind of demand pull, even if the economy is merely pulled out of a deep trough. If a strong upward pressure of wage rates is taken as a criterion of full employment, virtually any employment level or unemployment rate may qualify as full employment. We cannot really distinguish the various causes of wage increase: (a) restoration of the previous real-wage level after a period of price inflation, (b) defense against an erosion of real wages by anticipated price inflation in the next year or two, (c) participation in the gains from increased productivity in the economy as a whole or in a particular industry, or (d) an opportunity to obtain a more favorable wage contract from an industry expecting higher profits thanks to increased demand.

3. If demand-induced recovery is distinguished from supply-induced long-run real growth, a difference in the effects upon the balance of trade may be recorded. The expansion of demand (spending) during the recovery would almost certainly result in an increase in imports, whereas in the case of supply-induced growth not supported by an expansion of effective demand, the effects upon the trade balance would depend on a variety of conditions.

Counterargument: If, however, long-term growth is also supported by an expansion of effective demand, the effects upon the trade balance depend chiefly, though not exclusively, on the "relative expansiveness" of demand management, primarily monetary policy — relative to several variables, including demand management in the major trading countries.

Economic advisors who recommend policies designed to attain specified growth targets usually rely on the efficacy of fiscal and monetary policies to control what they (sloppily) call economic growth, namely, annual rates of increase of real GNP. Many believe that demand management can control not only recovery but also real economic growth, and that divergences of "growth rates" among countries are responsible for imbalances in the countries' trade accounts. Since they usually do not explicitly distinguish between recovery and long-run growth, and since, as I have tried to show, the distinction, though theoretically valid, is not operational (at least not within our present diagnostic powers), I next discuss the significance of divergent "growth rates" without the qualifications called for by different starting points of the upward movement of real GNP.

CONVERGENT OR DIVERGENT RATES OF GROWTH

There is no cogent reason for divergent rates of real GNP growth to induce imbalances in trade or instability of foreign exchange rates. It is conceivable that real GNP grows at a rate of 6 percent in Japan, 3 percent in West Germany, 2 percent in the United States, and 0 in Switzerland, without causing any substantial external imbalances or exchange rate movements. Indeed, this could well be a likely outcome in a world in which authorities abstain from monetary policies "aiming" to achieve faster growth.

Not divergence in rates of real growth but divergence in supposedly growth-inducing monetary policies leads to external imbalances and inordinate movements in exchange rates. Faster growth is said to have certain side effects, but these are in reality caused by so-called "growth policy"—that is, a policy claimed and believed to induce faster growth.

This so-called growth policy is neither a necessary nor a sufficient condition of real growth. Real growth can take place at falling prices and, in theory, is not incompatible with zero or negative growth of nominal GNP. However, one must admit that this has not happened in this century. Nowadays, when wage rates can easily go up but hardly ever go down, sustained growth calls for creation of monetary demand at least sufficient to induce the purchase of the labor that produces the additional output. This concession, however, does not imply that the demand expansion has to be larger than the growth in output. Many growth politicians[2] want monetary demand to be expanded enough to buy the intended increments of annual output at rising prices, and they aver that the creation of such additional monetary demand will actually bring forth the intended growth in real output. I submit that this idea of monetary growth policy has been largely responsible for the chronic price inflation that has become almost worldwide since the middle 1960s.

I further submit that the systematic adoption of growth targets to be achieved through demand management executed or supported by means of monetary expansion can lead to price inflations that may make demand expansion ineffective.[3] Large rates of growth of monetary demand are then translated into small rates of growth of real demand. Attempts to speed up the creation of monetary demand may actually result in zero rates or even negative rates of increase of real demand. Thus, the supposed growth policy may actually retard real growth some of the time. What a farce to give the name "growth policy" to a policy that may actually inhibit real growth. (It is like full-employment policy that reduces employment, and like stabilization policy that destabilizes the economy. Policies should never be named by what they are *intended* to achieve.)

2. By "growth politician" I mean an advocate of policies that, in his opinion, will ensure the attainment of specified targets of real economic growth considerably above the rates that would result without the proposed policies.

3. For an attempt to show that demand expansion requires monetary expansion and cannot be engineered for a sufficiently long period (say, a year or two) by fiscal policy alone (that is, unsupported by an increase in the stock of money), see my essay on fiscal policy (Machlup 1979). For an attempt to show that expansion of monetary demand may be overtaken by price inflation, see my article on different kinds of inflation (Machlup 1978).

NURTURE VERSUS CONTROL OF GROWTH

Growth of real output (sustained, say, over a period of ten years) is the result of using more productive factors and/or using productive factors more productively. This means that the following developments can contribute to larger outputs, that is, to outputs increasing year after year: increase in the labor force, increase in the labor effort per hour and in the number of hours worked per year, increase in capital equipment, improvement of management, use of better techniques of production, and reduction of nonproductive uses of productive factors (labor, land, and equipment). If it is product per labor hour, rather than total product, that one desires to grow faster, one is confined to the last four growth factors—more capital, better management, better techniques, and less waste. More capital can be obtained, for a time, through borrowing from abroad, but ultimately only through greater thrift and productive investment of nonconsumed income. Neither incresaes in saving nor improvements in the use of labor, land, and capital are effectively promoted by the "growth policies" recommended to our monetary authorities by national advisors as well as international organizations.

Developments that can promote real growth of measured output are possibly "nurtured" by certain government policies, none of which works in the short run: tax policies to encourage personal and corporate saving and productive investments; labor and wage policies to prevent capital consumption (inadequate replacement) and to avoid encroachments on profits (reducing the incentive to invest as well as internal generation of investible funds); industrial policies to avoid stifling regulations imposing expensive nonproductive activities and unproductive uses of investible funds; research policies to encourage and finance investments in research and development; and several kinds of policies to facilitate structural adjustments to changing conditions. Through none of these policies, however, can the government control the rate of real growth or achieve any growth targets considered desirable by its advisors, wise or unwise.

The notion that real growth can be controlled by any kind of government policy, including the mislabeled growth policy, is an illusion. Even worse, the well-meant urging that we "achieve more coordination in this field" is counterproductive. Particularly damaging is the advice that we coax surplus countries into "aiming" for higher growth rates and accelerating "the pace of economic expansion" in order to have their growth rates converge with those of deficit countries that have pursued more expansionary monetary policies. Such "coordination" is apt to support continuation of excessive monetary expansion and price inflation. It may do little to enhance real growth and may even inhibit it in the long run.

REFERENCES

Balogh, Thomas. 1946. "The U.S. and the World Economy." *Bulletin of the Oxford Institute of Statistics* 8 (October): 309–23.
_____. 1948. "The United States and International Economic Equilibrium." In Seymour E. Harris, ed., *Foreign Economic Policy for the United States*, pp. 446–80. Cambridge, Massachusetts: Harvard University Press.
_____. 1950. *The Dollar Crisis: Causes and Cure.* Oxford: Blackwell.
_____. 1954. "The Dollar Crisis Revisited." *Oxford Economic Papers* (N.S.) 6 (September): 243–84.
Clarke, Stephen V.O. 1980. "Perspective on the United States External Position Since World War II." *Federal Reserve Bank of New York, Quarterly Review* 5, no. 2 (Summer): 21–38.
Haberler, Gottfried. 1948. "Dollar Shortage?" In Seymour E. Harris, ed., *Foreign Economic Policy of the United States*, pp. 426–45. Cambridge, Massachusetts: Harvard University Press.
_____. 1961. "Domestic Economic Policies and the United States Balance of Payments." In Seymour E. Harris, ed., *The Dollar in Crisis*, pp. 63–72. New York: Harcourt, Brace and World.
Hicks, John R. 1953. "An Inaugural Lecture." *Oxford Economic Papers* 5 (June): 117–35.
Johnson, Harry G. 1954. "Increasing Productivity, Income–Price Trends and the Trade Balance." *Economic Journal* 64 (September): 462–85. (Reprinted in his *International Trade and Economic Growth.* Cambridge, Massachusetts: Harvard University Press, 1961.)
Komiya, Ryutaro. 1969. "Economic Growth and the Balance of Payments: A Monetary Approach." *Journal of Political Economy* 77 (January–February): 35–48.
Machlup, Fritz. 1954. "Dollar Shortage and Disparities in the Growth of Productivity." *Scottish Journal of Political Economy* 1 (October): 250–67.
_____. 1978. "Different Inflations Have Different Effects on Employment." *Banca Nazionale del Lavoro Quarterly Review* 31, no. 127 (December): 291–303.
_____. 1979. "The Effects of Fiscal Policy and the Choice of Definitions." In Harry I Greenfield et al., eds., *Theory for Economic Efficiency: Essays in Honor of Abba P. Lerner*, pp. 92–109. Cambridge, Massachusetts: MIT Press.
International Monetary Fund. 1978. *Summary Proceedings of the Thirty-third Annual Meeting of the Board of Governors*, September 25–28, 1978. Report by the Managing Director, pp. 14–22. Washington, D.C.
Robertson, Dennis H. 1954. *Britain in the World Economy.* London: Allen and Unwin.
Streeten, Paul. 1955. "Productivity Growth and the Balance of Trade." *Bulletin of the Oxford University Institute of Statistics* 17 (February): 11–17.
Williams, John H. 1952. *Economic Stability in the Modern World.* London: Athlone Press. (Republished as *Trade, Not Aid: A Program for World Stability.* Cambridge, Massachusetts: Harvard University Press, 1954.)

7 THE STATE OF EXCHANGE RATE THEORY
Some Skeptical Observations
James Tobin

My friend Robert Triffin, for more than a quarter century my wise tutor in matters of international finance and money, constantly urged me to broaden the scope of my macroeconomic and monetary models beyond the convenient bounds of a closed economy. He understood very early the immense change that currency convertibility and internationalization of money and capital markets would bring. He foresaw the constraints these developments would impose on national macroeconomic policies and the necessity for orderly coordination of those policies, as well as for other dimensions of economic integration that would exploit the mutual benefits and minimize the hazards of international capital mobility. Never one to assume that institutions do not matter or that monetary arrangements are neutral and thus irrelevant, Triffin devoted his energy and his exceptional architectural talent to the design of international monetary institutions. The world has moved in the opposite direction this past decade, toward monetary anarchy rather than order. But this is not because the premises of Triffin's analysis were proved wrong or the institutions he designed and advocated were shown to be undesirable.

Having taken Triffin's advice too little and too late, I find myself puzzled by current theories of exchange rates and therefore uncertain whether institutional changes could yield results superior to our current international monetary anar-

I am grateful to William Brainard, Stanley Black, and John·Campbell for discussions enlightening me on the subjects of this chapter. An unpublished critical review of recent literature by Campbell, "Exchange Rates and the Current Account in a World of Capital Mobility," has been very helpful. Even more than usual, all errors and misunderstandings are my own.

chy. A few years ago I boldly advanced the hypothesis that foreign exchange markets were largely speculative, so that the signals they provided to private agents and the constraints they imposed on national policymakers were not conducive to economic efficiency. Even more boldly, I proposed a solution—to throw sand in the all too perfect currency exchange mechanisms, in the hope of filtering out speculative noise and allowing national economies more macroeconomic independence (Tobin 1978). I share the attraction to "gimmicks" that Triffin once avowed, though I do not think he was attracted to this one of mine. Anyway, the hypothesis and the gimmick were admittedly speculation on my part.

EXCHANGE RATES AS ASSET PRICES

The theory of exchange rates has increasingly taken as its point of departure the observation that "an exchange rate is an asset price." The implication is that theories and models of portfolio choice and asset pricing can help us understand the determination of exchange rates. This shift of emphasis from the role of the exchange rate as an element in the relative prices of internationally traded goods was a natural response to the increasing international mobility of financial capital. Although the approach has grown in vogue in the 1970s during the floating rate regime, it is no less relevant to pegged rates. After all, the pegs were not forever frozen in granite or gold. Since they were adjustable—and often adjusted—portfolio managers had to consider the probabilities of devaluations and revaluations.[1] In the interims, asset demands and supplies had to be adjusted to clear the markets, and official interventions altered the supplies of assets denominated in different currencies to match the preferences of investors. Interventions, of course, occur with floating rates, too.

Exchange rates are not exactly asset prices. Rather, an exchange rate (say, Deutsche marks per dollar) is an element of the price to holders of one currency (dollars) of every asset denominated in a second currency (Deutsche marks). Likewise, the change in the exchange rate between purchase and sale or redemption is an element in the dollar rate of return on a DM–denominated asset.

Among other assets are the literal currencies—dollar bills and DM notes—and the exchange rate is their relative price. In a multi-asset world this fact is of limited significance. We should not expect the exchange rate to depend in any simple way on the relative supplies of national currencies or even of more broadly defined transactions moneys. The oversimplification, fostered by semantics, is analogous to a celebrated aphorism in closed economy monetary theory: "The [real] price of money is the reciprocal of the price level." Since everyone with even a smattering of economics finds it self-evident that the price of a commodity varies inversely with the supply, this definition of the price of money paves

---

1. Kouri (1976) has a model of the forward premium under adjustable and flexible rates.

the way for the quantity theory. The semantics obscures the fact that variation of commodity prices alters the real values not only of currency and other transactions moneys but also of near moneys and a host of other promises to pay amounts specified in the monetary unit of account.

THE VALUES OF FIAT CURRENCIES

Why fiat currency, intrinsically useless paper, has positive real value at all and how its value is determined are questions that continue to puzzle economic theorists (Kareken and Wallace 1980). A fortiori, determination of the relative prices of several fiat currencies seems to be a subject on which the utility-technology-resource-endowment paradigm of basic microeconomic theory has nothing to say.

Neil Wallace, John Bryant, and John Kareken have pointed out the essential arbitrariness of price levels and exchange rates in a world of fiat moneys (Wallace 1980; Bryant and Wallace 1979; Kareken and Wallace 1978). They find a function for fiat money, and a reason for its positive value, as a store of value for households with finite horizons in an infinitely lived economy with overlapping generations. The retired aged buy their consumption goods from the productive young. Given a foreseen path of money creation, intergenerational trade determines the path of prices and thus of real returns on money. The shape of the money path matters for real outcomes, but its scale does not. For example, the economy will have the same rate of deflation and the same consumption path with any constant quantity of money, whatever its size.

In this world there is no room for more than one fiat asset. Consequently, there can be only trivial differences between currency itself and promises of future currency payments by the issuing government; since government debt will be currency on maturity, it is essentially currency now. Likewise, there can really be only one fiat money—the one that promises the highest real return. If two or more currencies are being held simultaneously, they must be equivalent in nominal growth rates and real rates of return. Exchange rates between them simply preserve purchasing power parity. Exchange rates are just arbitrary conversions of units between equivalent fiat moneys, of no more significance than the exchange rates between dimes, quarters, and dollars.

Instructive and provocative as it is, the Wallace-Bryant-Kareken model, emphasizing the store of value function of money rather than the transactions function, does not do justice to the social convention that makes the national currency the generally accepted medium of transactions within the nation's boundaries. Neither foreign currencies nor any promises to pay the national currency not on demand but in future serve as equivalents. Other stores of value—land, capital, loans—are the principal vehicles of saving for retirement and bequest. Currency and promises to pay currency on demand are held for very short periods and circulate rapidly. They have positive real value because of their advantage in transactions, and the demand for them depends on this service yield plus the rate of change in their purchasing power. National currencies are far from perfect substitutes. They can and do coexist with widely different real rates of return. In the extreme, each nation holds no other currency but its own. If there are no other outside nominal assets, capital movements across exchanges are transfers of title to real property or the equivalent in private loans and debts.

These assumptions can support neutrality conclusions similar to those of the Wallace-Bryant-Kareken model. Real outcomes throughout the world are invariant to scalar changes in the paths of any or all currency stocks. These simply alter national price levels, to which exchange rates adjust as necessary to preserve purchasing power parity, without affecting intertemporal decisions. Saving, capital formation, and real international capital movements are unaffected. They imply current account imbalances, which in a multicommodity world in turn determine the real or relative prices that define purchasing power parity. Moneys are neutral in these abstract worlds, but they are not superneutral. The time shapes of currency supplies will in general affect saving, investment, international capital movements, and relative prices.

Neutrality amounts to nothing more than invariance to unit changes, like calling a dollar a new dime and ten dollars one new dollar. Models that reduce monetary policy essentially to splits of this kind naturally conclude that, like stock splits, they do nothing real. They merely alter prices and exchange rates in an obvious and trivial way. The all too common fallacy of misplaced concreteness is to identify real world monetary policies with unit changes. Money stock increases by open market operations or by printing currency to finance government expenditures are not neutral or trivial. They will in general change real interest rates and exchange rates.

PORTFOLIO BALANCE ACROSS CURRENCIES
AND CURRENT ACCOUNT IMBALANCES

The portfolio balance approach assumes that currency, future promises to pay currency, even by the government itself, and real assets are imperfect substitutes for each other and also that assets denominated in different currencies are imperfect substitutes. International financial and capital markets determine simultaneously the prices of the various assets and currencies, as well as domestic commodity prices or incomes. As shown in a previous article (Tobin and Macedo 1980), equations of asset demand and supply balance and intercurrency payments balance suffice to determine these variables.

Portfolio balance considerations suggest that asset values will depend ceteris paribus on their relative supplies and on the asset preferences of wealth owners. In the application of these considerations to the international scene, a key assumption is that wealth owners display home currency preference. At a given exchange rate between dollars and Deutsche marks, Americans will wish to hold a higher fraction of wealth, and of a given increment of wealth, in dollars than Germans will and a lower fraction in Deutsche marks.

As asset supplies and total wealth of the several countries evolve over time, so will their trade balances and their current account deficits or surpluses. These depend on prices, exchange rates, interest rates, and "absorption" of domestic outputs by consumption, investment, and government purchases. A country's portfolio allocations of new saving may, for example, favor accumulation of foreign assets over local capital investment and thereby generate a constellation of prices, exchange rates, and interest rates that leads to a current account deficit. Monetary and financial shocks may lead to international asset transfers whose counterpart is an imbalance in current account; a change in exchange rates is a likely, but not inevitable, part of the mechanism that brings this about. Shocks of taste and technology that alter the competitiveness of nations in trade may show up as shifts of wealth, accomplished by current account surpluses and deficits, which set in train adjustments of prices, interest rates, exchange rates, and international transfers of assets.

It is thanks to home currency preference that current account shocks move exchange rates at all (Kouri and Macedo 1978:142-48; Dornbusch 1975). A U.S. deficit matched by a German surplus shifts wealth from U.S. to German portfolios, lowering demand for dollar assets and raising demand for DM assets. If asset supplies are unchanged, then they must change hands; Germans must buy some from Americans. The yields of dollar assets must rise or those of DM assets fall or both in order to maintain portfolio balance on both sides. All this will be accomplished by an increase in the dollar value of the Deutsche mark, an increase in the DM price of DM assets (lower interest rates), and a fall in the dollar price of dollar assets (higher interest rates), in some combination. In the absence of the difference in asset preferences, the current account imbalance could be financed without any change in the exchange rate.

How does the appreciation of the Deutsche mark help to equilibrate the system? It lowers the DM value of Germans' dollar holdings and induces them, in the interest of maintaining diversification, to channel some of the new wealth corresponding to their current account surplus into dollar securities. This inducement is powerfully reinforced in case German investors expect the dollar to rebound. These inducements do not apply to Americans, who because of their loss in wealth, reflected in the current account deficit, are willing to sell. Similarly, the incentive to sell DM securities provided by an increase in the dollar price of Deutsche marks—an incentive that is strengthened if the increase is expected to be temporary—applies to Americans but not to Germans. Concurrently with these asset shifts, appreciation of the mark may, given well-behaved elasticities, tend to eliminate the current account imbalance.

Empirically, the exchange depreciations associated with news of current account deficits seem larger than can be explained by the small shifts of wealth they entail. An alternative explanation is that unexpected weakness in current account is an indicator of competitive difficulties that will spell trouble later (Dornbusch 1980:157-63). But what is the trouble? It is that current account deficits will shift wealth abroad and make exchange depreciation necessary. If actual wealth shifts are too small for the phenomenon they are supposed to explain, then are not the expected shifts also too small?

HOME CURRENCY PREFERENCE

Home currency preference is by no means an obvious implication of portfolio theory. To the contrary, it has been shown in a variety of models that risk can be reduced by diversification across currencies (Kouri and Macedo 1978: 118-26; Macedo 1981; Krugman 1981 and references therein). The risks of nominal assets are those of commodity price fluctuation, interest rate variation, and default. Economies with different currencies, geographies, and central governments will be more independent of each other in these dimensions than, for example, the states of a federal union.

Exchange risk may work either way. Here it is necessary to consider the correlations of deviations of exchange rates from expected trends with the other risks of nominal assets. If the foreign currency appreciates when home inflation accelerates and depreciates when foreign inflation is relatively high, foreign currency assets are a hedge. If the foreign currency depreciates when domestic interest rates move up, foreign securities are not a good hedge against capital losses due to interest rate increases at home. They offer some protection against domestic political difficulties and defaults, but expose the investor to risks of the same kind abroad.

In addition, exchange rates may move because of speculations unrelated to the properties of nominal assets relevant to owners of wealth. Even so, these independent movements would seem to offer opportunities for diversification, especially when nominal claims in home currency are subject to important inflation risk.

The great portfolio advantage of home currency assets is that they enable an investor to hedge against contractual obligations and predictable needs to pay out home currency in future. This advantage is eroded by uncertainty about future commodity prices, the more so the more distant the payments to be financed by disposition of assets. For this reason, we should expect foreign currency assets to play a bigger role in portfolios at times of high uncertainty about inflation.[2]

Home currency preference is probably due less to mean-variance calculus than to other dimensions of asset choice. Among these are that (1) information is more complete and less costly for home currency assets; (2) transactions costs, including not only costs of purchases and sales and currency conversions but also

2. This is borne out in the portfolios computed in Kouri and Macedo (1978:129) and Macedo (1981).

tax and legal complications, actual and contingent, are higher for foreign assets; and (3) foreign investments by institutions and intermediaries—savings banks, mutual funds, trusts, and pensions funds—are legally restricted. As in domestic financial markets, we should expect these obstacles to diminish as the basic portfolio investment advantages persist and become clearer. Eurocurrency markets, international banking, registration of foreign currency securities in domestic markets, mutual funds with international portfolios, multinational corporations, even the inclusion of foreign assets in university endowment portfolios—all testify to the growing internationalization.

Home currency preference is logically separable from geographical or political preference, though many of the reasons for one are also sources of the other. It is, of course, likely that shifts of wealth between countries bring in their wake shifts of preferences in equity investment. Wealth owners favor capital domiciled in their own countries. But the consideration that leads to home preference among currency-denominated assets—namely, that the investor thus avoids exchange risk in consuming the income or principal—applies with considerably less force.

DOMESTIC ASSET SUPPLIES AND EXCHANGE RATES

Current account surpluses and deficits are, of course, by no means the only source of change in national asset demands and supplies. Indeed, they are minor compared to domestic asset creation. Wealth at the disposition of private agents grows with domestic capital formation and with public sector deficits and by capital gains on existing assets.

A U.S. government deficit increases the supply of Treasury obligations. Some of them may be bought by taxpayers as the best hedge against the taxes they foresee will be needed to service the debt.[3] But most likely there is a net increase in private wealth, and at prevailing interest and exchange rates, U.S. investors will not wish to absorb all of it in government bonds or even in dollar assets. An increase in the dollar interest rate on bonds and a decline in the dollar against other currencies will place some of the bonds overseas. This is a rationale for the time-honored conservative view that loose fiscal policy endangers or actually depreciates the currency. If public debt is rising faster relative to wealth in the United States than in Germany, that might be a reason for the dollar to fall against the Deutsche mark (Frankel 1979a, 1979b; Dornbusch 1980:163-72).

But what of the assets that make up the difference? These are basically claims to the capital stock and its earnings, not to specified amounts of any currency. An extreme view is that goods are goods, capital goods are capital goods, factories are factories—wherever they are located. Earnings may in fact come from worldwide sales in numerous currencies. Neither the earnings nor the value of

---

3. The rationale for hedging of this kind is argued by Barro (1974). Reasons why it is incomplete are given by Tobin (1980).

the shares in any currency is particularly correlated with the price of the currency in which the company is domiciled. If this is the nature of equity—a currency-diversified asset earning the world marginal efficiency of capital—then accumulation of wealth in this form does not satisfy the appetite of local investors for assets denominated in their home currency. By this argument, if Germany has high real investment and a low public deficit, while the United States has low real investment and high government deficit, the Deutsche mark should appreciate.

But the argument needs to be qualified on two counts. First, capital investment is typically debt financed, at least in part. If the Modigliani–Miller theorem applies, debt finance does not matter; the equity owners are in effect in debt to themselves. But the aggregation may be excessive and misleading. The equity owners could be at a corner. Risk-lovers seeking leverage, they have quite different portfolio preferences from their creditors, those risk-averse diversifiers who make the debt and exchange markets. To the latter, corporate debt issues are like government debt in the same currency. It may even be that high real investment throws so much private debt issue into the international market that the currency must depreciate to get it absorbed. In sum, it is not self-evident that public debt is an adequate or reliable measure of the supply of a currency to the asset markets.

The second point is that equity investments are not as currency-neutral as the extreme view suggests. The principal location and the legal and tax domicile of the business do entangle its earnings with the domestic and exchange value of the currency. For both foreigners and local investors, equity in the country's businesses may be a closer substitute for home debt than for foreign debt securities.

EXPECTATIONS AND THEIR NEBULOUS ANCHOR IN FUTURE EQUILIBRIUM

The price of an asset is the market's valuation of the future returns, in cash or in kind, sure or unsure, to which the owner will be entitled. Among those returns are the gains or losses from changes in the asset price itself. The current price thus depends on expectations of the price tomorrow, and that, in turn, depends on expectations of the day after tomorrow, and so on through the life of the asset or ad infinitum. New information about future prices, even those in the far distant future, affects the price today. In principle, the whole future is relevant even for investors or potential investors who intend to hold the asset only for a short time, because expectations of remote events will affect their capital gains or losses.

The situation is even more complex because portfolio choices involve comparisons of returns on many assets and thus involve expectations and joint probability distributions of large dimension. The market prices that emerge today reflect those choices by many diverse investors and depend on their estimates of the price vector that similar market processes will generate in the future. Thus expectations, and expectations of expectations, are crucial determinants of asset prices. But they are unobservable in practice and elusive in theory. These difficulties are acute for exchange rates.

If expectations can be anything, we have little to say about asset prices or about exchange rates in particular. Rational expectations theory confines price-determining expectations to those that will in fact be realized, at least actuarially. Those expectations are supposed to be anchored in a future equilibrium on which the views of investors, fully informed on both data and mechanism, converge. In the case of exchange rates, economists and econometricians, and presumably market participants too, have especially great difficulty in identifying such an equilibrium and much more in estimating it empirically.

Purchasing power parity and current account balance are sometimes advanced as conditions of equilibrium, but there are at least two reasons why they are inadequate and treacherous. First, equilibrium real terms of trade themselves depend on many features of the trading economies, some of them endogenous to the future paths of prices, exchange rates, and interest rates. The real exchange rate is not independent of the trade balance, except in those mythical one-good worlds that neglect all reasons for trade. Neither trade nor the current account as a whole is necessarily balanced at zero in any practical long run. Capital movements, transfers of technology, and other adjustments can continue for decades without wiping out the differences in marginal efficiencies of capital that induce them, and even then they may have to continue for decades more to maintain parity of real interest rates among economies whose effective supplies of labor and other local resources are growing at disparate rates.

The second reason is more devastating. Even assuming that an equilibrium of the real balance of payments and of the terms of trade could be foreseen, how could it be translated into expectations of exchange rates? One does not have to agree completely with Wallace et al. to appreciate the force of their reminder that the relative price of two purely nominal "commodities" is quite arbitrary, certainly not deducible from the real economic forces involved in the difficult projections mentioned in the preceding paragraph. To guess at truly long-run equilibrium exchange rates, we would have to model the monetary and fiscal policies of the several countries, their political and social tolerances of inflation and unemployment, the evolution of their price- and wage-setting institutions and of their financial systems, and many other phenomena relating to nominal variables and their interactions with real economic outcomes.

SLOW PORTFOLIO ADJUSTMENT AS A SOURCE OF NOISE IN ASSET PRICES

When news leads portfolio managers to revise their estimates of the expected future returns or risks of holding an asset at its prevailing price, they will wish to change their holdings. The portfolio adjustments will alter the prices of this and other assets, until they are aligned to the new information about expected returns and risks. If these price responses to news were discontinuous and instantaneous, then they could be distinguished from those continuous price movements that realize prior anticipations of expected returns and of entire probability distributions. An econometric investigator could then hope to recapture the determinants of portfolio choice from time series cleansed of unexpected capital gains and losses, identifiable as jumps in the price series.

In practice, unfortunately, the market rarely absorbs news so suddenly. Portfolio adjustments are strung out over considerable time, because of lags and costs in the diffusion of information and in decisions and transactions and because of liquidity and borrowing constraints. The result is that price movements reflecting adjustments of portfolios to news are inextricably tangled with those that reflect price paths anticipated in market price settings themselves.

Examples are numerous, both in domestic financial markets and in foreign exchange markets. Holding Treasury bills is an alternative to holding common stocks, and it is to be expected that the returns on the two will be positively correlated. News of higher bill rates—for example, because of tighter monetary policy, actual or expected—should lower the prices of equities in order to keep their subsequent yields inclusive of capital gains in line with bill yields. But if the adjustment of equity prices takes weeks or months, the investigator will see a negative ex post relationship between the two rates of return.

In a similar manner, portfolio adjustments generate confusing signals for the investigator of foreign exchange markets. The slide of the dollar in 1977-78 has been attributed to news that led international investors, including the managers of oil wealth, to believe that dollar assets were less secure and less remunerative than assets denominated in other currencies. The slide was sustained for at least fifteen months, and observations during that period certainly contribute, in any calculation that includes them, to the conclusion that dollar assets were less attractive in a multicurrency portfolio than they had been previously. To include observations during the portfolio shift in optimal portfolio calculations designed to support the hypothesis that rational portfolio adjustment to new information caused the decline in the dollar is to lift oneself by one's own bootstraps (as done by Kouri and Macedo 1978; and Dornbusch 1980).

The steady rise of the dollar from September 1980 to May 1981 is another example. Again, interest rate news appears to be responsible. Yet contrary to simple efficient market models, the response of exchange rates to the high positive differential between U.S. and European or Japanese interest rates was gradual. Since interest arbitrage kept forward exchange premiums in line with interest differentials, the forward rates predicted almost daily appreciations against the dollar that turned out to be wrong in sign. Both during this period and during the persistent swing against the dollar two years earlier, the market did not appear to be using information contained in the trend of the spot rate.

If it had been used, if the differential interest rate news had been exploited all at once, then the dollar would have risen more sharply in 1980 and then depreciated at a pace consistent with the forward premium—that is, with the interest differential.

In sum, observations of multicurrency portfolios held during periods when ex ante exchange rate anticipations were so radically different from ex post realizations or when agents with expectations correct at least in sign were slow to act are not good data from which to infer the subjective probability distributions and risk preferences underlying portfolio choice. Likewise, sluggish and smooth adjustment to news casts doubt on theories that require prices to jump to that singular expectations fulfillment path that leads to equilibrium. This is an issue of some moment, for the rational expectations equilibrium in multi-asset markets is generally a saddle-point. Usually there is no continuous expectation-fulfilling path from the initial point to the newly displaced equilibrium.

The major alternatives to models of financial and asset markets that assume rational expectations and efficient use of information are models that assume slow adjustment periods and disequilibrium. Disequilibrium need not mean that markets are failing to clear, though it may take that form. It may be simply that portfolio investors are off their desired portfolios. They may be following rules of thumb that can be described as "bounded" rationality. Or they may be fully rational if market imperfections and costs of transactions and decisions are properly taken into account. In either event, the task of modeling their behavior is very difficult, perhaps beyond our present capacity, and the task of inferring behavior from market time series even more formidable. The slow adjustment disequilibrium approach does not finesse the problem of expectations formation. But while it does not necessarily imply stability of equilibrium, it does not make stability contingent on the market's jumping to a singular dynamic path, even to the extent of "overshooting" equilibrium.[4]

A possibly preferable approach to the calculation of the means, variances, and covariances relevant to portfolio choices and asset prices is to use "fundamental" data only. Capital gains and losses due to the movements of asset prices over the period of observation are excluded from the returns used in such calculations. It is a nonbootstrap approach in the sense that the market prices are not "explained" by market price observations themselves. The "fundamental" approach has been used to explain variations across firms in share prices, yielding some interesting results but leaving many puzzles unresolved, including variation over time in the general level of equity prices (Tobin and Brainard 1977; Brainard, Shoven, and Weiss 1980). For exchange rates, the analogous strategy would be to relate the prices of a cross-section of currencies to a set of underlying characteristics of their economies. But this approach requires specification of those

---

4. These issues are clearly and usefully clarified by Burmeister (1980).

"fundamental" determinants of nominal variables, precisely the subject on which we lack theoretical clarity and consensus.

One apparently robust conclusion of research on stock and bond prices is that their variability over time is far larger than the variability of their underlying fundamental determinants (Douglas 1969; Shiller 1979, 1981; Grossman and Shiller 1981). The markets appear to exaggerate the significance and permanence of bits of information, adding self-generated speculative risk to the basic risks of the securities. The same or perhaps even greater magnification is likely to occur in foreign exchange markets, given the elusiveness of the "fundamentals."

CONCLUDING REMARKS

Portfolio and asset-pricing models have not been very successful in explaining observed fluctuations of securities prices in domestic markets, and we should probably not expect them to do much better in empirical explanations of exchange rates. We know that an increase in interest rates in dollars, widening its differential above sterling or Deutsche mark interest rates, generally appreciates the dollar. We know that bad news about exports and imports usually depreciates the currency. Those regularities are roughly on a par with our empirical wisdom about stock markets, and maybe we cannot expect to do much better with currencies.

For reasons I have tried to explain, it is not really surprising that the portfolio and asset market approach to exchange rates turns out to have little to say about their levels and to concentrate on their changes in response to policies and other shocks. But that focus leaves us without an explanation of the expectational shocks that are probably responsible for more of the observed movements of exchange rates than those our theories do illuminate and without a soundly based way to distinguish the one kind of movement from the other. It leaves me where I came in, with the suspicion that a large part of the activity in foreign exchange markets is speculation on future speculation and with my proposal that governments cooperate to filter out the noise.

REFERENCES

Barro, Robert J. 1974. "Are Government Bonds Net Wealth?" *Journal of Political Economy* 82 (November–December): 1095–117.

Brainard, William C.; John B. Shoven; and Laurence Weiss. 1980. "The Financial Valuation of the Return to Capital." *Brookings Panel on Economic Activity* 2: 453–502.

Bryant, John, and Neil Wallace. 1979. "The Inefficiency of Interest-Bearing National Debt." *Journal of Political Economy* 87 (April): 365–81.

Burmeister, Edwin. 1980. "On Some Conceptual Issues in Rational Expectations Modeling." *Journal of Money, Credit, and Banking*, pt. 2 (November): 800–16.

Dornbusch, Rudiger. 1975. "A Portfolio Balance Model of the Open Economy." *Journal of Monetary Economics* 1 (January): 3–20.

_____. 1980. "Exchange Rate Economics: Where Do We Stand?" *Brookings Panel on Economic Activity* 1: 143–86.

Douglas, George W. 1969. "Risk in the Equity Markets: An Empirical Appraisal of Market Efficiency." *Yale Economic Essays* 9, no. 1 (Spring): 3–46.

Frankel, Jeffrey A. 1979a. "The Diversifiability of Exchange Risk." *Journal of International Economics* 9 (August): 379–93.

_____. 1979b. "On the Mark: A Theory of Floating Exchange Rates Based on Real Interest Differentials." *American Economic Review* 69 (September): 610–22.

Grossman, Sanford J., and Robert J. Shiller. 1981. "The Determinants of the Variability of Stock Market Prices." *American Economic Review* 71 (May): 222–27.

Kareken, John H., and Neil Wallace. 1978. "Samuelson's Consumption–Loan Model with Country-Specific Fiat Monies." Federal Reserve Bank of Minneapolis Staff Report No. 24, July.

_____, eds. 1980. *Models of Monetary Economics.* Minneapolis: Federal Reserve Bank of Minneapolis.

Kouri, Pentti J.K. 1976. "The Determinants of the Forward Premium." Seminar Paper No. 62, IIES, University of Stockholm, August.

Kouri, Pentti J.K., and Jorge Braga de Macedo. 1978. "Exchange Rates and the International Adjustment Process." *Brookings Panel on Economic Activity* 1: 111–50.

Krugman, Paul R. 1981. "Consumption Preferences, Asset Demands and Distribution Effects in International Markets." NBER Working Paper No. 651, March.

Macedo, Jorge Braga de. 1981. "Optimal Currency Diversification for a Class of Risk–Averse International Investors." Working Papers in Economics No. 11, Woodrow Wilson School, Princeton University, May.

Shiller, Robert J. 1979. "The Volatility of Long–Term Interest Rates and Expectations Models of the Term Structure." *Journal of Political Economy* 87 (December): 1190–1219.

_____. 1981. "Do Stock Prices Move Too Much to Be Justified by Subsequent Changes in Dividends." *American Economic Review* 71 (June): 421–36.

Tobin, James. 1978. "A Proposal for International Monetary Reform." *Eastern Economic Journal* 4, nos. 3–4 (July–October).

_____. 1980. "Government Deficits and Capital Accumulation." In D. Currie and W. Peters, eds., *Contemporary Economic Analysis*, vol. 2, pp. 23–45. London: Coom Helm. Reprinted as Chapter III of *Asset Accumulation and Economic Activity*, Oxford: Blackwell, and Chicago: University of Chicago Press, 1980.

Tobin, James, and W. Brainard. 1977. "Asset Markets and the Cost of Capital." In R. Nelson and B. Balassa, eds., *Economic Progress: Private Values and Public Policy* (Essays in Honor of William Fellner), pp. 235–62. Amsterdam: North Holland.

Tobin, James, and Jorge Braga de Macedo. 1980. "The Short-Run Macroeconomics of Floating Exchange Rates: An Exposition." In J. Chipman and C. Kindleberger, eds., *Flexible Exchange Rates and the Balance of Payments: Essays in Memory of Egon Sohmen*. Amsterdam: North Holland.

Wallace, Neil. 1980. "The Overlapping Generations Model of Fiat Money." In John H. Kareken and Neil Wallace, eds., *Models of Monetary Economics*, pp. 49–82. Minneapolis: Federal Reserve Bank of Minneapolis.

8 INTERNATIONAL PORTFOLIO DISTURBANCES AND DOMESTIC MONETARY POLICY

Edwin M. Truman and
Jeffrey R. Shafer

This chapter analyzes the implications for the formulation and execution of national monetary policy of a shift of significant size over a short period (a few days or weeks) in the Eurocurrency market from deposits denominated in dollars to deposits denominated in marks. We analyze the immediate and short-run implications of such a shift under alternative assumptions about the orientation of monetary policy in Germany and the United States and about official exchange market intervention policies. Our conclusion is that a strategy of sterilized intervention could virtually eliminate any real economic disturbance resulting from the assumed deposit shift. However, this may not be the best strategy from Germany's viewpoint alone, nor would it be an easy strategy to implement.

Since the early 1970s, policymakers and economists increasingly have focused their attention on the phenomenon of currency diversification or, more technically, on shifts in demands for financial assets denominated in different national currencies. Such shifts are frequently assumed to be unrelated to current or immediately prospective economic and financial conditions in the countries whose currencies are used to denominate the assets. In this respect they are conceptually distinct from shifts in quantities of assets demanded as a result of fundamental economic developments working through expectations. These two types of shifts are difficult to distinguish empirically, however.

This paper was prepared in the Division of International Finance, Board of Governors of the Federal Reserve System. Our thinking over the years about the issues analyzed in this chapter has been stimulated and informed by discussions with our colleagues, especially Klaus Friedrich and Dale W. Henderson. However, the views expressed are solely those of the authors and do not necessarily represent the views of the Board of Governors of the Federal Reserve System or its staff.

129

A number of developments have contributed to the increased interest in this topic—the move to a more flexible exchange rate regime and the observed exchange rate variability that has been associated with it, the build-up of financial wealth by OPEC investors, and the increased integration of national and international financial markets. One important aspect of the last phenomenon has been the growth and development of the Eurocurrency market.

Our approach is informal and verbal, but it is based on formal portfolio balance models of exchange rate determination such as that presented by Girton and Henderson (1977). We have three reasons for proceeding as we do—(1) to make the intuition concerning the diversification issue contained in the formal models accessible to a wider audience; (2) to illustrate how such models apply in a specific, complex institutional environment (one that includes the Eurocurrency markets, more than two countries, and the operational techniques employed in the conduct of monetary policy and exchange market intervention); and (3) to suggest how short-run developments in financial markets can exert an influence on real economic developments.

A few words on the framework we use will provide some background for the analysis that follows. First, our interest is in two countries, the United States and Germany, but we do not assume a two-country world. The rest of the world is treated explicitly as the location of the Eurocurrency market. Economic agents in the rest of the world participate in this market as depositors and borrowers, and their behavior is the source of the disturbance we study. Moreover, none of the three areas is treated as "small." Actions by economic agents and policymakers in one country have implications for economic developments elsewhere. The asset market adjustments we consider, however, are restricted to those involving the U.S. dollar and the German mark.

Second, in both the United States and Germany, monetary policy is expressed as a matter of practice in terms of the achievement of target growth rates for monetary aggregates over one-year periods. However, monetary policy in the short run may be primarily oriented in either country toward the supply of bank reserves (as has been the case for Federal Reserve policy since October 6, 1979) or toward interest rates (as was the case for Federal Reserve policy before October 6, 1979, and as generally is the case for Bundesbank policy). One of the purposes of our analysis is to explore the short-run implications of these two types of possible operating procedures in the context of the assumed deposit shift in the Eurocurrency market.

Third, we see the Eurocurrency market as an international banking market with links to banks in national markets and as doing business with nonbank depositors and borrowers in currencies other than that of the country in which the Eurobank is located. The Eurocurrency market is nurtured in large part by the absence of regulations that are applied in domestic banking markets, including importantly reserve requirements and interest rate ceilings. Some countries, including from time to time the United States and Germany, impose reserve requirements on their banks against borrowings from the Eurocurrency market. We view the Eurocurrency markets as normally having close links with the relevant domestic financial markets even with such regulations. In fact, the initial deposit shift is assumed to take place in the Eurocurrency market not only because that market has been the focus of much of the discussion of the potential for such shifts but also in order to illustrate how disturbances in that market are propagated to domestic financial markets.

Fourth, the time frame for our analysis might usefully be thought of in terms of months or, at most, a few quarters. This allows us to focus primarily on immediate impacts and on the techniques of monetary policy and to ignore in large part the longer run adjustments induced by the Eurocurrency market disturbance.

The next section considers the initial and short-run implications of the deposit shift in the Eurocurrency market, assuming no official exchange market intervention. In the subsequent section, we assume that official exchange market intervention (sterilized or unsterilized) maintains the dollar–mark exchange rate unchanged. The final section pulls together the implications of our analysis for policy choices.

CASE I: NO OFFICIAL EXCHANGE MARKET INTERVENTION

In this section we consider the effects of a shift from Eurocurrency deposits denominated in dollars to deposits denominated in marks when authorities choose not to use exchange market intervention to resist the resulting pressure on the dollar–mark exchange rate. We focus first on the initial disturbance in the Eurocurrency market and then examine the consequent financial and real adjustments in Germany and the United States. We consider two alternative short-run orientations of monetary policy in the United States and Germany – toward interest rates or toward bank reserves.

Initial International Financial Pressures

The assumed shift in the Eurocurrency market will create an excess demand for mark assets and an excess supply of dollar assets. These excess demands and supplies will place upward pressure on the foreign exchange value of the mark against the dollar, which may be accompanied by downward pressure on interest rates on assets denominated in marks and upward pressure on interest rates on assets denominated in dollars.

Changes in the exchange rate and interest rates will tend to eliminate the initial market disequilibrium in two ways: First, expected rates of return will be reduced on mark assets and increased on dollar assets. Second, the valuation of mark assets will rise relative to the valuation of dollar assets. This valuation change may lead some asset holders to restore the original shares of mark and dollar assets in their portfolios. In the absence of official exchange market intervention, the sum of all sales of mark assets and purchases of dollar assets induced in these ways must exactly offset the initial shift from dollar deposits to mark deposits in the Eurocurrency market.

The relative magnitudes of the exchange rate and interest rate movements cannot be determined from an analysis of the Eurocurrency market in isolation. However, before proceeding to wider ramifications, it is helpful to consider the nature of the partial adjustments in the Eurocurrency market. Three types of adjustments may occur: (1) Nonbank depositors and borrowers may respond to changes in expected yields. (2) They may also react to valuation effects. (3) Banks may alter their exchange risk exposures.

Any reduction in Euromark interest rates and rise in Eurodollar interest rates, combined with an appreciation of the mark to a level from which market participants would expect it subsequently to appreciate less than was expected before the shift in deposits occurred will reduce the expected yield on Euromark deposits relative to Eurodollar deposits. The change in expected relative rates of return will induce some depositors in the Eurocurrency market to shift from mark deposits to dollar deposits. The change will also induce borrowers to switch from borrowing dollars to borrowing marks. These responses by depositors and borrowers will bring supplies and demands for mark and dollar assets toward balance following the initial disturbance in the Eurocurrency market. Over an extended period of time, a significant proportion of a one-time exogenous shift in the denomination of Eurocurrency deposits might be accommodated by an adjustment in the currency composition of borrowing. However, in the short run, the size of this adjustment is likely to be small because of the relatively long maturities of many Eurocurrency credits.

The changes in valuation will induce different responses by net depositors and net borrowers. An appreciation of the mark will raise the relative value of mark deposits in the portfolios of the holders of these deposits. Depositors who were previously content with the share of mark deposits in their portfolios would be expected to sell some mark-denominated assets. This response will also act to bring supplies and demands for mark and dollar assets toward balance following the initial disturbance in the Eurocurrency market by offsetting part of the initial excess demand for mark deposits and excess supply of dollar deposits.

Net borrowers of marks and dollars may also be induced by changes in valuation to adjust the currency composition of their borrowing. The reduction in the relative value of borrowing denominated in dollars and the increase in the relative value of borrowing denominated in marks brought about by the appreciation of the mark will induce net borrowers to borrow more in dollars and less in marks. Thus, in contrast to the response by net depositors, the response by net borrowers to valuation changes will tend to exacerbate the initial imbalance in the Eurocurrency market.

Whether the stabilizing adjustments to changes in valuation of depositors or the destabilizing adjustments of borrowers predominate depends on the relative sensitivity of each group and on the relative size of the positions of the two groups. Theoretical work generally assumes that the sensitivity of net asset holders (depositors) and net debtors (borrowers) is the same. While in the Eurocurrency market assets equal liabilities, financial market participants as a group, other than the U.S. and German governments, are net holders of both mark and dollar assets representing the government debts of the United States and Germany. Consequently, general equilibrium models generally assume that the behavior of net asset holders predominates.

Banks in the Eurocurrency market may accept some change in their foreign exchange exposure as the result of taking more deposits in marks while continuing to lend in dollars. Banks would behave in this manner in response to a lower expected cost of Euromark deposits relative to the expected return on Eurodollar loans. This change in exposure may be spread widely among banks through interbank foreign exchange and Eurocurrency operations. Such a change in the exposure of banks would help to bridge the gap between the supply of mark deposits and the demand for dollar borrowing. However, available information on banks' behavior suggests that they do not normally accept large foreign exchange exposures in either the short or the long run.[1]

Adjustments in Germany

Initial Financial Market Adjustments. We turn now to the links between the Euromark market and German financial markets. A downward movement of Euromark interest rates is normally accompanied by a downward movement of interest rates in Germany. In the absence of a parallel movement of interest rates in Germany, German corporations (and nonresident borrowers) will shift the locus of their borrowing toward the Euromark market. Depositors in the Euromark market will shift from Euromark deposits to time deposits at banking offices in Germany. Banking offices in Germany will also have an incentive to raise funds for lending in Germany wherever the costs, adjusted for reserve requirements, are lower. The potential for such shifts means that interest rates in the Euromark market and in Germany, if they move in response to the disturbance under consideration, will move closely together.

Because of these linkages, the behavior of the general level of mark interest rates will be determined by the demand function for money in Germany, the derived demand function for central bank money, and the orientation of the Bundesbank in the execution of monetary policy. As we indicated earlier, we consider two alternative orientations of Bundesbank policy—toward interest rates and toward bank reserves. Whether the Bundesbank will be confronted with an immediate need to choose between maintaining the prevailing level of

---

1. For example, Lowrey and Smith (1980) found that the foreign exchange exposure of U.S. banks was small and relatively stable during the period of intense exchange market pressures from September through November 1978.

interest rates and maintaining its path for bank reserves unchanged will depend on whether mark interest rates would tend to fall as a result of the initial deposit shift in the Eurocurrency market with unchanged bank reserves in Germany. If mark interest rates do come under downward pressure and the Bundesbank's policy orientation is to maintain the level of interest rates, the Bundesbank will have to allow bank reserves to grow more slowly and to allow slower growth in central bank money.

Crucial to the determination of whether mark interest rates would tend to fall is the influence, if any, on the quantity of money demanded in Germany of changes in the expected rate of return on dollar assets or of changes in the wealth of German residents as the result of a change in the exchange rate. These factors are unlikely to have a significant impact on the demand for money in Germany. Consequently, the Bundesbank is unlikely to have to choose between maintaining the level of mark interest rates and altering the amount of reserves provided to the banking system. If downward pressure on mark interest rates is negligible, the appreciation of the mark will have to be large enough to maintain balance between supply and demand for assets denominated in marks.

Under these conditions, the mechanism through which balance is maintained relies heavily upon the assumption of stabilizing expectations in exchange markets: Following a sharp appreciation of the mark, market participants expect a weaker trend for the mark than they expected before the deposit shift in the Eurocurrency market. If exchange rate expectations contain a bandwagon element, the exchange rate movement will have to be even larger before the overvaluation of the mark is sufficiently evident to bring about a reversal of expectations and contribute to a reduction in the expected relative rate of return on assets denominated in marks. In any event, the adjustment of interest rates and exchange rates (actual and expected) must induce market participants in Germany, in the United States, or in the Eurocurrency market to shift their exposures to offset the initial exogenous deposit shift. No net capital flow will occur among the three areas, but some changes in gross asset and liability positions may and probably will occur.

Subsequent Real and Financial Adjustments. If mark interest rates do not decline or are not permitted to decline as the initial result of the deposit shift, the appreciation of the mark will work to reduce the growth of nominal income in Germany through three channels: (1) Prices will rise less, directly reducing nominal income below what it would otherwise have been. (2) A slower rate of price inflation will mean that unchanged nominal interest rates will imply higher real interest rates, reducing real domestic aggregate demand. (3) The contribution of the external sector to real aggregate demand will be reduced. Because of lower nominal income, the demand for money will be reduced and downward pressure on mark interest rates will emerge even if it was not initially present. To maintain the level of mark interest rates, the Bundesbank will have to reduce the stock of central bank money below what it otherwise would have been.

If the Bundesbank continues to provide reserves to maintain the growth of central bank money, some actual decline in mark interest rates will occur. Compared with an interest rate orientation of Bundesbank policy, the upward pressure on the mark exchange rate, both nominal and price adjusted, will be reduced; the reduction in nominal income will be smaller; and the reduction in inflation will also be smaller. Real output will be higher than under an interest rate orientation of Bundesbank policy. Indeed, real output might be higher than without the deposit shift. This ambiguous result arises from the possibility that a decline in real interest rates could occur in Germany, which would stimulate domestic demand and might more than offset the drag from the external sector arising from the mark's appreciation. Thus, by maintaining the growth of central bank money, the Bundesbank would offset some of the price effects and some or all of the output effects of the deposit shift.

Under both orientations of Bundesbank policy, the short-run change in the German current account is indeterminate without a quantitative specification of the influences arising from the appreciation of the mark and from changes in real aggregate demand in Germany—to say nothing of the influences of economic developments abroad. It is clear, however, that in the absence of official exchange market intervention, a change in net private capital flows and any change in the German current account must balance one another.

Adjustments in the United States

The financial and real adjustments in the United States following the deposit shift in the Eurocurrency market will be opposite to those in Germany. Since the United States is a larger economy, however, the relative size of the impacts on U.S. output and prices presumably will be less.

One additional financial adjustment is likely to be more important for the United States than for Germany for a policy oriented toward reserves. As dollar interest rates rise, the cost of satisfying domestic reserve requirements and the existence of interest rate limitations on some deposits will induce a movement from deposits bearing high reserve requirements to deposits bearing a lower or no reserve requirement and from deposits subject to interest rate limitations to assets not subject to such limitations. Other liquid asset holdings of nonbanks will also increase.

One manifestation of this phenomenon will be an increase in Eurodollar deposits held by U.S. nonbank residents. In the absence of official exchange market intervention, and ignoring the uncertain changes in the U.S. current account, any increase in Eurodollar deposits of U.S. residents will have to be matched by a private capital inflow to the United States through other channels. This could occur through several channels. If no reserve requirement is imposed on banks in the United States against their borrowings from the Eurodollar market, these banks will have an incentive to fund U.S. lending from reserve-free Eurocurrency deposits. If banks' Eurodollar borrowings are subject to a reserve requirement at a level comparable to the reserve requirement against domestic deposits, no incentive will exist for completing round trip flows through this channel. However, an increase in direct lending to U.S. residents from foreign offices of foreign banks could still occur. And other channels could be utilized.

Summary of No Intervention Case

The adjustments in Germany and the United States following a deposit shift in the Eurocurrency market are summarized in Table 8-1 for both monetary policy orientations, assuming no official exchange market intervention. Monetary policies oriented toward interest rates will result in larger adjustments of the exchange rate, prices, and output than monetary policies oriented toward reserves. With an interest rate orientation, the direction of adjustment is contractionary in Germany and expansionary in the United States. Policies oriented toward reserves not only will result in smaller price adjustments but may lead to an increase, a decrease, or no change in output in either country.

If the Bundesbank and the Federal Reserve have the same monetary policy orientation, the expansionary and contractionary results in the two countries will be roughly offsetting in their global impact, though presumably the relative impact on prices and output in Germany will be larger. With different orientations, a Eurocurrency deposit shift could have net inflationary or deflationary consequences for the global economy. For example, if the Bundesbank has an

Table 8-1. Effects of a Shift of Deposits from Eurodollars to Euromarks, No Official Intervention.

	Germany		United States	
	Interest Rate Orientation	Reserves Orientation	Interest Rate Orientation	Reserves Orientation
Exchange value of the currency	+	(+)	–	(–)
Interest rates	0	–	0	+
Monetary aggregates	–	0	+	0
Prices	–	(–)	+	(+)
Real output	–	(–), 0, +	+	(+), 0, –
Nominal income	–	(–)	+	(+)
Private capital flows, net	0 immediately; subsequent flows associated with changes in current account positions could be +, -, or 0			
Official capital flows, net	0	0	0	0

Note: Parentheses indicate that the quantitative effect is smaller than for the other policy orientation.

interest rate orientation and the Federal Reserve has a reserves orientation, the net result will be contractionary.

CASE II: OFFICIAL EXCHANGE MARKET INTERVENTION

In this section we consider the effects of a Eurocurrency deposit shift when authorities choose to use official exchange market intervention to maintain the dollar-mark exchange rate unchanged. We focus primarily on intervention that is sterilized in the sense that it is not associated with any change in bank reserves in either country.

To provide background for our analysis, we consider first a number of the techniques for sterilized intervention that are available to the Bundesbank and the Federal Reserve. These techniques have in common that they all change the net positions in dollars and in marks of the two central banks combined. We assume that this change in positions will suffice to maintain the dollar-mark exchange rate unchanged by altering the size of the net positions in the two currencies that must be taken up by other market participants. Our assumption that sterilized intervention can affect exchange rates by this mechanism is consistent with our fundamental premise that an exogenous shift of demand in the Eurocurrency market from deposits denominated in dollars to deposits denominated in marks would cause the dollar-mark exchange rate to change in the absence of such intervention. If demand shifts matter, then supply shifts must also matter!

Following our discussion of the techniques of sterilized intervention, we consider the economic and financial implications of a Eurocurrency deposit shift when sterilized intervention maintains the exchange rate unchanged. We then consider unsterilized intervention and compare the results with those for sterilized intervention.

The distinction between an interest rate orientation and a reserves orientation of monetary policy is not central to the discussion in this section. It will be shown that for the subcase of sterilized intervention, the differences between the two orientations are technical and not fundamental. If intervention is not sterilized, either orientation must be subordinated to the objective of stabilizing the exchange rate.

Techniques of Sterilized Intervention

Either the Bundesbank or the Federal Reserve could undertake exchange market sales of marks and purchases of dollars to maintain the dollar-mark exchange rate unchanged in the face of a Eurocurrency deposit shift from dollars to marks. The financial and economic responses will be the same regardless of which central bank does the intervention, as long as it is sterilized in both countries.

Intervention and sterilization can take many forms. For example, the Bundesbank could purchase dollars with marks in the spot market. To maintain bank reserves and central bank money unchanged, it would have to absorb the bank reserves supplied by the intervention operation. This absorption might occur automatically through a reduction in the use of Lombard credit by German banks as the supply of nonborrowed reserves increased. The Bundesbank could also undertake open market sales of mark assets from its portfolio, or it could engage in a simultaneous swap transaction, selling dollars spot for marks and buying them back forward. This last type of sterilization, in effect, converts the initial spot intervention into the equivalent of outright forward intervention.[2] The Bundesbank may be limited in the extent to which it can employ the first two types of sterilization techniques by the amount of Lombard credit outstanding or by the size of its holdings of mark assets. However, its scope for using the third technique, and variants upon it, is in principle unlimited.

Following its normal practice, the Bundesbank would invest the dollars it acquired through intervention in U.S. Treasury securities. If it bought these securities in the open market, no change would occur in the Federal Reserve's balance sheet. However, if the Bundesbank used the dollars to purchase the securities from the Federal Reserve, the Federal Reserve would have to undertake an offsetting open market purchase of securities to sterilize the effect of the transaction on the supply of bank reserves in the United States.

Intervention could also be undertaken by the Federal Reserve using marks held at the Bundesbank or obtained through its swap line with the Bundesbank. In the first case, the Federal Reserve would have to buy Treasury securities with the dollars acquired in intervention in order to sterilize; in the second case, sterilization would occur automatically.[3] The response required of the Bundesbank to sterilize the intervention would be the same as when the Bundesbank intervenes itself. If the Treasury issued mark-denominated debt on the German market (Carter notes), reduced its sales of dollar-denominated debt correspondingly, and immediately sold the mark proceeds for dollars, neither the Bundesbank nor the Federal Reserve would need to take any action to sterilize the intervention operation.

In all of the cases discussed above, the essential feature of the sterilized intervention is that no change occurs in bank reserves in either country. Alternatively, either central bank could change its reserve requirements following an intervention operation. The Bundesbank has on occasion raised required reserves to pre-

2. The Bundesbank could also either sell mark-denominated participations in its holdings of U.S. Treasury securities or sell the securities outright with a promise to repurchase them at a specified later date at a fixed price in terms of marks.

3. The sterilization is automatic because the U.S. bank reserves absorbed by the intervention operation are normally replaced by reserves created as part of swap transactions. Should the latter step not complete the sterilization, open market purchases will do so (Kubarych 1977–78).

vent an increase in bank reserves induced by intervention from leading to an increase in the money supply. This technique forces banks to lend interest free to the Bundesbank and to reduce their holdings of interest-earning assets. Hence, bank profits are squeezed, which limits the practical scope for using this technique.

Effects of Sterilized Intervention

Sterilized intervention using any of the techniques described above will enlarge private market participants' net holdings of mark-denominated assets and forward positions and will reduce their net holdings of dollar-denominated assets and forward positions. The amount of intervention required to keep the exchange rate unchanged will equal the initial, exogenous shift from dollar deposits to mark deposits in the Eurocurrency market, but this shift normally would be unobserved. Intervention will have to meet exchange market pressure for as long as the Eurocurrency deposit shift is thought to be continuing.

As a consequence of such sterilized intervention, the general level of mark interest rates and of dollar interest rates will be unaffected. Hence, either a reserves orientation of monetary policy (with technical adjustment of the reserves path for sterilization through changes in reserve requirements) or an interest rate orientation will essentially require no further central bank action once the intervention and sterilization operations were completed.

Real output, prices, and current account positions in both countries will be unaffected by the disturbance if intervention maintains the exchange rate and interest rates unchanged. Private and official international capital flows generally will occur, however. It is worthwhile to consider some of the forms such flows might take and to examine why they would not have expansionary or contractionary implications.

Most of the techniques of sterilized intervention discussed above would be recorded as official capital flows in the balance of payments—generally as an increase in official reserve assets for Germany (official capital outflow) and as either a decline in official reserve assets or a rise in official liabilities for the United States (official capital inflow). These official flows would balance a net private capital inflow to Germany and a net private capital outflow from the United States involving, directly or indirectly, the Eurocurrency market. These flows would eliminate the initial excess supply of dollar assets in the Eurocurrency market created by the deposit shift. The increased supply of mark assets and reduced supply of dollar assets created by the sterilized intervention in the two countries would reestablish equilibrium at an unchanged exchange rate without necessarily involving adjustments in the general levels of mark and dollar interest rates.

The principal channels for private capital flows from the Eurocurrency market to Germany would be German firms' increasing their borrowing from the Euromark market, German banks' raising funds in the Euromark market for lending in Germany, and nonresidents' switching from borrowing in Germany to borrowing in the Euromark market and from deposits in the Euromark market to deposits in Germany.

The net private capital inflows to Germany would add to credit available to German residents. However, total credit available to private German residents would be unchanged because credit available from domestic sources would be reduced by an equal amount. The process of sterilization would bring about this reduction. Credit would be absorbed by Bundesbank sales of mark securities to German banks, through reductions in Lombard credit taken up by German banks to fund lending to nonbanks or as a result of an increase in required reserves (against as unchanged stock of bank liabilities) that would necessitate a decline in other bank assets.

The financial flows that would occur involving the United States would generally correspond, but be opposite, to those involving Germany. An official inflow as a result of the sterilized intervention would be associated with a net private capital outflow from the United States to the Eurocurrency market. The private sector would hold fewer Treasury securities and more net claims on foreigners, probably largely in the form of a shift in the net position of U.S. banking offices vis-à-vis affiliates in the Eurodollar market.

Forward market intervention to maintain the exchange rate would be an exception to these general patterns of recorded international capital flows, but the economic consequences would be essentially the same. No official capital flow or net private capital flow would occur. Rather, such intervention would increase the supply of forward cover for short mark positions against dollars in the exchange market. Eurocurrency banks could take up such cover against the increase in their mark deposits and the decline in their dollar deposits. In this way they would be able to pursue an unchanged currency composition of their lending without incurring any change in their exchange rate exposures. Domestic financial markets need not become involved at all.

Unsterilized Intervention

A policy of unsterilized intervention would imply an increase in bank reserves in Germany and a decrease in the United States equivalent to the amount of the intervention. For example, intervention would be unsterilized in both countries if the Bundesbank purchased dollars in the spot market and used them to purchase Treasury securities from the Federal Reserve and the Federal Reserve did not undertake any offsetting purchases of Treasury securities. Some types of intervention operations might result in sterilization in one country and not in the other.

Mark interest rates would fall if the Bundesbank did not sterilize, and dollar interest rates would rise if the Federal Reserve did not sterilize. These interest rate adjustments would help to eliminate the excess supply and demand created by the initial disturbance. Hence, a smaller volume of intervention would be

Table 8-2.   Effects of a Shift of Deposits from Eurodollars to Euromarks, Official Intervention.

	Germany		United States	
	Sterilized in both Countries	Unsterilized in both Countries	Sterilized in both Countries	Unsterilized in both Countries
Exchange value of the currency	0	0	0	0
Interest rates	0	−	0	+
Monetary aggregates	0	+	0	−
Prices	0	+	0	−
Real output	0	+	0	−
Nominal income	0	+	0	−
Private capital flows, net	+	(+)	−	(−)
Official capital flows, net	−	(−)	+	(+)

Note: Parentheses indicate that the quantitative effect is smaller than for the sterilized case.

required to maintain an unchanged exchange rate than if the intervention were sterilized. The corresponding private capital flows would also be smaller.

Monetary growth would be more rapid in Germany and slower in the United States than otherwise. Upward pressure on output and prices would develop in Germany, and downward pressure would develop in the United States. Thus, the effects on the price level would be opposite to those in the case of no intervention; the effects on real output would be opposite (compared with monetary policy oriented toward interest rates) or unambiguous (compared with monetary policy oriented toward reserves). The German current account would move toward deficit, and the U.S. current account would move toward surplus. These current account developments would entail further net private capital inflows to Germany and net private capital outflows from the United States. If these flows did not occur at an unchanged exchange rate, the earlier intervention would have to be reversed at least in part to prevent a depreciation of the mark against the dollar. The adjustments in Germany and the United States following a deposit shift in the Eurocurrency market are summarized in Table 8-2 for sterilized and unsterilized intervention.

IMPLICATIONS FOR POLICY CHOICES

We conclude by making several observations concerning the domestic and international monetary policy choices available to the Bundesbank and the Federal

Reserve in the face of a Eurocurrency market disturbance such as the one we have analyzed. Our first observation is that the two central banks could, in theory, neutralize the economic effects of a deposit shift in the Eurocurrency market by undertaking sterilized intervention. Following such a policy might be difficult in practice, however. The Bundesbank and the Federal Reserve generally would not know to what extent a shift in asset preferences of the type we have postulated was the cause of pressure on the dollar-mark exchange rate and to what extent the cause of the pressure was some other disturbance. Exchange market pressures could result from monetary policies in two countries that were fundamentally inconsistent with an unchanged exchange rate, from disturbances involving the demand for money, or from real disturbances. These other causes of exchange rate pressures would entail monetary or real economic adjustments. The adjustments that would occur with a policy of sterilized intervention could be more disruptive than those that would occur if the exchange rate were permitted to move. Hence, our analysis should not be interpreted as a general argument in favor of maintaining fixed exchange rates. Nevertheless, it suggests that to the extent that exchange market pressures can be identified with shifts in asset preferences, economic stability would be improved by sterilized intervention.

One indication that a shift in asset preferences lay behind exchange market pressures might be given by the simultaneous behavior of interest rates. Our analysis shows that such a shift would put downward pressure on mark interest rates, upward pressure on dollar interest rates, and upward pressure on the exchange value of the mark—although we noted that the interest rate pressures might be slight or delayed. Most other disturbances that would put upward pressure on the exchange value of the mark would have opposite effects on interest rates. Indeed, appreciation of a currency is more often associated with rising interest rates on assets denominated in that currency, while depreciation is associated with falling interest rates. This correlation suggests that asset shifts are not the dominant explanation of exchange rate changes. It should also be noted that a contraction of nominal income in Germany relative to the money supply, for example, together with a sufficiently large decline in expectations of inflation in Germany, would generate a decline in the mark interest rate and an appreciation of the mark. It would be much less clear under such circumstances that maintaining an unchanged exchange rate and unchanged domestic monetary policies would be an appropriate response. Nevertheless, examining exchange rate movements in the context of other financial developments may provide useful evidence concerning their origins.

German and U.S. officials might obtain better information about asset demand shifts by providing, or favoring the international provision of, special investment facilities to official holders as an alternative to investment in the Eurocurrency market. However, this benefit from establishing such facilities would need to be weighed against the costs. For example, the costs of making such facilities attractive to potential official investors would have to be considered, as would the risk that asset shifts would be encouraged by offering such facilities. Moreover, it would be wrong to interpret all changes in asset holdings of official institutions as exogenous disturbances reflecting a change in preferences. Changes in official portfolios could also reflect responses to changes in interest rates and to the influence of changing expectations about prospective economic developments.

Efforts by the Bundesbank and the Federal Reserve to determine the origins of exchange market pressures would inevitably leave very large uncertainties. In the face of such uncertainties, the two central banks might modify the policies they would have chosen in a case when they knew for certain the underlying cause of the exchange market pressures. For example if they would have chosen to maintain the exchange rate unchanged, knowing for certain that a shift in asset demands had occurred, they might intervene to moderate, but not to prevent, an exchange rate movement, suspecting but not knowing that such a shift had occurred. This strategy would be an application of the principle of policy-making under uncertainty put forward by Brainard (1967).

Our second observation is that while sterilization would neutralize the economic effects of an exogenous asset shift, the Bundesbank might prefer other policies. For example, it could achieve a short-run reduction in German inflation with little change in output if no intervention occurred and its monetary policy was oriented toward reserves. For the Federal Reserve, no policy action would result in better combinations of inflation and output in the short run than the combinations that were available before the disturbance occurred. Thus, the Federal Reserve might be more favorably disposed toward intervention than the Bundesbank. On the other hand, the short-run advantage to Germany of an appreciation of the mark could well be offset by the longer run implications of a possible deterioration in the external competitive position of Germany.

The asymmetry in the short-run advantages from sterilized intervention, which arises because a policy of active intervention to drive the exchange rate is precluded by international convention, could be an obstacle to central bank cooperation in dealing with disturbances of the type we have analyzed. The uncertainty concerning whether such disturbances lay behind any particular episode of pressure on the exchange rate and the question of how the exchange risk that would result from intervention should be divided between the Bundesbank and the Federal Reserve might pose other obstacles.

Our third observation concerns the choice of domestic monetary policy techniques. On the whole, our analysis suggests that a reserves orientation would yield more favorable results than an interest rate orientation under the conditions we have considered. If the two central banks intervened and sterilized, either domestic monetary policy would lead to the same results. The economic effects of a shift in asset demands would be smaller with no intervention and a reserves orientation of monetary policy than with no intervention and an interest rate orientation or with intervention that was permitted to alter the supplies of bank reserves (unsterilized intervention). This is true even though the quantity of reserves or of money has no direct effect on output and prices in our analysis but only influences these variables indirectly through interest rates and the exchange rate.

The multipliers relating the supply of reserves to monetary targets (central bank money in Germany and the family of monetary aggregates in the United States) cannot be expected to be absolutely stable when the exchange rate and interest rates change. Moreover, the relationship between a given monetary aggregate on the one hand and output, prices, and even nominal income on the other hand may be altered by shifts in asset demands. Thus, our analysis highlights in this specific case a general conclusion of Bryant (1980): Central banks should review periodically both the reserves path appropriate to achieving their stated monetary targets and the monetary targets themselves in terms of the ultimate objectives of policy—stability of prices and output.

REFERENCES

Brainard, William C. 1967. "Uncertainty and the Effectiveness of Policy." *American Economic Review* 57 (May): 411-25.

Bryant, Ralph C. 1980. *Money and Monetary Policy in Interdependent Nations.* Washington, D.C.: The Brookings Institution.

Girton, Lance, and Dale W. Henderson. 1977. "Central Bank Operations in Foreign and Domestic Assets under Fixed and Flexible Exchange Rates." In P.B. Clark et al., eds., *The Effects of Exchange Rate Adjustments.* Washington, D.C.: U.S. Government Printing Office.

Kubarych, R.M. 1977-78. "Monetary Effects of Federal Reserve Swaps." *Federal Reserve Bank of New York Quarterly Review* 4.

Lowrey, Barbara R., and Ralph W. Smith, Jr. 1980. "U.S. Banks, Exchange Markets, and the Dollar, September–November 1978." *International Finance Discussion Paper* No. 151. Washington, D.C.: Board of Governors of the Federal Reserve System.

II THE INTERNATIONAL MONETARY SYSTEM FROM GLOBAL, REGIONAL, AND NATIONAL PERSPECTIVES

9 THE EVOLUTION OF CURRENCY AREAS
A Speculation On Monetary History
Robert Z. Aliber

INTRODUCTION

In the past several decades marked changes have occurred in the structure of international payments arrangements, the composition of international reserves, and the external domain of national currency areas. At the end of 1948, gold was the dominant reserve asset; monetary gold holdings totaled $33 billion while the reserves denominated in the dollar, sterling, and other national currencies totaled $14 billion. Reserves denominated in sterling were more than twice as large as reserves denominated in the dollar. Reserves denominated in sterling remained largely unchanged during the 1950s and the early 1960s and then declined in the later 1960s. In contrast, reserves denominated in the dollar increased steadily in the 1950s and most of the 1960s and then surged at the end of that decade; at the end of 1969, reserves denominated in the dollar were more than ten times larger than reserves denominated in sterling. In the 1970s, however, the volume of reserves denominated in the mark and the Swiss franc and in other currencies increased steadily and at the end of the 1970s were as large as reserves denominated in the dollar had been at the end of the 1960s.

Reserves denominated in the dollar, however, have continued to increase rapidly and are almost five times larger than reserves denominated in all other currencies. The increase in the demand for reserves denominated in currencies other than the dollar is frequently attributed to the increase in the U.S. price level and the depreciation of the dollar in the foreign exchange market. Yet the direction of causality in the relationship between the increase in the U.S. commodity price level and the depreciation of the dollar is not unambiguous. Thus the depreciation of the dollar was more rapid than might be inferred from the change in national price level differentials, with the consequence that there was upward pressure on the U.S. price level from the increase in the dollar price of tradable goods, both imports and exports. Moreover, the increase in the demand for reserve assets denominated in the German mark, the Swiss franc, and other currencies led to a more rapid appreciation of these currencies than was suggested by the differential changes in national price levels.

The increase in the demand for reserves denominated in currencies other than the dollar might be explained in several ways other than greater U.S. susceptibility to inflation. Some monetary authorities may seek to diversify the currency mix of their reserves: Diversification has been a major theme in the finance literature for several decades. Diversification of the currency mix of reserves may be a transient by-product as countries gradually seek to reduce the holdings of dollar-denominated assets in their reserves and ultimately concentrate on some other reserve asset. Alternatively, the increase in the demand for reserves denominated in currencies other than the dollar might be attributable to changes in the pattern of international trade and investment in the last several decades and especially to the decline in the economic importance of the United States as Germany, Japan, and other countries gradually assumed the role that they had had in the international economy prior to World War II. Hence the diversification of the currency mix of reserve assets might have occurred regardless of the U.S. price level performance, although the more rapid increase in the U.S. price level might have advanced or quickened a development that would otherwise have occurred more slowly.

At issue is whether the changes in the demand of official institutions for assets denominated in various currencies are primarily a monetary phenomenon or whether instead these changes are primarily a structural phenomenon. In the former case, the increase in the demand for assets denominated in currencies other than the dollar would reflect anticipated or realized changes in the net returns on assets denominated in different currencies, where the anticipated return includes the net foreign exchange gain (or loss) as well as the interest payment. In the latter case, the increase in the demand for reserves denominated in currencies other than the dollar would reflect the desire to enhance efficiency in the financing of trade and investment, where efficiency means minimizing the variance of the returns on assets held as reserves relative to the import consumption bundle. An identification problem is likely, for the shift by official institutions from holding assets denominated in the dollar into holding assets denominated in other currencies may occur because individual monetary authorities seek both to increase their returns and to increase their efficiency.

The central issue discussed in this chapter is whether the external domain of national currency areas shifts in response to monetary phenomena or in response to structural phenomena. A derivative issue raised by the expansion of a European currency area centered around Germany and the mark and perhaps by the expansion of a third currency area centered around Japan and the yen is whether the likelihood of international monetary instability may be increased if there are several major currency areas (Triffin 1960).[1] Thus it has been argued that in the period between World Wars I and II, when the economic power of the United States was increasing while that of Great Britain was declining, the actual and incipient flows of funds between New York and London in response to differentials in interest rates was a source of monetary instability.

THE EXTERNAL DOMAIN OF
NATIONAL CURRENCIES

The external domain of a national currency expands as foreign monetary authorities believe that the attributes of assets denominated in this currency are increasingly attractive relative to the attributes of comparable assets denominated in other currencies. The key question involves the factors that lead to changes in the relative attractiveness of comparable assets denominated in different currencies for reserve holdings.

Changes in the official demand for reserve assets denominated in particular currencies may parallel or follow changes in the private demand for assets denominated in these same currencies, especially the demand of nonresidents. Private investors alter the currency mix of their assets to accomplish several objectives. They seek to maximize anticipated returns, which include capital gains due to changes in exchange rates as well as interest income. Private investors may seek to minimize risk, which means minimizing the uncertainty of the anticipated returns. Firms choose the currency mix of their liabilities to minimize net borrowing costs, again after adjustment for capital gains and losses from unanticipated changes in exchange rates. Freedom from exchange controls, both current and prospective, is important, as are convenience and ease in transactions. While lenders and borrowers may have a preferred "habitat" currency for denominating assets and liabilities, they may shift into other currencies on the basis of these risk and return calculations (Ben–Bassat 1980). These risk and return attributes are often analyzed in terms of optimizing a portfolio; the well-elaborated theme is that diversification of a portfolio among assets whose returns are less than perfectly correlated reduces the risk of the portfolio. The growth of offshore deposits denominated in the German mark and the Swiss franc is partly a response to the demand of nonresidents for assets denominated in these currencies, although part of this demand, especially for mark-denominated assets, reflects a shift by German residents from domestic deposits to offshore deposits.[2]

1. The anomaly is that continental Europe might become one currency area with two currencies, the German mark and the Swiss franc. The Swiss franc serves as a store of value. However, its other international roles are limited. And too, the correlation between changes in the foreign exchange values of the Swiss franc and of the German mark is very high.

2. At issue is whether the growth in the demand for offshore deposits reflects the "tax" on domestic deposits implicit in non-interest-bearing reserves. The U.S. and the German reserve requirements are relatively high, while the British and the Swiss reserve requirements are low.

When choosing among assets denominated in different currencies, central banks consider several factors in addition to those that affect the choices of private investors. If central banks peg their currencies or intervene in the foreign exchange market while their currencies float, they must choose a currency for intervention. This choice is likely to reflect trade patterns and the institutional characteristics of the foreign exchange market. Central banks may find it convenient to acquire reserve assets denominated in the currency used for exchange market intervention. Moreover, central banks, unlike private investors, do not switch between their currency and a foreign currency as their estimates of future exchange rates change. Instead, they hold reserve assets until it is necessary to buy their own currencies in the foreign exchange market. Central banks may be less concerned to maximize the return on assets denominated in a foreign currency than are private investors, for they have other objectives. Central banks traditionally have been more willing to maintain an exposure in foreign currencies, at least in nominal terms (Aliber 1981b).

For central banks as well as for private investors, differences in the currency mix of assets would be important only if the international money market is not efficient or at least not efficient in a naive sense.[3] If the international money market is efficient, then differences in the interest rates on comparable assets denominated in different currencies will correspond to realized changes in the exchange rates. At the extreme, the return on a portfolio of reserve assets would be independent of the currency mix of these assets. If the risk characteristics of these assets differ, then the statement could be readily modified; the risk-adjusted returns in assets denominated in various currencies would be equal. If instead the international money market is not efficient, then holding assets denominated in some currencies might lead to significantly higher returns than holding comparable assets denominated in other currencies. While anticipated returns on comparable assets might not differ, the ex post returns could differ, especially in the short-run intervals of one, two, or even three years.

That central banks are not indifferent to the currency mix of reserve assets might reflect a belief, implicit if not explicit, that the international money market is not efficient in the naive sense. If central banks prefer certain currencies for the denomination of reserves, the question becomes how much potential return they might be willing to forgo to achieve some other objective (Makin 1971). In deciding on which currency might be used to denominate reserve assets, central banks can choose among the currencies used for exchange market support (the intervention currency), the currencies in which their imports are priced (the quotation currency), and the currencies in which payments are made (the vehicle currency). Since transactions costs of foreign exchange are trivial,

---

3. In this context, exchange market efficiency involves the return on comparable assets denominated in different currencies after recognition of capital gains and losses due to changes in exchange rates. The foreign exchange market is efficient if the risk-adjusted rates on return of assets denominated in different currencies are not significantly different.

reserves can be denominated in currencies other than the one used for these purposes: The dollar has been used extensively as the intervention currency, even by countries that traditionally held most of their reserves in gold (Aliber 1981a). And countries that hold reserves denominated in the mark or the yen probably do not use these currencies as intervention currencies (Magee et al. 1980). Similarly, the vehicle currency is held by firms that have payments to make in particular currencies; the monetary authorities may have little incentive to hold reserve assets denominated in this currency.

In the nineteenth century, the domain of "currency areas" was determined by whether a country pegged its currency to gold or to silver (Hicks 1969). In effect, the countries whose currencies were pegged to gold comprised one currency area; another much smaller currency area included those countries whose currencies were pegged to silver. In the twentieth century, the development of currency areas goes back to 1931. A number of countries, both in Europe and in the British Commonwealth, pegged their currencies to sterling when Great Britain severed the fixed price relationship between gold and sterling and permitted sterling to float in September 1931. If the monetary authorities in these countries had continued to peg their currencies to gold, as most currencies still were, then the value of their currencies would have varied in terms of sterling and sterling area currencies. Given that the price of sterling would vary in terms of the dollar, the monetary authorities in these countries had to decide whether the increase in uncertainty about exchange rates in the future should fall on the traders and investors involved in transactions with dollar area countries instead of on the traders and investors involved in transactions with sterling area countries.[4] One consequence of the decision of these countries to peg their currencies to sterling was that the value of their holdings of international reserves, primarily gold, would vary in terms of their currencies as the foreign exchange value of sterling varied in terms of the dollar. The inference from the decision to peg to sterling was that maintaining a stable domestic value for their primary reserve asset, gold, in terms of domestic currency was dominated by the importance of minimizing exchange rate uncertainty between their currencies and that of their major trading partner. Trade issues dominated monetary issues in the choice of whether to peg to sterling or to gold. Like private investors, the monetary authorities were moved to reduce the uncertainty about future exchange rates, but they did so by a change in the international asset to which they pegged their currencies rather than by an increase in the number of currencies used to denominate assets held as reserves.

In the 1950s and 1960s, the effective choice in the selection of reserves for most countries was between gold and the U.S. dollar; sterling had dropped out of the effective choice set, partly because Great Britain maintained an overval-

---

4. In both cases, traders and investors might be expected to pass on the higher costs to their customers.

ued parity behind an extensive array of exchange controls and partly because the importance of sterling in world trade had declined significantly. The arguments for holding dollar assets as reserves were of two types. One set included the multiple roles of the dollar as an intervention currency, as a quotation currency, and as a vehicle currency; while the second set included the importance of the United States in world trade and in setting the world price level.

That many countries, primarily in Western Europe, continued to hold a large part of their reserves in gold seemed nonmaximizing, given the opportunity cost in the form of the absence of any interest income on gold. Moreover, despite popular belief, there was little apparent relationship between changes in the world price level and changes in the gold price. Only once before in the last several centuries had there been an increase in the monetary price of gold. In previous centuries, the long-run stability of the price of a market basket of goods in terms of gold resulted from the alternation of increases and decreases in the world commodity price level.

Historically, the development of gold as a money reflected the fact that the variability of the price of a market basket of goods was smaller in terms of gold than in terms of any other commodity money (Jastram 1978). During the nineteenth century, the variability of the price of a market basket of world goods was smaller in terms of gold than in terms either of sterling or of the dollar, since both currencies floated in terms of gold for more than a decade. Thus, during periods of great stress—the Napoleonic wars for Great Britain and the Civil War for the United States—gold retained its purchasing power in terms of a market basket of goods better than sterling and the dollar. Gold was stable when national currencies were subject to extensive inflation and deflation. The official demand for gold in the twentieth century can be traced to these earlier experiences; the appropriate inference is that the central banks place a great weight on minimizing uncertainty about the future value of their reserves and are willing to give up substantial current income to satisfy this objective. Moreover, the wealthier a central bank (more specifically, the wealthier the residents of a country), the more willing it might be to forgo the return on assets denominated in one of several currencies to obtain the reduction in uncertainty associated with holding gold.

As a stylized fact, it might be argued that holding assets denominated in a national currency as part of official reserves was derived from the need for an intervention currency that developed in World War I when private international gold shipments were embargoed (Lindert 1969). For Great Britain and France the dollar was the obvious choice as an intervention currency, since their trade deficits were financed with the proceeds from dollar loans. Virtually all currencies other than the dollar were subject to exchange controls.

In the post–World War II period, holding dollar assets as reserves offered several advantages, even though a higher interest income might have been obtained by holding reserves denominated in some other currency. Dollar assets were not subject to exchange control, whereas assets denominated in most other currencies were. Moreover, central banks were willing to accept a lower interest rate on dollar assets than for any other currency. The share of U.S. exports and imports in world trade exceeded 30 percent, while the dollar area countries accounted for more than 50 percent of world trade.

The increase in reserves denominated in currencies other than the dollar in the 1970s might be explained in a number of ways—the weakness of the dollar and its depreciation in the foreign exchange market; the attempt by some monetary authorities to increase the return on their reserve assets; the increased political risk associated with dollar assets following the freezing of Iranian dollar balances; and the declining importance of the United States and of the dollar area in world trade (Laney 1978, 1979). The monetary authorities in some countries may believe that changes in the foreign exchange value of their currencies are more closely correlated with changes in the foreign exchange value of the currency of some other major industrial country than with the dollar. Some countries might have acquired reserves denominated in a currency other than the dollar because they started to intervene in the foreign exchange market in support of their own currency using a currency other than the dollar: They might seek to match the currency denomination of reserves with the currency used for exchange market intervention.

One inference from the asset demands of private investors and portfolio theory is that uncertainty about anticipated returns can be reduced by diversification; investors may hold twenty or more securities to reduce uncertainty. In contrast, there is very limited evidence that central banks, in their efforts to reduce uncertainty, have significantly diversified portfolios. Instead, the historical data suggest that some central banks have concentrated their reserves in gold and others in either dollar-denominated or sterling-denominated assets (Heller and Knight 1978). While some central banks may hold reserve assets denominated in several currencies, diversification for many central banks may be the transient by-product of efforts to shift from holding assets denominated in one currency to holding assets in some other currency deemed more capable of satisfying their needs.

The major structural explanation for the increase in demand for reserve assets denominated in a currency other than the dollar involves the decline in the share of the United States and of the dollar area countries in world trade. Once countries stopped pegging their currencies to the dollar, the strength of the correlation of changes in the foreign exchange value of their currencies relative to currencies other than the dollar became apparent. The risk attached to holding assets denominated in the dollar became large relative to the risk attached to holding assets denominated in the German mark or the Swiss franc.

The decisions that central banks have faced about the currency mix of reserve assets once currencies began to float are similar to those faced by the countries whose currencies followed sterling in 1931: Once their currencies were pegged to sterling, they had to decide whether to continue to hold gold as their primary reserve asset or to gradually acquire assets denominated in sterling as part of their reserves. One reason central banks might give for acquiring as reserves assets denominated in a currency other than the dollar is that the international money market has not been efficient: The return on dollar assets has been significantly lower than the return on assets denominated in the German mark, the Swiss franc, and the Japanese yen. However, the recognition that returns on comparable assets denominated in different currencies have diverged in the past provides no insight on the comparison of anticipated returns on assets denominated in different currencies in the future.

At any moment there is little reason to believe that the interest rates on dollar assets relative to the interest rates on comparable assets denominated in other currencies understate the rate of depreciation of the dollar asset. Thus, some central banks may have altered the currency mix of their reserve assets to minimize the variation of the price of a world market basket of goods or of their imports in terms of their reserve assets—very much the rationale that led to the choice of gold as money. The central banks might identify the currency mix of their imports (or perhaps of their imports together with their exports) or their consumption bundles and reallocate the currency mix of the reserves to reduce the uncertainty of the value of their reserves in terms of their import consumption bundles.

Monetary history suggests that central banks differ from private investors in that they place greater value on minimizing risk and less value on maximizing returns than do private investors (McKinnon 1969). The increased risk associated with the sharp changes in the foreign exchange value of the dollar has reduced the attractiveness of the dollar as a reserve asset, especially for countries whose currencies move more closely with that of some other country. In part, then, this demand for reserve assets denominated in the mark or in some currency other than the dollar is a reflection of the decline in the U.S. importance in world trade in the 1950s and the 1960s, which was inevitable, given the gradual increase in the trade shares of Western Europe and Japan after the war toward their prewar levels. To the extent that U.S. inflation and the subsequent depreciation of the dollar led central banks to acquire assets denominated in a currency other than the dollar, these monetary developments probably hastened a change that was otherwise inevitable.

MONETARY STABILITY IN A BIPOLAR CURRENCY WORLD

If the domain of a European currency area continues to expand in the 1980s, a concern about reduced international monetary stability may develop, based on an interpretation of the interwar experience when the dollar area was expanding relative to the sterling area (Triffin 1964). This argument can be examined when the relative size of the two currency areas is stable or when one currency area is expanding relative to the other. The argument about the instability of a bipolar currency system should be contrasted with the management of a monetary system dominated by a hegemonic power. Then changes in the monetary policy of the hegemonic power in response to changes in its holdings of international reserves altered the supply of trade financing and induced currency flows from the financial centers in periphery countries to the financial center in the hegemonic country. These currency flows might be visualized as between the center of a wheel and along various spokes.

The argument that a world with several currency areas is less stable than a world with one currency area is that both private parties and official institutions might shift funds between the financial centers in the two currency areas when interest rate differentials are large relative to the anticipated changes in exchange rates. Thus the authorities in the dominant financial center in one of the currency areas might feel constrained about following a more contractive or a more expansive monetary policy because of the impacts on losing or attracting reserves from the dominant financial center in the other currency area. Thus the U.S. authorities were reluctant to raise interest rates in the late 1920s because funds might be attracted to New York from London, with an adverse impact on the precarious reserve position of the Bank of England.

The problems of monetary management in Great Britain were intensified because of the overvaluation of sterling, attributable to the desire to peg sterling to gold at its pre-World War I parity. The British price level had risen significantly more than the U.S. price level from 1913 to 1921, and sterling was overvalued. But even if there had been no change in relative price levels, sterling was overvalued—and for two different reasons. One was the adverse movement in Britain's terms of trade as reflected in the decline in its shipbuilding, coal, and textile industries. The second was the sharp shift in Britain's international investment position during the war due to the substantial liquidation of overseas investment and the increase in external debt.

In a financial system with only one dominant financial center, changes in the differential in interest rates between the financial center and the periphery countries also lead to flows of financial capital. Thus if interest rates in New York had risen relative to interest rates in London before the United States became a reserve currency country, gold would still have flowed to the United States, primarily because some importers and exporters shifted the center in which they financed trade. At issue is whether the flows of funds between New York and London would be larger for a given change in the interest rate differential when both are reserve currency countries. The argument that the flows of funds are larger when there are two reserve currency countries might be based on the assumption that monetary authorities might shift funds from one center to another in response to a change in the interest rate differential. Monetary history lends very little support to this contention; few central banks alter the currency mix of their reserves to profit from short-term changes in the interest rate differentials.[5] Alternatively, private parties might also shift funds between assets denominated in the two currencies in response to the changes in the interest rate differential. Since shifts by private parties would have occurred even if there were only one dominant financial center, the argument is compelling only if the shifts by private parties might be larger for a given change in the interest rate differential. On an a priori basis, however, there is little reason to expect that the elasticity of short-term capital flows would have increased.

The secular change in the importance of the boundaries between two currency areas might be a source of monetary instability as the domain of one currency area expands and that of the other contracts, especially if changes in the foreign holdings of assets denominated in the two currencies must be accommodated by changes in the current account balances of the two reserve currency countries. In the twenties, for example, the expansion of the external domain of the dollar area might have required a large U.S. current account deficit so nonresidents could acquire dollars. In this case, the change in the current account balances might have required a change in the effective exchange rate. The historical data, however, suggest that the external domain of a currency area usually expands when the reserve currency country has a large current account surplus. The appropriate inference is that the expansion of the external domain of a currency has resulted from an increase in international financial intermediation.

Thus, the likelihood that the monetary instability of the interwar period reflects the bipolar character of the currency arrangements seems low. Rather, the instability is traceable to "the economic consequences of Mr. Churchill"— the decision to peg sterling at its historic gold parity rather than to adjust sterling's parity to monetary and structural changes. Although the financial power of Great Britain was declining so that monetary authorities and investors might have had an incentive to shift from holding sterling assets to holding dollar assets, these shifts were a response to the structural change rather than to changes in the differential between sterling interest rates and dollar interest rates.

CONCLUSION

The argument of this chapter is that the external domain of national currency areas expands and shrinks in response to changes in trade patterns. The expansion of the dollar area was a natural response to the sudden growth of the United States in world trade; the shrinkage of the sterling area was an inevitable outcome of the decline in Britain's importance in world trade and the disappearance

5. Perhaps the decision of the Bank of France to withdraw deposits from the Bank of England might be cited to support the contention. The French recognized that sterling was overvalued — and that an increase in the sterling price of gold was inevitable and would have occurred even if Great Britain had remained the financial hegemon.

of its empire. U.S. exports were 15 percent of world exports in 1938, 31 percent in 1947, and 24 percent in 1948. Currently U.S. exports are 12 percent of world exports.

The U.S. share of world trade is lower now than it was in 1938 and 1948. A major trading area is developing around Germany, encouraged by the elimination of trade and tariff barriers on intra-European trade. Moreover, the scope of this tariff area is expanding as more countries join the European Community. The expansion of the European currency area is inevitable, with the implication that the European countries will find their self-interest advanced by holding reserve assets denominated in other European currencies. Increasingly, intervention by European central banks will involve the currency of another European country rather than the U.S. dollar. Moreover, countries outside Europe whose trade is primarily with Europe might begin to hold more of their reserve assets denominated in one of the European currencies.

The development of the European currency area might be viewed as a two-stage process. During the first or transitional stage, individual countries whose reserve assets are now primarily either gold- or dollar-denominated assets will gradually increase the share of their total reserves held in the form of assets denominated in one of the European countries. In some cases, holdings of dollar-denominated assets might decline (a country might sell dollar-denominated assets when in payments deficit and acquire mark-denominated assets when in payments surplus). This stage might easily last a decade or even more for an individual country, and since countries might alter their currency preferences at different times, the process could last substantially longer from the viewpoint of the system. In the second or post-transitional stage, the adjustment to the transient excess holdings of dollars by countries that have altered the preferred currency for the denomination of reserves will have been accomplished. The external demand for dollar assets by countries that remain members of the dollar area will continue to increase, just as the countries that identify their commercial interests with the European currency area will add to holdings of reserve assets denominated in one of the major European currencies.

The likelihood that the move toward expansion of the bipolar currency area arrangement will be a source of monetary instability after the transitional period depends on many uncertainties about the development of national monetary policies. Instability might take the form of increased shifts of funds between comparable assets denominated in the several currencies used to denominate reserve assets in response to a change in interest rates or in the interest rate differential, or to a change in the exchange rate anticipations, or to some other, perhaps political, disturbance. The magnitude of such shifts remains conjectural. Shifts of funds between the major currency areas have already led to large movements in exchange rates. It is plausible that these shifts have been larger because some central banks are already shifting from reserve assets denominated in dollars to reserve assets denominated in one of the major European currencies. The shifts by central banks, however, do not appear large relative to those undertaken by private parties.

The historical data do not suggest that the development of a bipolar currency area system will lead to reduction in monetary stability internationally. Thus, the interpretation of the monetary instability of the interwar period in the form of a conflict in the "management of the system" between the U.S. monetary authorities and the British monetary authorities appears invalid. The traditional conflict between domestic economic objectives and external balance at the prevailing pegged exchange rates does not appear to have been significantly more acute in the context of a bipolar currency area arrangement. Both the British and the U.S. authorities encountered conflicts, but these conflicts had their origin in the structural changes that required a depreciation of sterling in real terms. In contrast, the decision to peg sterling at its prewar gold parity despite the more extensive inflation in Great Britain than in the United States meant that sterling was appreciated in real terms. The overvaluation of sterling because of monetary and structural developments may have led to a more rapid expansion of the external domain of the dollar area.

REFERENCES

Aliber, Robert Z. 1981a. "Transactions Costs in the Foreign Exchange Market." University of Chicago. Mimeographed.

_____. 1981b. "U.S. Policy Toward Foreign-Owned Dollars. University of Chicago. Mimeographed.

Ben-Bassat, Avraham. 1980. "The Optimal Composition of Foreign Exchange Reserves." *Journal of International Economics* 10: 285–95.

Heller, H. Robert, and Malcolm Knight. 1978. *Reserve-Currency Preferences of Central Banks.* Essays in International Finance No. 131. Princeton, New Jersey: International Finance Section, Princeton University.

Hicks, John. 1969. *A Theory of Economic History.* Oxford: Oxford University Press.

Jastram, Ray. 1978. *The Golden Constant.* New York: Halstead/Wiley.

Laney, Leroy U. 1978. "A Diminished Role for the Dollar as a Reserve Currency?" *The Voice* of the Federal Reserve Bank of Dallas (December): 1–23.

_____. 1979. "Currency Choice Under Uncertainty: Some New Evidence." *The Voice* of the Federal Reserve Bank of Dallas (May): 3–15.

Lindert, Peter H. 1969. *Key Currencies and Gold, 1900-1913.* Princeton Studies in International Finance No. 24. Princeton, New Jersey: International Finance Section, Princeton University.

Magee, Stephen P., and Ramesh K.S. Rao. 1980. "Vehicle and Non-Vehicle Currencies in International Trade." *American Economic Review* 70: 368–73.

Makin, John H. 1971. "The Composition of International Reserve Holdings." *American Economic Review* 61: 818–32.

McKinnon, Ronald I. 1969. *Private and Official International Money: The Case for the Dollar.* Essays in International Finance No. 74. Princeton, New Jersey: International Finance Section, Princeton University.

Triffin, Robert. 1960. *Gold and the Dollar Crisis.* New Haven: Yale University Press.

_____. 1964. *The Evolution of the International Monetary System: Historical Reappraisal and Future Perspectives.* Studies in International Finance No. 12. Princeton, New Jersey: International Finance Section, Princeton University.

10 FROM THE EUROPEAN PAYMENTS UNION TO THE EUROPEAN MONETARY SYSTEM

Guido Carli

In the period after the close of the Second World War, economic reconstruction and European political unity seemed an unrealizable dream. Since that time miraculous progress has been made toward this goal. Yet in joining this tribute to Robert Triffin, who contributed to make that dream a partial reality, it would be ingenuous not to note the fact that the main problems to be overcome in the pursuit of European unity are today the same as those that Triffin and our other colleagues involved in the creation and operation of the European Payments Union wrestled with some thirty years ago. That those thirty years have brought the economic reconstruction of Europe and the permanent return of unhindered trade and payments is testimony to the success of the system that evolved from our efforts in dealing with those problems—yet they have not been eliminated. Since one of Triffin's most important contributions to economic analysis has been in the area of regional economic and financial integration, I should like to take the opportunity of our common experience in the successful application of this concept in the European Payments Union to illustrate the similarity of the problems that we face in the creation and operation of a European Monetary System to those of thirty years ago.

It may seem strange, in present circumstances, to look back to the series of bilateral trading agreements that controlled postwar trade through quantitative and qualitative administrative restrictions and made the reestablishment of multilateral trading relationships one of the major preoccupations of those responsible for the postwar reconstruction of Europe. In practice, the reestablishment of multilateral trade in the postwar period meant the reestablishment of the multilateral discharge of debts in national currencies. The problem was thus not only

161

one of free trade, but more importantly, of full exchange convertibility. Many economists—especially, but not exclusively, in the United States—believed that economic reconstruction and the liberation of trade in Europe could be established only by free market forces and the adoption of market-determined rates of exchange. But others were cognizant of the fact that the structural factors required for the successful operation of such a system were not present in the economies that emerged from the war. The low level of gold and dollar reserves and of industrial productive capacity sharply emphasized the fact that the prerequisites of a system of free convertibility and those of free international exchange did not exist in postwar Europe. In addition, given the political instability in many countries, the social consequences of such policies were considered to be a major deterrent to their implementation.

Thus, under the transitory provisions of the Bretton Woods agreements, the European countries chose what appeared to be the opposite course to the IMF goals of an early return to free trade and currency convertibility by stipulating a series of bilateral trading agreements (examples of such agreements can be reviewed in Carli 1950b: 448–50). These agreements, which gave governmental control over imports and exports via licenses and permits of various sorts and limited the convertibility of currency to the available reserves, certainly met the criteria of those who wished to limit excessive movements in trade balances at administratively determined exchange rates. But such bilateral agreements were soon recognized as impeding the recovery of European industry by shielding national markets from external competition. They also impeded the operation of the "rules of the game," whereby conditions of equilibrium or disequilibrium in the balance of payments influenced internal conditions through changes in the creation of money (Carli 1950b: 446–47). Thus, the bilateral balancing of trade flows by administrative decree isolated domestic producers from foreign competition and eliminated one of the principal avenues by which market forces determine domestic expenditure via the automatic impact of balance of payments disequilibria on the ratio of money to goods.

Such agreements did little to satisfy the eventual implementation of the Bretton Woods system, yet they calmed the fears of those who realistically rejected an immediate return to free trade and payments. In assessing these agreements, it must be kept in mind that the trading position of postwar Europe comprised two diverse problems—first, the permanent deficit position vis-à-vis the rest of the world, in particular the dollar area; and second, an extreme imbalance in intra-European trade. In such conditions, any proposals that implied early return to complete convertibility would have produced a dollar exchange rate that would have been intolerable given the crucial role of the United States as a primary supplier of industrial output to Europe. Some external asset would have been required to settle European trade imbalances with the United States. But the "Keynes plan," which would have supplied this alternative asset, had not found acceptance at Bretton Woods.

The intra-European imbalances could have been denominated in terms of a fictitious unit of account and settled via internal multilateral clearing, leaving the national rates of exchange free to vary. But there were two problems with this alternative. First, the size of the imbalances made clearing virtually ineffective. Second, the intra-European exchange rates, in the absence of full dollar convertibility and free capital markets, would have been distorted by the different positions of the various European currencies vis-à-vis the U.S. dollar. In the absence of free convertibility between European currencies and the dollar, normal arbitrage, which equalizes cross-rates of exchange, could operate only through intra-European rates of exchange—that is, the adjustment against the dollar that would have resulted from changes in rates of exchange of individual currencies vis-à-vis the dollar would have been obtained by variations in intra-European rates. It is obvious that such variations would be much greater than those that would occur with dollar convertibility.

In the absence of free capital movements within Europe, moreover, even these intra-European exchange rate adjustments could not be fully effected. The resulting distortions in European relative prices would have produced major distortions in trade flows. It would be impossible to defend such a result as being superior to the protectionism implicit in administrative controls. In the particular context then prevailing of an undervalued dollar, there would have been a substantial increase in the deficit on dollar imports above that acceptable to each country. As I pointed out at the time, the resulting "distortions in exchange rates would lead to distortions in trade flows which instead of recreating the European money market would yield chaos (Carli 1950a: 170). There seemed little possibility of moving toward more market-oriented solutions, given the practical problems of reconstruction and the size of the trade deficits.

Robert Triffin was instrumental in breaking this deadlock. As director of the exchange control division of the International Monetary Fund, he had proposed unsuccessfully that the IMF establish formal arrangements for multilateral payments agreements within Europe. He was able to put these ideas into effect in his subsequent role as advisor to the European Cooperation Administration on intra-European payments arrangements, and he thus gave a determining impulse to the evolution of events that were already, if only hesitantly, under way.

Because of the low levels of gold and dollar reserves, most of the bilateral agreements included limited provisions for payments credits. Only imbalances beyond the available bilateral currency plus credits were to be settled in acceptable third-country currencies or gold. The fear of continued insufficiency of means of payment, coupled with the need to expand trade in items necessary for reconstruction, led many countries to propose raising the credit limits at which imbalances would have required payment in gold or dollars. These credit limits, even if only conceded on a bilateral basis, represented in aggregate a substantial addition to international liquidity not subject to any formal control. Although increasing the limits raised the volume of trade, it did not eliminate formal administrative controls over the composition of trade.

As a partial remedy to these problems, a number of European countries proposed in 1947 to take steps to increase the transferability of bilateral debts and credits in a multilateral exchange system. Such a scheme of multilateral monetary compensation was instituted by France, Italy, Belgium, Luxemburg, and the Netherlands in November 1947, with the Bank for International Settlements acting as clearing agent. It met the immediate need for means of payment by providing transferability at the end of each monthly accounting period while permitting bilateral credits to exceed the agreed bilateral limits within each period.

The system was not a success. The wide differences in the trading positions of the members, mentioned above, made the impact of multilateral settlement minimal. At the end of December 1947, the balances of the four member countries in the scheme were as shown in Table 10-1.

As the largest creditor, Belgium had most of its claims on the countries with large net debtor positions. There was little room for multilateral compensation. In the absence of convertibility, the accounts could be closed only by additional credits or by payments in gold or an acceptable third-country currency (i.e., the dollar). In the absence of any desire or capability to supply additional credits, the accounts could be closed without diminishing reserves only to the extent that the debtor countries on intra-European trade were creditors on their trade with the rest of the world (i.e., the dollar area) or vice versa. Since all countries were in deficit with the United States, there was no practical solution between the extremes of additional credits on the one hand and cutting back on the level of trade via quantitative restrictions on the other. Eventually, member countries of the European Recovery Program agreed that part of the U.S. Marshall Plan funds should be used for the purpose of balancing intra-European accounts. The failure of the monetary compensation agreements on a European level was thus salvaged by the injection of dollar funds and by Triffin, who was the cata-

Table 10-1. Balances in the Multilateral Compensation Scheme, End of 1947 (*in millions of dollars*).

	Belgium/ Luxemburg	France	Italy	Netherlands	Total
Belgium Luxemburg	–	+44.5	+1.8	+35.2	81.5
France	–44.5	–	–2.1	– 3.1	–39.3
Italy	– 1.8	+ 2.1	–	+ 1.0	1.3
Netherlands	–35.2	+ 3.1	–1.0	–	–33.1

Source: Carli (1948: 348).

lyst that converted the whole plan into what became the European Payments Union (EPU).

In effect, the EPU simply put into practice Triffin's belief that regional integration was the most efficient—perhaps the only—road to full international integration based on free multilateral exchange and full convertibility. As indicated above, this position was not widely accepted by economists, especially in the United States, and it was the United States, through the European Cooperation Administration, that was to be primarily responsible for the financing of the EPU. Indeed, in a note to the preface of his historic *Gold and the Dollar Crisis*, Triffin recalls his proposals for regional multilateralization of payments and "the strenuous objections raised at that time by most of my academic colleagues, and by many of our high officials and experts in Washington, against the formation of an 'autarkic, high-cost, soft currency area sheltering itself by discrimination from world-wide competition'" (1960:viii, n. 2). The similarity to the objections raised against single countries subject to bilateral agreements is striking.

In the absence of a coordinated European dollar policy and free capital movements, immediate European convertibility could not be advised as a viable course of action. The possible solutions to the postwar problem of European payments imbalances could then be summarized as (1) granting credits sufficient to underwrite possible imbalances; and (2) making transfers from net debtors to net creditors in currencies acceptable to the latter.

In fact, the EPU proposed a combination of the two. In answer to Triffin's detractors, it could be said that given the impossibility of promoting the growth of trade in Europe and at the same time opening the European market to the dollar area, the proposed system compromised by creating conditions of competition among the European member states while protecting them from competition from the dollar area through the preservation of quantitative controls. It was thus not as protective as the bilateral arrangements, while preserving the minimum of protection necessary given the structural weakness of the postwar economies and the absence of any semblance of a free money market.

The new intra-European payments system and the gradual elimination of restrictions that it presupposed did not resolve the problem of eliminating the trading imbalances among European countries and between them and the extra-European countries. In this respect, it was no different from the system based on restrictions to assure equilibrium on the balance of payments (cf. Carli 1950a: 174). Yet the successful operation of the EPU had greater future implications than a bilateral policy based on quantitative restrictions, implications that were relevant to the discussions concerning the full establishment of a Federation of European Communities.

Participation in the EPU implied the acceptance of an obligation on the part of the participants to equilibrate their own balance of payments without recourse, except in cases of extreme necessity, to the imposition of quantitative restrictions. The coexistence, in the same system, of countries which accept this obligation implies that they also accept responsibility for the coordination of their own economic and monetary policies in a manner which limits divergences in their internal economic performance (Carli 1951: 431).

The variations that were actually observed in the debtor and creditor positions of the member countries were a result of the fact that they "followed divergent economic and monetary policies" (ibid.). Thus, corresponding to the divergences in intra-European trade balances and the balance between Europe and the United States, there were divergences both in internal policy and in terms of each country's policy vis-à-vis the dollar.

Again, in assessing the performance of the EPU, it must be kept clearly in mind that there were well-defined limits to its action. It was never conceived to deal with dollar payments disequilibrium, and there was never any possibility that it could do so by itself. Indeed, as I expressed the problem in 1952 in relation to the proposal for a European federation: "It would be a step in the right direction if [the members] would be content to consider the European Federation as a pledge to conduct a common policy relative to the dollar and that this common policy should be put forward through the EPU" (Carli 1953: 144).

Thus, the first requisite of the European unity implied in the EPU solution and the first step in eliminating the dollar deficits was a common policy relative to the dollar administered through the EPU. The second was the need to coordinate internal economic and monetary policies in order to influence the relative payments imbalances settled within the EPU. The EPU could provide the forum, but not the wherewithal, for the solution, which required formal action to coordinate economic policies.

Thus, the European Payments Union eventually produced the results that were desired by those who had advocated a rapid return to free trade and convertibility but that in all probability could not have been achieved directly. This is not to deny that the convertibility of money constitutes the necessary basis of a system of multilateral payments, and that this is the necessary basis for the reconstruction of internationally competitive markets for goods. In the conditions then prevailing it had to be recognized that the equilibrium determined by the forces of the market would have required a reduction of the supply of goods necessary to maintain the existing standard of living such that the consequent social upheavals would have been prejudicial to the pursuit of the objective of economic integration.

In addition to its declared aims of (1) eliminating monetary incentives to bilateralism in trade and payments, (2) providing incentives for adjustment policies to check excessive payments disequilibria, and (3) providing sufficient credits to make (1) worthwhile yet not allowing (2) to be avoided, the EPU implied the acceptance of a European federation on both a political and an economic scale. Although we may be dissatisfied by the progress made since 1960, there seems no doubt that by that date all of these objectives had been fulfilled and that the EPU was to a large extent responsible for the decade of stable growth that followed.

There is no doubt, moreover, that this very success was in large part responsible for the eventual demise of the Bretton Woods system. Indeed, it is probable that Triffin's close involvement with and understanding of the EPU led to his early diagnosis of the ills that would eventually undermine the system of stable but adjustable exchange rates based on the dollar as the primary reserve asset. Nor is it surprising that he has been among those who have most strongly attempted to recreate an area of exchange rate stability within the morass that emerged from the unilateral declaration of dollar–gold inconvertibility in August of 1971.

There is no need to dwell either on the causes or the events that dissolved the Bretton Woods arrangements or on the creation and impact of the market for Eurodollars that grew up as a result and the role of the Eurobanks in the subsequent petroleum crises (cf. Carli 1978). Rather, in light of these events, I should like to outline how the EPU experience might aid in the creation of the EMS.

The EPU was instrumental in preparing the ground for the economic integration defined by the Treaty of Rome and visible in the rapid expansion of European Economic Community (EC) trade since 1958. Although the EC is by no means fully integrated in terms of flows of goods and capital, the most important barriers to competitive trade throughout the Community have been removed. From this point of view, the next step in the sequence would appear to be monetary unification. This goal has been advanced at various times in proposals for the creation of a single European monetary unit. As Triffin himself has emphasized from the beginning (Triffin 1953:207), a single European money would differ only in secondary respects from the existence of national moneys freely convertible at fixed and invariable rates. Movement toward monetary unification thus will initially require the creation of conditions that allow free convertibility at stable rates of exchange rather than the simple imposition of a single currency.

The achievements of the EPU were a primary step in the realization of these required conditions. The elimination of trade barriers, achieved with the establishment of the Community, was the second necessary step. In this succession of events, the European Monetary System simply represents the culmination of the combined achievements of the EPU and the EC. It should not be surprising that the EMS faces similar problems, although on a different level (and in different international conditions). Indeed, the experience of the process that led to the EPU indicates that the EMS is but a first step on the path to monetary integration.

In support of this contention, recall that the forerunner of the EPU, the scheme of multilateral monetary compensation, failed due to the extreme imbalance in payments and the lack of a reserve means of payment for settling accounts. The eventual creation of the successor, the EPU, was based on the use of dollar aid to fill this latter need. A similar solution is not open to the EMS, which has instead proposed the European Currency Unit (ECU) in this role. But the ECU is based on existing reserves and cannot be freely exchanged either internally or with the rest of the world. Since balance of payments positions of the member countries have been satisfactory, this restriction has had little direct effect on the operation of the system. In the same way as the EPU, however, the successful operation of the EMS faces two primary problems—the stability of internal exchange rates and the position of the EMS currencies as a group against the floating dollar. The very same weaknesses produced in the operation of the EPU by divergent policies vis-à-vis trade with the dollar area have their counterpart in the instability within the EMS caused by the divergent priorities attached by various countries to the objectives of their economic and monetary policies and by the impact of these divergent priorities on the policies they choose to follow vis-à-vis the currencies of third countries and mainly the U.S. dollar.

In the case of the EMS, the problem of "external" policy is also linked to the performance of the internal system. Judging from the experience of the EPU and accounting for the changed circumstances of the dollar, the need for a commonly agreed external policy with respect to the dollar is more than demonstrated. The problem of the reserve asset could be solved and the dollar policy problem alleviated if the ECU were allowed to become a full-fledged reserve asset that could replace the dollar in official reserves and private portfolios. Both aspects will be required before the problem of policy coordination capable of producing internal stability can be approached.[1]

Variations in internal exchange rates, independent of those caused by conflicting dollar policies, will be necessary, just as in the EPU, as long as there are substantial divergences in individual monetary policies. The increase in the divergence in national inflation rates during the first year of operation indicates that the formation of the EMS was not sufficient by itself to compel the coordination of monetary policies required for stability. The EMS is but a framework to facilitate such coordination; it cannot mandate compatible monetary policies, which still remain under national control. Yet this is the ultimate condition that will be required for meaningful monetary unification.

The early years of the EPU did not bring rapid results in terms of policy coordination, although the eventual alignment of policy was sufficient to secure success. Such alignment is the ultimate goal, not the first step, in the path to be followed. Emphasis must first be given to the problem of a coordinated dollar policy. This implies positive action to eliminate the problem, such as the creation of a European Monetary Fund with the ECU available as a reserve substitute for the dollar. These moves are complementary to any move by the IMF to go forward with the dollar substitution account (just as the EPU was complemen-

---

1. The problems discussed here are not novel. They were pointed out in reports presented by Triffin and myself at meetings of the Commission of the European Communities, 15–16 July 1969, and are summarized in Triffin (1969).

tary to the operation of the IMF). Only when these steps have been taken can serious discussion of coordinated or centralized community monetary and fiscal policy be undertaken, although individual governments must still attempt greater coordination of policies.

The path to be followed is clear. Yet it appears that some countries believe that the EMS can remain in place, as it is currently constituted, without the further evolution necessary for its success. This position, which is based primarily on a failure to agree on a common dollar policy, represents a sharp step away from the goal of European unity and simply postpones the day when the problem of internal policy coordination must be faced by member countries.

REFERENCES

Carli, Guido. 1948. "I pagamenti intraeuropei e la posizione dell'Italia." *Moneta e Credito* 1, no. 3: 346–51.

_____. 1950a. "Gli accordi per i pagamenti intereuropei e la constituzione dell'U.E.P." *Moneta e Credito* 3, no. 10: 166–74.

_____. 1950b. "L'evoluzione degli accordi internazionali di pagamenti dal 1945 al 1950." *Moneta e Credito* 3, no. 12: 445–56.

_____. 1951. "Problemi dell'U.E.P." *Moneta e Credito* 4, no. 16: 425–35.

_____. 1953. "Sistema monetario e politica monetaria dell'Europa Federata." Actes du Congrès International pour l'étude des problèmes économiques de la Fédération Européenne, Genoa, 1952. *Economia Internazionale* 6, nos. 1–2 (February–May): 137–50.

_____. 1978. "Perspectives on the Evolution of the International Monetary System." *Journal of Monetary Economics* 4: 405–14.

Triffin, Robert. 1953. "Système et politique monétaires de l'Europe Fédérée." Actes du Congrès International pour l'étude des problèmes économiques de la Fédération Européenne, Genoa, 1952. *Economia Internazionale* 6, nos. 1–2 (February–May): 207–12.

_____. 1957. *Europe and the Money Muddle.* New Haven: Yale University Press.

_____. 1960. *Gold and the Dollar Crisis.* New Haven: Yale University Press.

_____. 1969. "On the Creation of a European Reserve Fund." *Banca Nazionale del Lavoro Quarterly Review* 22, no. 91 (December): 327–46.

11 SOME HISTORICAL VICISSITUDES OF OPEN ECONOMIES IN LATIN AMERICA

Carlos F. Diaz Alejandro

Over half a century has elapsed since the Wall Street crash. If normality in the world economy is defined as a situation in which center countries engage in relatively free trade in goods and services and permit reasonable freedom of movement at least for capital, and there are widespread expectations that these circumstances will continue, then abnormality claims as large a share of this half-century as normality. Backtracking to August 1914 will not change the score by much. Alone among major regions in the periphery, Latin America had throughout these years at least nominal sovereignty and thus the potential to adopt economic policies tailored to external conditions. The area's long-run development has been pieced together to a large extent from short-run responses to shocks and stimuli arising from the world economy.[1]

This chapter will discuss how some Latin American countries fared during the 1930s and will point out new complexities in the interaction between Latin America and the world economy of the 1970s. The 1930s are widely regarded as a crucial turning point in the region's development, marked by the acceleration of import-substituting industrialization and the start of public policy committed to growth and other social objectives. The contrast between "before and after 1929" is often exaggerated, but there is little doubt that the events of the 1930s have profoundly influenced Latin American attitudes toward foreign trade and finance.

Cynthia Lee Arfken generated most of the data found in this chapter, and Virginia Casey efficiently typed it. My thanks to both and also to Paul Krugman, for remarks wise beyond his years.

1. Robert Triffin (1964) has noted that the international rules of the game enforced by core countries frequently contributed to the instability of the periphery.

From the outside, Latin American countries may all look the same, but the region, even in the late 1920s, contained a variety of open economies, some of which were less open and more industrialized than others. Indeed, the 1930s witnessed different economic responses that can be divided between those of small or passive economies and those of large or active ones.

What follows is built on the premise that optimum foreign trade and payments policy for a Latin American type of economy, whether large or small, depends on what is expected to happen in the rest of the world. Some may question this, noting the assumption of smallness. Trade theory asserts that a truly small country facing perfectly elastic demands and supplies for its exports and imports, respectively, should follow the same trade policy (e.g., free trade), regardless of what is going on in the rest of the world. Uncertainty as to the terms of trade will not change matters much unless one is willing to attribute to government insights unavailable to the private sector. International finance theory adds that a small country will (and should) have little control over exchange rate and monetary policy: Pegging to a key currency and following "gold exchange standard" monetary rules are the usual prescriptions for the small, regardless of external circumstances.

Like Walrasian auction markets, smallness in foreign trade and finance is a powerful theoretical construct that may be more insightful in some circumstances than in others. In a world of trade quotas, convertibility restrictions, or foreign tariffs that may be imposed if one's export drive is successful, it could be that not even Andorra is small. Optimum currency area theory, stimulating as it is, gives little practical guidance for drawing the line between small peggers and large flexers. It appears that smallness in foreign trade and finance is not an intrinsic and permanent characteristic of a country, but the result of specific conditions in the world economy and changing domestic circumstances.

THE 1930s: SHOCKS

For a number of exporters of primary products the late 1920s had been difficult years (Kindleberger 1973:ch 4), but on the whole it is useful to picture that period as one of reasonable balance of payments equilibrium in the major Latin American countries. A series of violent external shocks during 1929–1933 disrupted that equilibrium, and much of the economic history for the 1930s can be written around the attempts to adjust the balance of payments, and then the domestic economy, to the new environment.

The primarily exogenous shocks to the Latin American economies have been amply documented. Between 1929 and 1933, dollar export unit values fell more steeply than dollar import unit values; in the eight countries for which comparable data are available, the terms of trade fell between 21 and 45 percent (Naciones Unidas 1976). The export quantum held up better for most countries, except for the spectacular cases of Chile and Cuba.

The crisis disturbed the balance of payments also via the capital account. After 1930 gross capital inflows fell sharply. Furthermore, with the dollar price level falling unexpectedly by around one-quarter, debt repayments rose in real terms. By the mid-1930s, most countries had suspended normal debt servicing. Private portfolio capital was not to play an important role in the external accounts of Latin America until the 1960s.

During the 1920s critics of the prevailing free trade orthodoxy within Latin America pointed to signs of growing protectionism at the center. In Britain, imperial preferences were advocated by influential groups; in the United States, the 1928 presidential election was accompanied by a protectionist wave. These trends culminated with the passage of the Smoot-Hawley tariff in 1930, the British Abnormal Importations Act of 1931, and the Ottawa Commonwealth preferences of 1932. The Latin American periphery, unconsulted regarding these measures, could go hang. A North American author writing in 1935 about southern core countries in Latin America described the situation as follows:

> The trade barriers which have been erected in Europe and the United States against agricultural products and raw materials have placed these countries in the forefront of foreign trade decline. . . . Nationalistic tendencies are not dominant in these countries. National leaders fully recognize the desirability of a heavy volume of trade. . . . National self-sufficiency to a greater and greater measure was forced upon these countries by the governmental policies of the United States and European nations. (Phelps 1935: 273)

The emergence of a protectionist and nationalistic center was perhaps the greatest shock to Latin American economies during the early 1930s. The memory of this betrayal of Hume and Ricardo would last longer in the periphery than in the center.

THE 1930s: POLICIES

An ex post description of measures taken by a group of Latin American countries during the early 1930s risks attributing to "autonomous policy" a series of improvisations more or less forced by circumstances. Yet not all countries were in a position to improvise. The largest ones, such as Argentina, Brazil, Colombia, and Mexico, were at the forefront of experimentation. The smallest countries, such as Guatemala, Haiti, and the Dominican Republic, did little but wait for export-led recovery. In between there is an interesting contrast between Cuba, which was dragged down by the crisis as surely as Mississippi, and Chile and Uruguay, which in spite of their smallness broke away from the orthodoxy of the gold exchange standard and free trade.

Unfortunately, data for those years are scanty, particularly for the small or passive countries. There is enough information, however, to document several of the measures taken by the large or active countries.

By the end of 1931, the active nations were experimenting with balance of payments measures previously regarded as heterodox. As convertibility into gold was abandoned, exchange rates depreciated, particularly those applied to imports. Table 11-1 presents indexes of those exchange rates, defined as units of local currency per $1US. The rates have been deflated by each country's cost of living index or other available general index, relative to the U.S. cost of living index. (Data scarcity limits other possible estimations of the real exchange rate.) The real depreciations relative to the dollar for the countries shown range from 36 percent in Mexico to 87 percent in Chile. The depreciation trend appears to have been unaffected by whether a country was politically moving left (Mexico, Colombia) or right (Argentina, Uruguay).

As may be deduced from Table 11-2, most of the swing in the real import exchange rates arose from nominal depreciations, which had a surprisingly small effect on price levels. Nevertheless, for all countries shown, price indexes for 1935-1939 were higher relative to 1929 than that of the United States.

For the passive countries one may conjecture that there was no such real depreciation of the import exchange rates. Some of these countries (Cuba, Panama) did not even have a central bank, while others (Guatemala, Haiti) maintained their peg to the U.S. dollar throughout the crisis and on the whole remained committed to gold exchange standard rules.

Nominal exchange rate devaluations were not the only measures undertaken by the active countries to restore balance of payments equilibrium: There were also increased tariffs, import and exchange controls, and multiple exchange rates. Contrary to what would happen in the late 1940s and 1950s, exchange rate and protectionist policies reinforced each other as import-repressing mechanisms. Indeed, by the mid-1930s in many of the active countries there may have been some redundancy in this formidable battery of measures: P.T. Ellsworth (1945: 67) has argued this point in his valuable study of Chile in depression. The passive countries also appear to have been more timid regarding protection; Cuba actually lowered tariffs in 1934, undoing much of the protectionist effect of the Tariff Act of 1927.

Abandonment of convertibility stemmed the decline in money supplies that occurred even in active countries during the early stages of the crisis. By the late 1930s, money supplies in active countries exceeded 1929 levels. Table 11-3 contrasts the Cuban case, where money supply shrank by about 40 percent, with those of Argentina, Brazil, Chile, and Uruguay. Interest rates for 1935-1939 appear lower than those registered at the height of the crisis (1930-1932) and lower than those of the late 1920s. In Argentina, for example, interest rates on ninety-day time deposits were 6 percent at the end of 1929, averaged 4.3 percent during 1930-1932, and oscillated between 2 and 3 percent for the rest of the decade.

There has been some controversy as to whether, during the early 1930s, the active countries followed fiscal policies that could be characterized as "Keynesianism before Keynes." The argument has been most lively for Brazil and centers

Table 11-1. Average Real Import Exchange Rates $(1929 = 100)$.

	1925-1929	1930-1934	1935-1939
Argentina	101.5	137.2	133.2
Brazil	100.2	173.2	186.0
Chile	100.5 [a]	186.7	175.3
Colombia	98.8	145.6	158.6
Mexico	103.0	136.4	140.0
Peru	98.6 [b]	153.8	153.1
Uruguay	101.3	155.8	160.3

a. Refers only to 1928 and 1929.
b. Refers only to 1926, 1927, 1928, and 1929.
Sources and method: For definitions see text. Basic data obtained from League of Nations yearbooks and national sources.

Table 11-2. Cost of Living Indexes $(1929 = 100)$.

	1925-1929	1930-1934	1935-1939
Argentina	100.8	86.4	89.8
Brazil	96.9	74.5	94.0
Chile	99.2 [a]	112.1	155.5
Colombia	101.4	65.9	90.3
Mexico	95.7	87.1	111.4
Peru	106.6 [b]	87.9	93.3
Uruguay	98.7	96.7	98.2
United States	101.4	83.9	81.6

a. Refers only to 1928 and 1929.
b. Refers only to 1926, 1927, 1928, and 1929.
Sources and method: As in Table 11-1.

Table 11-3. Nominal Money Supply $(1929 = 100)$.

	1925-1929	1930-1934	1935-1939
Argentina	100.0 [a]	90.6	110.8
Brazil	91.9	108.8	175.0
Uruguay	90.7	103.2	130.4
Chile	97.8 [b]	109.0	213.4
Cuba	107.6	56.7	60.9

a. Refers only to 1926, 1927, 1928 and 1929.
b. Refers only to 1928 and 1929.
Sources and method: Cuban data from Wallich (1950: 38-76, 152). Chilean data from Ellsworth (1945: 171). Other data from national sources. Data refer to money supplies at the end of the year. Definitions of the stock of money vary slightly from country to country; definitions are closest to M_1.

on the magnitude of planned fiscal deficits and their financing. In his pioneering work, Celso Furtado (1963: ch. 31) argued that domestic coffee price support programs led to fiscal deficits having an expansionary effect on aggregate demand. Later research noted that much of this expenditure was financed either by new taxes or foreign loans. Nevertheless, 35 percent of coffee purchases were financed essentially by money creation.[2] Even in Brazil the authorities remained committed to the rhetoric of fiscal orthodoxy, certainly during the early 1930s. Large fiscal deficits financed by money creation occurred, but typically as a result of unusual circumstances, such as political turmoil in Chile during late 1931 and 1932, including a short-lived Socialist government; the war between Peru and Colombia over Leticia in 1932; and the Second Chaco War between Bolivia and Paraguay, also in 1932. In Brazil, the Sao Paulo rebellion in 1932 and severe drought in the northeast added to the deficits generated by the coffee purchase program. In some countries fiscal orthodoxy was buttressed by memories of massive public works and deficit financing (with foreign borrowing) during the 1920s by corrupt governments, such as the dictatorships of Leguia in Peru and Machado in Cuba.

Even if there is little evidence outside Brazil that the full employment fiscal surplus was reduced to maintain aggregate demand, in most activitist countries, public expenditures seem to have been reduced by less, or expanded more, than private expenditures. The share of government in GNP rose in all active countries during the 1930s. On the revenue side there were important changes, with the share of custom taxes falling, as may be seen in Table 11-4. Both Argentina and Brazil witnessed a remarkable expansion in noncustoms current public revenues, which by 1932 (Argentina) and 1933 (Brazil) exceeded the levels reached in 1929, at current prices.

One may conjecture that fiscal policy in active countries exerted at least a modest balanced budget multiplier type of expansionary effect on aggregate demand during the early 1930s. The authorities were certainly wise not to seek

Table 11-4.   Custom Revenues as Percentage of Total Current Revenues.

	Argentina	Brazil
1925-1929	58	51
1930-1934	44	43
1935-1939	33	42

Sources: Díaz Alejandro (1970:490); Villela and Suzegan (1977:346-49, tables 117, 118).

2. For a review of the controversy, and new interpretations, see Fishlow (1972); Cardoso (1979); and Silber (1977). Fishlow and Cardoso argue that the new taxes, or the exchange rate appreciation generated by foreign loans, improved the Brazilian terms of trade.

a balanced budget under the conditions of those years. During the second half of the decade such an effect was reinforced by a cautious increase in domestically financed deficits, a process encouraged by increasingly self-confident cheap money policies isolated from the rest of the world by exchange controls.

THE 1930s: PERFORMANCE

It has been generally recognized that several Latin American countries performed "reasonably well" during the 1930s. Those years belong to the pre-national-accounts era, so that pinning down what a reasonably good performance is remains tricky. Available calculations show GDP growth rates for the largest Latin American countries (Argentina, Brazil, Colombia, and Mexico) as well as for some small active countries (Uruguay) that exceed those for Canada and the United States. However, neither the absolute Latin American GDP growth rates for the 1930s nor their level relative to growth achieved during the 1940s are impressive. In Argentina and Colombia, GDP clearly grew faster during the 1920s than during the 1930s.

Economic performance during the 1930s for the large or active Latin American countries look better when attention is focused on manufacturing. Between 1929 and 1939 average annual manufacturing growth rates range from 3.1 percent for Argentina to an astonishing 8.8 percent for Colombia (the major source of data is Naciones Unidas 1978). In the important case of Brazil, manufacturing growth during the 1930s was significantly higher than during the 1920s. For most large or active countries, manufacturing expansion between 1933 and 1939 exceeded that between 1939 and 1945.

If there was an engine of growth in Latin America during the 1930s, that engine was import-substituting industrialization. Not surprisingly, the uneven performance by different sectors implied by such a proposition can also be found within manufacturing. Even as some manufacturing activities closely dependent on pre–1929 export-oriented prosperity were shrinking, other activities (sometimes a handfull) made dramatic advances during the 1930s. Such leading sectors typically included textiles, building materials (especially cement), petroleum refining, tires, toiletries, and food processing for the home market. Textiles appear as quantitatively the most important, often providing more than 20 percent of the net expansion of value added in manufacturing and growing at annual rates above 10 percent during the 1930s.

The industrialization drive of the 1930s appears to have been relatively labor intensive and based on small- and medium-sized firms. It has been estimated that from 1930 to 1937 total industrial employment in Sao Paulo grew at a rate of 10.9 percent per year; the output elasticity of employment was about 1 (Mendonca de Barros and Graham 1978:12). Installed capacity was squeezed; statistics show no upsurge in imports of machinery and equipment. There are indications that the import-substituting drive relied heavily on new entrepreneurs, including fresh immigrants from the troubled Europe of the 1930s. There was some direct foreign investment in import substitution (see the fascinating book by Phelps 1936), but its role seems relatively smaller than it was to be in later years.

Internationally comparable data are available for the cement industry, which can be taken as representative of the import-replacing 1930s industrial success stories (although it was more capital intensive and foreign dominated than the textile industry). Table 11-5 first presents apparent cement consumption; on the whole, it confirms the hypothesis that larger and active countries performed better than North America and the smaller and passive Latin American countries, even if the implied annual growth rate of apparent consumption is far from spectacular. What is spectacular is the evolution of the share of consumption supplied domestically (shown in the last two columns) and the implied growth rates in cement production between 1928-1929 and 1937-1938. During those nine years, cement output multiplied by more than fourteen times in Colombia, by more than six times in Brazil, and by almost four times in Argentina. By 1937-1938 the large and active Latin American countries had become practically self-sufficient in cement. Such rapid transformation, incidentally, leaves one a bit puzzled as to the barriers to greater local cement production during 1928-1929 in countries such as Brazil and Colombia, especially in contrast with the Cuban and Mexican cases. Proximity to the United States may have encouraged greater direct foreign investment in cement in the last two countries before the Great Depression.

Table 11-5. Cement: Consumption and Output.

	Apparent Cement Consumption in 1937-1938 (1928-29 = 100)	Domestic Output as a Percentage of Apparent Consumption	
		1928-1929	1937-1938
Argentina	153	37	92
Brazil	112	16	91
Chile	114	43	99
Colombia	118	6	74
Mexico	148	88	97
Peru	136	46	66
Uruguay	77	81	90
Cuba	34	93	93
Dominican Republic	74	0	0
Haiti	58	0	0
Central American Republics (six)	100	12	11
Canada	51	–	–
United States	63	–	–

Source: Basic data in physical magnitudes obtained from the European Cement Association (1974). Apparent consumption refers to cement production plus imports less exports.

To summarize, during the 1930s large and active Latin American economies showed an impressive "capacity to transform," generating new leading sectors within manufacturing. The performance of small and passive economies was poorer. By the late 1930s the large and active economies had become less open to trade. In spite of GDP growth, import volumes (with 1928-1929 = 100) by 1938-1939 had dropped to 72 in Argentina, 70 in Brazil, 87 in Colombia, 56 in Chile, and 72 in Mexico (Naciones Unidas 1976). Governments also became committed to managing the economy and promoting growth. The 1930s saw the creation of more or less autonomous public agencies to regulate agricultural markets and promote construction. Even before the outbreak of the Second World War a new self-confidence had spread among policymakers based more on the structural changes that had occurred in their economies during the 1930s than on overall GNP economic performance.

AN INTERPRETATION AND A DIGRESSION

The silver lining in a deterioration of the terms of trade for a primary producer is the incentive it gives for industrialization. The shift in relative prices induces a movement along the production possibility frontier if the country manages not to fall within it. This simple point tells only part of the 1930s story: One has to worry not only about hanging onto the production possibility frontier, but also about other sectors besides rural exportables and industrial importables—hence the emphasis given earlier both to aggregate demand and to the real import exchange rate, which may be taken as a proxy for the domestic price of importables relative to nontraded goods prices (or relative to wages). The profitability of import substitution depends not only on the domestic prices of importables and exportables, but also on nontradable goods prices.

Whether a country steadfastedly pegs to a key currency or more freely experiments with changes in its nominal exchange rate, in the long run one may expect that an exogenous deterioration in its terms of trade will lead to a changed configuration of domestic relative prices. One may hypothesize an increase in the domestic price of importables relative to nontraded goods prices. The path toward this long-run result will vary depending on the exchange regime. For example, take a country with a steady peg suffering an exogenously given drop in the price for its exportable good: Eventually this should lead to a drop in the nominal price of its nontraded good. A country with a more flexible exchange rate, faced with the same exogenous conditions, can achieve the same relative price change without having to deflate the nominal price of its nontraded good. Another hypothesis, which has guided earlier descriptive sections, is that such a dynamic process is less costly in terms of forgone output and growth than the "gold exchange standard" rules of pegging and deflating.

The relation between the real import exchange rate, taken as dependent variable, and the terms of trade, taken as exogenously given, can be tested for several Latin American countries for 1928 through 1972. The results are presented in Table 11-6. Other independent variables are included in these regressions—a time trend and a dummy of Second World War years having a value of 1 from 1939 through 1945 and a value of 0 for all other years. The time trend explores possible secular movements in the real exchange rate following changes in per capita income. Some experimentation with lagged values for the terms of trade is also included. The regressions presented are the "cleanest" ones obtained. The war dummy, for example, did not work well for Brazil, Chile, and Colombia, so it was dropped from the regressions of Table 11-6 for those countries.[3] Adjustment was necessary for serial correlation, as indicated at the bottom of the table.

The t-statistics, appearing in parentheses under each coefficient, on the whole confirm a negative relationship between the real import exchange rate and the terms of trade. The results are clearest for the two coffee countries, Brazil and Colombia: Indeed, for these two nations the coefficients for terms of trade are remarkably similar. Colombia is the only country approaching a significant long-term upward trend in its real exchange rate. The residuals for these regressions show that for the five countries, actual exchange rate values exceeded the fitted ones during 1930-1934. For 1935-1939 the fit is closer, and the residuals are negative for two countries.

Table 11-6. Regressions with the Logarithm of the Real Import Exchange Rate as Dependent Variable (*1928 through 1972*).

	Argentina	Brazil	Chile	Colombia	Mexico
Constant term	0.01	19.38	9.90	−17.39	1.16
	(0.00)	(1.63)	(0.36)	(0.97)	(0.11)
Time trend	0.0037	−0.0059	−0.0016	0.0129	0.0026
	(0.82)	(0.97)	(0.12)	(1.42)	(0.45)
Logarithm of terms of trade (same year)	0.12	−0.27	−0.23	−0.27	0.07
	(0.52)	(1.80)	(1.04)	(2.14)	(0.57)
Logarithm of lagged terms of trade (average of previous two years)	−0.66	−0.38	−0.20	−0.32	−0.36
	(2.16)	(2.14)	(0.63)	(1.40)	(2.02)
Dummy for Second World War	0.27	−	−	−	0.17
	(2.26)				(1.86)
Estimate of serial correlation	0.6	0.8	0.9	0.9	0.8
R^2	0.77	0.86	0.63	0.81	0.86
F-statistic (43 observations)	32.4	81.2	22.0	56.0	59.1
Durbin-Watson statistic	1.8	1.9	1.8	1.7	1.8

Note: t-statistics are given in parentheses.

3. Data sources are Naciones Unidas (1976), League of Nations yearbooks and national sources. Further experimentation with the specifications for the Argentine case are carried out in Diaz Alejandro (1980).

These results tend to confirm the expected link between changes in external terms of trade and domestic relative prices, including prices for nontraded goods; for the countries and period shown, that link appears to have worked reasonably fast. However, lack of evidence for countries that throughout maintained fixed exchange rates does not allow us to show that for them the link was more tenuous or implied longer lags.

SOME ISSUES OF THE 1970s

Policy stories about the 1940s, 1950s, and 1960s in Latin America are relatively abundant. Here it will be enough to note that most large and active countries saw their real exchange rates decline during the 1940s and 1950s from the levels reached in the 1930s. The protectionist system in those countries became stricter. Then, in fits and starts, a new trend began in the 1960s toward less protection and a greater reliance on exchange rate policy as an instrument to repress imports and encourage nontraditional exports. A prosperous and liberalizing world economy encouraged this process, with a lag. After the 1930s, small and passive countries on the whole experienced three decades of recovery and export-led expansion.

One characteristic of policymaking during the troubled second half of the 1970s in some South American countries is worth noting. Argentina, Brazil, Chile, and Uruguay, for example, in recent years have coupled more liberal trade and exchange rate policies (relative, that is, to those of the 1930s, 1940s, and 1950s) with some liberalization of domestic financial markets. Complete liberalization, of course, has not been achieved, but enough has been done to generate fresh dilemmas. Even as the world economy has turned more protectionist in trade matters in the 1970s, international capital markets have achieved a degree of mobility and liquidity not seen since at least the 1920s. For capital-importing countries this should be on balance a positive trend, but it complicates the management of liberalizing domestic policies.

The major dilemma can be stated as follows. The object of the trade liberalization reforms was to achieve a more depreciated and stable real exchange rate, so that there would be less need for protection, and to encourage nontraditional exports. The liberalization of domestic financial markets tends to increase real returns on domestic assets. After many years of rigid exchange controls that were more successful in keeping liquid capital out than in keeping it in, liberalization induces wealth owners to increase their holdings of domestic financial assets. While the portfolio adjustment is taking place, the real exchange rate will appreciate relative to what it would have been without financial liberalization. Eventually, the adjustment will be completed, and the larger debt will have to be serviced, so that the real exchange rate, to the delight of exporters, will have to depreciate relative to the days of the capital inflow. In a growing world, of course, some gross inflows will persist, but pressures on the exchange rate will be similar.

In practice, the transition is proving to be far from smooth. Many imperfections remain: Some segments of the domestic capital market are still controlled or subject to different reserve requirements, leading to large spreads in domestic interest rates. The exchange rate is not perfectly flexible, so that changes in official reserves reflect a good share of capital inflows, with implications for the domestic money supply that are difficult to sterilize. The link between domestic and foreign financial markets is partly obstructed with controls.

Under these circumstances, troublesome short-run dynamic processes can occur, as in the recent Argentine experience.[4] Domestic interest rates adjusted for expected exchange rate devaluation substantially exceed foreign interest rates. Authorities preannounce the pace of devaluation, hoping to lower inflation. Massive capital inflows take place, validating the slowdown in the pace of exchange rate devaluation by increasing central bank reserves. The increase in reserves, however, tends to increase the money supply. This expansion in the money supply puts pressure on domestic prices of nontradable goods; whether because of this effect, or because of uncertainty, or because of some form of downward rigidity, domestic interest rates react sluggishly to the capital inflow. The slowdown in the pace of exchange rate devaluation further increases the attractiveness of domestic financial assets, leading to a greater capital inflow. Exporters find these short-run dynamics singularly perverse and will clamor for faster exchange rate devaluation. Authorities will point to bulging reserves as evidence that faster devaluation is unnecessary. Financial liberalization during this period will work at cross-purposes with export promotion. If at the same time the authorities are dismantling import-repressing mechanisms, the import-competing sector will be doubly damaged.

One possible reaction to this situation would be to press for the elimination of remaining imperfections in domestic financial markets, to increase the flexibility of the exchange rate, and to eliminate all controls over exchange and capital transactions between domestic and foreign residents. It is worth noticing, however, that even robust industrialized economies (perhaps with the exception of Canada, the Federal Republic of Germany, and the United States) have not dared to follow this prescription all the way. And the trend may be going the other way:

> Specifically, the mobility of financial capital limits viable differences among national interest rates and thus severely restricts the ability of central banks and governments to pursue monetary and fiscal policies appropriate to their internal economies. ... I therefore regretfully recommend ... to throw some sand in the wheels of our excessively efficient international money markets. (Tobin 1978:154).

4. The recent Argentine experience and similar ones elsewhere have generated a large number of working papers from Argentine and non-Argentine authors. Among the former are Guillermo Calvo, Ana Maria Martirena-Mantel, and Carlos Alfredo Rodriguez. The latter include Rudiger Dornbusch and Paul Krugman.

Semiindustrialized economies lacking sophisticated policy instruments may be unable to do without their clumsy "sand machine"—for example, controls or restrictions over international capital and exchange transactions—for a long time.

REFERENCES

Cardoso, Eliana A. 1979. "Inflation Growth and the Real Exchange Rate: Essays on Economic History in Brazil." Ph.D. thesis, MIT, February.

Diaz Alejandro, Carlos F. 1970. *Essays on the Economic History of the Argentine Republic.* New Haven: Yale University Press.

_____. 1980. "Exchange Rates and Terms of Trade in the Argentine Republic 1913-1976." Yale Economic Growth Center Discussion Paper No. 341.

Ellsworth, P.T. 1945. *Chile: An Economy in Transition.* New York: The Macmillan Company.

European Cement Association. 1974. *World Cement Market in Figures.* Paris.

Fishlow, Albert. 1972. "Origins and Consequences of Import Substitution in Brazil." In Luis de Marco, ed., *International Economics and Development,* pp. 311-65. New York: Academic Press.

Furtado, Celso. 1963. *The Economic Growth of Brazil: A Survey from Colonial to Modern Times.* Berkeley: University of California Press.

Kindleberger, Charles P. 1973. *The World in Depression 1929-1939.* Berkeley: University of California Press.

Mendonca da Barros, Jose Roberto, and Douglas H. Graham. 1978. "The Economic Recovery and Market Deconcentration of the Paulista Textile Industry During the Great Depression: 1928-1937." March. Processed.

Naciones Unidas. 1976. *America Latina: Relacion de Precios del Intercambio.* Santiago de Chile: Cuadernos de la CEPAL.

_____. 1978. *Series Historicas del Crecimineto de America Latina.* Santiago de Chile: Cuadernos de la CEPAL.

Phelps, Dudley Maynard. 1935. "Industrial Expansion in Temperate South America." *American Economic Review* 25:273.

_____. 1936. *Migration of Industry to South America.* New York: McGraw-Hill Book Company.

Silber, S. 1977. "Analise da politica economica e do comportamento da economia Brasileira durante o periodo 1929-39." In F.R. Versiani and J.R.M. de Barros, *Formacão Económica do Brasil; A Experiencia da Industrializacão,* pp. 173-208. Sao Paulo: Sarawa S.A.

Tobin, James. 1978. "A Proposal for International Monetary Reform." *Eastern Economic Journal* 4, Nos. 3-4 (July-October).

Triffin, Robert. 1964. "The Myth and Realities of the So-called Gold Standard." In *The Evolution of the International Monetary System: Historical Reappraisal and Future Perspectives,* pp. 2-20. Princeton Studies in International Finance No. 12, Princeton, New Jersey: International Finance Section, Princeton University.

Villela, Annibal V., and Wilson Suzigan. 1977. *Government Policy and the Economic Growth of Brazil, 1889-1945.* Brazilian Economic Studies No. 3. Rio de Janeiro: IPEA.

Wallich, Henry C. 1950. *Monetary Problems of an Export Economy: The Cuban Experience 1914-1947.* Cambridge, Massachusetts: Harvard University Press.

12 GOLD AND THE DOLLAR CRISIS
Twenty Years Later
Herbert G. Grubel

Robert Triffin's best-known book, *Gold and the Dollar Crisis*, was published with perfect timing. It came off the press in 1960 just when the dollar came under heavy selling pressure for the first time since the 1930s. In his book Triffin not only predicted the coming of this event that seemed impossible for the general public, politicians, and most economists, he also diagnosed its fundamental causes in a broad theoretical and historical context and presented a blueprint for solving the basic problem. The blueprint was in the tradition of the period, when economists were beginning to build empires in Washington and elsewhere, driven by their euphoric conviction that all economic problems could be solved by the creation of new institutions and their operation according to obvious humanitarian principles and in a spirit of international cooperation. In this setting, Triffin's proposal for the creation of a genuine world central bank for the countercyclical creation of liquidity and the capturing of seigniorage for the benefit of the entire world caught the imagination of many intellectuals and visionaries. His rejection of market solutions to the problem in the form of flexible exchange rates and increases in the price of gold fitted the mood of the time and was considered to be fundamentally correct.

In this chapter, I will try to assess the intellectual and practical impact of the ideas for world monetary reform that Triffin presented in his book twenty years ago. I examine in part one Triffin's views on monetary gold, in part two his pro-

I would like to express my gratefulness to Robert Triffin, who supervised my dissertation at Yale University, awakened my interest in political economy, and gave me great moral support during a difficult period. S. Easton, P.B. Kenen and J.B. de Macedo made valuable comments on the first draft of this paper.

posal for the creation of fiat reserves to take the place of dollars, and in part three his analysis of the liquidity position of the United States and global reserve adequacy. The last part contains a summary and some conclusions.

THE ROLE OF MONETARY GOLD

Triffin's proposal for the reform of the international monetary system envisaged an evolutionary role for gold that was strongly influenced by his historical perspective on the development of modern national central banks. Thus, as he showed in chapter one of *Gold and the Dollar Crisis*, central banks of the modern industrial states initially issued fiduciary money in the belief that the value and acceptability of the money depended on its convertibility into gold at a rate of exchange specified in terms of weight of gold per unit of currency. In parallel with this step in the history of national monetary systems, he proposed that the international liquidity issued by a reformed IMF be convertible into gold at fixed exchange rates. Triffin believed that even at this early stage of evolution of the international monetary system, the reform would bring important welfare benefits to the world economy, just as had happened within national economies. These benefits would accrue through assured and planned growth in liquidity, independent of the haphazard discovery of gold deposits or technologies for mining them. There would also be potentially large savings in real resources as the world would obtain liquidity at a much lower cost of production.

The next step in the evolution of national monetary systems sketched by Triffin saw the public accepting fiduciary issues without frequent convertibility into gold, while monetary theory developed models explaining that fiduciary money could perform its function readily without gold convertibility, as long as certain conditions were met. One of these was public confidence in and familiarity with the operation of the money-issuing institution. These developments and ideas paved the way for the suspension of gold convertibility of fiduciary money in all modern industrial countries during the First World War or the Great Depression of the 1930s. Most countries simultaneously ceased defining the value of money in terms of gold weight and removed legal requirements for the backing of the fiduciary money by the central bank's holding of gold, though the United States did not take these last two steps of national gold demonetization until the late 1960s.

While Triffin described the history of national monetary systems with obvious satisfaction about the rationality of man in creating institutions that were increasingly more efficient and under the control of capable and well-meaning bureaucrats and politicians, his plans for reform of the international monetary system did not spell out any steps for the international demonetization of gold. I believe that this was due to his highly developed sense of political feasibility. He also seemed very strongly influenced by personal experiences in international institutions, which convinced him that through actually working together, people gained confidence in each other and in the government agencies employing them, so that ultimately they would be willing to remove more and more of the institutional constraints on policymaking, such as gold convertibility and values. Moreover, it was clear that as long as the reformed IMF created reserves in adequate quantities and through collective agreements, there was little danger of instability created by the convertibility, and the world would enjoy the major benefits of having reserves grow in correctly planned quantities at low social cost.

Triffin's views on the role of gold in the longer run are reflected in his opposition to increases in the price of gold (1960:18) in the face of the prediction that there would be inadequate supplies of gold to meet the world's liquidity needs under the dollar-gold exchange standard (pp. 50-52) as well as in the following quote: "Nobody could ever have conceived of a more absurd waste of human resources than to dig gold in distant corners of the earth for the sole purpose of transporting it and reburying it immediately afterward in other deep holes, especially excavated to receive it and heavily guarded to protect it" (p. 89).

Response of Economists

There was a mixed response by economists to Triffin's proposals for reform of the international monetary system, which would initially retain gold convertibility at fixed exchange rates. At one extreme were Angell (1963) and Yeager (1963),[1] who preferred a system planned from the outset to have no role for gold at all. Their theoretical arguments and empirical judgments reflected modern monetary theory and history, which showed that gold convertibility was neither a necessary nor a sufficient condition for efficient and stable national monetary systems. Machlup (1963:260) argued that "The golden Calf is now a full-grown sacred cow, and perhaps the time to slaughter it is not far off." To achieve this goal, he urged, perhaps with tongue in cheek, that the U.S. government discourage speculators and express its disdain of monetary gold symbolically by lowering the official price at which the U.S. Treasury would buy gold from the public and exchange it for dollars held by foreign monetary authorities. Several economists and bankers interested in shoring up the dollar-gold exchange standard, such as Rockefeller (1963), Bernstein (1963), Jacobsson (1963), Roosa (1963), and Wallich (1963), rejected proposals for the creation of fiat reserves and any changes that would cast doubt on the permanence of the existing system. Thus, they also rejected proposals for an increase in the price and changes in the role of gold.

At the other extreme of the range of opinions were Harrod (1963), who believed that the IMF gold exchange standard would benefit from gold price

1. Most of the papers analyzing the Triffin plan were reprinted in Grubel (1963). The references in this paragraph and the next are to this source rather than to their original publication.

increases, and Rueff (1963) and Heilperin (1963), who recommended a restoration of the gold standard. These last two economists rejected the collective solution proposed by Triffin partly on the basis of principle and partly on the basis of their interpretation of history, where they had seen little evidence that bureaucrats and politicians could be trusted to operate economic institutions efficiently without such restraints on their ability to create money as are provided by a pure gold standard.

Since these early contributions to the debate over the reform of the international monetary system and the role of gold in it that was sparked by Triffin's work, there has been relatively little academic interest in the subject. The economic turbulence of the 1970s that raised free market prices of gold to a peak near $1,000, the payments imbalances created by OPEC petroleum price increases, the rapid inflation and slow growth in Western economies, and the failure of negotiations for reform of the international monetary system seem to have created an atmosphere of crisis and caused a reordering of priorities in the concerns of economists. The creation of a new "system" does not seem feasible in practice until at least the seemingly extraordinary disturbances of the decade are brought under control. More fundamentally perhaps, in the light of the fact that the economic problems developed when most national economies were managed by people without significant institutional restraints and there were in place many institutions for international cooperation, there has evolved an intellectual atmosphere favoring more nationalistic and market-oriented solutions. Symbolic of this new mood are the proposals for increased reliance on the discipline created by a link of fiduciary money to gold (Niehans 1976) or even for the restoration of the gold standard (Laffer 1979).

Governmental Attitudes and Actions

Phase One. Governmental attitudes and actions concerning the role of gold in the international monetary system can conveniently be considered to consist of three phases. The first lasted until 1968 and was characterized by official attempts to maintain and strengthen the gold exchange standard. There were more or less formal agreements by major governments to hold dollars and strictly limit their exchange into gold by the U.S. Treasury. The private gold market in London was supplied by sales from South Africa and a pool created by several central banks. These supplies kept the market price of gold in London very close to the official one of $35 an ounce until 1968, when in the aftermath of a speculative attack on sterling and an expansion of the Vietnam War, and in spite of a sale of $3 billion of gold by the pool (Solomon 1977: 119), the price of the metal rose to $42. At this point a symbolically important agreement was reached establishing a two-tier market for gold. On one tier the central banks of the major Western countries (except France) consented to exchange gold among themselves at the price of $35 an ounce, while they agreed to stop buying from or selling to the private market. The second tier consisted of the free market for gold, where industrial and speculative demand for the metal was to be met by new production and sales from hoards by governments not participating in the agreement.

The establishment of the two-tier market was in some ways equivalent to the domestic policy of stopping convertibility of national currencies into gold. Therefore, the period up to 1968 represents an era when official policies were aimed at removing gold from its central position in the dollar-gold exchange standard system in fact at a rate more rapid than Triffin had envisaged. The policies were the outcome of an alliance of two forces serving their own ends. First, there was the U.S. financial community backed by the U.S. Treasury, which wanted a strengthening of the dollar-gold exchange standard through a modification of the gold exchange provision; and second, there were the technocrats at the IMF, intellectuals and economists who wanted a replacement of the market by collective institutions and who saw the removal of gold from its role in international liquidity and as a standard of value as a rational step in this direction. The relative stability and rapid economic growth of the period kept in check the private market forces, as well as the intellectuals and economists who distrusted collective solutions.

Phase Two. The second phase in the postwar history of gold in the international monetary system occurred during the period from 1968 to about 1979, when there was continued success by the forces moving toward official demonetization and collective solutions, while increasing strength was gained by the forces wanting a return to market solutions and a strengthened role for gold. The successes of the movement toward demonetization of gold came in the form of official policies that were designed to signal to private markets the determination of the U.S. government and of the community of nations acting through the IMF that gold was to lose completely its traditional role in the world's monetary affairs. In this spirit, the U.S. Treasury in 1971 suspended the conversion of dollars into gold held even by foreign monetary authorities. The U.S. Treasury and the IMF held regular gold auctions for private buyers. The crowning and ultimate success of this movement came in the so-called 1976 Jamaica Accords, which resulted in the second amendment to the IMF Articles of Agreement, under which the official price of gold and several provisions for its convertibility at the IMF were abandoned.

During this period the policies for the demonetization of gold were supplemented by the so-called 1968 Rio Agreements, which permitted the IMF to create SDRs. These assets in principle are just like fiduciary money issued by national central banks, and therefore they are capable of substituting for gold as reserves for countries. The Rio Agreements represent a major milestone in the evolution of the collective approach to international monetary problems. The supply of SDRs was increased in 1979-1981. This development suggested that regular growth of fiat reserves may take place to meet the growing world demand for reserves, in the spirit of the collective solution proposed by Triffin.

However, during the period 1968–1979, there have also been developments indicating greater strength of the forces away from collective to more market-oriented solutions. The increases in the official price of gold to $35 an ounce under the 1971 Smithsonian Agreements and two years later to $42.50 an ounce show that among the Western governments there was no unity about the planned future for gold, even after the Rio milestone. But most important during this period was the development of the price of gold in private markets. As can be seen from Figure 12-1, the price of the metal had risen gradually from 1969 through 1974, then fell moderately until 1976, when it rose at an accelerating rate through 1980.

This rise in London gold prices during the 1970s took place in spite of the U.S. and IMF official gold sales and in spite of all the IMF policies noted above that indicated international agreement in favor of collective and away from market solutions to the supply of international liquidity. The gold price increases appear to reflect a general, broadly based dissatisfaction with and distrust of collective solutions to national and international problems that was encouraged by certain intellectuals and economists. During the period they exposed the necessary shortcomings of these solutions and pointed to the inflation, unemployment, energy crisis, and slow growth of the 1970s as evidence in support of their theoretical arguments. In several major Western countries, the public

Figure 12-1. London Gold Prices.

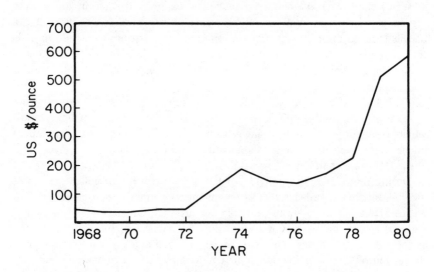

Note: Prices are end of year.
Source: International Financial Statistics, 1980 yearbook and February 1981.

elected national governments more committed to market solutions and increased nationalism.

Phase Three. As a result of these intellectual and political developments around the turn of the decade, the world appears to have entered a third phase in the evolution of the role of gold in the international monetary system. This phase is characterized by an official return to gold as a standard of value and source of liquidity. Thus, in 1980 the U.S. government and the IMF ceased the auctioning of monetary gold in their portfolios. Most countries began to value their gold reserves in terms of the market price of the metal and counted them officially together with holdings of dollars and SDRs. Even the IMF has begun to publish statistics of world reserves with gold valued at market prices. Importantly, the European Monetary System, created in 1979 as a collective institution serving the needs of the region, has given gold new status by requiring that member countries exchange 25 percent of their dollar and gold holdings for European Currency Units, which can be used like SDRs as liquid reserves within the system.

In sum, Triffin's 1960 proposals for the reform of the IMF into an institution capable of issuing fiduciary reserves were made in the spirit of the time, when collective solutions to national and international problems were sought with great hope and expectations for the betterment of human welfare. In this spirit, and helped by a coincidence of aims by those wanting to rescue the dollar–gold exchange standard and the proponents of a reformed IMF, the demonetization of gold proceeded at a pace more rapid than Triffin had envisaged, leading to the two-tier market, the cessation of dollar convertibility, the auctioning of gold holdings from monetary reserves, and the abandonment of gold valuation and convertibility by the IMF. However, simultaneously public opinion became skeptical of, if not hostile to, the increasing reliance on collective solutions for national and international economic problems. This trend was reflected in rapidly rising gold prices in private markets, the election of more conservative governments, and the resultant emergence of increased nationalism and market-oriented solutions, including the restoration of gold valued at market prices in reserve portfolios and in the European Monetary System.

FIAT RESERVES IN PLACE OF DOLLARS

One of the central objectives of Triffin's plan for reform of the IMF and the creation of fiat reserves was to stop the use of dollars as reserves. He had several reasons for suggesting this change. First, it would end the inevitable dilemma of the gold exchange standard, which depended on U.S. payments deficits to generate reserves for other countries, while these deficits necessarily caused a rise in the ratio of U.S. liabilities to gold. This deterioration in the U.S. net liquidity position, Triffin predicted, would cause periodic instabilities in foreign exchange markets of the kind observed in 1960. Importantly, gold production was not sufficient for the United States to maintain the gold-to-liabilities ratio. The inadequacy of new gold supplies for the United States was itself the inevitable consequence of the operation of the system, because in order to maintain public confidence in the value of the dollar, the gold price could not be raised. But at the fixed price through time, the growth in industrial demand for gold and in the costs of producing it would result in reductions in the supply of monetary gold (Triffin 1960:9-10).

Second, because the creation of world liquidity required U.S. deficits, the supply tended to be erratic and unpredictable (p. 67). Third, the overhang of dollars impinged on the freedom of U.S. policymakers to use monetary and fiscal policy in the pursuit of domestic objectives (p. 12). Fourth, the issue of short-term dollars to the rest of the world had as its counterpart the inflow of real resources or long-term assets that increased the real income and wealth position of the United States. Triffin considered this system to be inequitable.

In Triffin's view, the solution to the problems inherent in the dollar–gold exchange standard was the reform of the IMF in a manner that would enable it to create fiat reserves whose properties would dominate those of dollars in the portfolios of central banks. These reserves could be created to meet world liquidity demands in an orderly and planned manner, with the social savings implicit in the substitution of fiat money for gold accruing to the community of nations rather than to any large country or countries whose national currencies served as reserves.

Response of Economists and Bankers

Several economists analyzed more rigorously some of the arguments made by Triffin. Thus, Kenen (1960) formalized the dilemma of the gold exchange standard. Grubel (1964, 1969) and Johnson (1969) discussed the nature and magnitude of the gains, which came to be known as seigniorage, accruing to countries and institutions issuing liquidity and how this seigniorage can be distributed efficiently and equitably. Cohen (1971) demonstrated empirically that the net seigniorage gains to the United States and Britain during the postwar years were small and possibly zero. Others, such as Stamp (1963) and Fried (1969), as well as UNCTAD (1969), urged that the seigniorage be made available for the finance of world collective goods.

A number of bankers and economists in influential positions and with access to the inner councils of the U.S. Treasury, such as Rockefeller (1963), Roosa (1963), and Wallich (1963), refused to accept Triffin's diagnosis of a fundamental flaw in the gold exchange standard and suggested instead marginal changes in institutions and practices to shore up the system. In this recommendation they were supported by the Governor of the Bank of Greece (see Zolotas 1963). There is little doubt that the U.S. writers were influenced by concerns over the loss of business and prestige that the U.S. banking community expected to suffer if the U.S. dollar ceased to serve as an international reserve asset and was ultimately replaced by a collectively created fiat money in private international transactions. However, they may also have been motivated by a genuine belief that the market solution to liquidity creation implicit in the dollar-gold exchange standard was in the long-run interest of the world and superior to the Triffin approach, which placed too much power in the hands of politicians and international bureaucrats.

Opposition to Triffin's idea for the creation of fiat money by the IMF also came from Bernstein (1963) and Jacobsson (1963), who as a leading member of the IMF's technical staff and as managing director, respectively, had been involved intimately in the evolution of the institution and envisaged its further growth through the expansion of credit facilities rather than the creation of fiat money.

During the period 1963-1964, a group of distinguished economists from many countries (known as the Bellagio Group after the place of two of their meetings) deliberated the problems of the international monetary system and suggested how it could be improved. In their report (Machlup and Malkiel, eds., 1964), they attained consensus about the desirability of the centralized creation of international reserves, together with the introduction of increased exchange rate flexibility. Triffin's basic idea on the central creation of reserves thus had found strong support from a group of intellectuals, who gained significant influence on policymakers through persistent lobbying in several meetings that brought together senior officials and academics during the 1960s.

The analysis of the current operation and future of the international monetary system that was stimulated by Triffin's 1960 book did much to sort out the issues in a relatively short time. Most of the tough issues were political and ultimately came down to the central debate noted above—whether collective solutions were in the long run superior to market solutions. In the spirit of the times, most economists and intellectuals were very sympathetic toward Triffin's ideas.

Actual Developments

Table 12-1 shows the composition and growth of international reserves and lends itself well to an analysis of actual developments in the international monetary system since 1960. First the official holdings of foreign exchange, mostly dollars, which Triffin had argued should be reduced, grew from $17.6 billion in 1960 to $368.6 billion in 1980. The relative importance of these foreign exchange holdings in total reserves rose gradually, from 29.7 percent in 1960 to a high of 52.9 percent in 1972, and remained roughly constant until in 1980 it fell back to 33.1 percent, about where it was when Triffin argued that the growth in dollar reserves should be curtailed.

Balance of payments theory suggests that a country's holdings of dollars is a matter of choice insofar as any country faced by an excess supply of dollars in its foreign exchange market can simply cease purchasing them and let its exchange rate appreciate. According to this model, the observed growth in dollar

Table 12-1.   International Reserves (*in billions of dollars*).

End of Year	Gold at Market Prices	Foreign Exchange	IMF Positions	SDR	Total Value
1960	38.0	17.6	3.6		59.2
1962	39.3	19.9	3.9		63.1
1964	40.8	23.7	5.4		69.9
1966	40.9	24.6	6.2		71.7
1968	38.9	32.0	6.8		77.4
1970	37.2	44.8	7.7	3.1	92.8
1972	76.4	104.1	6.8	9.4	196.8
1974	219.7	154.9	10.8	10.9	396.2
1976	157.2	186.2	20.6	9.3	374.1
1978	259.9	288.0	19.3	10.6	577.8
1980	704.0	368.6	21.5	21.0	1,115.1

	Percentages of Total Value				Rate of Growth of Total
1960	64.2	29.7	6.1		
1962	62.3	31.5	6.2		6.5
1964	58.4	33.9	7.7		10.7
1966	57.0	34.3	8.6		2.5
1968	50.2	41.3	8.8		7.9
1970	40.1	48.3	8.3	3.3	19.9
1972	38.8	52.9	3.5	4.8	112.1
1974	55.5	39.1	2.7	2.7	101.3
1976	42.0	49.8	5.5	2.5	-5.6
1978	45.0	49.8	3.3	1.8	54.4
1980	63.2	33.1	1.9	1.8	93.0

Source: *International Financial Statistics*, 1980 Yearbook and December 1980.

reserves reflects a genuine demand for reserves by the countries of the world that could not be met from sources other than dollars. Triffin's arguments about the demerits of the dollar-gold exchange standard and especially the decrease in the U.S. liquidity ratio appear to have been convincing to economists, but did not prevent countries from satisfying their need for liquidity through access to the market. In this context it is ironic that the biggest increases in dollar holdings took place during the 1970s, when the United States had stopped the gold convertibility, the ratio of U.S. gold holdings to liabilities had become irrelevant, and institutional changes had permitted countries legally to let their exchange rates adjust freely to excess demand or supply in foreign exchange markets.

Second, Table 12-1 shows that gold reserves grew from $38 billion in 1960 to $704 billion at the end of 1980. The percentage of the total, like that of foreign exchange, was virtually unchanged at around 64 percent at the beginning and the end of the period. However, in developments exactly opposite to those for exchange reserves, gold decreased in relative importance until the share hit a low of 38.8 percent in 1972. Thereafter, the higher market prices of gold raised the percentage again. These data suggest that in clear contrast with Triffin's ideas and those of many other economists and intellectuals, gold did not play a role of decreasing importance in the international monetary system. Instead, over the full period, market forces returned it to the position of importance it had before the articulation of the ideas for its demonetization.

The reason for this state of affairs follows from the third outstanding feature of Table 12-1—namely, that the absolute quantity of resources provided by the IMF as substitutes for gold and dollar reserves remained a very small proportion of total reserves throughout the period. IMF positions, which are mostly borrowing facilities with some degrees of conditionality attached to them, grew rapidly in absolute size from $3.6 billion in 1960 to $21.5 billion at their peak in 1980. The fiduciary reserves issued by the IMF that in principle can be used without restrictions and therefore are almost perfect substitutes for dollars and gold also grew rapidly from $3.1 billion in 1970 to $21.0 billion in 1980. However, as the bottom half of Table 12-1 shows clearly, combined IMF resources constituted 11.6 percent of total reserves as a maximum in 1970 and have fallen ever since.

In light of the above facts, Triffin's proposal that fiduciary reserves created at a planned, steady, and adequate rate replace dollars and gold obviously has failed, in spite of the fact that the IMF had been put in the position in principle to carry out such a plan through the ability to create SDRs. What went wrong? The answer to this question is found in the analysis presented above in connection with the history of monetary gold. Just when the institutional conditions for collective international solutions had been put into place, the world became disenchanted with and began to distrust the collective approach. Instead, a search for market solutions to economic and social problems has begun. The creation of international reserves through increases in the price of gold and holding of dollars along with a decreased importance for IMF-supplied reserves are expressions of this new trend.

RESERVE ADEQUACY AND BANKER'S POSITION

In his 1960 book, Triffin presented a large set of ratios of reserves to trade of individual countries and groups of countries to indicate trends in the adequacy of reserve supplies, suggesting that the continuation of the trends of preceding years would lead to shortages and force countries into the imposition of balance of payments restrictions or greater exchange rate flexibility. While there are many well-known shortcomings to the use of ratios of reserves to trade as a measure of reserve adequacy (see IMF 1970; Grubel 1971), it is nevertheless interesting to study the development of the global ratio before and after 1960.

Table 12-2 shows in the last column the ratio of the sum of reserves held by all market economies over the sum of these countries' exports plus imports, all valued in U.S. dollars at current exchange rates and market prices for gold. As can be seen, the ratio fell from 0.41 in 1950 to 0.25 in 1960. This is the trend

Table 12-2. World Trade and Reserves (*in billions of dollars*).

Year	Exports plus Imports	Reserves	Reserves-Trade Ratio
1950	117	48	0.41
1952	156	49	0.31
1954	158	53	0.34
1956	194	55	0.28
1958	198	58	0.29
1960	236	60	0.25
1962	259	63	0.24
1964	315	70	0.22
1966	387	72	0.19
1968	440	77	0.18
1970	579	93	0.16
1972	766	197	0.26
1974	1,559	396	0.25
1976	1,831	374	0.20
1978	2,417	578	0.24
1979	3,053	632	0.20

Source: International Financial Statistics, 1980 Yearbook.

that had alarmed Triffin and that prompted him to predict a reserve shortage and suggest the reform of the IMF to prevent it. The data show that Triffin was justified in projecting the continuation of the trend, which occurred because the creation of reserves remained haphazard. By 1970 the ratio had fallen to its lowest level of 0.16. Thereafter, the market solutions to reserve supplies noted above gained strength, and the ratio rose back to the levels of about 0.20-0.25 that it had reached around 1960.

However, while this recovery of the reserve adequacy index in recent years is remarkable, some differences in basic conditions affecting the economic interpretation of this index should be mentioned, though lack of space prohibits detailed analysis. On the one hand, the distribution of reserve holdings in 1979 was more skewed than it was in 1960, since some of the OPEC countries had become disproportionately large holders of liquid assets, suggesting that the simple ratio overstates global reserve adequacy. On the other hand, the increased availability of Eurocurrency credits and the greater flexibility of exchange rates suggests that the world might have been able to get along with a lower reserves-to-trade ratio in 1979 than in 1960. Perhaps these two important influences are offsetting, but there is no simple way of establishing this point rigorously.

As a final comment on historical trends in the reserves-to-trade ratio, it is worth recalling that while Triffin was correct in predicting a declining ratio after 1960, he was wrong in predicting that balance of payments restrictions and controls would proliferate along with this fall in the ratio unless his collective solution was adopted. In fact, the world moved toward increased reliance on market solutions, as already noted above, with the growth in gold and dollar reserves, increased exchange rate flexibility, and the use of Eurocurrency credits for balance of payments financing. All of these developments, of course, do not invalidate Triffin's basic argument that the world would have been better off if the supply of reserves during the 1970s had come from the IMF in the correct amounts and at the proper time. The facts merely show that it is easier to propose rational, collective solutions to economic problems than it is to reach the political consensus needed to put them into effect.

The U.S. Liquidity Position

One of the key shortcomings of the dollar-gold exchange standard noted by Triffin in 1960 was the deterioration in the net liquidity position of the United States acting as the world's banker. For reasons already noted above, this position of necessity had to deteriorate as U.S. liabilities continued to grow and there were inadequate supplies of gold to add to U.S. holdings of the metal.

Figure 12-2 adapts and updates the graph that adorned the dust jacket of Triffin's book, which he used to support the analysis of the book. As can be seen, the key year 1960 is marked by the intersection of the two lines tracing the level of U.S. reserves and liquid foreign liabilities. The trend of the 1950s continued well into the 1960s. The reduction in the U.S. liabilities between 1966 and 1968 was caused by the adoption of a new approach to balance of payments presentation undertaken as a result of the recommendation made in the Bernstein Report (1965). Starting in that year, the liabilities shown are only those to central banks and governments, excluding liabilities to private foreigners. This seems a more reasonable measure of U.S. indebtedness, since if private obligations were to be included, then at least private U.S. short-term assets abroad should be used to offset them. However, because this argument was not accepted officially until 1968 and in order to preserve the part of the graph showing the developments that prompted Triffin's 1960 analysis, the time series on U.S. liabilities is not made consistent through the period and is shown with a break in 1966-1968. The subsequent improvement in the liquidity position of the United States occurred as the growth in the value of gold reserves at market prices exceeded that of external liabilities. This trend continued until in 1979, for the first time since 1960, U.S. reserves exceeded official liabilities. As in the case of the role of gold, foreign exchange, and the trend in reserves relative to trade, Triffin's predictions made in 1960 were realized in the following ten to fifteen years and then invalidated by market developments that he neither foresaw nor considered desirable.

SUMMARY AND CONCLUSIONS

Twenty years ago, in 1960, Triffin published a book that contained a brilliant diagnosis of the problems besetting the dollar-gold exchange standard, predicted the development of recurrent crises in the international monetary system, and presented a visionary plan for international cooperation in the creation of an

Figure 12-2. U.S. Liquidity Position.

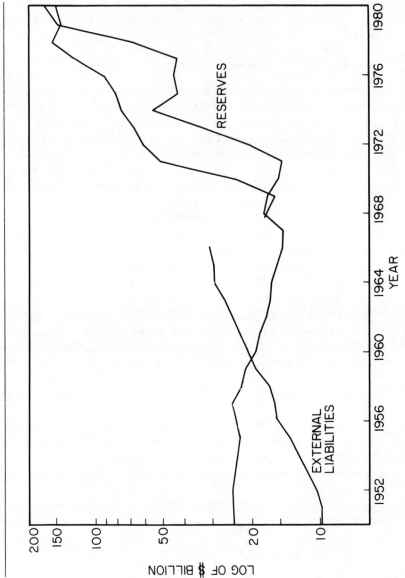

Note: Until 1966, external liabilities are to all foreigners. Thereafter, they are only to central banks and governments. Reserves consist of SDRs, IMF reserve positions, foreign exchange holdings, and gold valued at market prices.

institution that would issue fiat reserves in the right quantities and at low cost. He rejected gold price increases and flexible exchange rates as solutions that were irrational and socially too costly. During about four years[2] following the publication of Triffin's book, a lively debate ensued and led to a thorough understanding of the issues and economic and political trade-offs underlying his proposals. By and large, academic economists supported Triffin's plan, though there were some dissenting views from those who distrusted collective solutions and wanted a return to the gold standard. The U.S. financial establishment, including the relevant departments in the U.S. government, opposed Triffin's ideas because they did not want to diminish the country's role as the world's banker. Architects and insiders of the IMF wanted to see a continued evolution of that institution along the lines it had been following since 1945.

In my judgment, during the late 1960s the views of the academics in support of Triffin's ideas appeared to have won the day, as the two-tier system for gold and the creation of the SDR facilities represented at least symbolically significant steps toward the rational reorganization of the international monetary system. Unfortunately, however, the economic turbulences of the 1970s were so powerful that the evolutionary process started so hopefully a few years earlier came to a halt, some of the progress made earlier was reversed, and the world turned increasingly to the market and away from collective approaches for a solution to economic and social problems.

Thus, the demonetization of gold stopped, and the precious metal has regained to a very significant degree its role as the ultimate store and measure of value for private citizens as well as governments. The only rearguard action in this field was fought by the IMF and the U.S. government through sales of gold in private markets throughout the 1970s and through the refusal of the United States to report reserves with gold valued at market prices. (The IMF reports world reserves at market prices and at the $35 an ounce price.) The IMF has developed numerous programs for the extension of credit since 1960s, but they do not amount to a significant proportion of world reserves. SDRs similarly were created only in small quantities. In the face of rapidly growing nominal and real values of international trade, therefore, the world's need for liquidity was met by the creation of very large quantities of U.S. dollar obligations and the increase in the value of gold holdings. The increased flexibility of exchange rates and the development of Eurocurrency loans to countries with payments deficits have probably prevented the development of exchange and trade restrictions that otherwise would have resulted from the fall in the reserves-to-trade ratio that took place in spite of the growth in dollar and gold reserves. Gold price increases, greater dollar reserves, the growth in IMF credit facilities, and the

2. Most of the ideas in *Gold and the Dollar Crisis* were published a year earlier in the *Banca Nazionale del Lavoro Quarterly Review*, and much of the professional analysis of the Triffin plan was based on these publications.

greater flexibility of exchange rates were market developments that Triffin's plan was designed to avoid.

The analysis of this chapter has revealed the curious fact that in four important ways, the conditions of 1960 are replicated almost exactly in 1979-1980, after having changed substantially during the intervening years: The share of gold and foreign exchange in total reserves, the ratio of world reserves to trade, and the ratio of U.S. liabilities to reserves all went through large cycles during the twenty years under study. The big difference between the two periods is, however, that in 1960 the trends were pointing to the need for collective solutions while in 1980 the trends produced by market developments pointed in the opposite direction. Only the future will show whether market solutions can continue to serve the world community well or whether they will be inflexible or produce unexpected costs, or both, leading to renewed need for the kind of visionary plans for collective actions produced by Triffin in 1960.

If I were asked to engage in the precarious task of forecasting the future, I would suggest that for several years there will be a continued swing toward market solutions in all spheres of economics. Thereafter, the causes of the economic turbulence of the 1960s and 1970s will have been sorted out and a consensus will emerge on the proper role of collective policies and institutions. At that point the reliance on the market may have overshot the optimum and there will be renewed interest in the Triffin Plan. In the long run, gold may well remain the ultimate standard of value and a source of liquidity, while dollars, IMF credit, and SDRs compete successfully for places in countries' diversified reserve portfolios.

REFERENCES

Altman, Oscar L. 1963. "Professor Triffin on International Liquidity and the Role of the Fund." In Herbert G. Grubel, ed., *World Monetary Reform: Plans and Issues.* Stanford, California: Stanford University Press.

Angell, James. 1963. "The Reorganization of the International Monetary System: An Alternative Proposal." In Herbert G. Grubel, ed., *World Monetary Reform: Plans and Issues.* Stanford, California: Stanford University Press.

Bernstein, Edward M. 1963. "Proposed Reforms in the International Monetary System." In Herbert G. Grubel, ed., *World Monetary Reform: Plans and Issues.* Stanford, California: Stanford University Press.

Bernstein Report. 1965. *The Balance of Payments Statistics of the United States: A Review and Appraisal.* Washington, D.C.: U.S. Government Printing Office.

Cohen, Benjamin J. 1971. "The Seigniorage Gains of an International Currency." *Quarterly Journal of Economics* 85 (August): 494-507.

Fried, Joel. 1969. "International Liquidity and Foreign Aid." *Foreign Affairs*, October. 139-49.

Grubel, Herbert G., ed. 1963. *World Monetary Reform: Plans and Issues.* Stanford, California: Stanford University Press.

_____. 1964. "The Benefits and Costs of Being the World's Banker." *National Banking Review*, December.

_____. 1969. "The Distribution of Seigniorage from International Liquidity Creation." In Robert A. Mundell and Alexander Swoboda, eds., *Monetary Problems of the International Economy.* Chicago: University of Chicago Press.

_____. 1971. "The Demand for International Reserves: A Critical Review of the Literature." *Journal of Economic Literature* 9 (December): 1148-66.

Harrod, Sir Roy. 1963. "Liquidity." In Herbert G. Grubel, ed., *World Monetary Reform: Plans and Issues.* Stanford, California: Stanford University Press.

Heilperin, Michael A. 1963. "The Case for Going Back to Gold." In Herbert G. Grubel, ed., *World Monetary Reform: Plans and Issues.* Stanford, California: Stanford University Press.

International Monetary Fund. 1970. *International Reserves: Needs and Availability.* Washington, D.C.

Jacobsson, Per. 1963. "The Two Functions of an International Monetary Standard: Stability and Liquidity." In Herbert G. Grubel, ed., *World Monetary Reform: Plans and Issues.* Stanford, California: Stanford University Press.

Johnson, Harry G. 1969. "Comments on the Distribution of Seigniorage." In Robert A. Mundell and Alexander Swoboda, eds., *Monetary Problems of the International Economy.* Chicago: University of Chicago Press.

Kenen, Peter. 1960. "International Liquidity and the Balance of Payments of a Reserve-Currency Country." *Quarterly Journal of Economics* 74 (November): 572-86.

Laffer, Art. 1979. *Los Angeles Times*, October 30, p. 4.

Lutz, Friedrich A. 1963. "The Problem of International Liquidity and the Multiple Currency Standard." In Herbert G. Grubel, ed., *World Monetary Reform: Plans and Issues.* Stanford, California: Stanford University Press.

Machlup, Fritz. 1963. "Reform of the International Monetary System." In Herbert G. Grubel, ed., *World Monetary Reform: Plans and Issues.* Stanford, California: Stanford University Press.

Machlup, Fritz, and Burton Malkiel. 1964. *International Monetary Arrangements: The Problem of Choice.* Princeton, New Jersey: International Finance Section, Princeton University.

Mundell, Robert A., and Alexander Swoboda, eds. 1969. *Monetary Problems of the International Economy.* Chicago: University of Chicago Press.

Niehans, Jurg. 1976. "How to Fill an Empty Shell." *American Economic Review* 66 (May): 177–83.

Rockefeller, David. 1963. "International Monetary Reform and the New York Banking Community." In Herbert G. Grubel, ed., *World Monetary Reform: Plans and Issues.* Stanford, California: Stanford University Press.

Roosa, Robert V. 1963. "Assuring the Free World's Liquidity." In Herbert G. Grubel, ed., *World Monetary Reform: Plans and Issues.* Stanford, California: Stanford University Press.

Rueff, Jacques. 1963. "Gold Exchange Standard a Danger to the West." In Herbert G. Grubel, ed., *World Monetary Reform: Plans and Issues.* Stanford, California: Stanford University Press.

Solomon, Robert. 1977. *The International Monetary System 1945–76.* New York: Harper & Row.

Stamp, Josiah. 1963. "The Stamp Plan – 1962 Version." In Herbert G. Grubel, ed., *World Monetary Reform: Plans and Issues.* Stanford, California: Stanford University Press.

Triffin, Robert. 1960. *Gold and the Dollar Crisis.* New Haven: Yale University Press.

UNCTAD. 1969. "International Monetary Reform and Cooperation for Development." Report of the Expert Group on Monetary Issues, TD/V285, October.

Wallich, Harry C. 1963. "Cooperation to Solve the Gold Problem." In Herbert G. Grubel, ed., *World Monetary Reform: Plans and Issues.* Stanford, California: Stanford University Press.

Yeager, Leland B. 1963. "The Triffin Plan: Diagnosis, Remedy, and Alternatives." In Herbert G. Grubel, ed., *World Monetary Reform: Plans and Issues.* Stanford, California: Stanford University Press.

Zolotas, Zenophon. 1963. "Towards a Reinforced Gold Exchange Standard." In Herbert G. Grubel, ed., *World Monetary Reform: Plans and Issues.* Stanford, California: Stanford University Press.

13 INTERNATIONAL MONETARY REFORM IN THE NINETEENTH CENTURY

Charles P. Kindleberger

Next to Keynes, Robert Triffin is surely the most noted advocate of international monetary reform in the twentieth century. In honoring him by calling attention to proposals for international monetary reform in the nineteenth century, I am guilty of the venial sin of what Jonathan Hughes calls "colligation" — urging that the roots of a particular event or idea extend further back in time than is ordinarily thought. The practice is of course a form of antiquarianism, and if this be an impeachment, I plead guilty. If one were trying to compete, one could go further back — for example, to the monetary union of the Wendish towns of Lübeck, Hamburg, Wismark, and Luneberg, formed in 1379 — and later joined by Rostock and Pomeranian towns, with the Wendish standard later spreading to virtually all of Scandinavia (Dollinger 1970:207-208) — but it would be a mistake; Robert Mundell would find an example from the pre-Christian era. The nineteenth century is interesting enough.

Three related examples will be offered — all unsuccessful. These are decimalization of the pound sterling, the Latin Monetary Union, and "universal money" — that is, the production of uniform coinage in Europe and the United States. A case may be made that decimalization in Britain is not international but a national monetary reform. It should be remembered, however, that by the mid-nineteenth century, France, Lombardy, Sardinia, Rome, Tuscany, Naples, Holland, Switzerland, Russia, Greece, Portugal, the United States, Mexico, China, Egypt, and Persia had adopted the decimal system for money (O'Brien 1971:III, p. 1384). According to a representative to the International Monetary Conference in Paris in 1867, the government of Sweden had sought to introduce the metric system of weights and measures into the kingdom between 1847 and 1854, but had not been entirely successful because of the resistance of the clergy

203

and of agriculture. The metric system had been introduced, but the old units had been retained (U.S. Senate 1879:827). Had Britain followed, however, the calculation of most exchange rates through the pound would have been greatly eased. The Commission on Decimal Coinage reached its negative decision largely on domestic grounds, but pressure for decimalization came to a great extent from merchants with international purposes.

DECIMALIZATION OF THE POUND

The decimal system goes back to the fourteenth century, but interest in converting British currency from the traditional European system of pounds, solidus, and denier—in English, pounds, shillings, and pence—arose shortly after the French adoption of the metric system for weights and measures at the time of the French Revolution. The *franc germinal* replaced the *livre tournois* in 1803 and was divided into centimes rather than sous and deniers. Immediately after 1815 voices began to be raised in the British Parliament. John Wilson Croker suggested decimalization of British money in the debate on Lord Liverpool's coinage act of 1816 (Fetter 1965: 66). He received no support. A similar suggestion was put forward by Lord Stanhope in the House of Lords (Smart 1964: I, p. 508). A memorandum prepared for the Decimal Coinage Commissioners by Lord Monteagle, who strongly favored decimalization and was a member of the commission, picks up the history of the movement with the proposal for an inquiry into the applicability of the decimal scale to coins made by Sir John Wrottesley in the House of Commons in 1824 (O'Brien 1971: III, p. 1381). This was opposed by the master of the mint on the ground that the government planned to assimilate the currencies of Great Britain and Ireland. The question arose again in 1838 when the standard weights and measures of Britain had been destroyed in the fire at the Houses of Parliament and restoration of the standards was considered. Various inquiries followed, largely in the first instance by scientists, such as astronomers.

In 1847, Dr. John Bowring, an economist, moved the adoption of the coinage and issue of silver pieces equal to a tenth and one hundredth of the value of the pound. He withdrew the motion when the government proceeded with the initial step of issuing the florin, a two-shilling piece, equal to one-tenth of a pound, as the first experimental step in a process of decimalization.

The commissioners of 1843 reported again in 1853, urging the adoption of the decimal system not only for money but for the linear foot and the pound avoirdupois. This was followed by the appointment of a Select Committee of the House of Commons, which sat for fourteen days, examined twenty-eight witnesses, and recommended decimalization of the pound sterling. No legislation was introduced on the subject in 1854, but many declarations, petitions, and memorials favoring it were presented to the government and the Parliament in 1854 and 1855 by merchants, bankers, municipal government, chambers of commerce, and so forth. A considerable pamphlet literature on decimalization of coinage developed with works by Bowring and Rathbone (O'Brien 1971:II, p. 579) and by T. Wilson and Laurie (U.S. Senate 1879:760). In June 1855 further resolutions were introduced to accept the success of the florin and extend decimalization by the production of a silver coin equal to one one-hundredth of a pound and a copper coin of one one-thousandth. The government replied by appointing a new board of commissioners, consisting of J.G. Hubbard (later Lord Addington), Lord Monteagle (previously T. Spring–Rice), and Lord Overstone (previously Samuel Jones Lloyd). The most readily accessible source on the work of the commission is found in *The Correspondence of Lord Overstone* (O'Brien 1971), which included, along with a discussion of the work of the commission in Lord Overstone's letters, a summary analysis by the editor in Volume I and a number of papers–seven by Overstone, two by Monteagle (from the first of which the summary history in the preceding paragraph was drawn), and two by Hubbard–in an appendix in Volume III.

Lord Overstone opposed decimalization and defeated it so thoroughly in the commission that it was a dead issue for another fifty years (O'Brien 1971: I, p. 52). The commission was supposed to be a rubber stamp endorsing decimalization, but Overstone was a man of strong views–even prejudices–and of effective tactics. He started out by admitting that the decimal system was superior for "abstract calculations" like insurance and convenient for banking, affecting the rich, but argued that it did not fit the needs of everyday practicality. Tactics consisted of delaying action by the commission through various devices until the public lost interest and the movement lost momentum (O'Brien 1971: II, p. 886).

It seems hardly necessary to set forth the arguments in favor of decimalization. Against it was one quandary: How best to go about it–whether to keep the pound sterling as a unit of account and the florin and then adjust the shilling and the penny or to start with the penny and introduce a whole new set of coins at the upper end, such as the "dollar" of one hundred pennies. While one or two pundits favored the shilling or the penny as the basic unit, virtually everyone came out in favor of retention of the pound. This meant, first, "crying down" the shilling from twelve to ten pence and the sixpence to fivepence and, second, not stopping at the "cent" or one one-hundredth of a pound but going on to the mil, one-tenth of the cent. The cent would have been almost 2½ d and too large a unit. One-tenth of it was less than a farthing or quarter of a penny, but most proposals called for it.

Overstone's negation was first expressed as a series of questions, to which he finally gave his own answers. In essence, however, he objected to change and couched his opposition in the form of the adverse impact on the transactions of the poor. There were more abstract arguments:

1. A pound under the old system was divided into 240 pennies or 960 farthings, whereas a decimal pound would consist of 1000 mils. Nine-hundred

and sixty is divisible by twenty-seven numbers without a remainder, 1000 only by fifteen.

2. The binary system is "natural," as opposed to the decimal system, which is contrived. Weights and measures used by the British conform to binary reckoning, especially for quarts, pints, gills, or the pound avoirdupois, which is divided into 16 ounces. Hence it is natural to have a pound, crown, and half-crown and then, with a shift, the shilling, sixpence, and threepence, before another shift to the penny.

3. As an extension of the binary character of nature, he observed frequently that the United States had retained in circulation the 12½ cent and 6¼ cent Spanish coins—the bit and the half-bit.

4. To change the monetary system without changing the system of weights and measures would be confusing, as, for example, to charge 10 pennies for a dozen eggs.

5. The penny would be too large a coin in copper and too small in silver.

6. The poor would have great difficulty in adjusting to new values for the shilling and the penny and to the new coin, the mil.

It is not the position of the historian to seek to counter these arguments, although the binary nature of British weights and measures is somewhat dubious. The system is partly duodecimal and partly binary. It should be recalled that at one time British money had the "angel," a gold coin equal to one-third of a pound sterling, or 6s 8d. When the price of gold was raised in 1526, this coin was "called up" to 7s 6d, which was not a useful denomination, so it was replaced by the "noble" a lighter coin again at 6s 8d (De Roover 1949:74). One could make an argument for having world money on the duodecimal system, embracing first the arguments of Lord Overstone and covering also the linear measures of foot and inch and the avoirdupois measure of the troy pound, not to mention the temporal measures of months, hours, minutes, and seconds. It is clearly wrong to claim that the British system was consistent or binary throughout. It is also worth noting that the United States demonetized the 12½ cent and 6¼ cent foreign coins in 1857, at the same time that Lord Overstone was arguing from their existence.

Lord Overstone was clearly correct that any change in money is disturbing to the poor. Overstone, leader of the Currency School, and Thomas Tooke, leader of the Banking School, were at loggerheads on most things. Tooke did write Overstone, however, to assert that he had started his career as a merchant in the Russian trade in St. Petersburg and had found no difficulty in shifting to the combined binary, decimal, duodecimal system when he returned. He thought the experiment in changing standards imprudent (O'Brien 1971: II, pp. 738–40). But changing systems for less-educated and experienced calculators clearly was likely to pose difficulties, especially if a number of coins were changed at one time. The various commissions were aware of the problem and examined school officials as witnesses to discuss the education of children in the new money, were it to be adopted.

It is evident to most of us that the French people had difficulty in changing from the old to the new franc in the 1950s, with children and tourists calculating in new franc long before French adults had accomplished the task of converting from 10,000 old francs to 100 new francs, dividing by 100. A similar problem is posed for the United States today in the slow progress made in moving to the metric system—in temperature, liquid measures, and distance—with what we suppose to be a highly literate and educated populace. For the nineteenth century the difficulties were more formidable in light of limited education and circulation. Eugen Weber's brilliant *Peasants into Frenchmen* (1976), with the thesis that peasants remained stuck in the *ancien régime* until 1860-1880, when railroads, compulsory education, military conscription, and the press began to force them to become contemporary Frenchmen, has an early chapter entitled "The King's Foot" that describes the difficulties. In places like Limousin, the peasant counted by *pistola*, *louis*, and *escu* as late as 1895; in 1917 in Brittany, peasant vocabulary clung to fourteenth century *blancs*, *écus*, and a Spanish survival, the *real* (Weber 1976: 32-33). The same cultural lag obtained in dry, liquid, linear, and ounce weight measures: Fathom and foot; ell and bushel; quart, pound, and ounce; *poids de marc* and *poids de table* persisted into the twentieth century.

Changing standards is traumatic, even when the improvement is substantial. Adjustments have to be made all at once, everywhere, whereas the costs of the inadequate standard are regarded as sunk. It is not by accident that the French adopted the metric system for weights and measures, plus money, as a result of a revolution or that the United States and Britain adopted a common standard for the pitch of the screwthread during a war. A high national rate of interest puts the cost of nearby trouble above the benefits of far-off gains from the public good of an improved standard, unless there is trouble in abundance already, so that the addition from changing standards is not striking. It is not without relevance that Sweden made an extended study of the costs of shifting from driving on the left to driving on the right and decided, the first time, against change on cost-benefit grounds. In Austria, the switch was made abruptly by German order one day after Anschluss, with the problems posed by the passenger doors of buses and trolleys facing the street rather than the sidewalk to be worked out pragmatically over time. The Swiss change to the franc and the centime in 1852 and the metric system of weights and measures in 1857, characterized by O'Brien as much superior to the old chaos although causing some inconvenience to lower income groups (O'Brien 1971: II, p. 731), resulted from the close ties of Switzerland to the French economy.

It is curious that Lord Overstone should have been so opposed to change. As a banker, he could see the benefits from the gain in abstract reckoning—in insurance, foreign exchange, calculation of interest. Despite a strong Christian interest in the poor and the Poor Laws of 1834, he lacked contact with the ordinary poor and can hardly have been dominated by their concerns. While O'Brien withholds any attempt to calculate his motives, it seems evident from reading the 1500 pages of O'Brien's Introduction and Overstone's Correspondence that primarily he was a conservative. What existed, and worked more or less, should be left alone. Even when it did not work as well as he had anticipated—as for example, the Bank Act of 1844—keep it and do not try to improve it. It is hard for a modern academic economist to understand the adulation that, say, McCulloch and Torrens rendered Overstone. In Torrens' case, he "ventured on what may perhaps be regarded as heresy; inasmuch as I have placed in the category of Money, Deposits not actually represented by Bullion" (O'Brien 1971: II, p. 707). Overstone came back at him like a Dutch uncle: "If you publish this you let loose upon us the Floodgates of Confusion—It will be the Deluge of Monetary science, Tooke will be in third Heaven ..." (ibid.: 713). To which Torrens abjectly replied: "I have no confidence unless you approve. I throw Deposits to the dogs" (ibid.: 717). "Confusion" provides the key. Overstone had certainty and wanted to keep it. His support of the Bank Act of 1844 was directed to his Bullionist certainty. An evident reform to decimalize the pound sterling and help business and banking reckon introduced uncertainty. There was no merit in it.

Decimalization was rejected by a second royal commission in 1918 and finally came in 1971 after the favorable report of the Parliamentary Committee of Inquiry on Decimal Currency in 1963. The move came after a number of countries of the Commonwealth had adopted decimalization or recommended it and despite one suggestion that Britain adopt duodecimalization. The committee had been asked not to recommend for or against decimalization but to suggest how it be done—particularly how to rationalize the system of coinage.

Overstone was suspicious that decimalization of money was the thin end of the wedge to introduce the metric system of weights and measures more generally. We shall see below in the discussion of the universal money that he—or rather his alter ego, G.W. Norman—regarded the trivial adjustment in seigniorage required as an "Appendage to an International Coinage and Decimalization—the Metric System &c, &c." (O'Brien 1971: III, pp. 1183-84).

The story comes to an end in the nineteenth century with the passage of an act in 1862 that permitted the use of the metric system in contracts and dealings by declaring that any contracts or dealings contained metric measures shall not by that fact be deemed invalid or open to objection. Leone Levi, who hailed the memorial of the Lords Commissioners of the Great Exhibition of 1851, urging decimalization of money and metrication of weights and measures as a reflection of the growing intelligence and education of the British and a sweeping away of antipathy in international relations, regarded a permissive measure as doubtless insufficient. "Sooner or later," he continued, "we may anticipate the entire substitution of the metric system for the present practice. Considerable progress has also been made regarding international coinage" (Levi 1872: 469-60). Later, not sooner.

LATIN MONETARY UNION

A series of monetary steps were taken to unify currencies among the principalities and states of the Zollverein, including Austria, in the Coinage Treaty of Vienna of January 1857 and in Scandinavia in December 1872. The major step at the international level, however, was the Latin Monetary Union of December 1865, ratified by the four signatories—France, Belgium, Switzerland, and Italy— to take effect by August 1, 1866; acceded to by the Papal States that same year and by Greece and Rumania in 1867; and renewed in November 1878 after the collapse of the International Monetary Conference (U.S. Senate 1879:779-80). The immediate stimulus to the arrangement is of interest as it evokes echoes of the "optimal currency area" of Mundell and McKinnon. As the French economy grew in the 1850s and 1860s, the practice of settling large sums in sacks of silver 5-franc pieces became cumbersome, so that gold coins were introduced. Silver having been overvalued in the process, silver coins were melted down or exported, so that adjustment of the fineness of the 5-franc piece had to be undertaken. France, Switzerland, and Italy all moved to reduce the fineness of their coins from 9/10. When France and Italy chose 835/1000 for the grade of silver, Switzerland's choice of 800/1000 threatened to lead to replacement of French and Italian by Swiss coins. The French in 1864 prohibited the use of Swiss coins. Then Belgium saw the virtue of making its change in fineness conform to that of the neighboring states and proposed an agreement among the countries using the franc, but including also Italy, whose lira was equal to a franc.

Small countries have difficulty managing a national currency and preventing the intrusion and use domestically of the moneys of larger states. The fact was observed by Adam Smith at a time when Belgium was a large, not a small, state:

> The currency of a great state, such as France or Belgium, generally consists almost entirely of its own coin. . . . But the currency of a small state, such as Genoa or Hamburgh, can seldom consist altogether of its own coin, but must be made up, in a great measure, of the coins of all the neighboring states with which its inhabitants have a continual intercourse. (Smith 1937: Book IV, ch. III, pt. I, Digression)

Forty years later, the same phenomenon was observed in the Rhineland, where, in 1816, at least seventy coins from Holland, France, Belgium, and various German states were reportedly in local circulation, and Prussian coin was rarely seen (Tilly 1966:20). Some areas are too small to be optimum currency areas and must use moneys of other countries.

In 1865, the Swiss, Belgians, and Italians all favored going over from bimetallism to the gold standard, but French loyalty to the "double standard" carried the day. The French had been debating bimetallism with some fervor since the great flood of gold let loose by the discoveries of 1849 in California and 1851 in Australia. The question was settled regularly, but as regularly arose again. One commission met on the issue in 1857, a second in 1861, a third in 1867, and a fourth in 1869 (Wolowski 1869:183-98). Most of the members of the various commissions continued to vote in favor of bimetallism. Only Michael Chevalier and Esquirou de Parieu opposed it, Chevalier favoring silver in the light of the gold discoveries and de Parieu gold, presumably on the basis of the British de jure adoption of gold in 1816, following de facto adoption in 1717. De Parieu was a member of the French delegation to the 1867 International Monetary Conference and its vice-president, presiding in the frequent absence of the Prince Jerome Napoleon and of the foreign minister. He was also an indefatigable writer on international money between 1859 and at least 1878 (U.S. Senate 1879: 761-72).

The articles of the "Treaty Constituting the Latin Union" cover barely three pages and regulate the weight, title, form, and circulation of their gold and silver coins. Five-franc (lira) silver coins were held to 0.9 fineness; silver coins of 2 francs, 1 franc, 50 centimes, and 20 centimes were limited to a fineness of 0.835. Since the seigniorage on these coins was positive, it was agreed that each country would hold down the number of such coins issued to no more than 6 francs per inhabitant, lest one country would gain at the expense of its neighbors.

The Latin Monetary Union met some strain when Italy proved unable to sustain convertibility of the lira in May 1866 and adopted forced circulation of its banknotes (*corso forzoso*). The export of silver from that country prior to inconvertibility is sometimes held to have contributed to the decline in silver. This source of pressure was small, however, compared with the discovery of the Comstock load in Nevada in 1859, the electrolytic process for refining silver, and the more serious sales of silver by the German Reichsbank after the adoption of the gold standard in 1875. From 1865 to 1877 the Latin Monetary Union maintained bimetallism, restricting the coinage of silver in the latter year. In 1867 the success of the union was so widely recognized that it was thought useful to proceed from it to the adoption of a universal money.

UNIVERSAL MONEY

The term "universal" money was used as early as 1588 by Davanzati in his "Discourse on Coin" to the Florence Academy. He explained that while the prince could make money out of iron, leather, wood, cork, lead, paper, salt, or the like, as sometimes had happened, it could not circulate outside of his realm and thus could not be universal money (Vilar 1976:190). Francois Nicholas Mollien, Napoleon's minister of finance, approaches the idea, if not the term, in writing in his *Memoires* that it was desirable that all people adopt a uniform system of measures and that, of these measures, the uniformity that brings most to the convenience of nations is uncontestably that of money (Mollien 1845: III, p. 498). The pressure for a universal money in the second half of the nineteenth century came largely from France and especially from Esquirou de Parieu, an economist and vice-president of the Conseil d'Etat, who wrote prodigiously but whose reputation has not stood the test of time. De Parieu was intimately connected with the Latin Monetary Union. He was also a leading spirit in calling the International Monetary Conference of 1867 in Paris to explore the possibilities of extending the achievement of the union to more countries. The conference was held in connection with the Universal Exposition of 1867, also held in Paris, and the U.S. representative to the monetary conference was not a member of government or the director of the mint as in the case of other countries, but the U.S. commissioner to the Universal Exposition.

The idea behind "universal money" was partly to assist travelers by having coins interchangeable, but primarily for the sake of commerce (U.S. Senate 1879:817). There is an echo of Lord Overstone in the remark of a Norwegian delegate that it would be desirable to have international understanding with respect to subsidiary coinage, with equivalent subdivisions, for the sake of the laboring classes—but the point of view was international and long-run rather than domestic and focusing on maintaining the status quo.

De Parieu opened the conference by propounding a series of questions, again with echoes of Lord Overstone's technique. Again here, however, the purpose was different—to elicit agreement, rather than to prevent change. The first question is as relevant today as it was more than a century ago:

1. By what means is it most easy to realize monetary unification; whether by the creation of a system altogether new, independent of existing systems—and in such what should be the basis of such system,—or, by the mutual co-ordination of existing systems, taking into account the scientific advantages of certain types, and the number of the populations which have already adopted them? In this case, what monetary system should be principally taken into consideration, reserving the changes of which might be susceptible for making it perfect? (U.S. Senate 1879:811)

On this I fear that I disagree with Robert Triffin, who along with Keynes, the IMF, the European Monetary System, and the like would favor the creation of a new international money. In fact, the conference of June 1867 worked on how to create a universal money out of existing currencies. The negotiating problem strongly resembled the question of the decimalization of the pound— what denominations of existing coins to keep and what to cry up or call down.

Most of the discussion revolved around the French franc. One scheme, favored by the British, was to start with a new 25-franc piece, equal to the pound sterling after adjustment of the sovereign to change its fineness from 11/12 to 0.9 through a mintage charge of approximately (in French reckoning)

20 centimes (out of 2500). The mintage charge was discussed in 1869 by Lord Overstone and G.W. Norman of the Bank of England, who saw it as a new attempt by the routed proponents of decimal currency to institute international coinage and "ultimately Decimalization and the Metric System" (O'Brien 1971: III, p. 1184). Norman thought mintage the small end of the wedge: "At any rate I can not believe that a sovereign with a portion of gold abstracted from it will be worth as much as the present coin in foreign countries (ibid.). A third memorandum by Lord Overstone on gold coinage concludes "that the sovereign can not be tampered with as regards weight and fineness of the gold upon any plea. It is fraud in disguise" (ibid.: 1187).

The minting of a 25-franc piece and the adjustment of the sovereign through mintage called next for adjustment of the dollar from $4.8665 to the pound sterling to $5.00, a small devaluation which the American delegate to the 1867 conference, and later John Sherman as a U.S. senator (prior to becoming secretary of the treasury), thought entirely feasible. The former, one Samuel B. Ruggles, U.S. commissioner to the Paris Exposition of 1867, thought that the dollar could not be eliminated, but that its value might be altered 3.5 percent. The Portuguese representative then expressed the key currency notion: If agreement could be worked out among France, England, and the United States, other countries would sooner or later rally round (O'Brien 1971: III, p. 813).

Twenty-five francs was not very satisfactory to the French. They would have preferred the Napoleon of 20 francs or the 10-franc piece, once called the ducat, with its neater fit into the metric system. The British representative noted that the British might have preferred 20 francs as the standard as well, since they were used to dividing by twenty. There was thus a possibility that having adjusted the pound to 25 francs from 25 francs, 20 centimes, they would have to undertake a second recoinage. In addition, half of 25 francs is 12.5 francs, an awkward designation.

In a remark anticipating the distinction between national and international public goods, the French prince, who presided at the conference in the final days, said:

> Certainly, if France consulted only its own convenience, she [sic] would see no necessity for issuing this new [25-franc] coin; but to facilitate the work of unification, the object of the labors of the conference, it would make the concession requested by the United States. It also appeared that the 25-franc piece would equally accommodate both England and Austria. (U.S. Senate 1879:858)

Other countries were not content to let the issue be settled among France, Britain, and the United States. The Swedish delegate kept coming back to 10 francs as the standard and thought that the United States could issue a $2 gold coin, more convenient than the silver dollar. The Prussian representative suggested a 2.5-franc coin. Supported by South Germany and Wurtemberg, the

Dutch insisted on a 15-franc standard, which Austria opposed. Prussia abstained from voting on either the 25-franc or the 15-franc coin because its delegate had no instructions beyond voting for the gold standard, even though Prussia was on the silver standard.

Bimetallism was one issue. Although off the gold standard in 1867, the United States did not insist on bimetallism as it later did in calling the unsuccessful International Monetary Conference of 1878. The other issue was that to which so much attention has thus far been given—which national currency unit to follow. All agreed that it would occasion too much artificiality to start afresh with a brand new currency. Britain's leadership was not so clearly established, either in the calling of the conference, which had been done by the French, or in taking a lead in the discussion, to induce the Continent to follow.

The conference ended on July 6, 1867. It concluded in favor of the gold standard, with a gradual transition from bimetallism and the common denominator of the franc, especially the 5-franc gold piece (dollar), 0.9 fine, but with recommendation for the coinage of a 25-franc piece to equal the pound sterling, the half-eagle of $5, and a piece adopted by the Vienna conference of 1857 to represent 10 florins. No conclusion was reached on the gold piece of 15 francs. The recommendations were given to governments "with the hope that some decision may be reached by the middle of February 1868, or at least some instructive steps taken by governments" (U.S. Senate 1879:877). In the event, nothing happened. The outcome is reminiscent of the International Economic Conference of 1927, when all countries agreed to lower tariffs, but none did.

Discussion of monetary reform continued into the next years. Walter Bagehot wrote a series of articles in *The Economist* between October and December 1868, which were then assembled in a pamphlet entitled "Universal Money" and reproduced in his *Collected Works* (Bagehot 1978: XI, pp. 55-104).

Universal Money focuses less on the technical details of how to reach monetary unification and more on the purposes of reform. The author states:

A remarkable movement is going on in the world towards a uniformity of coinage between different nations. And it was begun in what seems the way of the nineteenth century; the way Germany was created, and the unity of Italy too; that is, not by a great number of states, of set design and in combination, chalking out something new, but on the contrary, by some great state acting first for its own convenience, and then other lesser and contiguous nations imitating its plan and falling in with its example. . . .

The advantages of a single coinage, which are explained in the following papers, seem to me fully equivalent. But I fear, when looked at strictly, it will be found that the difficulties of such a step are simply insurmountable. And if this is so, and we do nothing, what then? Why, we shall, to use a vulgar expression, be left out in the cold. . . .

Every person must see that the demand for uniformity in currency is only one case of the growing demand for uniformity in matters between nations really similar. . . . Commerce is everywhere identical; buying and selling, lending and borrowing, are alike all the world over, and all matters concerning them ought universally to be alike too. . . . Ultimately the world will see one *code de commerce*, and one money as the symbol of it. (Ibid.: 64–66)

In one chapter Bagehot shoots down a series of alleged advantages of a universal money—convenience of travelers, simplification of international remittances, and ease of statistical calculation internationally. Since foreign transactions are small in relation to internal ones, he concludes that the slight advantages do not outweigh the inconvenience to domestic trade. Moreover, he is not impressed by the arguments of Michael Chevalier in favor of the naturalness of the metric system. The advantage of a universal money lies in the unit of account function, in enabling foreigners to understand English *"price language"* (his italics—ibid.: 71) and in enabling British bankers to know how much bullion there is in the Bank of France: "Of course all English bankers can *turn* francs into pounds, and some think they *will*; but few ever do" (ibid.: 73).

But the exercise shatters on the same rock as the 1867 conference, to which he refers. Should the basic international coin be the sovereign equal to 25 francs (after adjustment) or the 10-franc piece equal to 8 shillings (after adjustment), which could be coined into a "gold florin" or "metrical pound" of 100 (originally 96) pence? The French, he is sure, would be unwilling to take the pound (25 francs). He is persuaded that a new 8-shilling gold piece in circulation with the old 10-shilling gold piece would create insuperable difficulties for bank cashiers and the public and discredit the plan. In the end he comes down to two systems—a great Anglo-Saxon system based on the sovereign and the half-eagle ($5) on the one hand and the Latin unit on the other. Germany, in his view, would choose to align itself with the former to constitute a Teutonic coinage league to go with the Latin coinage league.

One may wonder about the political feasibility of the scheme. On the economic technical level, two world moneys suffer the disability of being subject to Gresham's law, the warning implicit in Triffin's criticism of the gold exchange standard.

THE INTERNATIONAL MONETARY
CONFERENCE OF 1878

A footnote to the above cautionary tale of monetary reform in the nineteenth century should indicate that the 1878 conference, larger and more encompassing than that of 1865, was called by the United States to explore the possibility of restoring bimetallism. Political pressures from mining senators were intense. John Sherman, now Secretary of the Treasury, was now a political bimetallist, whereas he had been for gold as a senator. It proved impossible to get Humpty-Dumpty back together again. The Latin Monetary Union had left bimetallism. The new German Reichsbank had adopted the gold standard in 1875, selling off more silver to add to that pouring from Nevada mines. This was perhaps the significant monetary reform of the nineteenth century, taken long after 1774, when Britain demonetized silver; resisted by the United States; and defensive rather than positive.

Bagehot follows his introduction to *Universal Money* with a postscript to the long quotation given above, ending "One *code de commerce*, and one money as the symbol of it." "We are, as yet," he says, "very distant from so perfect an age" (Bagehot 1978: XI, p. 66). Despite the talent and the drive of Robert Triffin, we still are.

REFERENCES

Bagehot, Walter. 1978. *The Collected Works of Walter Bagehot.* Edited by Norman St. John-Stevas. 11 vols. Vols. IX–XI: *The Economic Essays.* London: The Economist.

De Roover, Raymond. 1949. *Gresham on Foreign Exchange.* Cambridge, Massachusetts: Harvard University Press.

Dollinger, Philippe. 1970. *The German Hansa.* Translated and edited by D.S. Ault and S.H. Steinberg. Stanford, California: Stanford University Press.

Fetter, Frank Whitson. 1965. *Development of British Monetary Orthodoxy, 1797-1815.* Cambridge, Massachusetts: Harvard University Press.

Great Britain. 1963. *Report of the Committee of Inquiry on Decimal Currency.* Cmnd 2145. London: Her Majesty's Stationery Office, September.

Levi, Leone. 1872. *History of British Commerce, and of the Economic Progress of British Nation, 1763-1870.* London: John Murray.

Mollien, François Nicholas. 1845. *Mémoires d'un ministre du trésor public, 1780-1815.* 4 tomes. Paris: Fournier.

O'Brien, D.P., ed. 1971. *The Correspondence of Lord Overstone.* 3 vols. Cambridge: Cambridge University Press.

Smart, William. 1964. *Economic Annals of the Nineteenth Century* (1911). Rprt. ed. 2 vols. New York: Augustus M. Kelley.

Smith, Adam. 1937. *An Inquiry into the Nature and Causes of the Wealth of Nations* (1776). Cannan, ed. New York: Modern Library.

Tilly, Richard H. 1966. *Financial Institutions and Industrialization in the Rhineland, 1815-1870.* Madison: University of Wisconsin Press.

U.S. Senate. 1879. *International Monetary Conference.* Washington, D.C.: Government Printing Office. (Reprinted in New York: Arno Press, 1978).

Vilar, Pierre. 1976. *A History of Gold and Money, 1450-1920.* Translated from the 1969 Spanish original by Judith White. London: NLB.

Weber, Eugen. 1976. *Peasants into Frenchmen, The Modernization of Rural France, 1870-1914.* Stanford, California: Stanford University Press.

Wolowski, Louis. 1869. *La question monétaire.* 2nd ed. Paris: Guillaumin.

14 CURRENCY SUBSTITUTION AND MONETARY INDEPENDENCE
The Case of Mexico

Guillermo Ortiz and
Leopoldo Solís

INTRODUCTION

When the "Triffin dilemma" was finally resolved in 1971 and the Bretton Woods system collapsed, the evolution of the international monetary system into a flexible exchange rate regime was widely regarded as an important step toward greater national autonomy. Following the work of Mundell (1968), one of the stronger arguments used by economists who favored greater exchange rate flexibility was that floating rates could insulate the domestic monetary system of a country from developments abroad. Under floating rates, the central bank no longer has to intervene in the foreign exchange market in order to maintain a certain exchange rate and consequently cannot be foreced to absorb an excess supply of (or to accommodate an excess demand for) the domestic currency. Clearly, this would amount to making domestic and foreign currencies perfect nonsubstitutes on the supply side, eliminating international flows and thus allowing the monetary authorities to follow an independent monetary policy.

The experience of the industrialized world with floating exchange rates during the 1970s—as Robert Triffin has repeatedly pointed out—has certainly shown that individual countries cannot follow independent policies without causing severe disruptions in the international monetary system (see Triffin 1978a, 1978b). This record has led to a reexamination of the notion that flexi-

The ideas contained in this chapter are the sole responsibility of the authors and do not reflect official views of Banco de México. The authors gratefully acknowledge the assistance of Patricia Abreu and the statistical advice and help of Víctor M. Guerrero and Gabriel Vera.

217

ble exchange rates provide an effective insulation from policy actions undertaken by other countries.

While it remains true that in the absence of central bank intervention in the foreign exchange market, domestic and foreign currencies are nonsubstitutes on the supply side, there is no reason to expect similar behavior on the demand side. In fact, if the domestic and foreign currencies are regarded as substitutes on the demand side, asset holders will include both types of currencies in their portfolios. Furthermore, the greater the degree of substitution between these currencies, the more difficult it will be for the monetary authorities to pursue independent policies. Although economists have long been aware of historical periods where more than one money circulates at the same time in a given country, the literature on "currency substitution"—that is, the conditions under which diversified currency portfolios will be held by the public—and its effects on domestic monetary policy is fairly recent (see, for example, Girton and Roper 1981; Miles 1978; and Brillembourg and Schadler 1980).

Mexico has had long experience with portfolio diversification across currencies. The large number of commercial and financial transactions carried on between Mexico and the United States—determined to a large extent by the geographical proximity—make the dollar a natural asset to hold for both firms and individuals in Mexico, especially those engaged in international exchange. On the other hand, although the historical record of the peso–dollar exchange rate has been reasonably stable (at least by Latin American standards), dollar holdings have traditionally been regarded by Mexicans as the most effective protection against expected fluctuations in the purchasing power of the Mexican peso over goods and services produced abroad.[1] However, in spite of this close association between peso and dollar holdings and the fact that Mexico maintained a fixed exchange rate with respect to the dollar from 1954 until 1976 (and no exchange controls), a number of economists have suggested that the Mexican monetary authorities were able to exercise a certain degree of independence during the 1960s. The next section examines this proposition more closely and reviews some empirical evidence connected with the literature on currency substitution mentioned above.

Section three focuses on the development of dollar deposits in Mexican banks (mexdollars) during the 1970s and the effects of this growing market on the formulation of monetary policy in Mexico, particularly after the liberalization of the mexdollar deposit rates that occurred a few months after the peso was officially floated. Using intervention analysis, we explore in section four the hypoth-

---

1. This is a logical consequence of the dollar dominance over Mexico's international transactions. Also, forward markets for the peso were only established in recent times, and there is a question about their operating efficiency, since the peso was consistently selling forward at a discount, while the spot rate remained fixed for a long period of time. For a discussion of the "peso problem" see Krasker (1980); Lizondo (1981) analyzed empirically the efficiency of the peso's forward market.

esis that the existence of a competitive dollar deposit market in Mexico has decreased substantially the volume of short-term capital flows between Mexico and the United States, providing an "insulation" effect that seems to have potentially enhanced the degree of short-run monetary discretion allowed to the central bank. As suggested in the conclusion, this experience may be of interest to other semi-industrialized countries in Latin America and other areas that have recently embarked on financial liberalization programs that include the creation of their own foreign currency deposit markets.

ASSET SUBSTITUTION AND CAPITAL FLOWS IN THE 1960s

During the period of stabilizing development[2] (which includes the last few years of the 1950s and the decade of the 1960s), a number of studies on the workings of monetary policy in Mexico were produced. Several authors observed then that due to the persistence of disequilibrium conditions in the credit market, the monetary authorities were able to exert a significant influence on the state of liquidity of the economy.

What became known as the "excess demand for loanable funds" hypothesis was developed by Sheldon (1964), Brothers and Solís (1966), Koehler (1968), and Bazdresch (1973), among others, and can be summarized as follows: First, the monetary authority fixed a nominal interest rate below the marginal productivity of investment. Second, the public sector deficit, together with the level of official net foreign borrowing, determined the amount of government spending to be financed with internal funds. These funds were then obtained through the reserve deposits that all financial institutions are required to maintain at the central bank. Third, the remaining financial savings were extended as credit to the private sector, which in turn complemented the financing of its investment projects with retained savings plus whatever amount it was able to borrow abroad. Finally, since the lending rates were fixed at lower than equilibrium levels, credit rationing was the market-clearing mechanism.[3]

In view of the fact that Mexico maintained a fixed parity with respect to the dollar throughout the 1960s (coupled with full convertibility of the peso for both current and capital account transactions), the question is, Why did Mexico not experience capital inflows sufficient to eliminate credit rationing and thus the excess demand for loanable funds? Although none of these authors attempted a formal empirical verification, the explanation suggested was that

2. The term "stabilizing development" was coined by the former Mexican secretary of the treasury, Antonio Ortiz Mena (1969), to describe the economic policies followed by the government during the 1960s.

3. Although lending rates were not fixed directly, Banco de México controlled these rates indirectly through the setting of deposit rates, since there is evidence that the spreads between lending and deposit rates remained quite stable in this period.

Mexican and foreign securities were not close enough substitutes in wealth holders' portfolios.

A more recent econometric study of private financial capital flows between Mexico and the rest of the world for the period 1962–1969 seems to support the above hypothesis. Hernández-Catá (1974) investigated movements of short- and long-term flows between Mexico, the United States, and the Eurodollar market, using a stock adjustment model and focusing mainly on the role of changes in domestic and foreign interest rates in inducing these flows. The empirical results show that during the 1960s Mexico was quite distant from the textbook case of perfect capital mobility. Although the study concludes that international movements of financial flows did respond to changes in interest rate differentials, the magnitude of the coefficients on the interest rate and lagged dependent variables suggest a highly imperfect degree of substitution between domestic and foreign assets during the sample period. This implies, of course, that portfolio adjusted only gradually and slowly to changes in domestic credit conditions.

An alternative method of measuring the degree of substitution between domestic and foreign financial assets is simply to include the appropriate foreign variable on the estimation of the demand for the relevant domestic aggregate. If domestic and foreign assets are indeed substitutes, one would expect that a stable demand for the domestic asset could not be obtained if the foreign variables are omitted.[4] In a recent paper, following an asset view of the demand for money, several specifications of money demand equations for Mexico were estimated using quarterly data from 1960 to 1972 (Ortiz 1980). In addition to conventional regressors, several foreign interest rates and other proxy variables for exchange rate risk were included.[5] The results of the regressions fail to show any statistically significant influence of foreign variables on the demand for money (both M_1 and M_2 turn out to be stable functions of real income and measures of domestic opportunity costs), thus supporting the above-mentioned conclusions of Hernández-Catá (1974).

It seems then that the stable world and domestic environment prevailing during the 1960s allowed the Mexican authorities to determine the level of domestic interest rates with a certain degree of independence from the short-run move-

---

4. This procedure was recently applied by Alexander (1980) with the idea of testing the importance of the currency substitution effects on Canadian data. There is a growing body of literature concerned with the influence of the international economy on the demand for domestic money (see, for example, the papers by Hamburger 1977; Frenkel 1977; Abel, Dornbusch, Huizinga, and Marcus 1980; and Akhtar and Putnam 1980).

5. The proxies utilized to capture foreign exchange risk were based on real exchange rate calculations. A more common measure of foreign exchange risk is the degree of variability of either the spot or the forward exchange rate. However, the exchange rate was fixed throughout the estimation period, and a forward market for the peso did not exist before 1972.

ments of interest rates experienced abroad, thereby maintaining disequilibrium conditions in the credit market. The central bank fixed the levels of domestic deposit rates a few points above the prevailing international interest rates, leaving a "buffer zone" in which the foreign rates could fluctuate without provoking financial flows that would force variations of the domestic interest rates.

In the above scenario, foreign borrowing and interest rate policy were used quite successfully for the purpose of maintaining external balance (compensating the structural current account deficits), while the use of reserve requirements was directed toward the control of domestic liquidity. In fact, given the cyclical nature of public expenditures, this allocation of instruments allowed private investment to play a stabilizing role on economic activity – that is, expanding when government expenditures were sluggish due to a greater availability of funds (typically during the first year or two of the incoming administrations) and contracting as public expenditures were crowding out private outlays.

DOLLARIZATION AND MONETARY INDEPENDENCE

The effectiveness of the monetary instruments available to the authorities depended not only on an imperfect degree of capital mobility between Mexico and the rest of the world, but also on the ability of the central bank to expand and contract the domestic credit demanded by the private sector. Naturally, this required a moderate reliance of the government on the central bank to finance its budget deficits. Throughout the 1960s, the level of the government's deficit was kept within reasonable limits, and foreign borrowing was also used with restraint (the foreign debt–GDP ratio increased by less than two percentage points). However, after 1972 the acceleration of government spending resulted in deficits that could not be financed out of domestic private savings. The result was a sharp increase in the monetization of the deficit, which in turn fueled inflationary pressures. The higher inflation rates turned real interest rates negative, discouraging financial savings and further eroding the base of noninflationary domestic resources available to the government (for a more detailed analysis of the events occurring in this period, see Ortiz and Solís 1979).

The effect of the higher inflation rates of the 1970s on the size and structure of financial savings was quite dramatic. The ratio to GDP claims on the banking sector held by the public fell from 35 percent in 1972 to 25 percent in 1976, while the share of nonmonetary debt of financial institutions in total debt (that is, holdings of time deposits plus *financiera* bonds) decreased from a high point of 61 percent in 1972 to less than 37 percent in 1976. The reduction of the real size of the financial sector forced the government to increase foreign borrowing substantially in order to finance its growing deficits and to maintain an adequate level of foreign reserves. The public sector's external debt grew from $4.7 billion in 1972 to $14.4 billion at the end of 1975. It was precisely this combination of a reduced flow of domestic savings channeled through the banking system and an excessive use of foreign credit that impaired the use of reserve requirements as an effective instrument of monetary control.

Also, a persistent outflow of capital has developed since 1973, reflecting an increasing fear of devaluation in view of the high inflation rates and the speed of accumulation of foreign debt. It became increasingly clear that the peso (fixed at a parity of 12.50 pesos to a dollar since 1954) was gradually appreciating in real terms.[6] From 1973 to 1975, short-term capital outflows amounted to almost $3 billion.[7] Reported claims of Mexican residents (households and firms) on U.S. banking institutions alone increased from less than $400 million at the end of 1972 to more than $1.5 billion by the third quarter of 1976.[8]

Devaluation expectations were also reflected in the composition of financial assets held by the public in the domestic banking system. The share of the total debt of the financial sector denominated in dollars increased from 16 percent in 1972 to 31 percent in 1976, an increase of $10.2 billion in domestic holdings of dollar-denominated bonds.

Finally, on August 31, 1976, the peso was formally floated. The magnitude of the depreciation (about 45 percent in terms of dollars) was much greater than generally anticipated, as reflected in a forward premium of about 4 percent. Not surprisingly, it had a profound inflationary impact on prices, coupled with a severe contractionary effect on aggregate demand.[9]

In spite of the greater than expected magnitude of the devaluation, speculation against the peso did not subside in the months following the announcement. Private short-run capital outflows exceeded $1 billion during the last four months of 1976 and the first quarter of 1977. Dollar deposits in U.S. banks held by Mexicans (households and firms) increased $240 million during the last quarter of 1976 and the first quarter of 1977, representing an increase of 12.6 percent of total holdings. Dollar deposits held in Mexican banks also increased substantially following the devaluation. Figures 14-1 and 14-2 repre-

6. It is interesting to note that when the Mexican money demand estimations (see Ortiz 1980) were extended to include the years 1973-1979, the coefficient of the real exchange rate index used as a proxy for exchange rate risk turned out to be negative and statistically significant.

7. Short-term capital flows are only partially registered in the Mexican balance of payments statistics. These flows, including foreign sales of domestic financial assets, appear in the residual term "errors and omissions," so that a positive balance of this item tends to reflect net short-term capital inflows and conversely.

8. The U.S. *Treasury Bulletin* reports monthly claims and liabilities of foreigners on U.S. banking and nonbanking financial institutions. The figures distinguish between public sector and banking institutions and the private nonbanking sector. Short-term claims include demand, time and saving deposits, Treasury bills, and negotiable certificates of deposit.

9. The forward three-month rate for the Mexican peso quoted in the Chicago Mercantile Exchange Market in June 1976 was 12.97, implying a premium on the dollars of only 3.73 percent per annum. For a discussion on the effects of the devaluation on aggregate demand, see Córdoba and Ortiz (1979).

Figure 14-1. Dollar Checking Deposits–Peso Checking Deposits
(*Mexican financial institutions*).

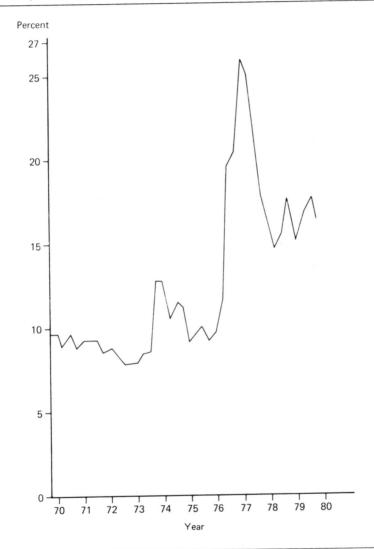

Source: Banco de México, S. A.

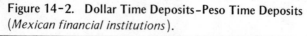

Figure 14-2.   Dollar Time Deposits-Peso Time Deposits
(*Mexican financial institutions*).

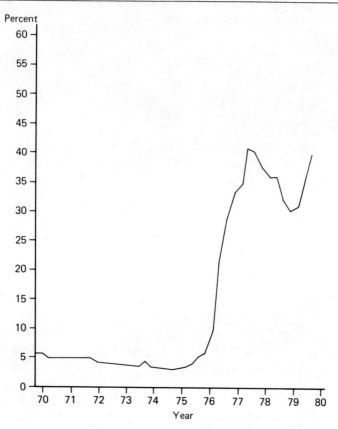

Source: Banco de México, S. A.

sent the proportion of dollar-denominated checking and time deposits to total peso deposits held in domestic financial institutions. From these figures it is apparent that the "dollarization" of demand deposits jumped sharply in 1976, declining again after the first quarter of 1977, while the proportion of dollar-denominated time deposits also increased substantially starting in early 1976, but accelerated rapidly after the September devaluation.

Mexican banking institutions have been authorized to receive dollar-denominated demand and time deposits since the 1940s. Interest rates payable on dollar time deposits—like those payable on peso deposits—were fixed by Banco de México and moved very little during the 1950s and most of the 1960s; during the 1970s, however, the more volatile behavior of world financial markets and interest rates forced the Mexican monetary authorities to adjust domestic interest rates more often. Finally, in March 1977, Banco de México announced that the interest rates payable on dollar deposits (of different maturities) received by financial institutions in Mexico would follow the daily fluctuations of the Eurodollar rates and pay a premium of one point above these rates. A few weeks later, the premium of one point was lowered to one-half of a percentage point, and in November 1978, this premium was totally eliminated.

The evolution of mexdollar rates and U.S. interest rates for six-month deposits since 1970 are depicted in Figure 14-3. From this figure, it is clear that large and persistent differences between rates occurred before 1977. These deviations of Mexican rates from those prevailing in international capital markets for the same type of deposits made mexdollar holdings imperfect substitutes for dollar deposits held abroad in a period when international capital markets were becoming even more integrated.

Figure 14-3.   Interest Rates on Dollar Deposits in the United States and Mexico.

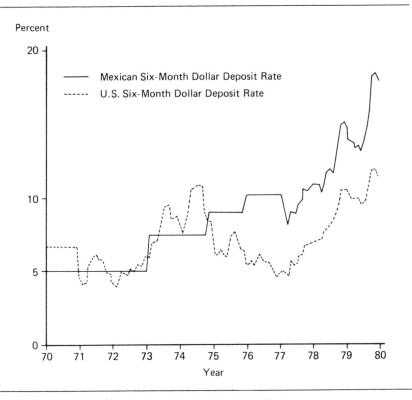

Source: Banco de México, S.A., and Federal Reserve Bulletin.

Along with the flexible mexdollar interest rate policy adopted, the monetary authorities allowed financial institutions to offer a more diversified choice of foreign-denominated deposits to the public (for example, in 1978, the *sociedades financieras* were authorized to receive one-month $100,000 dollar deposits). As a result of these measures, and except for political risk factors, current mexdollar deposits can be considered very close portfolio substitutes for dollar deposits offered in other major world financial centers. These measures were adopted in view of the instability introduced in domestic financial markets by the large short-term capital outflows that took place during the first few months of 1977. Naturally, the main objective was to provide Mexican residents with a competitive domestic menu of assets denominated in foreign currency to protect them from the risk of exchange rate fluctuations and thus to avoid the flight of speculative short-run financial funds.

Figure 14-4 illustrates the distribution of total dollar holdings of the Mexican private nonbanking sector between U.S. banking institutions and mexdollar deposits. It is apparent from this figure that the growth of the latter type of deposits has outpaced substantially the corresponding increase in U.S. banks' deposits, especially after the first quarter of 1977, when mexdollar interest rates were liberalized.

INTERVENTION ANALYSIS

A statistical method developed recently by Box and Tiao (1975) for the purpose of detecting and quantifying the effect of an exogenous event (such as the introduction of a new policy measure) on the behavior of a time series is a convenient tool for the analysis of the effect of the liberalization of the mexdollar interest rate on the distribution of dollar deposits between U.S. and Mexican banks. The procedure can be briefly described as follows.[10]

First, it is assumed that the series can be represented as a stochastic model of the Box-Jenkins (1976) type such as

$$y_t = f(\Omega, \xi, t) + N_t \tag{14.1}$$

where $y_t = F(Y_t)$ is an appropriate transformation of the data $Y_{t-1}, Y_t, Y_{t+1} \ldots$, which is obtained at equal time intervals; $f(\Omega, \xi, t)$ is a function that allows for deterministic effects Ω on y_t at time t; ξ is a vector of unknown parameters; and N_t represents a disturbance that can be modeled as an ARIMA process. Once the model is specified (according with the type of expected intervention), a dynamic intervention function is constructed, and the iterative Box-Jenkins technique is applied to estimate the complete model. Here we use

10. The basic reference is Box and Tiao (1975). In this paper the authors develop the basic methodology and apply it to evaluate the effects of Nixon administration Phase I and Phase II on the behavior of the U.S. Consumer Price Index. Two other applications of this technique can be found in Bhattacharyya and Layton (1979) and in Guerrero and Vera (1981).

Figure 14-4.   Dollar Deposit Holdings of Mexicans in U.S. and
Mexican Banks *(billion dollars)*.

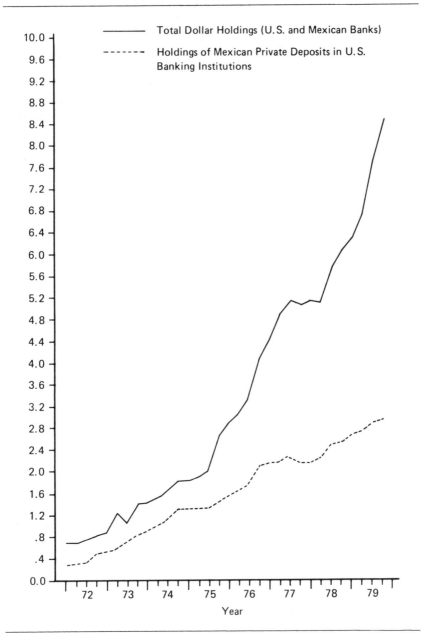

monthly data from January 1972 to December 1979 to analyze the effect of the pegging of the mexdollar rate to the Eurodollar rate on March 22, 1977, on the growth rates[11] of:

1. The holdings of dollar deposits by Mexicans on U.S. banks (USD_t);
2. The holdings of dollar deposits on Mexican banks (MXD_t); and
3. The ratio of mexdollar-to-U.S. holdings (RAT_t).

Given the type of intervention under consideration, one would expect a priori a portfolio redistribution of dollar deposits between U.S. and Mexican banks affecting not only the level of the deposits but also their rates of growth. This can be represented by the following intervention function:

$$\epsilon(t) = \left\{ \omega/1 - B \right\} P_t^I \qquad (14.2)$$

where B is the lag operator, ω is a parameter to be estimated, and P_t^I is a "pulse indicator" (see Box and Tiao 1975:71), such that

$$P_t^I = \begin{cases} 1 & \text{if } t = 1 \\ 0 & \text{if } t \neq 1 \end{cases} \qquad (14.3)$$

Note that equation (14.2) is a simple first-order difference equation $(1 - B)$ $\epsilon(t) = \omega P_t^I$. The solution of this equation, subject to the initial condition $\epsilon(t) = 0$ for $t < I$ (that is, there is no intervention effect before time I when it occurs) is

$$\epsilon(t) = \omega \qquad \text{for } t \geq I$$

and is illustrated in Figure 14-5.

The models constructed to represent the behavior of the series from January 1972 to March 1976 are reported in Table 14-1. The θs represent moving average parameters and the $\{a_t\}$ are white noise—that is, $\ldots a_{t-1}, a_t, a_{t+1} \cdots$, is a sequence of independently distributed random variables having mean zero and variance $(\sigma_a)^2$. All the parameters of Table 14-1 are significantly different from zero at two standard deviations (except for $\hat{\theta}_1$ of model 1.3, which is significant at 1.75 standard deviations).

The results of the estimations of the complete model (including the intervention function) for the period January 1972 to December 1979 are shown in Table 14-2. The coefficients of the ωs are all significantly different from zero at two standard deviations. Thus, bearing in mind the caveats of time series anal-

11. Let B be a lag operator, such that $BZ_t = Z_{t-1}$. Then $(1 - B) \ln(Z_t) = \ln(Z_t) - \ln(Z_{t-1}) = \ln(Z_t/Z_{t-1}) = \ln(1 + \gamma_t^z) \simeq \gamma_t^z$, where γ_t^z is the growth rate of Z_t. This transformation was performed since it is clear from Figure 14-4 that the levels of the original series are not stationary.

Figure 14-5. Intervention Function $\epsilon(t) = (\omega/1 - B)P_t^I$.

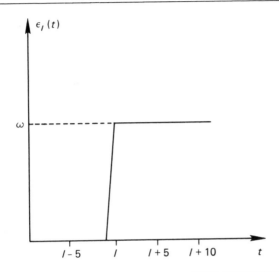

ysis, from this evidence it can be concluded that the effects of the mexdollar liberalization measures adopted in 1977 were

1. A decrease in the growth rate of the deposits held by Mexican residents in U.S. banks of about 2.1 percent;

2. An increase in the growth rate of mexdollar holdings of about 3.7 percent; and

3. A corresponding increase in the ratio of mexdollar holdings to deposits held by Mexicans in U.S. banks of 1.9 percent.

A CONCLUDING NOTE

One important finding from the previous section is that as the mexdollar market became more competitive, the outflow of funds to the United States was substantially reduced.[12] The lesson is, therefore, that the existence of a large mexdollar market gives the Mexican monetary authorities a certain degree of monetary independence in the short run, due to the insulation effect that this market provides from speculative capital flows.[13] It is obvious, on the other

12. The average quarterly figure for the "errors and omissions" items of the Mexican balance of payments from 1977 (II) to 1979 (IV) was $16.5 million compared with -$244.5 million for the 1975-1977 period.

13. In a recent paper, Ize (1981) analyzes the theoretical implications of a dual currency system on the financial equilibrium of an open economy.

Table 14-1. Estimated Models for the Period January 1972–
February 1977.

Model	Estimated Parameters and Standard Deviations	$\hat{\sigma}_a$	Q Statistic and (k) Degrees of Freedom[a]
1.1 $(1-B)\ln(USD_t) = \hat{\theta}_0 + a_t$	$\hat{\theta}_0 = -0.031 \pm 0.005$	0.0380	16.89 , (23)
1.2 $(1-B)\ln(MXD_t) = (1-\theta_1 B^4$ $-\theta_2 B^8 - \theta_3 B^{12}) a_t$	$\hat{\theta}_1 = -0.349 \pm 0.127$ $\hat{\theta}_2 = -0.772 \pm 0.109$ $\hat{\theta}_3 = -0.425 \pm 0.134$	0.0642	11.95 , (21)
1.3 $(1-B)\ln(RAT_t) = (1-\theta_1 B^7$ $-\theta_2 B^8 - \theta_3 B^{11}) a_t$	$\hat{\theta}_1 = -0.296 \pm 0.082$ $\hat{\theta}_2 = -0.495 \pm 0.090$ $\hat{\theta}_3 = -0.593 \pm 0.079$	0.0682	11.36 , (20)

a. The Q statistic should be compared with the values of a χ^2 with (k) degrees of freedom.

Table 14-2. Models Estimated for the Period January 1972–
December 1979.

Model	Estimated Parameters and Standard Deviations	$\hat{\sigma}_a$	Q Statistic and (k) Degrees of Freedom[a]
2.1 $(1-B)\ln(USD_t) = (\frac{\omega}{1-B})p_t^I$ $+ \theta_0 + a_t$	$\hat{\omega} = -0.021 \pm 0.004$ $\hat{\theta}_0 = 0.030 \pm 0.007$	0.0340	7.84 , (22)
2.2 $(1-B)\ln(MXD_t) = (\frac{\omega}{1-B})p_t^I$ $+ (1-\theta_1 B^4 - \theta_2 B^8$ $- \theta_3 B^{12})a_t$	$\hat{\omega} = 0.037 \pm 0.017$ $\hat{\theta}_1 = -0.299 \pm 0.101$ $\hat{\theta}_2 = -0.494 \pm 0.094$ $\hat{\theta}_3 = -0.313 \pm 0.103$	0.0564	21.81 , (20)
2.3 $(1-B)\ln(RAT_t) = (\frac{\omega}{1-B})p_t^I$ $+ (1-\theta_1 B^7 - \theta_2 B^8$ $- \theta_3 B^{11})a_t$	$\hat{\omega} = 0.026 \pm 0.0127$ $\hat{\theta}_1 = -0.228 \pm 0.100$ $\hat{\theta}_2 = -0.225 \pm 0.101$ $\hat{\theta}_3 = 0.250 \pm 0.101$	0.0621	18.02 , (19)

a. The Q statistic should be compared with the values of a χ^2 with (k) degrees of freedom.

hand, that mexdollar banking liabilities constitute potential claims against the foreign exchange reserves of Banco de México, with direct implications on exchange rate policy. Mexdollars will remain close substitutes for dollar deposits held abroad as long as the public believes in the commitment of the monetary authorities to full convertibility and unrestricted capital mobility.

It should also be mentioned that changes in the currency mix of bank deposits clearly affect the composition of financial institutions' portfolios on the asset side, since dollar deposits have to be balanced with dollar-denominated assets.[14] If dollar and peso deposits are not treated equally by the monetary authorities (different reserve requirements, for example), fluctuations in the deposit currency denomination will affect the available flow of credit and thus have potentially destabilizing real effects. However, in the absence of a functioning futures market, the mexdollar deposit market provides the monetary authorities with a good indicator of the state of expectations of the future evolution of prices and the exchange rate. With the dollar rate taken as given, the authorities can move the peso deposit rate in order to influence the composition of the public's portfolio between pesos and dollars.

14. This is a regulation of Banco de México. Currently, commercial banks are required to maintain 70 percent of their dollar liabilities as (interest-bearing) deposits in the central bank, and the remaining funds can be used to extend dollar-denominated loans at a market-determined rate of interest.

REFERENCES

Abel, Andrew B.; Rudiger Dornbusch; I. Huizinga; and A. Marcus. 1980. "Money Demand during Hyperinflation." *Journal of Monetary Economics* 5:98-103.

Akhtar, M.A., and Bluford H. Putnam. 1980. "Money Demand and Foreign Exchange Risk: The German Case, 1972-1976." *Journal of Finance* 6: 787-94.

Alexander, William. 1980. "Foreign Influence on the Demand for Money in an Open Economy: The Canadian Case." Paper presented at the XVII Reunión de Técnicos de Bancos Centrales del Continente Americano, Bogotá, Colombia, November 24-29.

Bazdresch, Carlos P. 1973. "La Política Monetaria Mexicana: Una Primera Aproximación," In Leopoldo Solís, ed., *La Economía Mexicana IV*, pp. 138-56. Mexico, D.F.: Fondo de Cultura Económica.

Bhattacharya, Mihir, and A.P. Layton. 1979. "Effectiveness of Seat Belt Legislation on the Queensland Road Toll—An Australian Case Study in Intervention Analysis." *Journal of the American Statistical Association* 74:596-603.

Box, G.E.P., and G.M. Jenkins. 1976. *Time Series Analysis, Forecasting and Control.* 2d ed. San Francisco: Holden Day.

Box, G.E.P., and George C. Tiao. 1975. "Intervention Analysis with Applications to Economic and Environmental Problems." *Journal of the American Statistical Association* 70 (March):70-79.

Brillembourg, Arturo, and Susan Schadler. 1980. "A Model of Currency Substitution in Exchange Rate Determination, 1973-78." *IMF Staff Papers* 3: 513-42.

Brothers, Dwight S., and Leopoldo Solís. 1966. *Mexican Financial Development.* Austin: University of Texas Press.

Córdoba, José, and Guillermo Ortiz. 1979. "Aspectos Contraccionarios de la Devaluación del Peso Mexicano de 1976." Documento de Investigación No. 9, Subdirección de Investigación Económica, Banco de México. In *Economía y Demografía*, in press.

Frenkel, Jacob A. 1977. "The Forward Exchange Rate, Expectations, and the Demand for Money: The German Hyperinflation." *American Economic Review* 4 (September): 653-70.

Girton, Lance, and Don E. Roper. 1981. "Theory and Implications of Currency Substitution." *Journal of Money, Credit and Banking* 1:12-30.

Guerrero, Victor, and Gabriel Vera. 1981. "Una Applicación del Análisis de Intervención a Series de Tiempo de la Economía Mexicana." Documento de Investigación No. 33, Subdirección de Investigación Económica, Banco de México, S.A.

Hamburger, Michael J. 1977. "The Demand for Money in an Open Economy. Germany and the United Kingdom." *Journal of Monetary Economics* 3: 25-40.

Hernández-Catá, Ernesto. 1974. "International Movements of Private Financial Capital. An Econometric Analysis of the Mexican Case." Ph.D. Dissertation, Yale University.

Ize, Alain. 1981. "Real Stabilization and Asset Substitution in a Bicurrency Financial System with Devaluation Expectations." El Colegio de México.

Koehler, John E. 1968. "Information and Policymaking: Mexico." Ph.D. Dissertation, Yale University.

Krasker, William. 1980. "The Peso Problem in Testing the Efficiency of Forward Exchange Markets." *Journal of Monetary Economics* 6: 269–76.

Lizondo, Saul. 1981. "Interest Differentials and Covered Arbitrage." Paper presented at the NBER/ITAM conference on Financial Policies and the World Capital Market: The Problem of Latin American Countries, Mexico City, March 26–27.

Miles, Marc A. 1978. "Currency Substitution, Flexible Exchange Rates, and Monetary Independence." *American Economic Review* 3 (June): 428–36.

Mundell, Robert A. 1968. *International Economics.* New York: Macmillan.

Ortiz, Guillermo. 1980. "La Estabilidad de la Demanda de Dinero en México." Documento de Investigación No. 30, Subdirección de Investigación Económica, Banco de México, S.A.

Ortiz, Guillermo, and Leopoldo Solís. 1979. "Financial Structure and Exchange Rate Experience, Mexico 1954–1977." *Journal of Development Economics* 6: 515–48.

Ortiz–Mena, Antonio. 1969. "Desarrollo Estabilizador – Una Década de Estrategia Económica en México." *El Mercado de Valores* No. 14.

Sheldon, Donald. 1964. "The Banking System." In *Public Policy and Private Enterprise in Mexico.* Cambridge, Massachusetts: Harvard University Press.

Triffin, Robert. 1978a. "The International Role and Fate of the Dollar." *Foreign Affairs* 57: 269–86.

_____. 1978b. "Gold and the Dollar Crisis: Yesterday and Tomorrow." *Essays in International Finance* 132. Princeton University.

15 GOLD AND THE DOLLAR: ASYMMETRIES IN WORLD MONEY STOCK DETERMINATION, 1959-1971

Alexander K. Swoboda and
Hans Genberg

INTRODUCTION

Two recurring themes in Robert Triffin's writings on the international monetary system have been, on the one hand, the inherent instability of a reserve currency system and, on the other hand, the inflationary potential of a reserve system based on the dollar. His *Gold and the Dollar Crisis* (1960) emphasized what has since become known as the "Triffin dilemma." The very fact that a strong currency becomes used as an international reserve asset weakens it. As the center country's ratio of owned international assets (e.g., gold) to external liabilities (e.g., dollars) declines, the Triffin dilemma arises: Either the growth of international liquidity is stunted in order to prevent a further deterioration of the gold-dollar ratio, thereby threatening a deflationary crisis, or dollar holdings are allowed to expand, thereby threatening a confidence crisis. In other writings, Triffin has emphasized and deplored the "explosion" of international liquidity — and the ensuing inflationary growth of domestic monetary aggregates—that has resulted from reliance on the dollar as the main source of growth of international reserves (see, for instance, Triffin 1979).

This chapter attempts to give more precise content to the second of these concerns—which we consider as perhaps more important than the "Triffin dilemma" in explaining the breakdown of the Bretton Woods system in the early 1970s (on this point, see, for instance, Swoboda 1978b). That breakdown can be viewed as resulting in part from an inability to agree on an appropriate common stance of macroeconomic policy, with the fixity of exchange rates ensuring convergence among national inflation rates and fairly close links in real cycles, and with the reserve currency status of the dollar imparting to the monetary policy of the United States a dominant role in the determination of the industrialized world's common macroeconomic trend. There are several components to this view — first, that fixed exchange rates enforce substantial convergence of national inflation rates; second, that world monetary aggregates play an important role in determining the average (or underlying) "worldwide" rate of inflation toward which national inflation rates converge; and third, that the monetary policy of the country whose currency is used as an international reserve asset by other countries plays a dominant role in determining world monetary aggregates.

It is on the last of these hypotheses that this chapter concentrates. To justify the chapter's focus on the determinants of the world money stock, section two begins with a brief outline of the underpinnings of the monetary view of the generation and transmission of worldwide inflation under fixed exchange rates. It then develops a simple model of the world money stock under fixed rates to give content to the hypothesis that the monetary policy of the United States played a dominant role in determining the evolution of world monetary aggregates under the Bretton Woods system. The results of empirical tests of the hypotheses yielded by the theoretical model are presented in section three. The concluding section draws some implications for the interpretation of postwar international monetary history.

THE ROLE AND DETERMINANTS OF THE WORLD MONEY STOCK

In the late 1960s and early 1970s, the period of major strain and eventual breakdown for the Bretton Woods system, inflation rose significantly in industrialized countries and took on worldwide character. To illustrate, the average of annual rates of inflation for ten industrialized countries rose from 2.3 percent per annum in 1955–1965 to 4.1 percent in 1965–1970 and to 6.9 percent in 1969–1974. At the same time, the standard deviation calculated for each year stayed within the narrow range of 0.7 to 1.8 over the entire period 1955–1973, with the exception of 1958 and 1963.[1] We have argued in some detail elsewhere that the convergence of national inflation rates from the return to convertibility in 1957 to the breakdown of fixed exchange rates was sufficient to confer both analytical and empirical content on the concept of a worldwide rate of inflation. We have also argued that the "world money stock," rather than individual national money stocks, plays a crucial role in determining the world rate of inflation.[2] Only the briefest summary of the argument is offered below before we

---

1. The figures are from Genberg and Swoboda (1977a), where a more detailed picture of worldwide inflation can be found. The ten countries are the G-10 countries minus Sweden plus Switzerland.

2. See, for instance, Genberg and Swoboda (1977a, 1977b). This section is partly based on the second section of the latter, unpublished paper.

turn to a discussion of symmetries and asymmetries in the determination of the world money stock.

Worldwide Inflation and the World Money Stock

National inflation rates will tend to converge under a system of fixed exchange rates. If the convergence were complete, one and the same inflation rate, the world rate, would prevail in all countries linked by fixed rates. Even if the convergence is not perfect, the common element in national inflation rates may be strong enough to warrant focusing on explaining the world rate of inflation, while for some purposes also investigating the sources of national deviations from the common inflationary trend.[3]

There are, of course, many reasons why national inflation rates should tend to converge under fixed exchange rates. Goods arbitrage provides one of the principal links among national price levels and rates of inflation. Such arbitrage should equalize the prices of homogeneous traded goods, expressed in the same currency unit, up to a margin representing transport costs and impediments to trade. Over a period long enough for adjustment to take place and for price rigidities not to play too important a role, the prices of nontraded goods will tend to move in the same direction as the prices of traded goods—and hence in unison across countries. The mechanism that brings the two sets of price changes into line relies on substitution effects in both consumption and production. To illustrate the mechanism of inflation transmission, consider a single country that faces a rise in the world price of traded goods. This creates an excess demand for nontraded goods, an excess supply of traded goods, and a payments surplus. The prices of nontraded goods begin to rise, as does the money stock; the process goes on until equilibrium is restored at initial relative prices, but with a higher money stock, price level, and nominal income.

In practice, one would not expect measured inflation rates to be exactly identical across countries, even under fixed exchange rates. Apart from differences introduced by adjustment lags, discrepancies may occur because of technical differences between countries in the measurement of inflation, on the one hand, and because of changes in the economies that alter the equilibrium-relative prices of traded to nontraded goods, on the other. Differences in measurement may stem, inter alia, from differences and changes in the quantity weights entering national prices indexes, from differences in sampling methods and frequency, and from differences in the treatment of changes in the quality of the goods entering the price indexes (see Genberg 1977).

Structural changes that alter the equilibrium-relative prices of traded to nontraded goods may also be a source of differences between countries in measured inflation rates. Such structural changes can result from externally imposed

---

3. In one way, this is similar to being interested both in why purchasing power parity should tend to hold and in why there should be deviations from it.

changes in the terms of trade, from differences in rates of growth of productivity, or from local changes in tastes; and they lead to less than exact convergence of measured inflation rates—namely, to equilibrium deviations from purchasing power parity.

Neither of the problems just discussed robs the concept of a world rate of inflation of its analytical meaning and usefulness under fixed rates, however. The empirical applicability of the concept, on the other hand, depends on the relative importance of movements in general price levels as compared to movements in relative prices. For the period and the sample of countries considered in this chapter, Genberg's previous work (1976, 1977) suggests that the concept of a world price level and rate of inflation is indeed empirically useful.

Convergence of national inflation rates to a worldwise rate leaves open the question of what determines the latter. It seems natural, here, to extend the monetary hypotheses concerning the relationship between money and prices in a closed national economy to the fixed exchange rate world economy, the only truly closed economy. To put it in somewhat simplistic fashion, the world price level adjusts in the long run and through a variety of mechanisms to bring into equality the world demand for money with the world supply. Just as arbitrage in goods, together with fixed rates, make it meaningful to talk about a world price level, so fixed rates, together with the payments adjustment mechanism, lend meaning to the concept of a world stock of money, defined as the sum of the money stocks in the hands of the public in various countries converted into a common currency unit at the ruling fixed exchange rates. National moneys can be aggregated into a Hicksian composite commodity by virtue of the exchange stabilization operations of central banks, which keep their relative prices constant.

The world demand for money, in turn, is the sum of national demands. Static equilibrium requires not only that the world demand equal the supply, but also that the demand for each national money stock be equal to the supply. It is the role of the world price level to satisfy the former equality and the role of the payments adjustment mechanism to satisfy the latter. From a national vantage point, the payments adjustment mechanism endogenizes the national stock of money; from an international point of view, it serves to endogenize the distribution of the world money stock (and of reserves) among nations. This long-run monetary view yields three simple hypotheses for empirical work—that there should be a broad correlation between secular changes in world prices and the world money stock; that "causation" should run from world money to world prices; and that for an individual small country, the supply of money should adapt to the demand for it. Empirical evidence is broadly consistent with these three hypotheses.[4]

---

4. On the correlation between secular changes in world prices and the world money stock, see, for example, Meiselman (1975), Heller (1976), and Genberg and Swoboda (1977a). The latter authors also apply Granger–Sims tests of temporal precedence and con-

This account, however, leaves open the question of what determines the world money stock. The argument implies that even though the world stock is the sum of national money stocks, a small country's monetary policy will not have a significant long-run influence on the world rate of inflation and hence on its own national rate, unless it can significantly affect world monetary aggregates.[5] To illustrate, consider an open market purchase of nontraded securities by the monetary authorities of a small open economy. Within the confines of a standard macromodel, this will put downward pressure on home interest rates, raising expenditure, income, and the price level. The effects will be only temporary, however, since the ensuing balance of trade (and capital account) deficit puts downward pressure on the home money supply. The rest of the world's reserves increase, as does its money stock. The home country's monetary policy has become generalized through the process of redistribution of international reserves—that is, through the process of payments adjustment. This generalization will occur faster the more integrated are goods and asset markets. Had the open market operation taken place in traded securities, the reserve loss would have been instantaneous for most practical purposes. Whether domestic monetary policy has a lasting impact on domestic prices and other variables thus depends on whether it has a significant impact on the world money stock, on foreign demand, and on foreign prices. This depends, of course, on the size of the domestic economy relative to that of the rest of the fixed exchange rate world, but also, as the next subsection emphasizes, on the institutional arrangements that govern the supply of international reserves.

Symmetries and Asymmetries in World Money Stock Determination

The world money stock has been defined as the sum of the national money stocks held by the world's public.[6] However, to analyze its determinants in terms of a simple sum of the determinants of national money stocks would be

---

clude that changes in the world money stock precede changes in world money income and prices. They find, in addition, that the temporal precedence of money relative to income and prices either vanishes or becomes much less strong for a number of single small open economies.

5. Empirically, the argument also suggests that "world," rather than national, aggregates are the relevant variables in determining the world rate of inflation—that is, the common element in national inflation rates. This is borne out by the authors' own work (see, especially, Genberg and Swoboda 1977b) and by work of members of the Manchester Inflation Workshop. See, in particular, Gray, Ward, and Zis (1976) for estimation of a stable world demand for money function and Duck, Parkin, Rose, and Zis (1976) for estimation of an expectations-augmented Phillips curve for the world economy.

6. All the usual problems concerning the definition of money arise in the present context. In addition, accounting for Eurocurrency deposits and deciding which portion of such deposits should be included raise many questions. These will be almost entirely ignored here for the sake of brevity. For further discussion, see Swoboda (1978a).

either misleading or not very informative (in the nature of a tautology). The reason is simply that national money stocks are not independent of each other; they are related through the payments adjustment mechanism. An alternative procedure is to model the world money stock as one would that of a closed economy – namely in terms of exogenous or policy controllable variables and of behavioral parameters. Such an approach is adopted in Swoboda (1978a), where the domestic source components of national monetary bases are treated as exogenous variables, together with the stock of outside international reserves (in practice, gold and IMF-created international reserves), and behavioral parameters include the desired ratio of commercial bank reserves to deposit liabilities, the proportions of different types of international reserves desired by central banks, and the preferences of the public for different types of monetary assets. The details of that analysis will not be repeated here, but some of its salient implications for an empirical investigation of the world money supply process are summarized below, emphasizing the asymmetries introduced by institutional arrangements such as the dollar standard, on the one hand, and by the neutralization of reserve flows, on the other.

It will be useful to start with the simplest case, in which the only international reserve asset is gold, to illustrate the basic symmetry of an outside reserve system. Consider a two-country world composed of the United States and Europe, and let variables that refer to Europe be distinguished by an asterisk. Let each country's money supply, M, be equal to a multiplier, m, times the monetary base, B, whose source components are the domestic assets of the central bank, A, and international reserves, IR, in this instance gold, G. The world gold stock is given and equal to $\bar{G}$: Its distribution among the two countries, G and G^*, however, is endogenous to the system. The demands for real money balances in the United States and Europe are denoted by L and L^*, respectively. For convenience, the exchange rate is assumed to be equal to 1 throughout this subsection.

Consider the effect of an open market purchase of securities in the United States – that is, an increase in A by, say, dA. For a constant stock and distribution of international reserves, the effect of the change (which could be dubbed the "impact" effect) would be to increase the U.S. money stock by mdA and, hence, the world money stock ($M^w = M + M^*$) by the same amount. For given values of the arguments of the demand for money functions, however, there is now an excess supply of dollars and a world excess supply of money. Adjustment requires both that the world demand for money increase (through a generalized increase in money income and/or decrease in interest rates) and that the excess supply of U.S. money be eliminated. The latter excess supply is eliminated because the generalized increase in money income and decline in interest rates increases the European demand for money until it matches the U.S. excess supply and gold flows from the latter to the former to reestablish payments equilibrium. As gold flows from the United States to Europe, moreover, the former country's money supply decreases by mdG, while the latter's increases by $m*dG*$ $(= -m*dG)$.[7] A redistribution of reserves changes the total world money stock if the two money multipliers differ.[8]

Full equilibrium requires that the world demand for money be equal to the supply and that each country's money stock be equal to the demand for it. Formally, this is equivalent to the satisfaction of the following three equations:

$$M^W = M + M* = PL + P*L*$$ (15.1)

$$M = PL$$ (15.2)

$$M* = P*L*$$ (15.3)

only two of which are independent.

Through substitution it is possible to express the world money stock as a function of exogenous variables $(A, A*, \bar{G})$ and of the ratio of national money demands:

$$M^W = \frac{1}{\beta(1/m) + (1 - \beta)(1/m*)} \cdot (A + A* + \bar{G})$$ (15.4)

where $\beta = L/[L + L* \cdot (P*/P)]$.

This formula expresses the world money stock as the product of a multiplier times the sum of domestic assets of central banks plus the world gold stock. The multiplier is a weighted average of the national money multipliers, the weights, β and $(1 - \beta)$, reflecting the "effective sizes" of the two countries. Here, effective size refers to the weight of each country in the total demand for money. In full equilibrium (but not at impact or during adjustment), these weights will be independent of changes in national money supplies and, provided some assumptions are satisfied, of the size of the world money stock.[9] That is, in equilibrium, β can be treated as exogenous, its long-run changes being governed by such factors as different long-term rates of growth of income across countries.[10]

---

7. More precisely, $DM = mDG$, where D indicates the differential operator with respect to time.

8. In the final equilibrium, however, equal changes in A and $A*$ have exactly the same effect on $M*$ even if m and $m*$ differ; see expression (15.4). The magnitude of the change in M^W, however, is affected by m and $m*$.

9. The relationship between β and the world money stock is outlined in Swoboda (1978a). β will be independent of M^W in a world of price flexibility and full employment. With price rigidities (a Keynesian world), additional conditions (essentially, similarity of income and interest elasticities of the demands for money across countries) must be imposed for β and M^W to be independent of each other. However, even if these conditions are not met, a stable functional relationship between β and M^W in terms of such elasticities can be derived.

10. It may be helpful to think of β as being subject to short-run changes due to variations in national monetary policies. Assume, for instance, that the Federal Reserve carries

In the present context, the one important lesson of equation (15.4) is that an increase in A and A^* of equal size has equal effects on M^W. This may seem surprising at first, since initially an increase of dA increases M by $m\,dA$, an increase of dA^* increases M^* by m^*dA^*, and the two increases will be different if national money multipliers differ. With payments adjustment, however, the initial increase in a national money stock is redistributed, and the final result is the same—that is, $dM^W/dA = dM^W/dA^* = dM^W/d\bar{G}$.

The symmetric gold standard case is illustrated in Figure 15-1. Panel (a) illustrates the case where $m = m^*$. The ray OH (in honor of Hume) shows the combinations of the two money stocks compatible with payments equilibrium: It represents equilibrium distributions of the world money stock between the two regions, and its slope is $\beta/(1 - \beta)$. Consider an initial equilibrium at point A. If gold were redistributed from one region to another, it would decrease the money stock of the first and increase that of the second by the same amount, since $m = m^*$, leaving the world stock unchanged. The effects of such redistributions of gold, given the total stock of the metal and given the domestic assets of the two central banks, are represented by the line M_0^W, with a slope of $45°$ since $m = m^*$. Consider, now, an open market purchase of securities by the European central bank, which initially increases the European money stock from M_0^* to M_1^*. The world money stock increases by the same amount, and, without payments adjustment, the U.S. money supply would remain unchanged; the system would move to point B. But this is not a full equilibrium point, since there is an excess supply of European money and excess demand for U.S. dollars. The ensuing redistribution of gold brings the system to full equilibrium at point D, along the new world money line M_1^W. Both the impact and final effect on the world money stock would have been the same had the initial open market purchase been made by the U.S. central bank. With $m = m^*$, $M_0 M_1 = M_0^* M_1^*$, and after having first moved to C, the system would have again settled at D. The major difference between the two cases is that the movement from A to B and then to D redistributes gold to the United States through a temporary American payments surplus, while the movement from A to C and then to D involves gold accumulation and a temporary surplus for Europe.

The symmetry in final equilibrium, though not on "impact," remains even if $m \neq m^*$. This is illustrated in panel (b) of Figure 15-1 for the case where $m > m^*$. In that case, the M^W lines are steeper than $45°$, since a redistribution of gold from Europe to the United States increases the U.S. money supply by more than it decreases the European one (hence, the world money stock

out an open market purchase that increases the U.S. money supply; β increases to, say, β_1, and then, through a complex adjustment mechanism that involves reserve flows, changes in the world money stock, and changes in interest, income, and price levels, adjusts back to its initial equilibrium level, say, β^*. The relevance of the theory outlined in the text to the real world hinges, of course, partly on the speed of that adjustment mechanism. Estimates in Genberg and Swoboda (1977b) indicate this adjustment to be quite rapid.

Figure 15-1. The Symmetric Gold Standard Case.

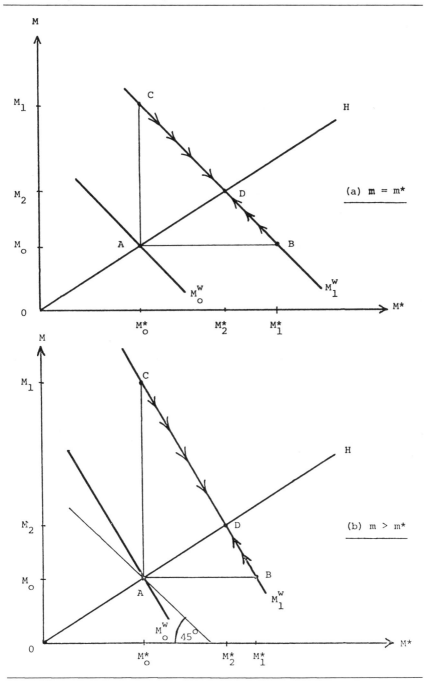

increases as one moves up an M^W line). The impact effects of U.S. and European open market purchases differ $(AC > AB)$. The final effects, after payments adjustment has taken place, are the same, however, as the system ends up at point B in both cases.[11] This basic symmetry of the gold standard (or of any system based on outside international reserves) is lost when a national currency is held as an international reserve.

Consider, for instance, a very simple model of the dollar standard. Assume that the European central bank holds all its international reserves in the form of deposits with U.S. commercial banks. The world money supply formula becomes[12]:

$$M^W = \frac{1}{\beta + (1 - \beta)(1/m^*)} \cdot (mA + A^*) \tag{15.5}$$

It is immediately apparent that European and U.S. monetary policies (changes in A^* and A, respectively) have very different effects on the world money stock. Whereas the (final) effect of U.S. monetary policy increases significantly, as compared with the symmetrical gold standard case, that of European monetary policy decreases dramatically. This asymmetry in response stems essentially from the fact that deposits at U.S. commercial banks, which are low-powered money there, are a source of high-powered money in Europe. The reserve outflow from the United States attendant on an increase in A creates a multiple expansion in the European money supply, but reduces (the increase in) the stock of dollars held by the U.S. public by only an equivalent and not a multiple amount. In contrast, an outflow of reserves from Europe attendant on an increase in A^* reduces (the increase in) Europe's money supply by a multiple amount, but increases the U.S. money supply in the hands of the public by only an equivalent amount. As a consequence, it is no longer possible to express the world money stock as the product of a given multiplier times an aggregated world money base. The origin of the change in base money plays a very important role in determining the change in the world money stock.

The same conclusion emerges even more dramatically if the European central bank keeps its international reserves entirely in the form of U.S. Treasury bills. In that case, expression (15.5) reduces to expression (15.6):

$$M^W = \frac{mA}{\beta} \tag{15.6}$$

American monetary policy is even more powerful than before, while European open market operations have no effect at all. Intuitively, the explanation is

11. Note also that if, other things equal, β increases (the line OH rotates upward), the world money stock increases or decreases depending on whether m is larger or smaller than m^*. This has an important bearing for the empirical testing undertaken in the next section.

12. For derivation of this and other results in this section, see Swoboda (1978a).

similar to that given above. As European monetary authorities buy European bonds from the public, European exchange stabilization authorities are selling U.S. bonds to that same public in order to acquire the dollars with which to buy back the European currency that is in excess supply in the foreign exchange market. In the end, the total amount of bonds outstanding is the same, the authorities having swapped U.S. bonds against European bonds with the public. Provided that the two types of bonds are perfect substitutes, the result described by equation (15.6) will hold exactly.[13] If the degree of substitutability were less perfect, however, the European open market purchase of domestic securities should lead to a fall in the interest rate on European securities and a rise in the interest rate on dollar assets. As a result, β would tend to fall, and the world and European money supply would tend to rise. Equation (15.6) would continue to hold, but A^* would enter the determination of M^W through β. The asymmetry between the effects of A and A^* on M^W would nevertheless remain.

Expression (15.6) also holds for the case in which the U.S. monetary authorities neutralize the effect of reserve flows on the money stock held by the U.S. public. Again, the sources of the asymmetry are easily explained. An expansionary open market purchase of bonds in Europe creates an excess supply of that region's currency that would normally be eliminated by a reduction in the total expansion of European money, which would have taken place in the absence of a reserve outflow and by a general expansion in the demand for money as interest rates fall, money incomes rise, and the U.S. money supply expands. With neutralization by the United States, that latter adjustment cannot take place; instead, Europe keeps losing reserves that do not result in an increase in the U.S. money supply. In contrast, when the United States engages in monetary expansion, the resulting reserve outflow does result in monetary expansion abroad, but fails to moderate monetary expansion in the United States because of the neutralization policy adopted by that country.

The strong asymmetry case of equation (15.6) is illustrated in Figure 15-2. For simplicity, the two money multipliers are assumed to be equal. Initial equilibrium is at point A. Consider the effects of an initial expansion of the European money stock from M_0^* to M_1^*. Without payments adjustment, we are, again, at B. The European payments deficit and corresponding U.S. surplus, however, are not allowed to affect the U.S. money stock (either because the European central bank sells U.S. Treasury bills or because the U.S. authorities do the selling to neutralize the reserve inflow). As a result, Europe will lose international reserves until its monetary base and money stock have decreased back to their original level and the system has returned to A. Consider now an expansion in the U.S. money stock from M_0 to M_1, which moves the system initially to

---

13. The result would be established instantaneously if capital mobility were perfect, but would only emerge over time in a model that assumes that interest rate differentials generate continuing capital flows.

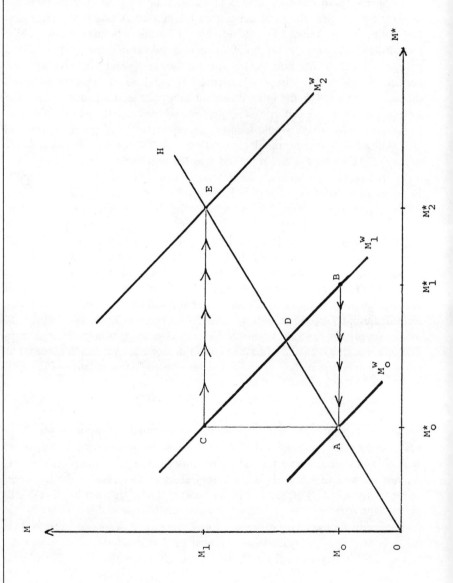

Figure 15-2. The Strongly Asymmetric Gold Standard Case.

point C. Under the gold standard, the resulting U.S. reserve loss and European reserve gain would move the two economies to point D, with world money stock M_1^w. With strong asymmetry, however, the U.S. deficit is not allowed to reduce the U.S. money stock, while the European reserves, monetary base, and money stock expand until an equilibrium distribution of the world money stock (M_2^w) is reached at point E.[14]

The preceding discussion carries two main messages for the purpose of this chapter. The first is that a change in national monetary policy becomes generalized at the world level through (1) the interaction of the adjustment of prices and incomes to an excess demand or supply of money in the world and (2) the adjustment of individual countries' money stocks to the demand for them through the process of payments adjustment. The second is that asymmetries are likely to arise as soon as low-powered money in one part of the system is used as high-powered money in other parts.[15]

One implication is that the process by which worldwide inflation is generated will differ depending on the particular institutional mode of organization of a fixed exchange rate system. In particular, a dollar standard imparts special importance to monetary policy in the United States in determining the course of world economic activity, for at least three reasons. There are, first, the asymmetries that arise from the practice by central banks abroad of accumulating inside (dollar) reserves and from U.S. neutralization of reserve flows. Second, it is easier for the United States to neutralize such flows, since the reserve currency country does not face the same reserve constraint as other countries, as long as the latter are willing to accumulate dollar reserves. Third, the sheer size of the United States implies a dominant influence on the world money stock and economic activity as compared with any individual country in the rest of the world.

The foregoing does not mean that any sustained change in the world money stock must have its origin in the United States. A balanced expansion of the domestic assets of both banking systems is not only possible but likely in some circumstances: It would tend to occur if policy reactions to common problems were similar in the two regions or if "Europe" was trying to maintain a given stock, or rate of growth, of reserves—or even a desired ratio of reserves to money supply. In addition, "Europe" can play at the neutralization game, too. It does mean, however, that over a longer term horizon, expansion of the domestic

14. Note that, under strong asymmetry, an increase in β unambiguously decreases the world money stock. In Figure 15-2, rotate OH upwards for a given U.S. money stock. The reader can satisfy himself that this will reduce M^*, and hence M^w, irrespective of whether $m > m^*$ or $m^* > m$.

15. The extent of such asymmetries in the "real world" is likely to be much more pervasive and complex than in the simple cases alluded to above. Some of these complexities are investigated in Swoboda (1978a), which develops a more general model, incorporating the Eurodollar market and central bank preferences as to the composition of their international reserve.

assets of the U.S. banking system is likely to be a necessary, though not sufficient, condition for expansion in the world money stock.

At an empirical level, the preceding analysis has two main implications. First, asymmetries induced by reserve-holding patterns and neutralization policies are worth investigating. Second, it is inappropriate simply to link the growth of the world money stock to the growth of a "world money base" composed of the sum of the domestic assets and international reserve holdings of national central banks, since part at least of international reserves is endogenous to the system and since the impact of a change in domestic assets on the world money stock is not independent of its national origin when asymmetries are present. The empirical work reported below takes these factors into account and thus differs from the few existing investigations of the world money supply process, which typically aggregate U.S. and non-U.S. monetary bases and treat foreign exchange reserves as being exogenously determined.[16]

EMPIRICAL TESTING

The preceding theoretical considerations attribute a very special role to U.S. monetary policy in the determination of the world monetary stock. The purpose of the empirical work reported below is to test for this asymmetry between the United States and the rest of the world in the world money supply process. The tests also shed some light on the extent to which sterilization of the effects of balance of payments deficits and surpluses on the U.S. money supply has taken place. Summarizing the outcome of the tests very briefly, the data strongly support the notion of an asymmetry between the role of the United States and that of the rest of the world. While it is not possible to affirm that "only the United States matters," is is quite clear that "the United States matters more." Furthermore, although it is not possible to assert that the effects of all reserve flows on the U.S. money supply have been effectively sterilized, the results clearly indicate that partial sterilization has regularly taken place.

Hypotheses to be Tested

The starting point of the empirical work was the specification of an equation for the world money supply capable of distinguishing between the special cases of

---

16. Heller (1976) expresses the world money stock as a distributed lag function of current and past world reserves. Changes in world reserves "explain" some 50 percent of the variation in the world money stock, with a mean lag of about one year. No explanation is provided, however, for the growth in world reserves. Parkin, Richards, and Zis (1974) relate the growth in the Group of Ten's aggregate money stock to the product of a multiplier and the sum of these countries' monetary bases (including gross international reserves). Under a partial adjustment hypothesis, the "world" money stock is seen as a distributed lag function of the "world" monetary base. Adjustment of the multipliers to their equilibrium value is, however, in our view, implausibly slow, a result that, we suspect, is due to the misspecification of the model.

symmetry, asymmetry, and full sterilization discussed in the previous section. With this in mind, consider equation (15.7):

$$M^W = F(A, A^*, \bar{R}, m, m^*, Y/Y^W, t) \qquad (15.7)$$

The notation in equation (15.7) is the same as that employed above, with the addition of t, which stands for a time trend, and $\bar{R}$, which represents "outside" international reserves (gold, SDRs, and the like). Y and Y^* are money income levels in the two regions, and $Y^W = Y + Y^*$.[17] This equation should not be thought of as a money supply identity. It incorporates explicitly both supply and demand factors and implicitly a balance of payments-adjustment process that ensures an equilibrium distribution of the world money stock. The first five arguments in the function are supply variables. In a perfectly symmetric world, an increase in domestic assets on the books of either monetary authority, an increase in "outside" reserves, and increases in either of the money multipliers should be expected to increase the world's nominal quantity of money for a given distribution among regions. Furthermore, under symmetry, A, A^*, and $\bar{R}$ would have equal quantitative effects, as would m and m^*. An increase in the relative income level of the United States would shift the equilibribum distribution of M^W toward the United States,[18] lead to a loss of reserves in the rest of the world at the expense of the United States, and increase or decrease M^W, depending on whether m was greater or less than m^*. The time trend, included as a catchall for omitted demand as well as supply factors, cannot be given an unambiguous interpretation, but to the extent that it captures mainly demand influences, its explanatory power would reflect changes over time in the demand for dollars relative to the composite currencies of the rest of the world.

In the extreme case of complete sterilization of all balance of payments influences on the U.S. money supply, equation (15.7) would be reduced to equation (15.8):

$$M^W = F^S(A, m, Y/Y^W, t) \qquad (15.8)$$

— that is, all supply factors in the rest of the world would disappear. This is a clear, testable proposition of the theory outlined above. The demand factors, operating via the balance of payments adjustment process, would now have unambiguous signs irrespective of the relative size of the multipliers. Any development that shifted demand away from the dollar would increase M^W, and vice versa.

The intermediate case of partial asymmetry also has precise testable implications. The general form of equation (15.7) would again be applicable, but the

17. The ratio of U.S. to world money income is a proxy for the "relative effect size" variable mentioned above, and, hence, for equilibrium β. As discussed above, it will be a relatively good proxy if interest rates are equalized and if the income and interest elasticities of the demand for money are similar across regions.

18. It is assumed implicitly that the income elasticities of the demand for money in the two regions are equal.

Table 15-1. Equation (15.7), Yearly Data, Sample Period of Dependent Variable, 1959–1970.

Dependent Variable	Functional Form	Constant	Time Trend	A	A*	R̄	Y/Yʷ	m	m*	D–W	R̄²
M_1^w	levels	-123336 (-.79)	-8666 (-4.59)	5.42 (8.39)	2.96 (9.59)	.59 (1.13)	-413596 (-3.65)	112616 (3.85)	25503 (1.01)	2.28	.9996
M_2^w	levels	94096 (.47)	-6634 (-.59)	7.96 (5.50)	4.48 (3.32)	2.10 (1.53)	-865228 (-2.67)	2155 (.08)	98861 (6.13)	2.72	.9997
ΔM_1^w	first differences	-6763 (-3.20)		5.03 (7.34)	2.86 (9.06)	.94 (2.07)	-320145 (-3.60)	102603 (4.30)	33177 (1.44)	2.10	.95
ΔM_2^w	first differences	-14450 (-2.22)		8.28 (8.22)	5.24 (5.29)	1.66 (1.34)	-1135904 (-5.31)	20498 (1.22)	95513 (6.70)	2.55	.95

Notes: Numbers in parentheses are t-values; D–W = Durbin–Watson statistic; $\bar{R}^2 = R^2$ adjusted for degrees of freedom.

Table 15-2. Equation (15.7), Quarterly Data, Sample Period of Dependent Variable, 1958I–1971I.

Dependent Variable	Functional Form	Constant	Time Trend	A	A*	R̄	Y/Yʷ	m	m*	Lagged Dependent Variable	h	R̄²
M_1^w	levels	-127076 (-3.01)	-1712 (9.42)	3.33 (8.66)	.81 (4.65)	.57 (2.58)	-252013 (-6.10)	69576 (7.49)	20590 (1.93)	.63 (9.75)	.82	.9995
M_2^w	levels	4309 (.06)	-4041 (-6.74)	4.76 (6.79)	.54 (1.60)	1.93 (3.33)	-636970 (-6.59)	21746 (3.18)	46200 (5.71)	.76 (12.50)	-.81	.9997
ΔM_1^w	first differences	-858 (-1.40)		3.72 (7.93)	.88 (4.05)	1.62 (3.62)	-71203 (-1.02)	75693 (8.00)	-98 (-1.68)	.48 (5.33)	1.35	.75
ΔM_2^w	first differences	-1882 (-1.54)		6.10 (6.56)	1.64 (3.68)	1.89 (2.08)	-158657 (-1.11)	66155 (8.03)	3.91 (.23)	.53 (6.66)	.45	.81

Notes: Numbers in parentheses are t-values; h = Durbin h-statistic; $\bar{R}^2 = R^2$ adjusted for degrees of freedom.

influence of A would be larger than that of $A*$, and the influence of m greater than that of $m*$. Without sterilization, moreover, $\bar{R}$ should have quantitatively similar effects as A, but its effect would be reduced if partial or full sterilization policies were systematically pursued in the United States. Finally, the consequences of demand shifts would depend on the degree of asymmetry. The greater the asymmetry, the more likely that a demand shift away from dollars would lead to an increase in M^W. The smaller the asymmetry, the more the influence of demand shifts would depend on the relative sizes of the multipliers. In the sample of countries considered here (see the next subsection), it turned out that the average U.S. multiplier over the sample period exceeded that of the aggregate in the rest of the world. Hence, the symmetry hypothesis would imply $\delta M^W/\delta\,(Y/Y^W) > 0$, whereas strong enough asymmetry and sterilization would imply $\delta M^W/\delta\,(Y/Y^W) < 0$. This provides another clear-cut hypothesis for testing.

Results

Linear versions of equation (15.7) were estimated using ordinary least squares and data on fourteen industrialized countries obtained from the International Monetary Fund's *International Financial Statistics*.[19] Both yearly and quarterly specifications were used, and the regressions were carried out both in level and first-difference form. The results for yearly data are contained in Table 15-1 and for quarterly data in Table 15-2. The implications of each set of results for the hypothesis concerning asymmetry and sterilization will be discussed in turn.

The information in Table 15-1 allows a clear rejection of both the symmetric case and the complete sterilization case. The latter hypothesis is invalidated by the consistent significance of $A*$, "domestic" credit in the rest of the world, which should not be an important explanatory variable under complete sterilization. The occasional significance of $m*$ conveys the same message. The symmetry hypothesis can also be rejected on two grounds. Recall that complete symmetry implies that a shift in demand toward the currency of the country with the higher multiplier would increase M^W. For the countries included here, the U.S. multiplier is larger, and hence an increase in Y/Y^W should lead to an increase in M^W. But the sign of the coefficient on this variable is consistently negative and significantly different from 0. This is at variance with the symmetry hypothesis and in agreement with a certain amount of asymmetry. Furthermore, for the M_1 definition of money, the coefficient on A is significantly greater than that on $A*$ at the 97.5 percent level using a one-tailed t-test. For the M_2 definition, the point estimates of these two coefficients are also quite different, but the difference is not statistically significant.[20] Finally, it can be stated that

19. For a detailed description of the data, see the chapter appendix.

20. Note that the high value of the Durbin–Watson statistic in the M_2 case may to some degree invalidate hypothesis testing based on the t-values reported in lines 2 and 4 of the

changes in "outside" reserves were partially prevented from having a one-for-one influence on the monetary bases of the two regions and hence on M^w. The coefficients on $\bar{R}$ are significantly smaller than those on A in each of the four cases.[21]

The results presented in Table 15-2, based on quarterly data, tell essentially the same story as those in Table 15-1, and they do so even more forcefully. The hypothesis that "only the United States matters" can be rejected by reference to the significance of A^* and m^* as explanatory variables. The symmetry hypothesis is rejected by the significantly negative effect of relative income and by the significantly greater influence of A as compared to A^*. Partial sterilization of "outside" reserve changes is also evidenced by the smaller effect of $\bar{R}$ as compared to A.

Table 15-2 reveals another pattern not discussed in connection with Table 15-1, although it was present there — namely, the consistent negative sign on the time trend in the "levels" regressions and of the constant in the first-differences regressions. As already noted, to the extent that the time trend picks up demand factors, this negative sign implies that there was a trendlike shift in demand toward the U.S. dollar at the expense of the rest of the world as measured here. This is consistent with the hypothesis that the dollar was becoming increasingly used as an international currency during the 1960s.

Finally, the significance of the lagged dependent variable in Table 15-2 indicates the possible existence of a partial adjustment mechanism at work. Some caution should be exercised in accepting this interpretation too readily, however, since there are theoretical reasons for believing that the adjustment paths to changes in A and A^* (to take only the most obvious cases) should be quite different and not constrained to be identical, as in this simple Koyck lag specification. Experimentation with Almon lag formulations for the influences of A and A^* seemed to suggest such differences, but, due either to the inherent limitations of this particular estimation technique or to the lack of enough information in the data, the results were not of good enough overall quality to be worth reporting in addition to those in Table 15-2.[22]

In order to confront the various hypotheses with what seem intuitively to be slightly more discriminating tests, all regressions were recalculated using M^*, the non-U.S. money stock, as the dependent variable. The equation that was the basis for the new regressions was:

$$M^* = G(A, A^*, \bar{R}, m, m^*, Y/Y^*, t) \qquad (15.9)$$

---

table. A shortage of degrees of freedom prevented experimentation with different lag structures to remove the apparent serial correlation.

21. Keep in mind the proviso that the previous footnote implies for this statement.

22. Problems included low Durbin-Watson statistics in a number of cases and sometimes implausible configurations of the lag pattern on A^*. As concerns the symmetry, asymmetry, and sterilization hypotheses, the regressions, including the Almon lags, contained the same message as those in Table 15-2.

Table 15-3. Equation (15.9), Yearly Data, Sample Period of Dependent Variable, 1959-1970.

Dependent Variable	Functional Form	Constant	Time Trend	A	A*	R̄	Y/Y*	m	m*	D-W	R̄²
M_1^*	levels	-114980 (-.93)	-3488 (-1.75)	2.58 (4.25)	1.59 (5.74)	.91 (1.95)	-84984 (-3.52)	33485 (1.23)	43331 (1.84)	2.42	.9993
M_2^*	levels	-84394 (-.94)	-4853 (-.68)	3.41 (3.84)	3.31 (4.13)	2.78 (3.83)	-190858 (-4.55)	-24805 (-1.63)	90456 (10.31)	3.46	.9998
ΔM_1^*	first differences	-1805 (-.84)		2.24 (3.33)	1.49 (4.82)	1.15 (2.69)	-69770 (-3.84)	25811 (1.10)	48056 (2.04)	2.49	.87
ΔM_2^*	first differences	-6909 (-1.60)		3.60 (5.36)	3.41 (5.29)	2.64 (3.38)	-205030 (-7.22)	-19652 (-1.52)	91674 (9.27)	3.41	.96

Notes: Numbers in parentheses are t-values; D-W = Durbin-Watson statistic; $\bar{R}^2 = R^2$ adjusted for degrees of freedom.

Table 15-4. Equation (15.9), Quarterly Data, Sample Period of Dependent Variable, 1958I-1971I.

Dependent Variable	Functional Form	Constant	Time Trend	A	A*	R̄	Y/Y*	m	m*	Lagged Dependent Variable	h	R̄²
M_1^*	levels	-132788 (-4.03)	-979 (-6.08)	1.85 (5.46)	.39 (2.93)	.63 (3.17)	-42969 (-4.76)	33922 (4.53)	24193 (2.56)	.65 (6.53)	1.53	.9992
M_2^*	levels	-94490 (-2.36)	-1291 (-3.25)	1.24 (2.99)	.15 (.76)	1.03 (2.74)	-38940 (-2.42)	2788 (.59)	22888 (3.83)	.90 (15.54)	.04	.9996
ΔM_1^*	first differences	237 (.43)		2.02 (4.27)	.43 (2.09)	1.12 (2.59)	-13974 (-1.02)	26942 (3.00)	-40 (-.70)	.35 (2.71)	-7.17	.47
ΔM_2^*	first differences	298 (.31)		2.18 (2.98)	.83 (2.39)	.83 (1.14)	-2853 (-.12)	17746 (2.75)	1.72 (.13)	.63 (5.99)	-2.49	.60

Notes: Numbers in parentheses are t-values; h = Durbin h-statistic; $\bar{R}^2 = R^2$ adjusted for degrees of freedom.

This equation has exactly the same implications for the various hypotheses concerning asymmetry and so forth as did equation (15.7), with the exception that the relative income variable should now have a negative influence on M^* regardless of the relative sizes of m and m^*, even in the symmetric case.

The results presented in Tables 15-3 and 15-4 corroborate the essential conclusions drawn from the previous regressions. Complete sterilization can be rejected for both yearly and quarterly data. Symmetry can likewise be strongly rejected in favor of asymmetry in Table 15-4. There is also evidence of partial sterilization of "outside" reserve changes and some form of adjustment mechanism spread out over time.

Possible Extensions of the Empirical Tests

A number of extensions and improvements of the empirical work presented here can be envisaged. The data could no doubt be refined to take account of differences in the structure of policy and banking systems in each of the countries involved. Additional demand side variables might also be included in attempts to capture what is now explained by the trend term and the relative income variable. Introducing monetary policy instruments, such as reserve requirements, that affect the multipliers rather than asset stocks, may also provide additional insights, as would the inclusion of variables capturing the preferences for reserve assets by central banks and for currency holdings (including Eurodollars) by the public.

At a more basic level, there may be high returns to specifying explicitly the adjustment mechanisms that bring about the equilibrium distribution of the world money stock and estimating what would then look more like a structural model of the processes involved. This would remove the ad hoc Koyck type lag structure used in the present study and would allow inferences to be drawn about the efficacy of the balance of payments adjustment mechanism under fixed exchange rates.[23] It would also allow testing of the hypothesis that the effects of non-U.S. policy measures are only of short-run nature and will give way to complete dominance of U.S. policies in the longer run. In principle at least, a somewhat more structural approach would also be able to handle possible simultaneity biases arising from the reactions of non-U.S. policy authorities to changes in their international reserve position and to externally imposed changes in their money supplies.

CONCLUSION

Both theoretical and empirical considerations support the assertion that U.S. monetary policy played a dominant role in determining the course of world monetary aggregates in the basically fixed exchange rate world of 1957 to 1971.

23. Some attempts along these lines were made in Genberg and Swoboda (1977b).

We suspect that the asymmetry would appear even more strongly if one allowed for lagged adjustment that reverses the short-run effectiveness of non-U.S. monetary policy.[24] Again, this does not mean that only U.S. monetary policy matters, but it does mean that it matters more.

Recognition of the special role of U.S. monetary policy in setting the growth of world monetary aggregates and of the convergence of inflation rates under fixed exchange rates has implications both for attempts at "reform" of the international monetary system and for the interpretation of the demise of the Bretton Woods system. The asymmetries inherent in any fixed rate system where a national currency is used as international reserve asset imply that it is illusory to treat countries' obligations and roles symmetrically in such a system. More concretely, the acceleration of worldwide inflation that took place in the mid-1960s focused dissatisfaction with the existing system. The endogenous creation of international reserves and the accelerating growth of monetary aggregates could not have been moderated without a change in the course of U.S. monetary policy, even if policy has been more restrictive elsewhere. For us—and we imagine for Robert Triffin, too—this asymmetry should be a basic ingredient in any attempt to explain the breakdown of the Bretton Woods system.

APPENDIX: DATA

In this chapter, the group of countries that the International Monetary Fund in *International Financial Statistics* calls "fourteen industrial countries" was used as a representation of the "world." The countries included are Austria, Belgium, Canada, Denmark, France, Germany, Italy, Japan, The Netherlands, Norway, Sweden, Switzerland, the United Kingdom, and the United States.

Data series for all individual countries were, with the exception of some GNP series, collected from the IFS data tape. To get "world" and "non-U.S. world" aggregates for all variables, the country series were first converted into $US equivalents, using the appropriate spot exchange rates, and then added over the fourteen (thirteen in the case of the non-U.S. world) countries.

The exact definition of each series, together with the corresponding symbol, is given in Table 15-5. The sample period was 1958I-1971I. The data were deseasonalized before the estimation.

---

24. In the short run, unless payments adjustment is instantaneous, European monetary policy will affect significantly the world money stock (cf. the movement from A to B in Figure 15-2), even though payments adjustment may reverse the initial effect in the long run (cf. the movement back from B to A). Some evidence on reversal effects is provided in Genberg and Swoboda (1977b).

Table 15-5. Symbols and Data Sources.

Symbol	Interpretation	Data Source	Aggregation
e	$US exchange rate (end of period)	IFS : Line ae	None
e'	$US exchange rate (average during period)	IFS : Line af	None
A	Domestic credit in the U.S.	IFS: Line 14, line 1	None
B	Monetary base in the U.S.	IFS : Line 14	None
B^*	Monetary base in ROW[a]	IFS : Line 14	$\displaystyle\sum_{i=1}^{13} (B^*_{i,t}/e_{i,t})$
IR^*	International Reserves in ROW	IFS : Line 1	$\displaystyle\sum_{i=1}^{13} IR^*_{i,t}$ [b]
A^*	Domestic credit in ROW	$B^* - IR^*$	$\displaystyle\sum_{i=1}^{13} A^*_{i,t}$ [b]
$\bar{R}$	"Outside" reserves for the world	IFS : Line 1, line 1d	$\displaystyle\sum_{i=1}^{14} R_{i,t}$ [b]
M^*	World money stock	IFS : Line 34 for M_1 and lines 34 and 35 for M_2	$\displaystyle\sum_{i=1}^{14} (M_{i,t}/e_{i,t})$
Y	Nominal GNP in the U.S.	IFS : Line 99a	None
Y^*	Nominal GNP in ROW	IFS : Line 99a or other[c]	$\displaystyle\sum_{i=1}^{13} (Y^*_{i,t}/e'_{i,t})$

a. ROW stands for the rest of the world, by which we mean the thirteen non-U.S. countries in our sample.

b. There is no exchange rate conversion for these series, since the raw data are in terms of $US.

c. The series can be obtained from the authors upon request.

REFERENCES

Duck, Nigel W.; Michael Parkin; D. Rose; and G. Zis. 1976. "The Determination of the Rate of Change of Wages and Prices in the Fixed Exchange Rate World Economy, 1956–71." In M. Markin and G. Zis, eds., *Inflation in the World Economy.* Manchester: Manchester University Press.

Genberg, Hans. 1976. "Aspects of the Monetary Approach to Balance-of-Payments Theory: An Empirical Study of Sweden." In J.A. Frenkel and H.G. Johnson, eds., *The Monetary Approach to the Balance of Payments.* London: Allen & Unwin.

_____. 1977. "The Concept and Measurement of the World Price Level and Rate of Inflation." *Journal of Monetary Economics* 3, no. 2: 231–52.

Genberg, Hans, and Alexander K. Swoboda. 1977a. "Causes and Origins of the Current Worldwide Inflation." In E. Lundberg, ed., *Inflation Theory and Anti-Inflation Policy.* London: Macmillan.

_____. 1977b. "Worldwide Inflation under the Dollar Standard." GIIS–Ford Discussion Paper No. 12, January.

Gray, Malcolm R.; T. Ward; and G. Zis. 1976. "The World Demand for Money Function: Some Preliminary Results." In M. Parkin and G. Zis, eds., *Inflation in the World Economy.* Manchester: Manchester University Press.

Heller, H. Robert. 1976. "International Reserves and World–Wide Inflation." *IMF Staff Papers* 23 (March): 61–87.

Meiselman, David I. 1975. "World–Wide Inflation: A Monetarist View." In Art Laffer and David I. Meiselman, eds., *The Phenomenon of World–Wide Inflation.* Washington, D.C.: American Enterprise Institute.

Parkin, Michael; I. Richards; and G. Zis. 1974. "The Determination and Control of the World Money Supply under Fixed Exchange Rates: 1961–1971." Paper presented at the Third Money Study Group Oxford Seminar, September.

Swoboda, Alexander K. 1978a. "Gold, Dollars, Euro–Dollars, and the World Money Stock under Fixed Exchange Rates." *American Economic Review* 68 (September): 625–42.

_____. 1978b. "Lessons from the 60's or, 'How the Dollar Standard Really Worked.'" March. Mimeographed.

Triffin, Robert. 1960. *Gold and the Dollar Crisis.* New Haven: Yale University Press.

_____. 1979. "The Future of the International Monetary System." Mimeographed.

16 ALGEBRAIC PROPERTIES AND ECONOMIC IMPROPRIETIES OF THE "INDICATOR OF DIVERGENCE" IN THE EUROPEAN MONETARY SYSTEM

Luigi Spaventa

INTRODUCTION

The "Resolution of the European Council on the Establishment of the European Monetary System (EMS) and Related Matters" of December 5th 1978, defines a European Currency Unit (ECU) as a basket of currencies identical, at the outset of the system, with the preexisting European Unit of Account (paragraph 2.1). It then states that "each currency will have an Ecu-related central rate," which will be used to establish a grid of bilateral exchange rates. For the currencies participating in the exchange rate mechanism (all the EMS currencies except the pound sterling), compulsory intervention points are fixed at ± 2.25 percent (6 percent for Italy) around the bilateral rates (paragraphs 3.1, 3.4) (see European Communities 1979: 40–41).

If this were all, it would be hard to find any difference, except for the number of the participating countries, between the EMS and the "snake" or indeed any other system based on restricted floating margins around central bilateral parities: The definition of ECU-related central rates is totally useless for the definition of the grid of bilateral parities and is, if anything, a result of the latter.

Paragraphs 3.5 and 3.6 of the resolution contain, however, what is considered to be a major novelty of the EMS:

> An Ecu basket formula will be used as an indicator to detect divergences between Community currencies. A "threshold of divergence" will be fixed at 75% of the maximum spread of divergences between currencies. . . . (Paragraph 3.5)

When a currency crosses its "threshold of divergence," this results in a presumption that the authorities concerned will correct the situation by adequate measures. . . . (Paragraph 3.6)

These two paragraphs of the resolution are very important in the history of the negotiations for the establishment of the EMS, as they embody a two-stage compromise on the old issue of symmetry of obligations between weaker and stronger countries.[1] The first compromise was that between the two possible interpretations of the passage in the annex to the conclusions of the Bremen European Council of July 1978, which stated that the ECU "will be at the centre of the system" (European Communities 1979:39). Those who thought that compulsory intervention points at given margins around bilateral parities impose a heavier burden on the weaker currency interpreted the Bremen annex as a decision to set fixed margins to the movements of a currency's ECU price around its central ECU parity. It would thus be possible to single out the currency that, diverging from the weighted average of the ECU basket, could be considered responsible for the disequilibrium and impose, if needed, the entire burden of intervention and adjustment on one country alone. This interpretation, however, met with both insurmountable political obstacles and intricate technical difficulties, into which we need not go (see especially Baer 1979; and Masera 1980b: ch. 4 and Appendix). The compromise was to set the margins around bilateral parities, as in the "snake," but to define an indicator of a currency's divergence in terms of the movements of its ECU price and recognize officially the need for unilateral corrective action if the indicator exceeds a certain threshold.

Agreement on this point still left another issue open: How binding was the obligation to take corrective action (in the form of market interventions or internal policy measures) to be for the country whose currency had reached the ECU threshold of divergence, though not the maximum bilateral margin against any other currency? The compromise here was "a presumption" that the authorities concerned would take adequate measures, with the further proviso that some justification for lack of action should be provided to the other partners (Paragraph 3.6).

This last issue and its solution (a disappointing solution in the view of a majority of official experts and external observers) only concern the consequences that should follow upon the flashing of the ECU alarm, but not the nature and the working of the alarm itself and of the indicator of divergence on which the alarm is based. The technical details of the actual modus operandi of the indicator were specified in article 3 of the agreement of March 13, 1979, between the central banks of the member states of the EC, laying down the operating procedures for the EMS (see European Communities 1979:56). Thus

---

1. Excellent accounts of the disputes that preceded this compromise are in Thygesen (1979a) and in Masera (1980b: ch. IV). For the more political aspects of the debate and the negotiations, see Ludlow (1980) and Spaventa (1980).

the indicator of divergence, whatever its policy implications, became the distinguishing feature of the exchange rate agreements of the EMS, with respect to any other system of restricted floating margins around bilateral parities.

The ministers and most officials of the participating countries, echoed by the press, hailed this as a major innovation and as a proof that the EMS was not – as many thought – merely an enlarged edition of the "snake." Similar views were expressed by many economists.[2] The merits of the indicator were seen to be that it "is an unambiguous (though in some respects arbitrary) number which can be easily monitored," "it fulfills the requirements for becoming an objective indicator," and "it represents for the first time in Community and world monetary history an agreement on the use of an *objective indicator as a trigger for policy coordination*" (Thygesen 1979a: 111, 112, italics in original).

After the start of the EMS, however, some doubts began to arise as to the significance of the signals coming from the indicator. It was thus realized that, as pointed out by the Deutsche Bundesbank (1979) even before the inception of the EMS, "individual currencies may reach their bilateral intervention rates without having crossed their thresholds of divergence first" (see also Rieke 1979). An official EC source thought that as a general rule this would not happen, but added somewhat loosely that such a possibility depends "on the pattern of exchange rates obtaining at the time and will occur notably where two currencies are at opposite poles and where all the other currencies are 'in the middle,' i.e. equidistant from the two currencies in question."[3]

The possibility that the ECU alarm might remain silent as two currencies reach their intervention margins may or may not, in itself, be considered a defect of the new mechanism. It does, however, raise a more crucial issue. Can the indicator, as it was conceived, fulfill the role of signaling the extent of a currency's absolute divergence and, as it approaches the threshold, the need for unilateral corrective action? To serve this purpose, its behavior should reflect mostly, if not entirely, the individual currency's strength or weakness. If, on the other hand, the movements of the indicator were commonly (and not only in the fluke case when all other currencies are "in the middle") affected by factors intrinsic to the movements of other currencies, then the economic significance, as well as

2. For an official's view, see van Ypersele de Strihou (1979b). Official and experts' views are well represented by Thygesen (1979), van Ypersele de Strihou (1979a), Bourguinat (1979), and Triffin (1979).

3. Commission of the European Communities (1979: 88). For a description of the behavior of the indicator after the beginning of the EMS and of the case of the Belgian franc, which reached the lower intervention margin in April 1979, one month before its indicator crossed the threshold, see Thygesen (1981) and Masera (1980a). Masera (1980b) takes a critical view of the indicator because it may not cross the threshold before the bilateral rate reaches the intervention margin. This is not the view of Thygesen, who thinks that the indicator must have "the role of signalling more lasting divergences" than those requiring official interventions in the foreign exchange markets" (1979: 114). For a criticism of this latter view, see below.

the practical usefulness, of the distinguishing feature of the EMS exchange rate agreements could be questioned.

A formal analysis of some rules of behavior of a currency's ECU price and, especially, of its divergence indicator is a necessary step in order to examine this issue. In the next section we first establish the relationships between the changes of these magnitudes and the changes in the constellation of bilateral rates of all currencies.[4] We then derive some properties of ECU prices and indicators. Such properties, as we argue in section three, are distinctly odd, in view of the task that the indicator is expected to perform: Two currencies can never reach the threshold together in an opposite direction, but up to four currencies can do so in the same direction. Neither of two currencies at their opposite intervention margin will reach the threshold for a whole range of the other currencies' bilateral rates (and not merely when the latter are "in the middle"), and such range is different for each different pair of currencies concerned. With two currencies at their opposite intervention margin, neither of which reaches the threshold, a third currency, not at the margin, may reach the threshold. As two or more currencies reach the maximum margin with respect to all others, the indicator will or will not reach the threshold according to the combination of the currencies concerned.

It thus appears that the indicator of divergence is a very arbitrary measure and may provide wrong or economically meaningless signals. It is therefore ill-suited to be used as a criterion for policy action. This does not depend merely on technical imperfections, which could be eliminated by suitable adjustments, as we argue later in the section, "Economic Improprieties." The indicator represents an attempt to graft some features of a system of restricted floating of ECU prices onto one of fixed margins around bilateral parities: It is an operation that is bound to produce inconsistent results. Further, the possibility of detecting an individual currency's divergence below the surface of the movements of bilateral rates, and of providing a meaningful measure thereof, should rest on some explanation of divergence and on a definition of its symptoms and should therefore follow from a set of relevant hypotheses. The indicator, however, possesses no such foundation and is no more than an unsatisfactory accounting device. As such, we conclude, it can hardly be the appropriate answer to the problem of policy coordination.

SEVEN PROPERTIES OF THE INDICATOR
OF DIVERGENCE

In this section we first define ECU prices and indicators of divergence and establish the relationships between movements of ECU prices and movements of bilat-

---

4. A thorough formal analysis of the ECU and of the relationship between a system of margins around central ECU parities and one of margins around bilateral parities can be found in Baer (1979) and in Masera (1980b: Appendix 1). The approach followed at the beginning of the next section owes a great deal to Masera's work.

eral rates. After setting the constraints to such movements under a regime of maximum bilateral margins, we prove some properties concerning the behavior of ECU prices (Properties A and C) and indicators (Properties B and D through G), providing numerical examples for each. For simplicity of presentation, our formal analysis deals with the continuous case, but the examples are calculated allowing for the effects of discrete changes. Also, since we are interested in the general properties of the ECU alarm, we neglect the complications arising from the wider (6 percent) band for the lira and from the fact that the pound sterling, though part of the ECU, floats freely[5] and accordingly assume that the same maximum bilateral margin of 2.25 percent applies to all the EC currencies.

The ECU is a basket of eight currencies, with a fixed amount of each currency entering the basket.[6] We number each currency from 1 to 8, in increasing order of its weight in the basket, as defined by equation (16.4). The list of currencies and their weights are given in Table 16-1.

We can thus write:

$$\Sigma_i \, p_i \, q_i \, = \, 1 \qquad (i = 1, \ldots, 8) \tag{16.1}$$

where q_i is the (fixed) quantity of currency i entering the basket, and p_i its price in terms of ECU. Let p_{ji} be the price of currency j in terms of currency i. Then:

$$p_j \, = \, p_i \, p_{ji} \tag{16.2}$$

and

$$p_i \, q_i \, + \, \Sigma_j \, p_i \, p_{ji} \, q_j \, = \, 1 \qquad (j \neq i) \tag{16.3}$$

We define the weight of currency j in the basket as

$$\pi_j \, = \, p_i \, p_{ji} \, q_j \tag{16.4}$$

Then:

$$\pi_i \, + \, \Sigma_j \, \pi_j \, = \, 1 \qquad (j \neq i) \tag{16.5}$$

5. In the actual working of the EMS, the indicator of divergence of the six currencies floating within the 2.25 percent band must be corrected to eliminate the influence of movements of the lira and the pound exceeding 2.25 percent. Using the notation explained in the text, the system chosen is the following: Suppose that, say, the pound appreciates (depreciates) by more than 2.25 percent with respect to one of the other six currencies, s: this means that p_s falls more or grows less (grows more or falls less) than if the pound had been in the narrower band. The corrected $\dot{p}_s$ to be used in equation (16.10) is obtained by adding $\pi_£(\dot{p}_{£_s} - 0.0225)$ to the actual $\dot{p}_s$, if $\dot{p}_{£_s} > 0.0225$ or by adding $\pi_£(\dot{p}_{£_s} + 0.0225)$, if $p_{£_s} < -0.0225$. The same adjustment must of course be operated on the indicators of the other five currencies even if their bilateral rate with the pound has not exceeded 2.25 percent (see Commission of the European Communities 1979: 90). The indicator for the lira has to be corrected in the same way for movements in the lira–pound rate exceeding 6 percent; further, in the denominator of equation (16.10) $\mu = 0.06$ (see Masera 1980b: Appendix 1).

6. We consider the Belgian franc and the Luxemburg franc as one currency, since they exchange at par, and we add up accordingly the amounts of each entering the basket.

Table 16-1. The ECU Basket and the "Indicator of Divergence."

Currencies	Weights π_i	$1 - \pi_i$	$D_i = \bar{\gamma}\mu(1 - \pi_i)$
Ireland (Ir£)	0.0113589	0.9886411	0.0166833
Denmark (DKr)	0.0280966	0.9719034	0.0164009
Italy (L)	0.0941449	0.9050551	0.0152728
Belgium (FB)	0.0955021	0.9044979	0.0152634
Netherlands (F1)	0.1042418	0.8957582	0.0151159
United Kingdom (£)	0.1363825	0.8636175	0.0145735
France (FF)	0.1966821	0.8033179	0.0135560
Germany (DM)	0.3335912	0.6664088	0.0112456

Note: The weights are those resulting after the realignment of September 1979 and after the devaluation of the Danish kroner of December 1979. The values of the indicator of divergence for the United Kingdom and for Italy have been calculated on the assumption that both countries are subject to the 2.25 percent margin.

The ECU price of currency i will thus be:

$$p_i = \frac{1}{q_i + \Sigma_j \, p_{ji} \, q_j} \qquad (j \neq i) \qquad (16.6)$$

Manipulating the definitions, we find the percentage rate of change (denoted henceforth by a dot) of this price to be:

$$\dot{p}_i = -\Sigma_j \, \pi_j \, \dot{p}_{ji} \qquad (j \neq i) \qquad (16.7)$$

Suppose $\dot{p}_{ji} = \alpha$ for all js $\neq i$, so that all currencies appreciate or depreciate by the same percentage with respect to currency j; then equation (16.7) becomes:

$$\dot{p}_i = -\alpha \, \Sigma_j \, \pi_j = -\alpha(1 - \pi_i) \qquad (\alpha \gtrless 0) \qquad (16.8)$$

Let μ be the maximum bilateral margin allowed by the exchange rate agreements, so that $-\mu \leq \alpha \leq \mu$; then the range within which the ECU price of currency i can vary if that currency appreciates or depreciates by the same percentage with respect to all other currencies is given by:

$$-\mu(1 - \pi_i) \leq \dot{p}_i \leq \mu(1 - \pi_i) \qquad (16.9)$$

The indicator of divergence of currency i is defined as:

$$\gamma_i = \frac{\dot{p}_i}{\mu(1 - \pi_i)} \qquad (16.10)$$

where

$$-1 \leq \gamma_i \leq 1$$

The threshold of divergence is reached when $\gamma_i = \bar{\gamma} = 0.75$. We shall call D_i the (absolute value of the) rate of change of the ECU price of currency i at which the latter reaches its threshold of divergence, or:

$$D_i = \bar{\gamma} \mu (1 - \pi_i) \tag{16.11}$$

With $\bar{\gamma} = 0.75$ and $\mu = 0.0225$, $\bar{\gamma}\mu = 0.016875$. Table 16-1 also gives the values of D_i for the eight currencies.[7] Thus, a presumption of action on the part of the authorities concerned arises when the ECU price of a currency appreciates or depreciates by more than 75 percent of the rate of appreciation or depreciation corresponding to an appreciation or depreciation of that currency with respect to all other currencies by the full bilateral margin.

We note that, if together with currency i we consider separately currency s, we can rewrite equation (16.7) as:

$$\dot{p}_i = -\pi_s \, \dot{p}_{si} - \Sigma_k \, \pi_k \, \dot{p}_{ki} \qquad (k \neq i, s) \tag{16.12}$$

From equation (16.2):

$$\dot{p}_s = \dot{p}_i + \dot{p}_{si} \tag{16.13}$$

so that

$$\dot{p}_s = (1 - \pi_s) \, \dot{p}_{si} - \Sigma_k \, \pi_k \, \dot{p}_{ki} \qquad (k \neq i, s) \tag{16.14}$$

Further:

$$\Sigma_k \, \pi_k \, \dot{p}_{ks} = \Sigma_k \, \pi_k \, \dot{p}_{ki} - \Sigma_k \, \pi_k \, \dot{p}_{si} \qquad (k \neq i, s) \tag{16.15}$$

and finally:

$$\Sigma_k \, \pi_k = 1 - \pi_i - \pi_s \tag{16.16}$$

If bilateral rates are not to exceed a margin μ ($\dot{p}_{si} \leqq |\mu|$), the following constraints must hold, in addition to equation (16.9) (and its equivalent for s):

$$|\Sigma_k \, \pi_k \, \dot{p}_{ki}|, \; |\Sigma_k \, \pi_k \, \dot{p}_{ks}| \leqq \mu (1 - \pi_i - \pi_s) \tag{16.17}$$

If $\dot{p}_{si} = \pm\mu$, constraints (16.9) and (16.17) become:

$$0 \leqq \pm\Sigma_k \, \pi_k \, \dot{p}_{ki} \leqq \mu (1 - \pi_i - \pi_s) \tag{16.18}$$

7. In the examples, account is taken of the fact that the D_is are applied to central ECU parities defined as prices of the ECU in terms of individual currencies, denoted as $1/p_i$ (rather than p_i). Hence, if the exchange rate of currency j with respect to currency i, p_{ij}, appreciates by $\Delta p_{ij} = \mu_a$, the exchange rate of currency i with respect to currency j, $1/p_{ij}$, will depreciate by $\mu_d = -\mu_a/(1 + \mu_a)$. In the EMS, since the agreed band is $\mu_a - \mu_d = 0.045$, we obtain $\mu_a = 0.022753$, $\mu_d = 0.022247$. In the EMS, the difference between the margin of appreciation and the margin of depreciation is conventionally neglected when calculating the thresholds, and hence the values D_i, for each currency: Expression (16.11) remains therefore unchanged. The thresholds are, however, applied to the central prices of the ECU in terms of individual currencies, so that currency i will reach the thresholds when $\Delta p_i/(1 + \Delta p_i) = \pm D_i$. To obtain the results in the examples, the expressions in the text have been modified to account for discrete changes.

$$-\mu(1 - \pi_i - \pi_s) \lesseqgtr \pm\Sigma_k \pi_k \dot{p}_{ks} \lesseqgtr 0 \tag{16.19}$$

$$-\mu\pi_s \gtreqless \pm\dot{p}_i \gtreqless -\mu(1 - \pi_i) \tag{16.20}$$

$$\mu(1 - \pi_s) \gtreqless \pm\dot{p}_s \gtreqless \mu\pi_i \tag{16.21}$$

It can be easily checked that, in this case, if any one of the four constraints is verified, the other three are also verified.

We are now equipped to establish some properties regarding the behavior of ECU prices and of the indicators of divergence.

Property A

For any value different from 0 of the rate of change of the bilateral rates of currencies s and i, there is always one value, different from 0, of the weighted rate of change of the bilateral rates of the other currencies, at which the rates of change of the ECU prices of s and i have the same absolute value and opposite sign.

Proof. If $\Sigma_k \pi_k \dot{p}_{ki} = 0$, from equations (16.12) and (16.14) we have that $-\dot{p}_i = \dot{p}_s$ requires that $\pi_s = 1 - \pi_s = 0.5$, which cannot happen in the EMS, as shown in the first column of Table 16-1. However, from equations (16.12) and (16.14), $\Sigma_k \pi_k \dot{p}_{ki} = (0.5 - \pi_s)\dot{p}_{si}$, which, with the weights of the same column, always respects constraint (16.17). Further, $\Sigma_k \pi_k \dot{p}_{ks} = (\pi_i - 0.5)\dot{p}_{si} > -\mu(1 - \pi_i - \pi_s)$.

Example. If the French franc (s) appreciates by 1 percent with respect to the Belgian franc (i), the ECU price of the French franc will move up and that of the Belgian franc will move down by 0.5 percent when the weighted rate of appreciation of the other currencies with respect to the Belgian franc is 0.3 percent.

Property B

There is always a value of the rate of change of the bilateral rate of currencies i and s and an associated value of the weighted rate of change of the bilateral rates of the other currencies at which the indicators of divergence of i and s have the same absolute value and opposite sign. The maximum absolute common value of the indicator is higher, the greater the weights of the two currencies, but will always be lower than the thresholds.

Proof. Let $-\gamma_i = \gamma_s = \gamma$, so that, from equations (16.10) and (16.11), $\dot{p}_i = -\gamma\mu(1 - \pi_i) = -D_i\gamma/\bar{\gamma}$, $\dot{p}_s = \gamma\mu(1 - \pi_s) = D_s\gamma/\bar{\gamma}$. Then, from equation (16.13), $\dot{p}_{si} = (D_s + D_i)\gamma/\bar{\gamma}$. Given the constraint $\dot{p}_{si} \leqq \mu$, γ can be higher, the smaller D_s and D_i and hence the greater π_s and π_i. Note also that the constraints on $\Sigma_k \pi_k \dot{p}_{ki}$ and on $\Sigma_k \pi_k \dot{p}_{ks}$ are always satisfied, since $\Sigma_k \pi_k \dot{p}_{ki} =$ $- [(1 - \pi_s)D_i - \pi_s D_s] \; \gamma/\bar{\gamma}$ and $\Sigma_k \pi_k \dot{p}_{ks} = - [(1 - \pi_i)D_s - \pi_i D_i] \; \gamma/\bar{\gamma}$. Suppose now that $\gamma = \bar{\gamma}$. The above constraint then requires that $D_s = D_i < \mu$, which cannot happen in the EMS shown in the third column of Table 16-1.

Examples. We let currency s appreciate by the full bilateral margin with respect to currency i; we impose the condition that the indicators of i and s should have the same value and opposite sign. Then from the discrete version of equations (16.12) and (16.13), we obtain the maximum common absolute value of the indicator and the associated weighted rate of appreciation of the other currencies with respect to i shown in Table 16-2.

Property C

The rates of change of the ECU prices of any two currencies can have the same value and sign only if their bilateral rate remains unchanged.

Proof. From equations (16.12) and (16.14), if $\dot{p}_{si} \neq 0$, $\dot{p}_i \neq \dot{p}_s$; if $\dot{p}_{si} = 0$, $\dot{p}_i = \dot{p}_s = -\Sigma_k \pi_k \dot{p}_{ki}$.

Property D

There is always a value of the rate of change of the bilateral rate of currencies i and s and an associated value of the weighted rate of change of the bilateral rates of the other currencies at which the indicators of divergence of i and s have the same value and the same sign. The maximum common value of the indicator is higher, the smaller the weights of the currencies. It is possible, under appropriate conditions, for the indicators of two, three, and up to four currencies to reach simultaneously the threshold of divergence.

Proof. Let $\gamma_i = \gamma_s = \gamma$. Then, from equations (16.10) and (16.11), $\dot{p}_i = D_i \gamma/\bar{\gamma}$, $\dot{p}_s = D_s \gamma/\bar{\gamma}$ and, from equation (16.13), $\dot{p}_{si} = (D_s - D_i)\gamma/\bar{\gamma}$, which, given the values in the third column of Table 16-1, always satisfies the constraint $\dot{p}_{si} < \mu$. From equations (16.14), (16.15), and (16.16), $\Sigma_k \pi_k \dot{p}_{ki} = - [(1 - \pi_s) D_i + \pi_s D_s] \gamma/\bar{\gamma}$ and $\Sigma_k \pi_k \dot{p}_{ks} = - [(1 - \pi_i) D_s + \pi_i D_i] \gamma/\bar{\gamma}$. As constraint

Table 16-2.   Example of Property B.

Currencies		Maximum Common Absolute Value of γ for s (+) and i (-)	Percentage Rate of Appreciation of Other k Currencies against i
i	s		
FF	DM	0.68	+ 0.47
FB	Fl	0.55	+ 0.88
DKr	Ir£	0.51	+ 1.09

(16.17) must be satisfied, γ can be higher, the smaller π_i and π_s. In the EMS, as appears from the values of Table 16-1, such constraints can be satisfied with $\gamma = \overline{\gamma}$ for any pair of currencies, unless one of them is the Deutsche mark.

For more than two currencies, we proceed along the same lines. Let the indicators of currency i and of h other currencies ($h = n - m - 1$) assume the same value γ, so that for each of the h currencies $\dot{p}_{hi} = (D_h - D_i)\gamma/\overline{\gamma}$. Then the constraints $\Sigma_m \pi_m \dot{p}_{mj} \geqq -\mu \Sigma_m \pi_m$ must simultaneously be observed for each currency j belonging to the group comprising currency i and currencies h, which assume together the common value γ of the indicator.[8] With $\gamma = \overline{\gamma}$, the possibility that the indicators of more than two currencies reach together the value $\gamma = \overline{\gamma}$ is obviously more limited, as we can see from the examples.

Examples. For the currencies considered we shall set the common value of the indicator at $\gamma = \overline{\gamma} = 0.75$. Consider first two currencies. With the Deutsche mark and the Irish pound both at the threshold in the same direction, the weighted rate of change of the other currencies with respect to one of the two exceeds the constraint. The same must therefore apply if we consider, together with the Deutsche mark, any other currency with greater weight than the Irish pound. We now take the French franc and the British pound: Both can reach the threshold without the weighted rate of change of the other currencies with respect to them exceeding the constraints. The same must therefore apply to any other pair of currencies with smaller weights.

Consider now three currencies, say the French franc, the Irish pound, and the Danish kroner. If they reached the threshold together, the weighted rate of change of the other currencies with respect to one of the three would exceed the constraint. The same must therefore apply to any group of currencies, including the French franc. It can be verified that any three of the five smaller currencies can reach the threshold together in the same direction, as the associated rates of the other currencies with respect to each of the three do not exceed the constraint. It is impossible for the British pound, the florin, and the Belgian franc to reach the threshold together, but any two of these currencies can reach the threshold together with another smaller currency.

A necessary condition for four currencies to reach the threshold together is that two of them be the two smallest, the Irish pound and the Danish kroner. The other condition is that the group not include both the British pound and the florin. A group comprising the British pound and the Belgian franc, as well as the Irish pound and the Danish kroner *can* reach the threshold, however.

Property E

When the bilateral rate between two currencies is at the maximum margin, their indicators will not reach the threshold for a range of values of the weighted rate

---

8. We have $\Sigma_m \pi_m \dot{p}_{mi} = -[(1 - \Sigma_h \pi_h = D_i + \Sigma_h \pi_h D_h]\gamma/\overline{\gamma}$. If currency s is one of the h currencies and if h' is now the group comprising all the h currencies minus s plus i, $\Sigma_m \pi_m \dot{p}_{ms} = -[(1 - \Sigma_{h'} \pi_{h'})D_s + \Sigma_{h'} \pi_{h'} D_{h'}]\gamma/\overline{\gamma}$.

of change of the other currencies with respect to the currencies considered. Such range is greater, the smaller the weights of the two currencies. The value of the weighted rate of change of the other currencies at which the ECU prices of the two currencies considered have the same value and opposite sign falls within the range, unless one of the two currencies is the Deutsche mark.

Proof. Let $\dot{p}_{si} = \pm \mu$. We wish $\overline{\gamma} > \gamma_i > -\overline{\gamma}$ and $\overline{\gamma} > \gamma_s > -\overline{\gamma}$, or, considering equations (16.10) and (16.11), $D_i > \dot{p}_i > -D_i$ and $D_s > \dot{p}_s > -D_s$. Using equation (16.13), these conditions are both satisfied when $D_s - \mu > p_i > -D_i$, for $p_{si} = \mu$, and $D_i > p_i > -D_s + \mu$, for $p_{si} = -\mu$. In the EMS, as appears from Table 16-1, we always have that $D_i > -D_s + \mu$, and these constraints can always be respected. The range for the weighted rate of change of the other currencies can be derived from equation (16.12) and from the above conditions—$-D_s + \mu(1 - \pi_s) < \Sigma_k \pi_k \dot{p}_{ki} < D_i - \pi_s \mu$, for $\dot{p}_{si} = \mu$, and $-D_i + \pi_s \mu < \Sigma_k \pi_k \dot{p}_{ki} < D_s - \mu(1 - \pi_s)$, for $\dot{p}_{si} = -\mu$. This range falls within that set by equation (16.18). Therefore also $\Sigma_k \pi_k \dot{p}_{ks}$ falls within the range set by equation (16.19).

Further, we know from Property A that $-\dot{p}_i = \dot{p}_s$ when $\Sigma_k \pi_k \dot{p}_{ki} = (0.5 - \pi_s) \dot{p}_{si}$. With $\dot{p}_{si} = \pm \mu$, we have $\dot{p}_i = \pm 0.5 \mu$, $\dot{p}_s = \pm 0.5 \mu$. Such value exceeds the D value only in the case of the Deutsche mark.

Examples. We suppose that the first of the two currencies considered in Table 16-3 appreciates by the full bilateral margin with respect to the second. We then give the range of the percentage-weighted rate of change of the other currencies with respect to the second, within which neither of the two currencies considered reaches the threshold. We give in brackets the value of the weighted rate of appreciation for which the ECU prices of the two currencies have the same value $|0.5 \mu|$ and opposite sign.

Property F

The bilateral rate between two currencies is at the maximum bilateral margin, but neither currency reaches the threshold because the conditions specified

Table 16-3. Example of Property E.

Currencies			
s	i	Range of $\Sigma_k \pi_k p_{ki}$ Percent	$|0.5 \mu|$
DKr	Ir£	0.53–1.60	(1.07)
FF	DM	0.43–0.68	(0.68, outside the range)
Ir£	DM	0.53–1.10	(1.11, outside the range)
Fl	FB	0.47–1.29	(0.90)

under Property E are observed. A third currency, though not at the maximum bilateral margin with respect to any other currency, may reach the threshold in either direction.

Proof. Let us consider three currencies—i, s, and z—on the one hand and another $m = n - 3$ currencies on the other. Let $\dot{p}_{si} = \mu$. From equation 16.13), $\dot{p}_{zi} = \dot{p}_z - \dot{p}_i$, and from equation (16.14), $\Sigma_m \pi_m \dot{p}_{mi} = -\dot{p}_i - \pi_s \dot{p}_{si} - \pi_z \dot{p}_{zi}$. Let $\dot{p}_{si} = \mu$. We know from Property E that the condition $D_s - \mu > \dot{p}_i > -D_i$ insures that both s and i do not reach their threshold.

Consider first the case $\dot{p}_z = D_z$. For z not to reach the upper margin with respect to i, $\dot{p}_{zi} < \mu$. Whence $\dot{p}_i < D_z - \mu$. Note that, with the values of Table 16–1, $D_z - \mu > -D_i$. This condition also satisfies the right-hand side of constraint (16.18) for $\Sigma_m \pi_m \dot{p}_{mi}$. The left-hand side of (16.18) requires that $\Sigma_m \pi_m \dot{p}_{mi} > 0$ (which also insures that the bilateral rates of the m currencies with respect to s and z do not exceed the margin). Whence $\dot{p}_i < -(\pi_z D_z + \pi_s \mu)/(1 - \pi_z)$. It cannot, however, be established a priori whether such ratio is greater or smaller than $D_s - \mu$.

Consider then $\dot{p}_z = -D_z$. For z not to reach the lower margin with respect to s, $\dot{p}_{zi} > 0$. Whence $\dot{p}_i < -D_z$. Note that $-D_z < D_s - \mu$. This condition also satisfies the left-hand side of constraint (16.18). The right-hand side of (16.18) requires that $\Sigma_m \pi_m p_{mi} < \mu \Sigma_m \pi_m$. Whence

$$-\dot{p}_i < \frac{-\mu \Sigma_m \pi_m + \pi_z D_z - \mu \pi_s}{1 - \pi_z} = \frac{-\mu(1 - \pi_i - \pi_z) + \pi_z D_z}{1 - \pi_z}$$

(since $\Sigma_m \pi_m = 1 - \pi_i - \pi_s - \pi_s$). It cannot be established a priori whether such a ratio is greater or smaller than D_i.

The conditions for $\dot{p}_{si} = -\mu$, $\dot{p}_z = -D_z$ are the same as those of the first case, with the signs changed; those for $\dot{p}_{si} = -\mu$, $\dot{p}_z = D_z$ are the same as those of the second case, with the signs changed.[9] Thus, summing up, when two currencies s and i are at the margin, without reaching the threshold, a third currency, z, may reach its threshold, without reaching the margin, if the following conditions hold:

$$D_z - \mu < \pm \dot{p}_i < \min \begin{cases} -\dfrac{\pi_z D_z + \pi_s \mu}{1 - \pi_s} \\ \\ D_s - \mu \end{cases} \tag{16.22}$$

9. The basic constraints from which the conditions are obtained if $\dot{p}_{si} = -\mu$ are for $\dot{p}_z = -D_z$, $\dot{p}_{zi} > -\mu$, which also satisfies $\dot{p}_i < D_i$, $\dot{p}_s > -D_s$, $\Sigma_m \pi_m \dot{p}_{mi} < 0$; for $\dot{p}_z = D_z$, $\dot{p}_z > 0$, which also satisfies $\dot{p}_s > -D_s$, $\dot{p}_i < D_i$, $\Sigma_m \pi_m p_{mi} > -\mu \Sigma_m \pi_m$.

For $\dot{p}_{si} = \pm\mu$, $\dot{p}_z = \pm D_z$:

$$-D_z > \pm\dot{p}_i > \max \begin{cases} \dfrac{-\mu(1 - \pi_i - \pi_z) + \pi_z D_z}{1 - \pi_z} \\ \\ -D_i \end{cases} \tag{16.23}$$

Condition (16.22) implies $\pi_s < (1 - \pi_s)(1 - \overline{\gamma})$ or $D_s > D_z$ (and hence $\pi_s < \pi_z$), according to whether the upper or the lower part of the right-hand side inequality holds, while condition (16.23) implies $\pi_i < (1 - \pi_z)(1 - \overline{\gamma})$ or $D_i > D_z$ ($\pi_i < \pi_z$), according to whether the upper or the lower part of the right-hand side inequality holds.

The associated ranges of values for $\Sigma_m \pi_m \dot{p}_{mi}$ are obtained by substituting the extreme values of $\dot{p}_i$ into the expression for $\Sigma_m \pi_m \dot{p}_{mi}$ derived from equation (16.14).

With the weights of the currencies in the EMS as given in Table 16-1, there can be no currency z reaching the threshold, when the Deutsche mark is currency s in case (16.22) and currency i in case (16.23). In other words, no currency moving in the same direction as the Deutsche mark can reach the threshold with respect to that other currency which is at its full bilateral margin with the Deutsche mark.

Examples. In Table 16-4, currency s appreciates (sign + in brackets) or depreciates (sign − in brackets) by the full bilateral margin with respect to currency i. Currency z is the one whose bilateral rate against any other moves by less than the full margin but reaches the upper (sign +) or the lower (sign −) threshold. This happens when the percentage appreciation or depreciation of the other m currencies with respect to the first three is within the range shown in the table.

Property G

With two or three currencies at their maximum bilateral margin with respect to the others, it is possible that no currency reaches its threshold.

Proof. Let two currencies, i and s, reach the upper bilateral margin with respect to all others.[10] Hence, $\dot{p}_{si} = 0$, $\Sigma_k \pi_k \dot{p}_{ki} = -\mu \Sigma_k \pi_k = -\mu(1 - \pi_i - \pi_s)$ and, from equations (16.12) and (16.14), $\dot{p}_i = \dot{p}_s = \mu(1 - \pi_i - \pi_s)$. Let us first show that no other currency except i and s can reach the threshold. Consider

---

10. The same argument applies if two or three currencies reach their lower bilateral margin.

Table 16-4. Example of Property F.

Currencies			Percent Rate of Change of Other m Currencies with Respect to					
s	i	z	s		i		z	
Fl	FB (+)	DM (+)	-1.04	-0.91	0.00	0.13	-0.95	-0.91
DKr	L (+)	FB (+)	-1.41	-1.32	0.33	0.43	-1.33	-1.32
FF	£ (+)	DM (-)	-0.08	0.00	0.67	0.76	0.68	0.72
DM	DKr (+)	FB (-)	-0.46	-0.34	0.77	0.88	0.76	0.85
Fl	DKr (-)	FB (+)	0.35	0.45	-1.38	-1.28	-1.29	-1.28
L	FF (-)	Fl (-)	1.066	1.08	-0.30	-0.29	-1.066	1.07

first a currency r, belonging to the $n - 2$ currencies at the maximum bilateral margin against i and s. Hence, from equation (16.7), $\dot{p}_r = -\mu(\pi_i + \pi_s)$. We know from equation (16.11) that such currency will reach the threshold when $-\mu(\pi_i + \pi_s) \leq -D_r$. But given the weights in the EMS, this is impossible. Currencies i and s, on the other hand, will not reach the threshold if $D_s, D_i > \mu(1 - \pi_i - \pi_s)$ or (from equation 16.11) $\pi_i > (1 - \overline{\gamma})(1 - \pi_s)$, $\pi_s > (1 - \overline{\gamma})(1 - \pi_i)$. In the EMS, these two conditions are simultaneously verified only for the French franc and the Deutsche mark, as can be seen from Table 16-1.

Consider now three currencies—i, s, and z—reaching together the upper bilateral margin with respect to all others. Hence $\dot{p}_i = \dot{p}_s = \dot{p}_z = \mu(1 - \pi_i - \pi_s - \pi_z)$. Also, in this case none of the other $n - 3$ currencies can reach the threshold, since in the EMS, $-D_r < -\mu(1 - \pi_i - \pi_s - \pi_z)$, always. The first three currencies will not reach the threshold if $\dot{p}_i < D_i$ or $\pi_s + \pi_z > (1 - \overline{\gamma})(1 - \pi_i)$; $\dot{p}_s < D_s$ or $\pi_i + \pi_z > (1 - \overline{\gamma})(1 - \pi_s)$; $\dot{p}_z < D_z$ or $\pi_i + \pi_s > (1 - \overline{\gamma})(1 - \pi_z)$. These conditions are more easily verified than the ones for two currencies only.

Examples. If the Deutsche mark and the French franc are at the full bilateral margin with respect to all other currencies, the weighted rate of depreciation of the latter is 1.045 percent, so that neither the Deutsche mark nor the French franc reach the threshold. If the two appreciating currencies are the French franc and the British pound, the weighted rate of depreciation of the other currencies is 1.179 percent: The Deutsche mark is above the threshold, the British pound is not. In general, if the two appreciating currencies are the Deutsche mark and any other except the franc, only the mark will cross the threshold. For any other pair, both currencies will cross the threshold.

In the case of three appreciating currencies, if the group of the latter includes any three of the four currencies with the greater weight, no currency will cross the threshold. All the three appreciating currencies will instead cross the threshold if the group includes any three of the four smaller currencies. In the intermediate cases, the currency with the greater weight will cross the threshold but the other two will not (e.g., the Deutsche mark will, but the Irish pound and the

Danish kroner will not; the British pound will, but the florin and the Belgian franc will not).

ECONOMIC IMPROPRIETIES

The tiresome analysis of the previous section has shown that the alarm mechanism set up in the EMS possesses some distinctly odd features. In this mechanism, the indicator is supposed to measure divergence, and there is an official recognition of a currency's divergence as that currency's indicator crosses the 0.75 threshold. At this stage we can, however, legitimately pose the following questions.

First, why should it be impossible for two currencies to be "officially" divergent in an opposite direction (Property B) when it is possible not only for the ECU prices of the same two currencies to have the same value and opposite sign (Property A), but also for two, three, and even four currencies to be "officially" divergent in the *same* direction (Property D)? Though it is not clear what kind of imbalance the indicator is supposed to reveal, it is in any case quite conceivable that two countries may display opposite symptoms, due to economic policies deviating in an opposite direction from the norm of other countries. It is hard to find a reason why the possible effects on exchange rates of a relatively lax monetary policy in one country and of a relatively restrictive monetary policy in another should not, in principle, be recognized as symptoms of two situations that both require corrective interventions of opposite sign. The answer cannot be that the indicator's task is to single out one, and no more than one, diverging currency, for as we have seen, the writing on the wall may instead appear for two or three or four sinners at the same time, if the sin is of the same nature (collective incontinence or collective overrestraint) and provided that a large-sized sinner does not belong to the group.

Second, it has been argued that the possibility that divergence may not be signaled before two currencies reach their intervention margin should not be considered as an intrinsic drawback of the mechanism: The indicator's role, according to Thygesen (1981), should be that of "signalling more lasting divergences," while two currencies may find themselves at the margin for temporary reasons that require no corrective action other than compulsory intervention. But the mere fact that the alarm may not flash as two currencies reach their margin is certainly not proof that the indicator satisfies the requirement of signaling "more lasting divergence," unless it is also shown that, in general, the indicator will recognize divergence when the movement of the bilateral rate depends on lasting rather than on temporary causes. But this is not the case, judging from Property E. Two currencies at the margin may or may not reach the threshold according to whether the weighted rate of change of the other currencies does or does not exceed a certain interval, which is different for any different pair of currencies at the margin.

How can we decide when the weighted rate of change of the other $n - 2$ currencies is itself the symptom of temporary rather than deep-seated disequilibrium? The disequilibrium may well be temporary and still be such that the weighted rate of the other currencies exceeds the range, bringing one of the two currencies to the threshold, or it may be deep-seated, in spite of the fact that the behavior of one of the other currencies keeps their weighted rate within the range. Further, the difference of range for different pairs of currencies cannot be accounted for in terms of the nature of the underlying disequilibrium, as it depends only on the weights of the two currencies at the margin. Before divergence is signaled for either the Irish pound or the Danish kroner, when one is at the top and the other at the bottom of the band, the weighted bilateral rate of the other six currencies with respect to either of the two can move within an interval of one percentage point, but the range is little more than a half point when the two currencies are the Irish pound and the Deutsche mark and only a little more than one-fifth of a point when they are the French franc and the mark.

Third, queries and doubts about the economic significance of the indicator mechanism are strengthened by Property F. Here two currencies are at their opposite intervention margins, but their indicator is below the threshold, because the movement of the other $n - 2$ currencies is confined within the range defined by Property E. It is, however, possible that the indicator might signal divergence for one of these other currencies, which are all below the margin. This property does not seem to possess any economic justification. Why should the underlying disequilibrium of the third currency be considered more important than the other two, and why should corrective intervention be required for the former but not for the latter? Further, the possibility described by Property F also depends crucially on the weights of the currencies concerned.

Finally, Property G shows an additional oddity of the indicator, complementary to that of Property D examined above. The Deutsche mark and the French franc, or any three of the four larger currencies, or some combination of three large and medium-sized currencies, may move together, appreciating or depreciating by the full margin with respect to all others, without any alarm signal coming from the indicator. If this happens to any three of the four smaller currencies, however, the indicator will register official divergence, but it will not do so for two smaller currencies if they are in the company of a larger one. Again, it is difficult to offer economic justification for this divergent behavior of the divergence indicator.

What is wrong, then, with the indicator and the alarm system? Is it only a question of technical imperfections, which could in principle be remedied by suitable alterations? Certainly some odd effects may be due to the fact that there is not enough room between the threshold and the bilateral margin, and a few would disappear if the threshold were lower relative to one margin. But while a lower threshold would make the alarm flash very often—a not necessarily desirable consequence—it would be no remedy to the economic arbitrariness that we have noted in the behavior of the indicator.

The trouble lies deeper and so cannot be cured by simple technical adjustments. First, whatever the relative merits of a system of margins around ECU parities and one of margins around bilateral parities, each one has an internal consistency. The indicator of divergence attempts to capture some features of both systems, but the resulting hybrid loses the internal consistency of either. The indicator is a ratio between a moving numerator and a denominator that is fixed but different for each currency. The numerator is the currency's ECU price, which moves, as ECU prices do, with very great freedom with respect to the movements of specific bilateral rates and depends on the entire constellation of the bilateral rates among all the currencies included in the basket. The denominator, against which the movement of the ECU price of the individual currency should be gauged, is, on the other hand, a number reflecting one peculiar—and indeed very unlikely—situation for an ECU price in a regime of given bilateral margins—one where the individual currency appreciates or depreciates by the full margin with respect to all other currencies and where therefore the bilateral rates among all the other $n - 1$ currencies remain unchanged. The whole complexity of the relationships between the movements of ECU prices and those of bilateral rates being thus lost, that limiting case can hardly serve as a yardstick to assess the extent of a currency's divergence.

But there are other, and perhaps more fundamental, reasons why the indicator, or any similar device, cannot in principle provide an economically meaningful measure. The problem that the various proposals following the Bremen Council attempted to solve has some similarity with another time-honored problem, well known in the theory of value and distribution since Ricardo's days. In Piero Sraffa's words,

> the necessity of having to express the price of one commodity in terms of another which is arbitrarily chosen as standard, complicates the study of price movements which accompany a change in distribution. It is impossible to tell of any particular price-fluctuation whether it arises from the peculiarities of the commodity which is being measured or from those of the measuring standard. (Sraffa 1960: 18)

Similarly, as one currency appreciates or depreciates with respect to another, it is impossible to tell whether that particular movement of the exchange rate depends on the "peculiarities" of one or the other currency.

In the theory of value and production, a consistent solution was provided by Sraffa's "standard commodity"—"a standard capable of isolating the price-movements of any other product, so that they could be observed as in a vacuum" (Sraffa 1960: 18). Currency prices in terms of a currency basket and the connected notion of an indicator were thought to be at least a partial solution to the problem of identifying the "divergent" currency in the field of exchange rates.

There is, however, a fundamental difference between the two solutions. The former is the outcome of meaningful theory—that is, of a consistent model based on a set of hypotheses that could, in principle, be verified or refuted. The latter, instead, is little more than an accounting device, connected neither to a relevant explanation of a country's external disequilibrium nor even to a satisfactory identification of its symptoms. The remarkable size of intramarginal and "intrathreshold" interventions in the EMS and the resulting changes in official reserve assets and/or in commercial banks' liabilities are the most obvious examples of the inability of the EMS indicator (or of any similar measure) to capture all the relevant manifestations of divergence and to serve as a signal for policy action.

The introduction of mutually agreed criteria for assessing the external consequences of a country's internal policies is an important prerequisite of coordination at the international level. Political considerations more than pure theory will dictate the choice of such criteria. But the spurious precision of a ratio void of theoretical significance is neither the only nor the best compromise between the abstract precision of rigorous theory and the need for politically workable solutions.

REFERENCES

Baer, Gunter D. 1979. "Some Technical Implications of Pegging Exchange Rates Against a Basket of Currencies." *De Economist*, 127, no. 3.

Bourguinat, Henry. 1979. "Written Comments." In Robert Triffin, ed., *EMS: The Emerging European Monetary System*. Offprint of *Bulletin* of National Bank of Belgium (April).

Commission of the European Communities. 1979. "The European Monetary System." *European Economy* 3 (July).

Deutsche Bundesbank. 1979. "The European Monetary System: Structure and Operation." *Monthly Report of the Deutsche Bundesbank* 31, no. 3 (March): 13–14.

European Communities, Monetary Committee. 1979. *Compendium of Community Monetary Texts*. Brussels.

Ludlow, Peter. 1980. "The Political and Diplomatic Origins of the European Monetary System, July 1977–March 1979." *Bologna Center Occasional Paper* No. 32. Research Institute, the Johns Hopkins University, June.

Masera, Rainer. 1980a. "The EMS and European Monetary Integration." Paper prepared for a seminar on Arab Monetary Integration: Issues and Pre-requisites, November.

_____. 1980b. *L'unificazione monetaria europea*. Bologna: Il Mulino.

Rieke, Wolfgang. 1979. "Written Comment." In Robert Triffin, ed., *EMS: The Emerging European Monetary System*. Offprint of the *Bulletin* of the National Bank of Belgium 1 (April).

Spaventi, Luigi. 1980. "Italy Joins the EMS: A Political History." *Bologna Center Occasional Paper* No. 32. Research Institute, the Johns Hopkins University, June.

Sraffa, Piero. 1960. *Production of Commodities by Means of Commodities*. Cambridge: Cambridge University Press.

Thygesen, Niels. 1979. "The Emerging European Monetary System: Precursors, First Steps and Policy Options." In Robert Triffin, ed., *EMS: The Emerging European Monetary System*. Offprint from *Bulletin* of the National Bank of Belgium (April).

_____. 1981. "The European Monetary System – An Approximate Implementation of the Crawling Peg?" Paper prepared for a conference in Rio de Janeiro, October 1979. In John Williamson, ed., *Exchange Rate Rules: The Theory, Performance and Prospects of the Crawling Peg*. London: Macmillan.

Triffin, Robert. 1979. "Concluding Remarks." In Robert Triffin, ed., *EMS: The Emerging European Monetary System*. Offprint of the *Bulletin* of the National Bank of Belgium 1 (April).

van Ypersele de Strihou, Jacques. 1979a. "Written Comments." In Robert Triffin, ed., *EMS: The Emerging European Monetary System*. Offprint of *Bulletin* of National Bank of Belgium (April).

_____. 1979b. "Le Système Monétaire Européen: un premier bilan et les tâches de demain." November 26. Mimeograph.

17 THE EUROPEAN MONETARY SYSTEM
Past Experience and Future Prospects

Jacques van Ypersele

INTRODUCTION

From the beginning the European Monetary System has found in Robert Triffin one of its most careful observers and lucid commentators (see, e.g., Triffin 1979, 1980), and one feels somewhat inhibited in trying to honor him with a modest contribution to a subject that he could handle with so much more mastery himself. Insofar as deeds are better than words, the EMS itself could be seen as a more fitting tribute to Triffin, since, imperfect as it may be, it gives weight and substance to two ideas that he has repeatedly stressed in his writings over the past twenty-five years—the need to cooperate in the monetary field in order to compensate for the "inadequacy of national sovereignty as a framework for policy decisions and their administrative implementation in an interdependent world" (Triffin 1957) and the need, in such efforts at greater international cooperation, to be pragmatic and to rely on regional groupings wherever they can elicit from like-minded countries closer cooperation than would be feasible in broader groups. "Closer regional agreements of this type," wrote Triffin in 1960 in reference to the then newly born European Economic Community (EC), "can usefully supplement and support the looser agreements attainable on a worldwide level, and pave the way, under favorable conditions, for a complete merger of economic sovereignty among the participating countries" (Triffin 1960: 147).

The goal of monetary cooperation is duly inscribed in the birth certificate of the EMS: The heads of state and government of the European Community, meeting in Bremen in July 1978, decided to establish "a scheme for the creation of closer monetary cooperation leading to a zone of monetary stability in Europe." As of this writing, twenty months have elapsed since the EMS actually started operating in March of 1979, months in which the international environment and the circumstances surrounding the functioning of the EMS have changed noticeably, thus making our experience with it, though still short, nevertheless diversified enough to bear a retrospective look and to yield lessons for the future.

At the time of the European Council meetings in Bremen and Brussels that resolved to set up the EMS, the economic outlook for the Community during the 1980s was undoubtedly brighter than it is now: The European Community as a whole had eliminated the current deficit caused by the 1973–1974 oil price increase and was indeed running a combined current account surplus of some $17 billion, while the current surplus of the OPEC countries had virtually disappeared; the terms of trade of industrialized countries as a whole, and of the European Community within that group, had registered a considerable improvement since 1974 and were fairly stable; rates of inflation in member countries, though still much too high in some cases, had fallen from the 1974–1975 peaks; and finally, there had been some narrowing of inflation differentials between member countries, and the sharp divergence in balance of payments performance among them, which had been characteristic of the early 1970s, had been substantially reduced.

In brief, the external position of the European Community as a whole was quite strong, and conditions for exchange rate stability among member countries were more favorable than they had been for a number of years. As many observers have remarked, the good performance of the EMS during its first year was partly due to the favorable circumstances under which it was launched.

There is now a rather different set of circumstances. The doubling of crude oil prices during 1979 pushed the OPEC current surplus in the vicinity of $70 billion last year. A surplus of this size, or even larger, is likely to persist for several years in view of the OPEC countries' apparent determination to resist any reduction in the real price of oil, by cutting production if necessary, and in view of their lower capacity to absorb imports rapidly from industrialized countries.

The implications for the EMS are twofold: On the one hand, the European Community's terms of trade have once again sharply deteriorated; most of its member countries have been thrown into current deficits, and inflationary pressures have been rekindled. But the balance of payments impact of this new oil price increase has been unevenly distributed, since some member countries are more dependent on imported oil than others. Furthermore, because of differences between countries regarding their capacity or resolve to control inflationary pressures, national inflation rates are diverging once again within the Community. On the other hand, OPEC countries once again have to dispose of vast surpluses, which they will seek to invest partly in short-term assets within the European Community, but with a tendency to direct their capital to those countries with the strongest financial performance, thus possibly aggravating exchange rate strains within the Community.

In this swiftly changing international environment, the performance of the EMS to date has to be appraised in relation to the fixed set of goals that its creators envisioned for it. I will first review those goals, before examining the results achieved by the EMS so far, outlining the prospects it faces for the near future, and finally, proposing what I consider to be some important future tasks for the EMS.

OBJECTIVE: A ZONE OF MONETARY STABILITY IN EUROPE

The Bremen communiqué of 1978 referred to the creation of "a zone of monetary stability in Europe"; by this was meant a zone wherein stable exchange rates between national currencies would be maintained, preferably not in a superficial and artificially constraining way, but above all through a convergence of the member countries' internal economic performances toward internal stability. Western Germany's minister of finance, Hans Matthöffer, clearly expressed the purpose when he said that the stability of exchange relationships within the EMS was not to be pursued for itself but rather as "the point of crystallization of a community of stability" (Matthöffer 1980). Furthermore, the enhancement of monetary stability within such a zone was viewed as a positive contribution to the stability of the international monetary environment and in particular to the relationship with the dollar.

This move toward a greater degree of exchange rate fixity among European currencies came about largely as a result of a growing dissatisfaction with exchange rate flexibility and with the great measure of instability it seemed to impart to foreign exchange markets. Such instability was felt to be harmful to investment and growth prospects in European economies. European business executives often complained that because of ever-present exchange risks and uncertainty about inflation rates, they were unable to give their companies a full European dimension and to reap the potential benefits of a market as large as Western Europe. But monetary instability is not necessarily a permanent feature of exchange rate flexibility. A number of influential voices, among prominent economists in particular, continue to extol the virtues of flexible exchange rates, for the adoption of which they had long campaigned, and to hail their near generalization in the spring of 1973 as a great step forward in international economic relations. Since the arguments they used still underlie most of the criticisms directed at exchange rate fixity in general and at the EMS in particular, they deserve careful consideration.

In a world of independent nations but interdependent national economies, flexible exchange rates could in principle perform two irreplaceable functions— adjustment on the one hand, insulation on the other. Whenever a balance of payments disequilibrium develops in a country and throws the demand for foreign exchange out of balance with the supply, exchange rate flexibility should allow a quick and automatic variation in the price of foreign exchange to restore external equilibrium swiftly and painlessly.

Since the demand for and supply of foreign exchange, within a country, are much influenced by the country's macroeconomic policy relative to the policies of other countries, both through the effect of aggregate demand on imports and the response of short-term capital movements to intercountry interest rate differentials, exchange rate flexibility makes compatible, to some extent, national economic policies that are pursued in uncoordinated fashion. Exchange rate fixity on the other hand implies that some other mechanism of accommodation—running down reserves, deflating aggregate demand, or controlling imports and capital outflows—has to be found whenever an excess demand for foreign exchange develops, thus placing obvious constraints on the ability of a country open to trade and capital movements to pursue certain domestic policy objectives.

As to the insulation function performed by flexible exchange rates, it is obviously related to their capacity to restore equilibrium in the foreign exchange market: A country can afford to ignore external constraints and to pursue national economic objectives in a relatively autonomous manner only to the extent that the exchange rate mechanism takes care of external imbalances engendered by its own actions. Thus, for instance, a more expansionary policy than in one's trading partners would rapidly bring about growing trade deficits under fixed exchange rates, depleting the country's reserves and possibly leading to the erection of protective barriers. Under flexible exchange rates, by contrast, the more rapid expansion can simply translate into a continuous depreciation of the country's currency vis-à-vis the less inflationary countries. By the same token, countries that are more oriented toward internal price stability can be insulated by an appreciating currency from the inflationary tendencies that develop outside of them, which tendencies would surely contaminate them under exchange rate fixity. Thus, exchange rate flexibility was said to "bottle up" inflation in the countries where it originated. According to Milton Friedman's classic essay (1953), flexible exchange rates "are a means of permitting each country to seek for monetary stability according to its own lights, without either imposing its mistakes on its neighbors or having their mistakes imposed on it."

In a world where rates of inflation have a tendency to diverge wildly, as in the 1973 boom and subsequent episode of stagflation–recession, while balance of payments were thrown sharply into disequilibrium by the oil price increases, exchange rate flexibility played the role of a safety valve. Thus, wrote Marina v. N. Whitman (1977), "There can be little doubt that the avoidance of a wholesale retreat into competitive protectionism in the face of accelerating and divergent rates of inflation, the oil crisis, and the subsequent widespread recession, was made possible by the shift from pegged rates to managed floating."

More recently, prominent critics of the EMS and of the relative exchange rate fixity built into it have deplored the fact that countries with relatively stable prices, such as Germany, might have to accept a certain amount of imported inflation from the more inflationary ones. Thus Dr. Otmar Emminger, former president of the Deutsche Bundesbank, recently remarked at an American Enterprise Institute Conference in Washington: "Our experience in Germany has clearly shown that in the past free floating, far from having an inflationary effect, shielded us from imported inflation. Germany and Switzerland went over to floating in early 1973 not primarily with the aim of adjusting their payments balances but mainly in order to shield their monetary systems from destabilizing inflows of foreign exchange" (Emminger 1980).

Why is it, then, that the practical experience with generalized floating among the major currencies has not been satisfactory enough to give this system permanent credibility and acceptability? Contrary to what its advocates expected, flexibility has been accompanied by much instability in exchange markets, and exchange rates have fluctuated much more widely than appeared to be warranted by underlying economic conditions and by inflation differentials, while balance of payments imbalances between industrial countries, far from being swiftly eliminated, remained on the average very important after 1973.

First of all it appears that the adjustments under flexible exchange rates did not take place in the manner predicted by simple theoretical models focused on the trade balance. Flows of international trade appear to be influenced only slowly by exchange rate variations, but react rapidly to variations in aggregate demand. There is a new mood of "elasticity pessimism" that is borne out by a number of empirical studies. For instance, a recent econometric analysis by Miles (1979) finds that in almost all of the sixteen cases studied in the period 1962-1967, the trade balance was not affected by a devaluation; indeed, it worsened initially, and the small improvement in the year following the devaluation was not large enough to recoup the initial worsening. There is a temporary improvement in the *balance of payments*, which appears to be a stock adjustment lasting about two years and which is explained in this study by the devaluing country's desire to rebuild its real balances. These are reduced by a devaluation and are rebuilt by an exchange of bonds for money resulting in a net capital inflow. One may add that in today's conditions, where trade deficits are mostly due to oil price increases, exchange rate variations are even less effective for adjustment, given the low price elasticity of oil in the short run, and more emphasis should be laid on adjustment by means of internal economic policies.

Of course, such evidence is not sufficient to invalidate the case for flexible exchange rates. One can still claim that exchange rate variations will work for adjustment if they are accompanied by the right supporting measures aimed at aggregate demand. In the case of countries with a chronic deficit and a high rate of inflation, a currency depreciation can presumably be effective if it is accompanied by measures to control aggregate demand and the money supply. On the other hand, currency appreciation can reduce a balance of payments surplus if it goes hand in hand with expansionary measures at home.

The question becomes then whether such supporting measures, which are necessary in any case, are more likely to be taken with a variation in the exchange rate than without. The record of the recent experience with flexible exchange rates among major currencies leaves one skeptical on that score. As Henry Wallich (1980) puts it concisely: "The promise of speedy adjustment of payment imbalances through exchange rate movements has remained unfulfilled, perhaps because the very ease with which exchange rates could move has diminished political pressure to adopt appropriate fiscal and monetary policies."

Along the same lines, it has been argued that exchange rate variations will be effective for adjustment provided they lead to "real" changes in exchange rates and are not offset by an increase in the inflation differential (see, for instance, Cooper 1980). But as we shall see, such offsetting movements in the form of "vicious" or "virtuous" circles have shown a tendency to appear under exchange rate flexibility.

A crucial factor in altering the adjustment function that was expected from exchange rate variations has been the importance assumed by short-term capital movements. As Fritz Machlup (1979) commented recently: "Few of us realized before the 1960s that capital movements would swamp the foreign-exchange market to such an extent that transactions associated with the flows of merchandise could become relatively insignificant."

The fact that asset markets react much more rapidly than the flows of trade, so that exchange rates are more and more often determined by portfolio adjustments, is undoubtedly behind the prevalence of the phenomenon of "overshooting." Under flexible exchange rates, a country whose currency appreciates because of, say, a favorable trade balance, will not necessarily see its trade surplus being corrected very fast by the exchange rate appreciation, but it is likely to attract in the meantime short-term foreign capital that speculates on the chances of a further appreciation, and the surplus that appears in the balance of capital flows will in effect cause a new appreciation, thus confirming ex post the speculators' expectations. The reverse phenomenon will of course occur in a country whose currency initially depreciates because of a deficit on current account.

This capital mobility, coupled with the tendency of asset markets to adjust more rapidly than goods markets, is what causes "overshooting" and also reduces the effectiveness of the insulation that exchange rate flexibility was supposed to provide. Imagine a country that takes advantage of the "license to inflate" that exchange rate flexibility supposedly gives and that lets its currency depreciate accordingly. If overshooting occurs, the exchange rate depreciation will exceed the inflation differential. But the rising prices of imported goods will feed the inflationary process, and a vicious circle of depreciation-inflation is likely to get started. Excessive movements in the exchange rate thus tend to be accommodated ex post by price movements.

Thus, under flexible exchange rates, capital movements make it difficult for a country to keep under control an inflationary process that, under fixed exchange rates, would at least be disciplined by the external constraint. The freedom to inflate under the false protection of a flexible exchange rate may rapidly turn into an uncontrollable addiction. The fear of being thrown into such vicious circles, coupled with a growing recognition of the short-run ineffectiveness of exchange rate variations in correcting fundamental disequilibria, helps to explain the very strong resistance to devaluation shown by all member countries of the EMS when their currencies come under pressure.

As a postscript to this section, I would like to point out that "overshooting" and "vicious circles" are merely new additions to the economist's jargon. The phenomena they purport to designate were thoroughly analyzed by Robert Triffin more than twenty years ago. The following quotation from his famous *Gold and the Dollar Crisis* should perhaps persuade the casual reader to drop this *Festschrift* and go back to the classics.

Under convertibility conditions, an excessive rate of credit expansion, particularly in a small country, may spill out very quickly into balance-of-payments deficits, long in advance of any substantial price increases, these being held down anyway by the competition of imports from abroad. The depreciation of the national currency under the free interplay of market supply and demand would, however, stimulate increases in import prices which would, in turn, affect internal price, cost and wage levels in general. Speculation would accelerate and amplify these disequilibrating movements without, of and by itself, correcting the internal financial policies which lie at the root of the balance-of-payments deficits. If, however, such policies were continued indefinitely, the accelerated currency depreciation and price rises could hardly fail either to end in a currency collapse, or, more probably, to induce the authorities to resort to stringent trade and exchange restrictions, bringing to an end the flexible exchange rate experiments. If, on the other hand, the authorities decide, instead, to arrest their inflationary rates of monetary and credit expansion, price and wage rigidities will make it difficult to reverse the intervening cost increases. The new "equilibrium" exchange rates, even in the absence of renewed inflationary forces, will be lower than would have been the case if exchange flexibility and speculation had not previously driven exchange rates, import prices, and overall wage and cost levels further than they would have gone under a system of pegged exchange rates. Resistance to downward cost and wage adjustments would tend to impart a "devaluation bias" to any system of exchange rate flexibility, and this bias could not fail to make private exchange speculation far less "stabilizing" than envisaged by the proponents of exchange rate flexibility. (Triffin 1960: 82–83)

THE EMS PERFORMANCE DURING ITS FIRST YEAR AND A HALF

Has the EMS succeeded so far in fostering closer monetary cooperation and creating a zone of monetary stability in Europe? I propose to answer this complex question in three steps:

- First, I will claim that the EMS was quite successful in promoting greater exchange rate stability among member countries.

- Next, I will admit that unfortunately this greater exchange rate stability was not accompanied by a greater convergence of member countries' economic results, although the exchange rate mechanism imposed a certain amount of discipline on member countries.

- Finally, I will argue that the EMS' relatively unsatisfactory performance with regard to convergence, and in particular the persisting divergence of inflation rates among member countries, has not, so far, caused the inconvenience for the more price stable countries that its detractors like to stress.

For the sake of brevity I will not describe here the specific mechanisms of the EMS, which by now have been amply covered, analyzed, and illustrated in many official documents and financial publications. I will concentrate instead on the results achieved by the operation of those mechanisms. The interested reader can consult another article in which they are described in some detail (van Ypersele 1979).

Greater Exchange Rate Stability

First of all, it appears that the EMS has succeeded in eliminating the phenomenon of "overshooting" among member countries' currencies and thus contributed to much greater exchange rate stability, without at the same time making the system and the parity grid as rigid as some had feared. The exchange mechanism, which specifies the authorized limits of fluctuations between currencies, has performed well.

Since the EMS came into force on March 13, 1979, the fluctuations in the exchange rates of the currencies participating in the system have been the most moderate recorded for eight years, even taking into account the realignments of September 23 and November 30, 1979. For the Community currencies taken together, the annual average fluctuation against the ECU was 1.9 percent, compared with 2.7 percent in 1978 and the 5.2 percent average over the period 1973–1978. One has to go back to 1972 for a lower figure (1.2 percent). A similar pattern emerges when one considers bilateral exchange relationships in the EMS.

This satisfactory start for the EMS was partly due to a set of favorable circumstances: First, the balance of payments situations of France and Italy, two countries whose currencies had shown some weakness in the years preceding the EMS, were quite strong in 1979. Second, the dollar was fairly stable against EMS currencies during the first six months of the EMS, following the improvement in the U.S. balance of payments and the strong measures taken by the Carter administration in November of 1978 in support of the dollar, and it is often when the dollar weakens and when short-term capital takes refuge in the Deutsche mark that tensions between this currency and other European currencies have a tendency to appear.

Tensions grew stronger in September of 1979, as the dollar weakened under the sudden acceleration of U.S. inflation. On September 23, a realignment of EMS central rates took place: The Deutsche mark was revalued by 2 percent, and the Danish kroner devalued by 3 percent against all other currencies within the system. On November 30, the Danish kroner was devalued again by 5 percent, as part of a new set of policy measures taken by the new Danish government following elections.

The fact that these realignments were accomplished quietly and swiftly, without any kind of crisis, indicated that even for a group of countries larger than the former "snake," the EMS was not a rigid system. To be sure, some commentators have argued that the September 23 realignment came too late and in any case was insufficient to accommodate the important differentials existing between member countries' rates of inflation (Scharrer 1980). But one has to observe that, until now, tensions within the EMS have been provoked less by inflation differentials than by balance of payments situations: The Belgian franc, for instance, was rather weak and kept close to its "threshold of divergence" during most of 1979, while the inflation rate in Belgium was equal and sometimes below the German rate of inflation. By contrast France and Italy, with much higher inflation rates, remained strong with the EMS, thanks to their favorable balance of payments situations.

Did the EMS also contribute to greater monetary stability between zones and in particular between the dollar and European currencies? There is little one can say about this as of now. Europeans still lack a common policy toward the dollar. One can presume, however, that first the conception and then the creation and successful operation of the EMS did contribute toward the change of attitude displayed by U.S. authorities vis-à-vis the dollar and their shift from "benign neglect" to growing concern.

In addition, there is one particular feature of the EMS that is likely to help stabilize the dollar. This is the replacement of the dollar by Community currencies in principle at least for market interventions and by the ECU in the settlement of mutual credits. Triffin has noted that "Americans have often justifiably complained of the dominant use of the dollar for both of these purposes, as strong—even though unintended—upward or downward pressure could be exerted on the market rates of the dollar, irrespective of any development in the underlying balance of payments of the United States, whenever Community countries' surpluses or deficits switched from eager to reluctant dollar holders, or vice versa" (Triffin 1979: 68). Interventions in Community currencies amounted to 6.9 billion ECU in the period April 1979–August 1980. But one has to recognize also that in practice, dollar interventions were still very important and in some cases were not in line with the EMS agreement.

An initial supply of ECUs to serve as reserve and as means of settlement was provided at the start of the EMS. Central banks deposited with the European Monetary Cooperation Fund (EMCF) the equivalent of 20 percent of their reserves in gold and dollars in exchange for a total of about 23.3 billion ECUs. Out of this total, 13.3 billion ECUs were issued against gold and 10 billion against dollars. This operation took the form of revolving swap arrangements. The gold and dollars thus deposited are valued on the basis of their market prices. Every three months, when they renew the swap arrangements, central banks make whatever adjustments are necessary to maintain with the EMCF deposits corresponding to at least 20 percent of their gold and dollar reserves, while the amounts of ECUs issued are adjusted according to the changes that have taken place in the market value of the gold or dollar exchange rate. As of September 1980, the ECUs held by the EMS central banks amounted to 45.5 billion, of which 36 billion were issued against gold and 9.5 billion against dollars.

The fast progression in the total amount of ECUs held by European central banks was the result mainly of the upsurge in the price of gold. Since the ECU is transferable between central banks in the EMS, the ECU mechanism has allowed a certain mobilization of gold reserves to take place and has thus increased the liquidity of their reserves. At the end of September 1980, ECU transfers had resulted in a net increase of ECUs held by France (1.35 billion) and net losses for Belgium (990 million), Germany (210 million), and Denmark (150 million).

Insufficient Convergence Toward Internal Stability

As I stressed earlier, stable exchange relationships in the EMS should be the sign and the consequence of a greater harmonization of national policies and a better convergence of economic performances toward stability. On this score, the EMS has not yet produced very satisfactory results. This relative failure appears most visibly in the fact that the divergence among member countries' inflation rates has increased.

The difference between the rates of the two countries with the highest and lowest consumer price inflations went up from nine percentage points in the second quarter of 1978 to seventeen points in the last quarter of 1979. Over a slightly longer period, it appears that the maximum divergence among the EC countries' inflation rates was reached in 1975, that it decreased thereafter, but that it started increasing again in 1979 (Vaubel 1980).

Should one therefore draw the conclusion that the EMS mechanisms did not function properly in this respect and that monetary cooperation was lacking? Not necessarily. I believe that the existing mechanisms did function properly, but that they may be insufficient, and one should consider supplementing them. In addition, particular external circumstances are partly responsible for the increasing divergence of inflation rates.

The operation of the so-called "divergence indicator" was typical in these respects. As is well-known by now, this is a kind of early warning system that signals whether a currency has a different movement from the average of the other currencies. It flashes when a currency crosses its "threshold of divergence," which is set at 75 percent of the maximum spread of divergence allowed for each currency, and this results in a presumption that the authorities of the country in question will take adequate measures to correct this situation, failing which they must submit to a consultation with their partners within the EMS.

It appears that the divergence indicator played a useful role in the cases of Belgium and Denmark. The authorities of both countries played correctly by the rules when their currencies crossed their respective divergence thresholds. The Belgian authorities in particular took the three types of prescribed internal policy measures: First, the central bank intervened in EC currencies within the margins; then, monetary policy was significantly tightened, in particular by raising the central banks' discount rate; and finally, the government took important restrictive budgetary measures, first to limit the budget deficit for 1979 and then to present a tight budget for 1980 and to decrease the financing needs of the social security system.

Thus, the divergence indicator has encouraged the self-discipline that is a necessary component of any effort toward a greater harmonization of national policies. It was interesting to note in this respect that in a speech to the Belgian parliament in October 1979, in which he presented the budgetary and social security measures proposed by the government, the prime minister, Wilfried Martens, specifically mentioned the divergence indicator, the presumption of action that the crossing of the "divergence threshold" entailed, and the specific actions that had been taken.

But the divergence indicator played this useful role only to the extent that external stability was in danger, and in 1979, as I mentioned before, tensions in the EMS exchange mechanism were provoked less by inflation differentials than by balance of payments disequilibria. This undoubtedly is the main factor that allowed the divergence among inflation rates to increase without until now creating new tensions within the system.

The increasing divergence of inflation rates is due partly to the fact that the new round of oil price increases does not affect all EMS member countries in the same manner. But there remain important national differences with regard to the extent to which inflation is tolerated or can be subdued by stabilization measures: Internal stabilization is not being pursued with the same intensity everywhere, nor is it followed with the same results. These differences appear not only when one considers the divergence of inflation rates, but also when, more directly, one asks whether there was any convergence of monetary policies. One could indeed argue that, given the time lag with which inflation reacts to expansion of the money supply, the divergence among inflation rates observed in 1979 was already implied by monetary developments in 1978.

Thus, to determine whether there was any convergence of monetary policies among EMS countries in 1979, one should not look simply at the rates of inflation in 1979, but at the behavior of monetary aggregates in 1979. This was recently done by Roland Vaubel (1980). The index of monetary policy he uses for each country is the differential between the rate of growth of the monetary stock (M_1) and the growth rate of real GNP. It appears then that monetary policies have become increasingly divergent since 1975 and that this movement was not interrupted in 1979; on the contrary, there are indications that it accelerated.

Were More Stability-oriented Countries Forced to "Import" Inflation Under EMS Rules?

According to many prominent critics of the EMS, the pursuit of exchange rate stability and the resulting commitment on the part of member countries to intervene in order to preserve the agreed upon parity grid leads those among them that are more attracted to internal price stability and more successful in attaining that goal to give it up partially by "importing" the inflation that originates within laxer partners. This can occur both as an effect of the tendency toward uniformity of price displayed by internationally traded goods and because the strong currency countries, through their interventions on foreign exchange markets, may be induced to expand their money supplies beyond what they deem appropriate for internal stability.

In response to that argument, which is of course perfectly respectable on a theoretical plane, I think it is appropriate to make the following points:

1. The two realignments of central rates that occurred in 1979 proved that the EMS was not as rigid as was feared by many initially. A major concern in Germany had been that it would be impossible under EMS rules to achieve in time the unavoidable parity readjustments.

2. While it is true that speculative flows of capital lead strong currency countries to intervene in order to prevent appreciation of their currencies beyond the authorized limits, as happened several times during the first year of EMS, the volume of those interventions was never such as to prevent the objectives of internal monetary growth from being achieved in the intervening coun-

tries. For there are ways to neutralize the effects of such interventions on the monetary base, and the Bundesbank in Germany, among others, used them. During the third trimester of 1979, as I mentioned earlier, the tensions within the EMS were strongest, because of the renewed weakness of the dollar, and during that period the Bundesbank had to purchase foreign exchange worth DM 20 billion. But the effect of these speculative capital inflows on the monetary base in Germany was largely offset by internal credit restrictions (cf. van Ypersele 1980). And data on the growth of the monetary stock in Germany do not indicate that it accelerated during that period — on the contrary.

3. The operation of the EMS did not prevent a definite appreciation of the Deutsche mark in 1979, with favorable effects on German import prices. During that period, according to the Bundesbank, the Deutsche mark rose in value by 3.7 percent relative to a basket of the currencies of Germany's main twenty-three trading partners and by 2.3 percent with respect to a basket of EMS currencies.

4. Finally, the turnaround in the current account of Germany's balance of payments, with a DM 9 billion deficit in 1979 and an expected deficit of DM 25 billion in 1980, as well as the outflow of German short-term capital toward the dollar in the first months of 1980, have pushed the Deutsche mark toward a median position within the EMS. Thus one can no longer claim that the exchange mechanism prevented an appreciation of the Deutsche mark. Since the end of 1979, the value of the mark has remained fairly stable vis-à-vis a basket of EMS currencies, as well as vis-à-vis the currencies of Germany's main twenty-three partners.

Having thus responded to a major criticism of the EMS and an important concern that has been expressed, particularly in Germany, I should immediately add that I concur with the critics of EMS in deploring the fact that the divergence of inflation rates has persisted or even increased, and I agree that this lack of convergence should not be allowed to go on too long, for otherwise it will create problems and tensions.

Where I part with the critics is in the conclusion to be drawn from this diagnosis. Whereas many tend to see it as a reason to abandon the EMS, I definitely see a reason to consolidate the EMS, to strengthen it, and to make it operate more in the spirit in which it was conceived, for the alternative of going back to exchange rate flexibility between EC currencies does not appear to me to be feasible. Certainly, the divergence of inflation rates would then increase further, because overshooting and vicious circles of depreciation–inflation would resume on a large scale in the rather turbulent international environment that we have once again. Exchange rate flexibility would make this increasing divergence more tolerable, but as I tried to argue earlier on the basis of our past experience with exchange rate flexibility, it does not seem to be a tenable option in the long run.

PROSPECTS

Having dealt with the past experience of EMS, let us now turn toward its future, first cautiously trying to predict what is in store for the near future. We saw that the persisting and even increasing divergence among member countries' inflation rates had not yet created any noticeable tensions in the exchange relationships, because some important members with higher inflation rates, such as France and Italy, also had more favorable balance of payments situations in 1979. Is this peculiar conjunction likely to persist? Balance-of-payments prospects are still relatively good for France and Italy, in the sense that the deterioration that affects the Community as a whole will remain moderate for these two countries. The latest figures and forecasts from the OECD show this to be the case (see Table 17-1).

The pattern of current account balances should undoubtedly contribute toward maintaining a fair degree of exchange rate stability within the EMS despite the divergence of inflation rates. Another factor likely to have similar effects is that countries whose currencies weaken display increasing resistance to downward readjustments of their parities; there is a growing preference for adjustment through internal measures.

Table 17-1.   Current Accounts and Inflation.

	Current Account of the Balance of Payments (billion of dollars)			Consumer Price Deflator (percent variation)	
	1979	1980	1981 (first semester, annual rate)	1980	1981 (first semester, annual rate)
France	1.5	−4.0	−1.0	13.2	11.0
Germany	−5.7	−16.0	−13.2	5.5	3.5
Italy	5.2	−2.7	4.7	19.6	15.5
United Kingdom	−5.2	−2.5	−2.5	20.3	14.2
Denmark	−3.0	−3.6	n.a.	11.5	n.a.
Belgium−Luxemburg	−3.8	−4.2	n.a.	7.0	n.a.
Ireland	−1.3	−1.4	n.a.	19.5	n.a.
Netherlands	−2.5	−1.6	n.a.	6.5	n.a.
Total European Economic Community	−14.8	−36.0		12.3	
Total European Economic Community minus United Kingdom	−9.6	−33.5			

Sources: Current account – OECD, *Economic Prospects*, July 27, 1980; Consumer price deflator, 1981 – ibid.; Consumer price deflator, 1980 – Commission of the European Economic Community, May 1980.

Two recent episodes are likely to strengthen these tendencies. In Denmark, the two consecutive devaluations of the kroner within the EMS do not seem to have had the expected positive results on the balance of payments, while having adverse consequences for price stability. On the other hand, the March 1980 speculation wave against the Belgian franc gave Belgian authorities an opportunity to demonstrate that monetary authorities can defeat speculation and relieve downward pressures on the exchange rate. Since then, the Belgian franc is once again comfortable within the EMS, and its divergence indicator has remained well on this side of the divergence threshold.

But divergent inflation rates will in the end create tensions if they persist too long. One can only be in agreement with one of the conclusions of the latest annual report of the Bank for International Settlements (1980), where it is said: "Countries where inflation spreads more rapidly than in their principal trading partners cannot prevent their currency from depreciating in the long run. Therefore, in order to consolidate the greater exchange rate stability that obtained last year, one will have to achieve a better convergence of inflation rates, at an appreciably lower level than the one which prevails now."

FUTURE TASKS

Thus, among the EMS' future tasks, a major one will be to secure a greater degree of convergence among member countries' national economies and possibly to devise new mechanisms for achieving it. Member countries should give priority to domestic policies, particularly monetary and budgetary policies, to achieve this better convergence.

Among these efforts at convergence, the coordination of monetary policies deserves a special role. The purpose is to insure the compatibility of member countries' domestic monetary objectives with the exchange rate objective. The focus should be on the coordination of the expansion of domestic credit. Policies relating to the evolution of incomes can be significant too, and coordination of budgetary policies can also play an important role.

The divergence indicator should continue to induce countries to take the necessary measures when their currencies cross the divergence threshold, in which case there is a presumption of action on the part of the authorities of the country in question. One could consider also whether to devise another indicator, for the divergence of inflation rates. It too would imply a presumption of action, this time when the inflation rate of one country diverges upwards and significantly from its partners' average rate. At a recent European summit in Luxembourg, the Belgian prime minister, Mr. Martens, made a proposal in that direction.

The EMS agreement provides also for "coordination of exchange rate policies vis-à-vis third countries and, as far as possible, a concertation with the money authorities of these countries." It seems to me that monetary authorities of the

EMS countries should try to adopt, together with the United States, a common view on a target zone for the dollar and that authorities on both sides of the Atlantic Ocean should then take measures that would facilitate staying within this target zone. This zone could be modified at regular intervals and would in no way imply the automatic defense of a fixed dollar rate. Given the attitude of the U.S. authorities, the present context appears favorable for such a discussion.

If the EMS is reinforced in the ways that I have outlined and succeeds also in decreasing fluctuations with third countries, it seems clear to me that it will exert a strong power of attraction, first, vis-à-vis sterling, which at present does not participate in the exchange rate mechanism, and then on other currencies, such as the Austrian schilling or some Scandinavian currencies that earlier abandoned the association with the snake.

Finally, steps toward the creation of a European Monetary Fund should proceed as foreseen in the December 1978 agreement of the European Council. As was stated then:

> We remain firmly resolved to consolidate, not later than two years after the start of the scheme, into a final system the provisions and procedures thus created. This system will entail the creation of the European Monetary Fund as announced in the conclusions of the European Council meeting in Bremen on 6/7 July, 1978, as well as the full utilization of the ECU as a reserve asset and a means of settlement. It will be based on adequate legislation at the Community as well as the national level.

Considerable attention has been paid to the question of whether this calendar should be adjusted, but this is not the most important question. Of greater significance is the question of whether there is still a firm commitment to create a real European Monetary Fund. The technical discussions are under way, and in no way does one get the impression that the commitment to the Fund has weakened.

I will not deal here with the technical issues that are still being debated, but I will simply underline a few points:

1. The creation of the EMF should represent an important qualitative step forward and not merely a minor adjustment of the present European Monetary Cooperation Fund, which is mostly an accounting device for transactions between central banks.

2. The mechanism should incorporate sufficient evolving elements, which would make it possible to keep a certain parallelism between the functions of this institution and the progress of monetary integration. In other words, it should contain a number of enabling clauses.

3. It will be important to make the ECU a full-fledged asset. This implies the abandonment of a number of constraints on its use and attractiveness.

4. The ultimate goal should be to create a sort of European central bank, which could effectively contribute to the harmonization of monetary policies in Europe and stimulate a greater degree of monetary stability.

CONCLUSION

The European Monetary System is still very much a human construction in progress. It was not made perfect and unalterable from the start, nor was it ever meant to be so. One year of operation of the EMS in a turbulent international environment has already revealed some of its shortcomings, and I have indicated some of the ways in which the gaps should be filled and the foundations strengthened. As it is now, nevertheless, the EMS has already achieved positive results, not only in promoting greater exchange rate stability among European currencies, but also in bringing out in the open the necessary conditions of convergence for sustaining exchange rate stability, thus reinforcing the case for deeper monetary and economic integration in Europe.

Finally, the functioning of the EMS has proved a useful learning experience for all those who, since the collapse of the Bretton Woods agreement, have tried to formulate a viable reform of the international monetary system. The EMS, as some have noted (see Triffin 1979), incorporates in its construction principles that were put forward in the discussions on reform of the IMF that took place in the early 1970s. In particular, by adopting an abstract numeraire, the ECU, both as a common denominator for exchange rate quotations and readjustments and as an asset for reserve and settlement purposes, it answers the need for a greater symmetry in the pursuit of exchange rate stability that the Bretton Woods system lacked. The EMS exchange mechanisms are meant to involve both the strong and the weak currency countries in the defense of their exchange rate, and the divergence indicator based on the ECU provides them with an objective and clear signal of the moment when measures have to be taken.

Thus, the existence and operation of the EMS and the management of the relationship between the EMS and the dollar should be inserted, as Robert Triffin suggested, "into the broader framework of world monetary reform. . . . I consider," he wrote in 1979, "that a successful functioning of the E.M.S. and of the links to be established between it and the dollar area may provide invaluable guidelines for the reforms that will be negotiable and feasible on a global scale" (Triffin 1979:73). Both Western Europe and the rest of the world have thus much to gain from a successful continuation of the EMS experience.

REFERENCES

Bank for International Settlements. 1980. *Fiftieth Annual Report.* Basle, June 9.

Cooper, Richard N. 1980. "Flexible Exchange Rates: An Assessment." *Impact* 30.

Emminger, Otmar. 1980. Remarks at a Conference of the American Enterprise Institute in Washington on 28 February 1980." *Deutsche Bundesbank – Auszüge aus Presseartikeln* 28 (27 März).

Friedman, Milton. 1953. *Essays in Positive Economics.* Chicago: University of Chicago Press.

Machlup, Fritz. 1979. "Comment at a Conference on the Emerging European Monetary System." *Bulletin de la Banque Nationale de Belgique* 4 (Avril).

Matthöffer, Hans. 1980. "Reden in der Feierstunde anlässlich des Wechsels in der Leitung der Deutschen Bundesbank, Frankfurt am Main, 20. Dezember 1979." *Deutsche Bundesbank – Auszüge aus Presseartikeln* 2 (4 January).

Miles, Marc A. 1979. "The Effects of Devaluation on the Trade Balance and the Balance of Payments." *Journal of Political Economy* 87, no. 3 (June).

Scharrer, Hans–Eckart. 1980. "Gefährlicher Zeitzünder." *Wirschafts Dienst* (January).

Triffin, Robert. 1957. *Europe and the Money Muddle.* New Haven: Yale University Press.

_____. 1960. *Gold and the Dollar Crisis: The Future of Convertibility.* New Haven: Yale University Press.

_____. 1979. "The American Response to the European Monetary System." In Philip H. Trezise, ed., *The European Monetary System: Its Promise and Prospects.* Washington, D.C.: The Brookings Institution.

_____. 1980. "The Future of the International Monetary System." *Banca Nazionale del Lavoro Quarterly Review* (March).

van Ypersele, Jacques. 1979. "Operating Principles and Procedures of the European Monetary System." In Philip H. Trezise, ed., *The European Monetary System: Its Promise and Prospects.* Washington, D.C.: The Brookings Institution.

_____. 1980. "Bilanz und Zukunftperspektiven des Europäischen Währungssystems." *Integration* (Institut für Europäische Politik) 2.

Vaubel, Roland. 1980. "Der Test steht noch aus." *Wirtschafts Dienst* (January).

Wallich, Henry C. 1980. "Exchange Rates, Inflation and the Dollar." *Impact* 30.

Whitman, Marina v.N. 1977. "Sustaining the International Economic System." *Essays in International Finance* No. 121, Princeton, New Jersey: International Finance Section, Princeton University.

18 THE FAILURE OF WORLD MONETARY REFORM
A Reassessment
John Williamson

INTRODUCTION

A dozen years before the Bretton Woods system collapsed – indeed, at the very time that it was entering its golden age – Robert Triffin diagnosed the system's inherent fragility and proposed reforms intended to permit its orderly evolution to something more robust. It is a tribute to his analytical and persuasive powers that his diagnosis and prescription not only stirred the official world into the negotiations that ultimately led to establishment of the SDR, but that they continued to dominate the Committee of Twenty (C-20) negotiations that were supposed to design a coherent successor system to Bretton Woods. As is well known, that attempt failed, with the result that the world now muddles through with a "nonsystem." I have already (Williamson 1977: ch. 7) offered an explanation of why the reform attempt failed; I return to the topic because of a growing dissatisfaction with my earlier analysis.

The chapter starts with a brief consideration of the fundamental purposes of an international monetary system. The next section sketches Triffin's vision of a desirable system, which one might term a "civilized gold standard" or an "SDR standard." There then follows a similar sketch of the principal competitor to the Triffinesque solution – namely, the dollar standard. That sets the stage for the reassessment in the final section of the chapter.

THE PURPOSES OF AN INTERNATIONAL MONETARY SYSTEM

Just as money exists to permit bilaterally unbalanced transactions between economic agents, so international monetary arrangements are necessary because

297

payments between countries are not always, continuously, and bilaterally balanced. Exactly where in the balance of payments accounts the line should be
drawn to define an imbalance is not clear. On a narrow definition, one would
take the official settlements balance; on a wide concept, the current account
balance; and on an intermediate concept, the balance on nonmonetary transactions. I tend to use the wider definition, since the narrower ones exclude some
of the most interesting and important problems, although I concede that a more
appropriate term for what one thus defines might be the "international financial
system." The scope of the international monetary (or financial) system concerns
the terms on which national currencies are traded for each other (which influences the size of imbalances), the assets used to finance those imbalances, and
the arrangements governing when and how imbalances should be adjusted.

One reason for regarding these questions as significant is that there are a series
of constraints that face a closed economy but that do not, by virtue of the scope
that the system provides for imbalances, confront each nation individually. For
example, absorption may exceed or fall short of output in an open economy—
but cannot do so for the world as a whole. An individual country may be able
to decelerate inflation without much loss in real income by varying the fiscal-
monetary mix so that its currency appreciates—this is not an option in a closed
system, such as the world. Credit creation need not equal monetary expansion in
a single country, but it does so for all countries together.

The consequences of a set of national policies that collectively fail to add up
to a result consistent with a real global constraint are, it goes without saying,
prone to be unfortunate. Inadequate world aggregate demand leads to world
recession; an excess, to demand inflation. Generalized attempts to combat inflation by playing the fiscal-monetary mix lead to high interest rates, low investment, and low growth, not to a cut price deceleration of inflation. Excessive
credit creation in a single country may simply leak out through a (reversible)
payments deficit, but excessive credit creation in the whole system cannot but
generate inflation. Inconsistency in balance of payments objectives, either in
the sense that reserve accumulation ambitions do not sum to the increase in the
global supply of reserves or in the sense that the sum of targeted current surpluses and deficits be different from zero, might provoke competitive payments
policies—escalating trade restrictions, competitive devaluations or deflation, or
an interest rate war. A major test of a set of international monetary arrangements must surely be their success in ensuring that the policies chosen by the
several nations add up to a total result that is appropriate in the light of the constraints that cannot be sidestepped in that closed economy, the world.

TRIFFIN'S PARADIGM AND
THE C-20 MAINSTREAM

I have suggested already that Triffin's vision of a desirable international monetary system might be characterized as a "civilized gold standard." This is not
because he displayed any tendency to worship at the feet of the "barbarous

relic"; on the contrary, he could be accused of wishing to civilize gold in part by supplementing it with a fiduciary reserve asset to the point where the metal itself was driven out of active use as a reserve asset by Gresham's Law. The central similarity with the gold standard arises, rather, from the idea that a limited stock of world reserves acts as a world "monetary base" that ultimately governs the world money stock and regulates the adjustment process, thus providing a mechanism for coordinating national policies to produce a globally satisfactory outcome.

Triffin's writings (especially 1960, 1964) suggest that he envisaged the process of civilizing the gold standard as requiring two major amendments to the pre-1914 classical gold standard (in addition to the secondary question of disposing of gold itself). The first was the ability to change exchange rates in exceptional situations, such as after a war or a period of populist misgovernment. Triffin always—even back in the 1950s (e.g., Triffin 1955, 1957: ch. 2), when contemporary monetarist legend would have one believe that no one understood the significance of the distinction between internal and external sources of monetary expansion—displayed considerable faith in the ability of automatic monetary forces, when not thwarted by sterilization, to correct payments disequilibria at tolerable cost without an exchange rate change. But he did not regard it as reasonable to impose on the monetary mechanism the task of realigning seriously disaligned price levels, as was attempted with such sorry results in Britain in the 1920s. In such circumstances, an exchange rate change was appropriate. Since this ability had been provided by Bretton Woods, no further reforms were in his view necessary in that direction.

The second major civilizing change involved establishment of an ability to regulate the stock of world reserves with a view to stabilizing the world economy. The Rio Agreement to create the SDR marked a start in that direction, since it permitted deliberate reserve creation to alleviate a reserve shortage. What remained was to eliminate or control other sources of reserve growth, as well as the potential impact of reserve switching on the supply of reserves—in other words, to construct an SDR standard.

That provided the basic agenda for the C-20 negotiations, in the view of the C-20 mainstream—Europe, Japan, and the international bureaucracy. The Bretton Woods system had, in this view, collapsed because of the inherent contradictions of the gold exchange standard, and a coherent successor system demanded essentially the replacement of those fragile arrangements by more robust provisions regarding reserve supply—a substitution account, one or another form of asset settlement, and appropriate controls on the Euromarkets. The pace of world reserve growth would then be governed by SDR allocations, which could be wisely determined by the IMF, with a view to striking a balance between world pressures toward inflation and deflation.

It was rather taken for granted that an appropriate rate of growth of reserves would be sufficient to resolve the several potential dimensions of policy inconsistency mentioned earlier (the need for global demand to equal productive capacity, for an appropriate fiscal–monetary mix and credit expansion, and for consistency in payments objectives). In fact, however, this is not as farfetched as it might seem by facile appeal to the "theory of economic policy." Suppose that reserve growth were set, as it was envisaged it should be, at the level needed to preserve constant reserve ease with world growth equal to the growth of supply capacity and with minimal inflation. Suppose also (as did in large measure actually happen in the good old days of Bretton Woods) that each country directed its fiscal policy at an objective of noninflationary full employment, while accepting (as happened with less regularity under Bretton Woods) some deliberate trimming of demand management policy in the light of its balance of payments situation. So long as payments imbalances were broadly symmetrical, the world as a whole would not deviate from full employment because of payments imbalances. Indeed, as Triffin often emphasized, payments deficits usually stem from excess demand and therefore provide both an early warning that deflation is needed and a safety valve that limits the extent to which temporary excess demand is translated into hard-to-stop inflation, as well as an incentive to take corrective action promptly.

Furthermore, conflict over the proper fiscal–monetary mix could not arise from a competitive desire to import price stability under a fixed rate system, while credit expansion would be limited by the stock of reserves. Reserve accumulation objectives would be consistent by virtue of the rule chosen to govern reserve creation. Thus the one potential source of conflict left would be over current balances—but even this would evaporate either if countries did not have current balance targets (as the United States used to argue in the C-20 that they should not) or if their current balance targets were chosen with a view to securing their reserve accumulation objectives in the medium term (which was the predominant European conception of what the targetry was about).

This is perhaps a somewhat more articulated version of the basic logic that seems to me to have underlain Triffin's vision of a reformed international monetary system, which in turn provided the basis for the mainstream view in the C-20. A question that needs asking is the range of circumstances under which the paradigm is relevant. At one extreme, it would clearly be relevant with rigidly fixed exchange rates and flexible internal prices. It made good sense also with Triffin's postulate that monetary policy normally can and should be guided by the dictates of maintaining a fixed exchange rate and that this would involve no significant sacrifice of internal objectives.

At the other extreme, as I have recently argued elsewhere (Williamson forthcoming), controlling the quantity of reserves cannot be expected to influence any important variable in the type of high capital mobility, floating rate world in which we now live. (A reserve shortage can be relieved by borrowing or depreciation, rather than requiring any significant adjustment of domestic policy.) In between, the notion of deliberate control of a world monetary base as a mechanism for securing international monetary harmonization still makes sense in a crawling peg system such as I favored at the start of the C-20, since monetary policy has to be assigned to the balance of payments to make such a system viable. Whether it made such sense in the sort of nominal par value system that was popular in the C-20, in which par values were supposed to be changed quickly at the first sign of any conflict between monetary policy and the exchange rate, is with hindsight rather doubtful.

THE DOLLAR STANDARD AND THE U.S. POSITION

While there may thus have been a certain logical inconsistency in the position of the C-20 mainstream, there was one major power that was clearly hostile to the idea of a world monetary order requiring the assignment of national monetary policies to external targets. That country was the United States, and the reason lay in the national attractions of a dollar standard.

The postwar monetary system agreed at Bretton Woods was not a dollar standard, but a gold exchange standard. Keynes failed to secure the strengthening of the obligations on surplus countries to contribute to adjustment in the way that he originally sought—by the interest charges to be levied on excess holdings of bancor—but he won the compensation prize of the scarce currency clause, which was regarded as deliberately aimed at the United States. And (however irrelevant it may have been at the time) there was no suggestion that reserve centers did not have the obligation of defending their currencies and thus adjusting their payments position. When the United States first experienced a deficit that was large enough to pose a problem, in the late 1950s, it reacted much as any other country was expected to do, with cautious monetary policies and restraints on capital outflows. The result was a substantial strengthening of the U.S. payments position, especially on current account, through the first half of the 1960s. And by 1965 the administration endorsed the Triffinesque position that consolidation and extension of that improvement would lead to a systemic problem of liquidity shortage without creation of a new reserve asset to supplement or substitute for gold, with the result that the United States led the movement that culminated in establishment of the SDR.

However, the mid-1960s also witnessed the emergence of an alternative paradigm that saw the world as already having slipped unconsciously to a dollar standard, and international monetary reform as the process of learning to like it. This view maintained that gold had already become an irrelevance, that the dollar was the ultimate reserve asset, that other countries took the responsibility for maintaining the payments balance, and that the United States set the pace of world monetary expansion to which other countries adjusted, while treating its own payments position with "benign neglect." These views were never officially endorsed, but there was a good deal of sympathy for them in the Nixon administration that took office in 1969. There was in particular a belief that the U.S. payments deficit was a reflection of the payments objectives being pursued by other countries, which the United States was in no position to correct by conventional payments policies. The administration did not, however, share the relaxed attitude toward a deficit recommended by the advocates of the dollar standard.

The United States therefore came to the C-20 negotiations with a deep ambivalence about the type of world monetary order it wished to see established. On the one hand, there was a realistic awareness of the national advantages of a dollar standard, in terms particularly of the freedom from external constraints on monetary policy. On the other hand, there was a desire to secure a mechanism for correcting U.S. payments imbalances that seemed inconsistent with the concept of a dollar standard. There was also a consciousness that the rest of the world was not prepared to accept an official dollar standard and would therefore require some form of convertibility if an agreement was to be reached at all. The reserve indicator proposal can be viewed as an ingenious way of attempting to reconcile these conflicting interests, by building in pressure for other countries to pursue policies consistent with U.S. payments needs, which might have made it possible for the United States to accept at least the form (if without much of the substance, in terms of discipline over U.S. monetary policy) of convertibility.

A REASSESSMENT

In my previous discussion of why the C-20 failed to negotiate a reform (Williamson 1977: ch. 7), I rather took it for granted that an SDR standard or a "civilized gold standard"—with one further civilizing amendment, the replacement of the adjustable peg by the crawling peg—provided a generally acceptable, because generally advantageous, basis for the construction of a reformed system. My explanation of failure was therefore directed (1) at the intellectual failure to appreciate that the adjustable peg had become unworkable because of the growth of capital mobility; (2) at the lack of political will (particularly on the part of the United States) manifested in a reluctance to concede points clearly required by the basic paradigm assumed to be directing the exercise; and (3) at the incompetence of the negotiators in failing to refashion differing proposals in a manner capable of reconciling the conflicting interests of the proponents within the framework provided by the agreed paradigm. The questions that I now believe need raising are whether the SDR standard in fact provided either a generally accepted or a generally advantageous base for a reformed international monetary system.

I consider first the question as to whether the SDR standard would have been generally advantageous. As one who is convinced that exchange rate changes have a legitimate and important role in economic policy, both as a way of neutralizing the external impact of deep-rooted inflationary movements that cannot be broken at tolerable cost simply by pegging the exchange rate and as a way of facilitating payments adjustment when that requires expenditure switching, I cannot conceive of an SDR standard being generally beneficial without making provision for inclusion of the crawling peg. I therefore take as the basis of comparison a system incorporating both the crawling peg and an obligation to direct monetary policy to external objectives, with an internationally controlled stock of world reserves.

One obvious question is whether such a system would not have been dominated by the dollar standard so far as the United States was concerned. Under the conventional assumption that any constraint on monetary policy is nationally disadvantageous, the answer is obviously that it would have been. But the implication of the previous section is that the conventional assumption needs questioning (and not only on the basis of the rather jaded and inconclusive "discipline" argument). Payments imbalances do not happen just because of random shocks, but more frequently because of events that demand a change of policy. The events of 1977-1978 and the arguments about the "locomotive approach" and the "convoy approach" provide a perfect example. The United States pressed ahead with what turned out (in view of the collapse in productivity growth) to be a grossly overexpansionary policy, despite the warning signal provided by an exploding payments deficit. Meanwhile the other two locomotives stayed resolutely in the engine shed until the convoy finally set to sea in 1978, by which time the leading locomotive was already running off the rails. Can one doubt that an automatic restraining influence on the United States and automatic expansionary pressures on the surplus countries, such as a functioning monetary mechanism would have provided, would have produced a markedly better outcome for everyone, including the United States?

A second obvious question is whether the "nonsystem" that emerged from the rubble of the C-20 may not be preferable to the system being considered. Present arrangements involve no mechanism intended to promote automatic or even presumptive policy harmonization, but instead rely on a mixture of market mechanisms and ad hoc policy discussions in summit meetings, the OECD, and the IMF. As the example cited in the previous paragraph demonstrates, the sort of ad hoc argument divorced from any framework of agreed principles that presently serves for international policy coordination is of very limited value in securing prompt, consistent action. The crucial question is whether floating exchange rates and private capital markets provide sufficient assurance of broad global policy consistency to make the absence of effective formal arrangements to that end a matter of little consequence.

There is a third option that it now seems to me natural to compare with the system under consideration, although this is an option that was most certainly not in the minds of the C-20 negotiators. This option involves a deliberate and formal coordination of monetary policy achieved through an agreed set of rules governing domestic credit expansion (DCE) rather than through control of the stock of reserves (see Williamson 1980, forthcoming). Now that gold has been demonetized in all but name, the world money supply rises only as a result of DCE in some country or other; thus a uniform and consistent set of rules governing DCE would permit international control of world monetary growth at least as well as a Triffinesque reform would have done. There are three advantages and one disadvantage that I can see in this alternative. The first advantage is that given the large margin for slippage in the reserves-to-money supply ratio, control could in fact be far more effective if sought directly by targeting DCE. The second advantage is that this approach would not require the prior establishment of effective control over international reserves, which looks something of a lost cause. The third advantage is that a combination of DCE limits and effectively unlimited reserves for countries that respect those limits would offer the possibility of making the system invulnerable to confidence crises, thus removing the great doubt about the feasibility of pegged rate systems in an era of high capital mobility. The disadvantage is that the required encroachment on monetary sovereignty would be greater than the model under the Triffinesque solution.

So, would an SDR standard have been generally advantageous? The answer I am led to is that it was in fact less attractive than we regarded it at the time. It would have been technically inferior to a system in which monetary coordination was sought by an agreed set of rules governing DCE. And it required acceptance of external constraints on monetary policies of a sort that the United States could avoid by a dollar standard and that other countries also came to escape by the "nonsystem."

However, what determines the outcome of a negotiation is not so much countries' actual interests (although these are relevant in determining the scope for persuading countries to modify their positions in the interest of achieving agreement), but rather their perceptions of those interests. The crucial question in assessing my previous explanation for the failure of the C-20 is whether the Triffinesque solution did in fact provide the generally accepted vision of where the negotiations were supposed to lead.

At least at the outset of the negotiations, the main reason for doubting the generality of support for an SDR standard lay in the attitude of the United States. (The developing countries were not part of the C-20 mainstream in that they gave less priority to securing control of global liquidity than to defending their particular interests, but they were among the strongest supporters of the SDR.) Of course, the United States never pressed for a dollar standard in any formal way. On the contrary, it led the rhetoric for a more symmetrical system (albeit emphasizing the need for symmetry between deficit and surplus countries rather than between reserve centers and others). Nevertheless, the facts are that a dollar standard was more in keeping with U.S. national interests, at least under the conventional assumption that all constraints on monetary policy are irksome; that the United States had followed an externally unconstrained monetary policy for most of the postwar period (the exception being the early 1960s) and grown accustomed to the luxury; and that U.S. negotiators showed clear signs of wishing to safeguard monetary policy from external pressures.

The aspect of the C-20 negotiations that displayed this most clearly is the remarkably low key debate about whether the reserve indicator system sought by the United States should have been based on gross or net reserves. When the Dutch pressed the U.S. delegates to specify which they had in mind, they received the reply that there were arguments both ways and that the question should be left open for the ministers to decide. The United States insisted that agreed documents express complete agnosticism, even when it was clear that they were alone in believing there was any sort of case for an indicator system based on gross reserves. Now a gross reserve indicator system with the dollar remaining the dominant reserve currency and without convertibility could never have signaled a need for U.S. adjustment, since the United States would not have gained or lost reserves. Indeed, since the countries gaining reserves corresponding to a U.S. deficit would have been exposed to adjustment pressures, the system would have remedied the one aspect of the dollar standard that the United States had found irksome. A gross reserve indicator with convertibility but without asset settlement—the preferred U.S. combination—could in principle have signaled a need for U.S. adjustment, although the U.S. proposal for "primary-asset-holding limits" might have emasculated that signal. But it might have done this even in the absence of a U.S. deficit, as a result of a desired portfolio shift out of dollars. Can one wonder that others found the U.S. position unintelligible, on the basis of their implicit assumption that the object of the negotiations was the construction of an SDR standard?

Under a net reserve indicator, in contrast, a U.S. deficit would have signaled a need for adjustment even in the absence of convertibility or asset settlement. Had the Europeans been smart, they would have jumped at the reserve indicator proposal, if necessary forgetting about asset settlement, just insisting on the little "technical" proviso that the system be based on net rather than gross reserves. That could have provided a way of giving effect to a "civilized gold standard" in which world monetary expansion was guided by a process of conscious international decisionmaking (focused in this case on the establishment of reserve norms and their growth, rather than on reserve creation, as under the SDR system) and all countries were expected to guide their monetary policies with an eye to reserve changes, thus (presumptively) ensuring a measure of consistency in demand and adjustment policies. Moreover, it would have been diplomatically embarrassing to the United States to have resisted. Hence the argument in my 1977 book that the lack of ingenuity of the negotiators deserves a major share of the blame for the failure of the C-20.

However, the assumption that the United States would have been reluctant to allow itself to be seriously embarrassed rested on the premise that it was prepared to go along, if somewhat more reluctantly than other countries, with the basic vision of an SDR standard. If instead the United States conceived its national interests to demand the preservation of complete freedom of monetary policy, the only doubt about the outcome of the negotiations was the precise issue on which they would break down.

Indeed, as the negotiations wore on, other countries came to share the U.S. concern for the ability to pursue a monetary policy untrammeled by external constraints. Germany, in particular, came to regard floating as an alternative to world monetary control in relieving it of the former pressure to import inflation. But the unwillingness to allow monetary policy to be subjected to serious external constraints was actually rather general—from the patent refusal of Australia to accept the principle, by way of the rather general "of course we can make an adjustable peg work, you see if we can't change par values before the market has thought of it," to the resistance of the developing countries to any constraint on their own actions.

And so the world ended up by getting exactly what is implied by those attitudes—a nonsystem with no coherent mechanism for monetary coordination, but relying instead on markets to reconcile the uncoordinated. We are still learning how high a price in terms of economic efficiency has been paid for the triumph of monetary nationalism. But looking back on the attempt at world monetary reform, the remarkable fact is not that monetary nationalism should have triumphed in a world as nationalistic as ours, but rather that Robert Triffin's internationalist vision should have inspired a reform movement at all.

REFERENCES

Triffin, Robert. 1955. "Adjusting Features in the Mechanism of Payments and Exchange Rates." Hearings before the Subcommittee on Foreign Economic Policy. 79th Congress. Washington, D.C.

_____. 1957. *Europe and the Money Muddle*. New Haven: Yale University Press.

_____. 1960. *Gold and the Dollar Crisis*. New Haven: Yale University Press.

_____. 1964. *The Evolution of the International Monetary System: Historical Reappraisal and Future Perspectives*. Princeton Studies in International Finance No. 12, Princeton, New Jersey: International Finance Section, Princeton University.

Williamson, John. 1977. *The Failure of World Monetary Reform, 1971–74*. London: Nelson; and New York: NYU Press.

_____. 1980. *International Monetary Reform: A Survey of the Options*. Report to the Group of Twenty-Four, UNDP/UNCTAD Project INT/75/015.

_____. Forthcoming. "The Growth of Official Reserves and the Issue of World Monetary Control." In J. Dreyer, ed., *The International Monetary System under Stress*. Washington, D.C.: American Enterprise Institute.

AUTHOR INDEX

SUBJECT INDEX